Judge Thomas R. Simpson, Jr.

Maryland Criminal Procedure

Professor Byron L. Warnken

University of Baltimore School of Law

2013

Volume III

27Legal, LLC endeavors to provide accurate information in these pages related to Maryland Criminal Procedure. However, information in these pages may not have been, in all circumstances, prepared by persons licensed to practice law in any jurisdiction. Moreover, law is constantly changing and open to interpretation. Nothing in these pages is intended to be legal advice by author Professor Byron L. Warnken or the publisher. 27Legal, LLC is not engaged in the business of providing legal advice. A book is not a substitute for the advice of competent, licensed counsel. If you require legal advice, you should seek the services of a qualified attorney.

27Legal, LLC may be reached at 410-929-3353 or 27legal.com

Library of Congress Control Number: 2013949034
ISBN #: 978-0-578-13012-5 (three-volume set)

Table of Contents

Volume I

Chapter 4:
Mens Rea

Chapter 5:
Right to Counsel

Chapter 7:
Fourth Amendment Applicability

Chapter 8:
Search & Seizure by Warrant

Chapter 9:
Arrest & Stop & Frisk

Chapter 10:
Search & Seizure Warrant Exceptions 10-437

Chapter 11:
Fourth Amendment Remedies

Volume II

Chapter 12:
Fifth Amendment Applicability

Chapter 13:
Interrogations & Confessions

Chapter 14:
Fifth Amendment Remedies

Chapter 15:
Eyewitness Identifications 15-687

Chapter 16:
Grand Jury & Charging Documents

Chapter 17:
Jurisdiction & Venue 17-759

Chapter 20:
Incompetency, NCR, & Intoxication 20-845

Chapter 21:

Double Jeopardy

Chapter 23:
Discovery

Chapter 26:
Burden of Persuasion

Chapter 27:
Fair Trial

Chapter 28:
Confrontation

Volume III

Chapter 30:
Sentencing

Chapter 32:

Appeals 32-1335

Chapter 33:
Collateral Review

Sentencing

§ I. Policies & theories of sentencing

Md. Code Ann., Crim. Proc. § 6-202, provides:

The General Assembly intends that:

(1) sentencing should be fair and proportional and that sentencing policies should reduce unwanted disparity, including any racial disparity, in sentences for criminals who have committed similar crimes and have similar criminal histories;

(2) sentencing policies should help citizens to understand how long a criminal will be confined;

(3) sentencing policies should preserve meaningful judicial discretion and sufficient flexibility to allow individualized sentences;

(4) sentencing guidelines be voluntary;

(5) the priority for the capacity and use of correctional facilities should be the confinement of violent and career criminals; and

(6) sentencing judges in the State should be able to impose the most appropriate criminal penalties, including corrections options programs for appropriate criminals.

Id.

Sentencing goals include (a) fostering respect for the law; (b) deterring criminal conduct; (c) incapacitating and punishing offenders; (d) providing restitution or reparation to crime victims; and (e) rehabilitating offenders.

§ II. Sentencing authority

Imposition of sentences is a judicial function to be performed by sentencing courts. *See Resper v. State*, 354 Md. 611, 620 (1999). A sentence must be within the legislative authorization. *See DeLeon v. State*, 102 Md. App. 58, 62 (1994). A sentence should be appropriate to both the offense and the offender. In most jurisdictions, the jury's role is limited to a determination of "guilty" or "not guilty," and the jury plays no role in sentencing, except in death penalty cases. *See ABA Standards for Criminal Justice—Sentencing* Standard 18-1.4. The trial judge should generally be the sentencing judge. Md. Rule 4-342(c).

In Maryland, subsequent to the abrogation of the death penalty, the sentencing authority is always the court and never the jury. *See* 2013 Md. Laws ch. 156.

§ III. Right to counsel at sentencing

Because sentencing is a critical stage, the Defendant has a Sixth Amendment right to counsel at sentencing. *Gardner v. Florida*, 430 U.S. 349, 358 (1977); *Mempa v. Rhay*, 389 U.S. 128, 134-37 (1967); *Townsend v. Burke*, 334 U.S. 736, 740-41 (1948). A Defendant who appears for sentencing without counsel should be afforded a meaningful opportunity to explain appearance for sentencing without counsel prior to the court finding a waiver of the right to counsel by inaction. In *State v. Brown*, 342 Md. 404, 428-29 (1996), the Court of Appeals held that there is no requirement for strict compliance with Md. Rule 4-215 when inquiring about counsel after the trial commences. In *Catala v. State*, 168 Md. App. 438 (2006), the Court of Special Appeals held that the Defendant was entitled to a new sentencing because the sentencing judge failed to give the Defendant a meaningful opportunity to explain why he did not have counsel. The Court stated:

> Based on *Brown*, the sentencing judge was justified in failing to comply with the strict requirements of Rule 4-215. But, the court was still required to give [the Defendant] some meaningful opportunity to explain why he had not retained counsel and then make a decision as to whether the right to counsel had been waived due to inaction.

Id. at 469.

§ IV. Sentencing considerations

A. Broad discretion of the sentencing judge

The primary objectives of sentencing are punishment, deterrence, and rehabilitation. *Jennings v. State*, 339 Md. 675, 682 (1995). The sentencing judge has broad discretion in deciding what factors to consider in sentencing. In *United States v. Tucker*, 404 U.S. 443, 447 (1972), the Supreme Court stated that sentences imposed within the statutory limits are generally not subject to review. In *Williams v. New York*, 337 U.S. 241 (1949), the Supreme Court stated:

The belief no longer prevails that every offense in a like category calls for an identical punishment without regard to the past life and habits of the particular offender. This whole country has traveled far from the period in which the death sentence was an automatic and commonplace result of convictions— even for offenses today deemed trivial. Today's philosophy of individualizing sentences makes sharp distinctions for example between first and repeated offenders. Indeterminate sentences, the ultimate termination of which are sometimes decided by non-judicial agencies have to a large extent taken the place of old rigidly fixed punishments.

Id. at 247-48.

In *Pennsylvania v. Ashe*, 302 U.S. 51 (1937), the Supreme Court stated: "For the determination of sentences, justice generally requires consideration of more that the particular act by which the crime was committed and that there be taken into account the circumstances of the offense together with the character of the [Defendant]." *Id.* at 54. *See Gary v. State*, 341 Md. 513, 516 (1996); *Teasley v. State*, 298 Md. 364 (1984); *Logan v. State*, 289 Md. 460, 480 (1981) (sentencing judge vested with virtually boundless discretion).

In *Bartholomey v. State*, 267 Md. 175 (1972), the Court of Appeals stated: "[The] sentencing judge is encouraged to consider information about the Defendant's reputation, past offenses, health, habits, mental and moral propensities, social background, etc." *Id.* at 193; *see Graves v. State*, 133 Md. App. 97, 105 (2000), *rev'd on other grounds*, 364 Md. 329 (2001). The fact that a sentencing judge consistently imposes harsh sentences does not mean that the judge fails to exercise his or her discretion. *Holland v. State*, 122 Md. App. 532, 548-49 (1997).

The Defendant's right to a fair trial includes an impartial and disinterested judge. *Jackson v. State*, 364 Md. 192, 206 (2001). Md. Rule 4-342(g) provides that sentencing judges should ordinarily state on the record the reasons for imposing a sentence. However, "[t]he rule does not require judges in all cases to give their reasons." *Id.* at 206; *see Brashear v. State*, 90 Md. App. 709, 724 (1992); *accord State v. Dopkowski*, 325 Md. 671, 682 (1992) (judge not required to give reasons for a sentence imposed at a probation revocation hearing); *see McElroy v. State*, 90 Md. App. 48 (1992).

1. Supreme Court

Williams is considered a seminal case regarding a trial judge's discretion during sentencing to consider a wide variety of factors. 337 U.S. 241. In *Williams*, the Defendant challenged the judge's consideration, for sentencing purposes, evidence that was not introduced at trial, primarily the Defendant's probation report. The Court recognized that is was "present[ed with] a serious and difficult question[,] relat[ing] to the rules of evidence applicable to the manner in which a judge may obtain information to guide him in the imposition of a sentence on an already convicted Defendant." *Id.* at 244.

The Defendant was convicted of murder, and the jury recommended a life sentence. The sentencing judge imposed the death penalty. The Supreme Court upheld his sentence and explained that the trial judge may consider evidence during sentencing that was not admissible during the guilt-innocence phase. The Court stated:

> Modern changes in the treatment of offenders make it more necessary now than a century ago for observance of the distinctions in the evidential procedure in the trial and sentencing process. [I]ndeterminate sentences and probation have resulted in an increase in the discretionary powers exercised in fixing punishments. [A] strong motivating force for the changes has been the belief that, by careful study of the lives and personalities of convicted offenders, many could be less severely punished and restored sooner to complete freedom and useful citizenship. This belief to a large extent has been justified.

> Under the practice of individualized punishments, investigation techniques have been given an important role. Probation workers making reports of their investigations have not been trained to prosecute but to aid offenders. Their reports have been given a high value by conscientious judges who want to sentence persons on the best available information rather than on guesswork and inadequate information. To deprive sentencing judges of this kind of information would undermine modern penological procedural policies that have been cautiously adopted throughout the nation after careful consideration and experimentation. We must recognize that most of the information relied upon by judges to guide them in the intelligent imposition of sentences would be unavailable if information were restricted to that given in open court by witnesses subject to cross-examination. And the modern probation report draws on information concerning every aspect of a Defendant's life. The type and extent of this information make totally impracticable if not impossible open court testimony with cross-examination. Such a procedure could endlessly delay criminal administration in a retrial on collateral issues.

Id. at 248-50.

2. ABA Standards

ABA Standards for Criminal Justice—Sentencing Standard 18-6.1 provides that the sentence should be no more severe than necessary to achieve societal purposes and to be consistent with the gravity of the offense, the culpability of the Defendant, and the Defendant's criminal history and personal characteristics.

B. Permissible sentencing considerations

1. Offense & offender

The sentencing judge should consider the facts and circumstances relevant to both the offense and the offender, i.e., both the crime and the criminal. *See Williams*, 337 U.S. at 251; *Jackson*, 364 Md. at 199; *Poe v. State*, 341 Md. 523, 532 (1996). In *Owens v. State*, 352 Md. 663, 687 (1999), the Court of Appeals held that, although mistake of age is not a defense to statutory rape, it is a proper sentencing consideration.

In *Mack v. State*, 69 Md. App. 245, 254-55 (1986), the Court of Special Appeals held that the Defendant's age, youth, and immaturity may be considered as mitigating factors, but the sentencing judge is not required to consider them. *See Williams v. State*, 77 Md. App. 411, 424 (1988); *Anthony v. State*, 117 Md. App. 119, 130 (1997). In *Hamwright v. State*, 142 Md. App. 17, 42-43 (2001), the Court of Special Appeals held that the trial court may consider charges over which only the juvenile court had jurisdiction.

2. Illegal confessions to other offenses

The sentencing judge may consider illegal confessions to other offenses when the statements were obtained by the State for purposes of prosecution and not for sentencing enhancement. *Logan v. State*, 289 Md. 460, 487-89 (1981).

3. PSI report

The sentencing judge should consider information obtained during the preparation of the PSI report. *See Borchardt v. State*, 367 Md. 91, 133 (2001) (may consider other crimes evidence, prior bad acts evidence, and evidence of the Defendant's institutional misconduct); *Colvin-el v. State*, 332 Md. 144, 166-67 (1993) (may consider the mental health portion of the PSI report); *Collins v. State*, 318 Md. 269, 294-95 (1990) (may consider the Defendant's juvenile record and institutional record in the PSI report); *Hunt v. State*, 321 Md. 387, 432-33 (1990) (may consider information in the PSI report about the Defendant's escape attempts and misconduct while incarcerated); *Huffington v. State*, 304 Md. 559, 576 (1985) (may consider the Defendant's statement regarding events surrounding a crime contained in the PSI report).

In *Conyers v. State*, 345 Md. 525, 568 (1997), the Court of Appeals held that the entire juvenile record is not automatically admissible because it is in the PSI report, and admissibility is limited to "reliable information" that is probative and relevant to the sentencing, with the Defendant having a fair opportunity to rebut the information.

4. Prior acquittals

The sentencing judge may consider facts and circumstances surrounding charges for which the Defendant was acquitted and the Defendant's failure to reform his conduct despite prior incarceration. *Henry v. State*, 273 Md. 131, 151 (1974); *Hamwright*, 142 Md. App. 17; *Harrod v. State*, 65 Md. App. 128, 140-41 (1985).

In *Curry v. State*, 60 Md. App. 171, 184 (1984), the Court of Special Appeals recognized that there is a fine line between impermissibly punishing the Defendant because he was acquitted of another crime and permissibly considering the facts and circumstances surrounding the offense for which the Defendant was acquitted. *See Middleton v. State*, 49 Md. App. 286, 292-93 (1981) (consideration of a theft charge for which the Defendant was acquitted not erroneous when the court was considering only the Defendant's failure to reform despite prior incarceration).

5. Lack of remorse

The sentencing judge may consider the Defendant's lack of remorse, so long as that is not explicitly linked to the Defendant's claim of innocence, a plea of not guilty, or the exercise of the right to remain silent. *Jennings*, 339 Md. 675, 688 (1995); *Saenz v. State*, 95 Md. App. 238, 250-51 (1993). In *Vogel v. State*, 76 Md. App. 56, 69-70 (1988), *aff'd*, 315 Md. 458 (1989), both Maryland appellate courts upheld the sentence because the trial court did not sentence the Defendant to a harsher sentence based on his claim of innocence, but rather considered the Defendant's claim of innocence as a limitation on the prospects for rehabilitation. In *Johnson v. State*, 274 Md. 536 (1975), the Court of Appeals explained:

> Even though we firmly believe that the judge at sentencing can and should take into account a broad spectrum of considerations, there do exist, in order to protect the fundamental rights of the offender, restrictions on this latitude. Thus, in view of what is at stake for one who is charged with a crime, it is improper to conclude that a decision, constitutionally protected, not to plead guilty and in doing so to require the State to prove the Defendant's guilt beyond a reasonable doubt, is a factor which ought to, in any way, influence the sentencing judge to the detriment of the accused.

Id. at 542-43.

6. Defendant's candor

The sentencing judge may consider the Defendant's demeanor and veracity before the court. *Johnson v. State*, 274 Md. 536, 540 (1975); *Atkins v. State*, 40 Md. App. 461, 465 (1978).

7. Judge's personal knowledge

Although the court is prohibited from relying on bias derived from his or her own personal circumstances in imposing a sentence, a sentencing judge may consider the perspective of the victim, the community, and other factors. *Ellis v. State*, 185 Md.

App. 522, 557-58 (2009). The sentencing judge may consider knowledge gained from living in the same community as the Defendant. *Johnson*, 274 Md. at 541.

8. Victim impact statement (VIS)

The sentencing judge may consider any VIS. *Hurley v. State*, 60 Md. App. 539, 564 (1984). The VIS should be limited to the impact of the crime on the victim and the victim's family members. *Ball*, 347 Md. at 198; *Reid v. State*, 302 Md. 811 (1985); *Tibbs v. State*, 72 Md. App. 239, 259 (1987). If the VIS goes beyond the impact of the crime on the victim and the victim's family, defense counsel must preserve the issue by objecting. If objected, the error is subject to the harmless error rule. *Hurley v. State*, 60 Md. App. 539, 560 (1984).

In *Evans v. State*, 333 Md. 660, 711-12 (1994), the Court of Appeals held that it was error to admit, from the PSI report, that the Defendant refused to speak with the investigator, but the error was harmless. In *Reid*, 302 Md. at 822-23, the Court of Appeals held that the trial court's consideration of a VIS was not am impermissible consideration and was not prejudicial to the Defendant.

9. Prior bad acts & other crimes evidence

In *Johnson v. State*, 75 Md. App. 621, 641 (1988), the Court of Special Appeals held that the sentencing judge may consider reliable evidence of prior bad acts and other crimes for which Defendant has not been convicted. In *Alston v. State*, 89 Md. App. 178, 184-85 (1991), the Court of Special Appeals held that the sentencing judge may consider crimes for which the Defendant has been found guilty and is awaiting sentencing.

In *Anthony v. State*, 117 Md. App. 119, 133 (1997), the Court of Special Appeals held that the sentencing judge may consider the Defendant's prior PBJ's. In *Muir v. State*, 308 Md. 208, 218 (1986), the Court of Appeals held that the fact that the Defendant's prior convictions were for offenses committed as a juvenile did not preclude their use as predicate felonies under the enhanced punishment statute.

10. Parole eligibility

The sentencing judge may consider parole eligibility in determining the length of time that the Defendant should be incarcerated. In *Reiger v. State*, 170 Md. App. 693 (2006), the Court of Special Appeals stated:

> A Defendant's parole eligibility date is relevant, without regard to whether parole will ever be granted, because it allows the court to determine the Defendant's minimum period of incarceration. Assessing what length of time a Defendant should be incarcerated for the crime he committed lies at the very heart of the court's constitutional duty to sentence.

Id. at 704.

11. ABA aggravating factors

ABA Standards for Criminal Justice, Fair Trial, & Free Press Standard 18-3.2(b) suggests that the following aggravating factors may be considered: (a) the Defendant was the leader among multiple participants; (b) the victim was particularly vulnerable; (c) the Defendant treated the victim with cruelty; (d) the Defendant injured the victim or threatened violence to gratify the Defendant's desire for pleasure or excitement; (e) the Defendant caused, attempted, or threatened bodily harm that was substantially greater than typical for that offense; (f) the Defendant caused, attempted, or threatened economic harm that was substantially greater than typical for that offense; and (g) the amount of drugs possessed by the Defendant or under the Defendant's control was substantially greater than typical for that offense.

12. Untried criminal conduct

In *Smith v. State*, 308 Md. 162, 173-75 (1986), the Court of Appeals held that the sentencing judge may consider criminal conduct for which the Defendant has been charged, but has not been tried, without violating the Double Jeopardy Clause. In *Khan v. State*, 115 Md. App. 636, 647-49 (1997), the Court of Special Appeals held that the Defendant may be prosecuted in state court in Maryland for conduct previously used in federal court to enhance the Defendant's sentence for a similar, but unrelated crime. In *Huffington v. State*, 304 Md. 559, 577-78 (1985), the Court of Appeals held that the sentencing judge may consider the Defendant's institutional history of infractions, even though they did not lead to criminal prosecution.

13. State's recommendations

The sentencing judge may consider the State's recommended sentence, but the judge is bound by the recommendation only if the judge previously agreed to that sentence as part of a three-party plea agreement. *Epps v. State*, 52 Md. App. 308, 315-16 (1982).

14. Evidence barred by the exclusionary rule

The sentencing judge may consider evidence that was excluded at trial because of the exclusionary rule, unless there is evidence that the evidence was obtained for the purpose of enhancing the Defendant's sentence. In *Logan*, the Court of Appeals held:

> [I]f the exclusionary rule were extended to sentencing in the ordinary case, its additional deterrent effect would be so minimal as to be insignificant. Generally, law enforcement officers conduct searches and seizures and seize evidence for purposes of prosecution and conviction not for the purpose of increasing a sentence in a prosecution already pending or not yet begun. If they are to be deterred from official lawlessness, it would seem obvious that the only effective deterrence is the threat that the prosecution arising out of the specific search and seizure in which they acted illegally would be ren-

dered ineffective. The additional threat that a future sentence might be less severe because they acted unlawfully can be predicted to have little practical effect to accomplish its main objective.

289 Md. at 485-87 (quoting *United States v. Lee*, 540 F.3d 1205, 1211 (4th Cir. 1976)).

15. Impact on the victim

"Certainly the effects of the crime on the victim whether economical, physical, psychological, or all three fall within [the] relevant permissible considerations." *Reid v. State*, 302 Md. 811, 820-21 (1985).

C. Impermissible sentencing considerations

1. Race, religion, or political affiliation

In *Zant v. Stephens*, 462 U.S. 862, 885 (1983), the Supreme Court held that the sentencing judge may not consider the Defendant's race, religion, or political affiliation. In *Jackson*, 364 Md. at 208, the Court of Appeals held that the sentencing judge may not base the sentence on where the Defendant lives, has lived, or was raised.

In *Burgess v. State*, 89 Md. App. 522, 554-55 (1991) the Court of Special Appeals affirmed the sentence when the sentencing judge stated: "Looking at your background, I would not consider you to be one of the young black males who the media is always talking about as part of the generation that is trying to kill itself off." The Court may consider whether race was a motivating factor for the Defendant when committing the crime, *see, e.g., Barclay v. Florida*, 463 U.S. 939, 949 (1983) (judge could consider elements of racial hatred in the murder).

In *Dawson v. Delaware*, 503 U.S. 159, 166 (1992), the Supreme Court stated: "Because the prosecution did not prove that the Aryan Brotherhood had committed any unlawful or violent acts, or had even endorsed such acts, the Aryan Brotherhood evidence was also not relevant to help prove any aggravating circumstance. [T]he inference which the jury was invited to draw in this case tended to prove nothing more than the abstract beliefs of the [Defendant's] chapter [of the Aryan Brotherhood].").

2. Gender, sexual orientation, national origin, or marital status

ABA Standards Standard 18-3.4 suggests that the sentencing judge may not consider the Defendant's gender, sexual orientation, national origin, or marital status.

3. Exercise of constitutional rights

The sentencing judge may not consider that the Defendant exercise of constitutional rights, such as (a) the Fifth Amendment privilege against compelled self-incrimination, *Ridenour v. State*, 142 Md. App. 1, 15-16 (2001); (b) the right to trial by jury, *Tellington v. State*, 336 Md. 567, 568 (1994); or (c) the exercise of appellate rights. *North*

Carolina v. Pearce, 395 U.S. 711, 718 (1969). *See* Md. Code Ann., Cts. & Jud. Proc. § 12-702(b) (Maryland's codification of the *Pearce* doctrine). *But see Alabama v. Smith*, 490 U.S. 794, 803 (1989) (holding that a greater sentence may be imposed after a trial following an initial sentence imposed after a guilty plea that was vacated).

In *United States v. Grayson*, 438 U.S. 41 (1978), the Supreme Court held that consideration by the sentencing judge of the Defendant's false testimony did not impermissibly "chill" the Defendant's constitutional right to testify on his own behalf. The Court stated: "Assuming, *arguendo*, that the sentencing judge's consideration of Defendant's untruthfulness in testifying has any chilling effect on a Defendant's decision to testify falsely, that effect is entirely permissible. This is no protected right to commit perjury." *Id.* at 54.

In *Mitchell*, 526 U.S. 314, the Defendant pleaded guilty to cocaine distribution as part of a 22-person drug ring. The Defendant reserved the right to contest the amount of cocaine attributable to her. At sentencing, the Defendant remained silent and the sentencing court stated: "I held it against you that you didn't come forward today and . . . explain your side." *Id.* at 319. The Third Circuit held that the judge's actions were permissible because sentencing proceedings were not part of the criminal case, and the Fifth Amendment privilege against self-incrimination did not apply. The Supreme Court reversed, holding:

> The Fifth Amendment by its terms prevents a person from being "compelled in any criminal case to be a witness against himself." To maintain that sentencing proceedings are not part of "any criminal case" is contrary to the law and to common sense. As to the law, under the Federal Rules of Criminal Procedure, a court must impose sentence before a judgment of conviction can issue. As to common sense, it appears that in this case, as is often true in the criminal justice system, the Defendant was less concerned with the proof of her guilt or innocence than with the severity of her punishment. [The Defendant] faced imprisonment from one year upwards to life, depending upon the circumstances of the crime. To say that she had no right to remain silent but instead could be compelled to cooperate in the deprivation of her liberty would ignore the Fifth Amendment privilege at the precise stage where, from her point of view, it was most important.

Id. at 327.

4. The *Pearce* presumption

In *North Carolina v. Pearce*, 395 U.S. 711 (1969), the Supreme Court indicated that there is a presumption of vindictiveness created by a harsher sentence imposed in a second trial after a Defendant succeeds in reversing his conviction on appeal or in a post conviction proceeding. In *Pearce*, the Court stated:

> In order to assure the absence of such a [vindictive] motivation, we have concluded that whenever a judge imposes a more severe sentence upon a Defendant after a new trial, the reasons for his doing so must affirmatively appear. Those reasons must be based upon objective information concerning identifiable conduct on the part of the Defendant occurring after the time of the original sentencing proceeding.

Id. at 726. *See United States v. Goodwin*, 457 U.S. 368, 374 (1982).

The factual data on which the increased sentence is based must be made part of the record, so that the constitutional legitimacy of the increased sentence may be fully reviewed on appeal. In *Texas v. McCullough*, 475 U.S. 134, 141 (1986), the Supreme Court held that a trial judge's harsher sentence, following a second trial, was permissible because it was based on new and objective information revealed in the second trial.

In *McCullough*, 475 U.S. 134, the Defendant was convicted of murder and sentenced to 20 years. The Defendant's motion for a new trial was granted based on prosecutorial misconduct. Upon a second conviction, the judge imposed a 50-year sentence, stating that he was relying on information not revealed during the first trial, including two new State's witnesses who implicated the Defendant directly in the murder. The Supreme Court held that the *Pearce* presumption of vindictiveness did not apply following the judge granting the Defendant's motion for a new trial, stating:

> The facts of this case provide no basis for a presumption of vindictiveness. In contrast to *Pearce*, McCullough's second trial came about because the trial judge herself concluded that the prosecutor's misconduct required it. Granting McCullough's motion for a new trial hardly suggests any vindictiveness on the part of the judge towards him. Unlike the judge who has been reversed, the trial judge here had no motivation to engage in self-vindication. In such circumstances, there is no justifiable concern about institutional interests that might occasion higher sentences by a judge desirous of discouraging what he regards as meritless appeals.

Id. at 139 (internal citations, quotations, & alterations omitted). Moreover, the Court held that even if the *Pearce* presumption of vindictiveness applied, the judge had rebutted that presumption based on his findings, which provided new and objective information justifying the harsher sentence. *Id.* at 141.

In *Alabama v. Smith*, 490 U.S. 794 (1989), the Defendant pleaded guilty. After his Defendant plea was vacated, he was re-tried, re-convicted, and received a harsher sentence. The Supreme Court refused to apply the presumption of vindictiveness, stating:

While the *Pearce* opinion appeared on its face to announce a rule of sweeping dimension, our subsequent cases have made clear that its presumption of vindictiveness does not apply in every case where a convicted Defendant receives a higher sentence on retrial. As we explained in *Texas v. McCullough*, "the evil the [*Pearce*] Court sought to prevent" was not the imposition of "enlarged sentences after a new trial" but "vindictiveness of a sentencing judge."

Id. at 799 (some internal citations & quotations omitted).

In *Chaffin v. Stynchcombe*, 412 U.S. 17, 29 (1972), the Supreme Court recognized that imposition of a harsher sentence, after a successful collateral attack, may have a "chilling effect." The Court stated: "The Court [in *Pearce*] intimated no doubt about the constitutional validity of higher sentences in the absence of vindictiveness despite whatever incidental deterrent effect they might have on the right to appeal." *See Colten v. Kentucky*, 407 U.S. 104, 116 (1972) (trial court on a "de novo" appeal did not have to justify imposition of a harsher sentence).

5. Prejudice

The sentencing judge may not be motivated by ill will, prejudice, or other impermissible considerations. *Jennings*, 339 Md. 675, 683 (1995); *State v. Dopkowski*, 325 Md. 671, 679 (1992).

6. False information

In *Townsend*, 334 U.S. at 740-41, the Supreme Court held that the sentencing judge may not consider false information.

7. Judge's personal beliefs

The sentencing judge may not consider his or her personal beliefs. If the judge does, the judge fails to make the sentence responsive to the offender and the offense. *United States v. Bakker*, 925 F.2d 728, 740 (4th Cir. 1991). In *Poe v. State*, 341 Md. 523, 533-34 (1996), the Court of Appeals held that the sentencing judge's comments during sentencing about his personal religious beliefs did not require a new sentencing because the sentence was based on the facts and circumstances of the case.

8. Defendant's plea of not guilty

The sentencing judge may not consider the fact that the Defendant denied guilt, pleaded not guilty, and made the State prove its case beyond a reasonable doubt. *Johnson*, 274 Md. 536, 543 (1975); *Colesanti v. State*, 60 Md. App. 185, 194-95 (1984) (sentence may not be based on having pleaded not guilty). In *Passamichali v. State*, 81 Md. App. 731, 747 (1990), the Court of Special Appeals held that the sentence was not influenced by the decision to plead not guilty.

In *Holmes v. State*, 209 Md. App. 427 (2013), the Court of Special Appeals held that a trial judge's comments about the Defendant rejecting a plea offer, made before trial, did not show that the Defendant's sentence was based on the his election of trial by jury, especially when the trial court, during sentencing, stated: "Whatever was discussed before trial is of no import to this court." *Id.* at 460.

9. Prior arrests not resulting in conviction

The sentencing judge may not consider a list of prior arrests that did not result in convictions, without evidence that supported those arrests. *Craddock v. State*, 64 Md. App. 269, 278 (1985).

10. Refusal to testify against a Co-Defendant

The sentencing judge may not consider the Defendant's refusal to testify against a Co-Defendant. *See Roary v. State*, 385 Md. 217, 245-48 (2005).

11. Failure to appear at sentencing

In *Tweedy v. State*, 380 Md. 475, 482-83 (2004), the Court of Appeals held that if there is a three-party plea agreement, with no variables other than to impose the agreed upon sentence, if the Defendant's presence at sentencing is not a condition of the plea agreement, the court cannot impose a greater sentence based on the Defendant's failure to appear at sentencing.

12. Victim impact statement (VIS)

In *Harris v. State*, 312 Md. 225, 236-37 (1988), the Court of Appeals held that the VIS impermissibly focused on the impact of the crime on the family, and not the victim, and such error was not harmless in a capital sentencing proceeding. In *Miller v. State*, 67 Md. App. 666, 674-75 (1986), the Court of Special Appeals remanded for re-sentencing when the sentencing judge heard additional VIS in chambers, without the Defendant or defense counsel being present.

13. Ex parte communication between the sentencing judge & the prosecutor

If the prosecutor and the sentencing judge engage in ex parte communication regarding the sentencing and the interrelationship of various Defendants' culpability, the Defendant is prejudiced, even if the communication was made in good faith. *Caldwell v. State*, 51 Md. App. 703, 709 (1982); *see Scott v. State*, 289 Md. 647, 653-54 (1981) (ex parte communications between judge and representative of the medical office).

14. Imposition of the statutory maximum sentence solely because the prior sentencing judge imposed the maximum sentence

In *Sanders v. State*, 105 Md. App. 247, 256-57 (1995), the Court of Special Appeals reversed a re-sentencing, holding that the re-sentencing judge's apparent feeling of constraint, following the original sentencing judge's decision to impose the maximum sentence, was an impermissible consideration.

15. Convictions obtained in violation of the right to counsel or right to effective assistance of counsel

In *United States v. Tucker*, 404 U.S. 443 (1972), after the Defendant was found guilty of bank robbery, the sentencing court, relying on the Defendant's previous convictions for bank robbery, sentenced the Defendant to the maximum sentence. After sentence was imposed, two of the previous convictions, on which the sentencing court relied, were overturned.

The Supreme Court held that the consideration of these unconstitutional convictions was impermissible and remanded for reconsideration, holding that the "real question" was not whether the result of the trials where the Defendant was convicted without counsel would have had different results had counsel been provided, "but whether the sentence in the [instant] case might have been different if the sentencing judge had known that at least two of the [Defendant's] previous convictions had been unconstitutionally obtained." *Id.* at 447-48.

In *Burgett v. Texas*, 389 U.S. 109 (1967), the Supreme Court stated: "To permit a conviction obtained in violation of *Gideon v. Wainwright*[, 372 U.S. 335 (1963)] to be used against a person either to support guilt or to enhance punishment for another offense is to erode the principle of that case. Worse yet, since the defect in the prior conviction was denial of the right to counsel, the [Defendant] in effect suffers anew from the deprivation of that Sixth Amendment right." *Id.* at 115 (internal citations omitted)).

However, in *Nichols v. United States*, 511 U.S. 738 (1994), the Supreme Court upheld the Defendant's conviction even though the sentencing court had considered a misdemeanor DUI conviction against the Defendant, obtained when the Defendant had not been represented by counsel. The Court stated:

> [C]onsistently with due process, [the Defendant] in the present case could have been sentenced more severely based simply on evidence of the underlying conduct that gave rise to the prior DUI offense. And the state need prove such conduct only by a preponderance of the evidence. Surely, then, it must be constitutionally permissible to consider a prior uncounseled misdemeanor conviction based on the same conduct where that conduct must be proved beyond a reasonable doubt.

Id. at 748. In *Custis v. United States*, 511 U.S. 485, 497 (1994), the Defendant challenge imposition of an enhanced sentence based on state convictions when the Defendant alleged he received ineffective assistance of counsel. The Supreme Court held that the Defendant had no right to collaterally attack his state convictions during a federal sentencing proceeding. Instead, the Defendant was required attack those proceedings through federal habeas corpus, and if successful, then apply for reopening federal sentences enhanced by the state sentences. *Accord Daniels v. United States*, 532 U.S. 374, 382 (2001).

16. Defendant's exercise of the right to a de novo appeal in Circuit Court

At sentencing, after conviction in a trial *de novo* in Circuit Court, a Defendant may be sentenced to a harsher sentence than he or she received in District Court. Md. Code Ann., Cts. & Jud. Proc. § 12-702(c). However, the sentencing court may not consider, as a sentencing factor, the fact that the Defendant exercised his right to a *de novo* appeal. *Abdul-Maleek v. State*, 426 Md. 59, 73-74 (2012).

§ V. Sentencing guidelines

Sentencing guidelines are discretionary. Md. Code Ann., Crim. Proc. § 6-211(b). The sentencing judge may follow the sentencing guidelines, but is not required to do so. If the judge does not adhere to the sentencing guidelines, there is no requirement to state on the record the reasons for not adhering to the guidelines. In *Teasley*, 298 Md. at 370, the Court of Appeals noted that the sentencing "guidelines are not mandatory; instead, they 'complement, rather than replace the . . . proper exercise of judicial discretion." *See Lee v. State*, 69 Md. App. 302, 311-12, *aff'd on other grounds*, 311 Md. 642 (1986). If a judge elects to follow the sentencing guidelines, but does so incorrectly, the sentence will not be disturbed if it is a valid sentence otherwise. *Teasley*, 298 Md. at 370.

In 1984, Congress enacted mandatory sentencing guidelines for all federal offenses. To save the statute from a finding of unconstitutionality, in *United States v. Booker & Fanfan*, 543 U.S. 220, 245 (2005), the Supreme Court held that federal sentencing guidelines are advisory only and are not mandatory. The Court explained that the Sentencing Reform Act of 1984 requires federal sentencing courts to consider guideline ranges and permits them to tailor the sentence to individual cases. *Id.* at 246.

In *Kimbrough v. United States*, 552 U.S. 85, 104-05 (2007), the Supreme Court held that crack cocaine sentencing guidelines, like all federal sentencing guidelines, are advisory only. In *Nelson v. United States*, 555 U.S. 350, 350-52 (2009), the Supreme Court stated that, not only are sentencing guidelines not mandatory, they are not even presumptively reasonable.

§ VI. Pre-sentence investigation (PSI) report

A. Confidentiality

PSI reports are confidential. Md. Rule 4-341. However, PSI reports are available (1) upon court order; or (2) for use by a correctional institution, defense counsel, and/or the State's Attorney's office. *Haynes v. State*, 19 Md. App. 428, 432-33 (1973).

Nonetheless, in *Germain v. State*, 363 Md. 511, 515 (2001), the Court of Appeals held that it was error to preclude the Defendant from using his cellmate's PSI, from prior conviction, to refresh the cellmate's recollection of his prior offenses when they were relevant and material to alleged attack by cellmate on the Defendant. The Court held that a probation officer's testimony, based on a PSI interview, was admissible to impeach the Defendant's statement: "The confidentiality of a PSI is primarily directed to protect against 'public inspection.' It is not absolute." *Id.* at 540.

B. Whether to order a PSI report

The ordering of a PSI report and the use of a PSI report are controlled by Md. Rule 4-341.

1. Discretionary PSI report

Whether to order a PSI report is a decision that is normally within the discretion of the sentencing court. *Callahan v. State*, 30 Md. App. 628, 636 (1976). If the court decides that a PSI report would assist the court in determining the appropriate sentence, the court may order the Department of Parole and Probation (DPP) to prepare and submit a PSI report. Md. Code Ann., Corr. Serv. § 6-112(b). In *Armstead v. State*, 195 Md. App. 599, 615 (2010), *cert. denied*, 418 Md. 191 (2011), the Court of Special Appeals held that the trial court abused its discretion by never ordering or using a PSI report, except in cases for which a PSI report is mandatory.

In *Somers v. State*, 156 Md. App. 279, 318-19 (2004), the Court of Special Appeals held that it was not an abuse of discretion to deny the Defendant's PSI request when there was no showing of a need for a PSI report. *See Sample v. State*, 33 Md. App. 398, 406 (1976); *Church v. State*, 5 Md. App. 642, 646 (1969). In *Ware v. State*, 170 Md. App. 1, 31-35, *cert. denied*, 396 Md. 13 (2006), *cert. denied*, 549 U.S. 1342 (2007), the Court of Special Appeals held that there can be only one PSI report per case. *See Armstead*, 195 Md. App. at 615-16 (if the court abused its discretion in failing to order a PSI report, the error was harmless).

2. Mandatory PSI report

Ordering and using a PSI report is mandatory in cases of life without parole. Md. Code Ann., Corr. Serv. § 6-112(c); *Nelson v. State*, 315 Md. 62, 70-72 (1989). In *Sucik v. State*,

344 Md. 611, 616 (1997), the Court of Appeals held that failure of the trial court to consider a PSI report before sentencing the Defendant to prison for life without the possibility of parole warranted vacating the sentence, notwithstanding the fact that the Defendant did not ask the court for the PSI required by statute.

C. Notification to Defendant, counsel, & State

The PSI report must be delivered to the Defendant or defense counsel and the State with sufficient time to allow a reasonable opportunity to review the PSI report and investigate its contents. Md. Rule 4-341.

In *Scott v. State*, 289 Md. 647, 652-54 (1981), the Court of Appeals held that the rule requiring the PSI report to be delivered to the Defendant or defense counsel and the State was violated when the Medical Examiner, when conducting the court ordered examination, recommended that the Defendant receive the maximum sentence, which was not known to the Defendant, defense counsel, or the State, because that report was not included in the PSI report. If a PSI report is not available to the Defendant, Defendant's counsel, who may see the report, may discuss the information in the report with the Defendant to the extent necessary to allow the Defendant to refute that information. *Haynes v. State*, 19 Md. App. 428, 434 (1973).

D. State's pre-sentence disclosures

The State must disclose information that it intends to present at sentencing. It must be disclosed with sufficient time for the Defendant to have a reasonable opportunity to investigate, or the Defendant is entitled to a continuance. Md. Rules 4-342(d) & 4-343(c). In *Dove v. State*, 415 Md. 727, 740 (2010), the Court of Appeals held that the State violated the pre-sentence disclosure requirement when it failed to disclose a fingerprint card that it intended to use at sentencing, which had been used as substantive evidence of the Defendant's identity in a prior conviction. If the State fails to disclose required information, it is a harmless error if the Defendant receives the most lenient sentence possible. *Id.* at 741.

Md. Rule 4-342(d) applies to all criminal trials, including felonies and misdemeanors, jury and non-jury trials, and guilty pleas. *Brown v. State*, 11 Md. App. 27, *cert. denied*, 261 Md. 722 (1971).

The Defendant is entitled to notice regarding the information that will be considered by the sentencing judge in formulating the sentence in capital cases. In *Gardner*, 430 U.S. at 359-60, the Supreme Court held that the Defendant was denied due process when the sentencing judge imposed the death penalty based, in part, on confidential information in the PSI report, which was not disclosed to the Defendant prior to sentencing. *See Lankford v. Idaho*, 500 U.S. 110, 127 (1991) (vacating a death penalty when defense counsel did not have adequate notice the Defendant could be sentenced to death).

Md. Rule 4-342(d) provides that the State's Attorney must disclose to the Defendant all evidence the State plans to present during sentencing and, if such notice is not provided, requires that the Court to postpone sentencing.

E. Availability to the Defendant

The DPP must make the PSI report available, upon request, to (1) the Defendant; (2) defense counsel; (3) the State; (4) the correctional facility; (5) the DPP pre-trial release officer; (6) a public health or mental health facility; and (7) the community substance abuse treatment program that is evaluating or treating the Defendant as a condition of probation. Md. Code Ann., Corr. Serv. § 6-112(a)(2).

F. Victim impact statement (VIS)

If required under Md. Code Ann., Crim. Proc. § 11-402, a PSI report must include a VIS. The court conducting the sentencing proceeding must consider the VIS report. Md. Code Ann., Corr. Serv. § 6-112(b)(3). A VIS stapled to a PSI report satisfies "included." *Ball v. State*, 347 Md. 156, 193 (1997). If the Defendant, in committing a felony, caused physical, psychological, or economic injury to the victim, a PSI may include a VIS. Md. Rule 4-341; Md. Code Ann., Corr. Serv. § 6-112; Md. Code Ann., Crim. Proc. § 11-402.

A typical VIS (1) identifies the victim; and (2) itemizes and identifies any economic loss, physical injury, or psychological injury, and other such information relating to the impact of the offense on the victim and the victim's family. *Id.* A trial court is not required to follow the recommendations made by pre-sentence investigators. *Glass v. State*, 24 Md. App. 76, 81 (1974).

G. Confrontation Clause

The right of confrontation is not violated by admission of a PSI report, even if the person who prepared the PSI report is not subject to cross-examination. *Ball*, 347 Md. at 201; *Tichnell v. State*, 290 Md. 43, 58-59 (1981); *Driver v. State*, 201 Md. 25, 32 (1952).

H. Contents of the PSI report

A PSI report often involves a "broad-ranging inquiry into a Defendant's private life, not limited by traditional rules of evidence." *United States v. Corbitt*, 879 F.2d 224, 230 (7th Cir. 1989) (citation omitted). The American Bar Association recommends that agencies preparing a PSI report should be required to adhere to uniform standards relating to content, preparation, and substantiation of information presented in a PSI report. *See ABA Standards for Criminal Justice, Fair Trial, & Free Press* Standard 18-5.4. In *Gatewood v. State*, 15 Md. App. 450, 460-62 (1972), the Court of Special Appeals held that a sentencing judge may consider anything, and a PSI report may include anything about the Defendant's reputation, past offenses, habits, health, etc.

The PSI report typically contains the following: (1) the crime and the aggravating and/or mitigating factors; (2) the Defendant's prior convictions and juvenile adjudications; (3) the Defendant's personal characteristics, even if not material to culpability; (4) information about programs or resources, e.g., treatment centers, residential facilities, vocational training services, educational and rehabilitative programs; (5) information about the physical, psychological, economic, or social effects of the crime on any victim; (6) authorized sanctions and sentencing guidelines; (7) assessment of the impact of sanctions and collateral consequences; (8) a summary and, if requested, a sentencing recommendation; and (9) the VIS.

§ VII. Allocution

A. What & when

Prior to being sentenced, the Defendant has the right to personally address the court, in addition to having defense counsel address the court. The Defendant addressing the court is called "allocution." Md. Rules 4-342(f) & 4-343(g); *Shifflet v. State*, 315 Md. 382 (1989); *Harris v. State*, 306 Md. 344, 352, 357 (1986). In *Miller v. State*, 67 Md. App. 666, 674-75 (1986), the Court of Special Appeals held that the purpose of allocution is to provide the Defendant with an opportunity to refute or explain any information presented and to speak in mitigation. Allocution is not subject to cross-examination. *See Booth v. State*, 306 Md. 172, 199-200 (1986).

The trial court is not required to inform the Defendant of the right of allocution. The court is required only to provide the Defendant with an opportunity to address the court and to make a statement. *Jones v. State*, 414 Md. 686, 698-99 (2010). In *Clermont v. State*, 348 Md. 419, 452, *cert. denied*, 523 U.S. 1141 (1998), the Court of Appeals held that the trial court, and not the Defendant, controls the timing of allocution at sentencing.

In *Brown v. State*, 11 Md. App. 27, 34 (1971), the Court of Special Appeals held that although the court erred by sentencing the Defendant, without granting the right of allocution, the error was harmless because the court allowed the Defendant's counsel to make an argument in mitigation after the sentence was imposed and the judge gave consideration to that argument. In *Hill v. United States*, 368 U.S. 424 (1962), the Supreme Court held that the failure to allow the Defendant to speak during allocution "is not a fundamental defect which inherently results in a complete miscarriage of justice, not an omission inconsistent with the rudimentary demands of fair procedure." *Id.* at 428.

In *Shifflett v. State*, 315 Md. 382, 387-88 (1989), the Court of Appeals held that it was an abuse of discretion for the court to deny the Defendant's request for allocution, which was made for the first time after the State's final argument, during which the State raised new substantive issues. The court may curtail irrelevant or unreasonably long allocution. *Harris*, 306 Md. at 359.

In *Henry v. State*, 324 Md. 204 (1991), the Court of Appeals held that the Defendant may not present inadmissible evidence during allocution: "Although [the Defendant has] a right to insist on presenting his allocution . . . , he did not have the right to present a transcript of extraneous, out of court statements made by a person who did not testify at trial." *Id.* at 245-47. However, the factual content of the allocution is not generally limited to the record in the case. *Booth v. State*, 306 Md. 172, 198 (1986), *rev'd on separate grounds*, 482 U.S. 496 (1987).

1. Contempt cases

A Defendant held in direct contempt is entitled to allocution. *Mitchell v. State*, 320 Md. 756, 769-70 (1990) (Defendant held in contempt for giving the judge a single-finger gesture). However, in *Thomas v. State*, 99 Md. App. 47 (1994), the Court of Special Appeals held that a Defendant held in direct contempt may be denied allocution if allocution would invite additional invective and the nature of the contemptuous speech leaves little room for "helpful explanation." Id. at 52-59 (Defendant told the judge to "fuck himself").

2. Violation of probation (VOP) hearings

In *Sellman v. State*, 47 Md. App. 510 (1981), the Court of Special Appeals held that the Defendant has a right of allocution in a VOP hearing.

3. Hearing on a motion for modification or reduction of sentence

In *Collins v. State*, 69 Md. App. 173, 195-96 (1986), the Court of Special Appeals held that the Defendant does not have a right of allocution in a hearing on a motion for modification or reduction of sentence.

4. Sentencing on remand

In *Jones v. State*, 414 Md. 686, 701 (2010), the Court of Appeals held that, because sentencing on remand is a new sentencing, the Defendant has a right of allocution, even if the Defendant made allocution at the original sentencing, and even though the remand was for the purpose of merging the Defendant's sentences.

B. Testimonial

Allocution is testimonial for Fifth Amendment purposes. Thus, the State may not compel the Defendant to speak at sentencing or comment on the Defendant's exercise of the Fifth Amendment privilege against compelled self-incrimination at trial or at sentencing. *Mitchell v. United States*, 526 U.S. 314, 324-25 (1999); *Ridenour v. State*, 142 Md. App. 1, 15 (2001). Like the decision to whether to testify, the Defendant makes a tactical decision whether to provide allocution. *Thanos v. State*, 330 Md. 77, 89-90 (1993).

C. State's response to allocution

In *Hunt*, 321 Md. at 435-37, the Court of Appeals held that, after the Defendant presents allocution, the court may permit the State to respond, including why the information provided in the allocution should not be considered.

D. Waiver of allocution

The right of allocution is not of constitutional dimension, and failure to present allocution before sentencing waives the right. *Hill v. United States*, 368 U.S. 424, 428 (1962); *State v. Calhoun*, 306 Md. 692 (1986); *Logan v. State*, 289 Md. 460, 487 (1981); *Robinson v. Warden*, 242 Md. 171, 172 (1966). If there is neither a request for allocution before sentencing, nor an objection to the absence of allocution immediately after sentencing, allocution is waived. *Calhoun*, 306 Md. at 704; *Perry v. State*, 150 Md. App. 403, 445-46 (2002). Prior to 1984, the failure of a trial judge to inform a Defendant of the right of allocution resulted in a re-sentencing. *See Kent v. State*, 287 Md. 389, 393-94 (1980); *Rome v. State*, 236 Md. 583, 589 (1964).

The requirement to inform the Defendant of allocution was removed when the Court of Appeals promulgated Md. Rule 4-342. In *State v. Lyles*, 308 Md. 129, 133 (1986), the Court of Appeals held that there is no requirement for the court to inform the Defendant of the right of allocution, but there is a requirement for the court to provide an opportunity for allocution. In *Shiflett*, 315 Md. at 387-88, the Court of Appeals held that the Defendant was entitled to respond to the State's allegations made just before sentencing, even if the Defendant previously waived the right of allocution.

E. Remedy for denial of allocution

If the Defendant is denied the right of allocution, the sentence is vacated, and the Defendant is re-sentenced. *Jones v. State*, 414 Md. 686, 707 (2010); *Shiflett*, 315 Md. at 388.

§ VIII. Incarceration

A. Authority to impose &/or to execute the sentence

In Maryland, for the vast majority of offenses, the legislature gives the trial judge, who becomes the sentencing judge, the authority to (1) impose any sentence, up to the statutory cap; and (b) execute any portion of the imposed sentence. *See* Md. Code Ann., Crim. Proc. § 6-219.

Occasionally, the legislature takes the sentencing imposition decision away from the sentencing judge, in part or totally. For example, the maximum sentence for use of a firearm in the commission of a felony or crime of violence is 20 years, and the sentencing court is required to impose at least five years of the 20-year maximum. Md.

Code Ann., 4-204(c)(1). Occasionally, the legislature takes the sentencing execution decision away from the sentencing judge, in part or totally. For example, for use of a firearm in the commission of a felony or crime of violence, the sentencing court is not only required to impose no less than a five-year sentence, the court may not suspend the first five years, and must execute at least five years.

Under federal law, 18 U.S.C. § 924 provides for a mandatory minimum sentence of ten years for the discharge of a firearm during a crime of violence, even if the discharge is accidental. *See Dean v. United States*, 556 U.S. 568, 577 (2009).

Moreover, in addition to the imposition and execution limitations placed by the legislature on the sentencing judge, the legislature may also place limits on the parole commission, i.e., not only must five years be imposed and five years be executed for use of a firearm in the commission of a felony or crime of violence, the parole commission may not parole the Defendant for at least five years.

B. Sentencing options for offenses subject to incarceration

In *Benedict v. State*, 377 Md. 1, 7-8 (2003), the Court of Appeals outlined the options available to a trial court when sentencing a Defendant to a crime punishable by incarceration.

1. Impose & execute a sentence, suspending none of the sentence

The trial court may impose a prison sentence, up the maximum term allowed, and execute the entire sentence. This means that the court suspends none of the sentence. In that case, the entire sentence must be served, unless the Defendant is released earlier because (a) the Defendant is released on parole; or (b) the Defendant is not granted parole but, based on accumulated diminution credits, the Defendant is entitled to release. In either (a) or (b), the Defendant will be on mandatory supervision until the entire sentence has been served.

2. Impose a sentence & suspend some or all of the sentence, executing none or some of the sentence

The trial court may impose a sentence, up to the maximum term allowed, and execute none of the sentence or execute part of the sentence but less than the entire sentence. This means that the court suspends some of the sentence or the entire sentence.

If the court suspends part of the sentence and executes part of the sentence, this is referred to as a "split sentence." If the court suspends the entire sentence, the court almost always places the Defendant on probation. If the court suspends some of the sentence, the court almost always places the Defendant on a period of probation upon release from the unsuspended portion of the sentence. It is possible, but highly unlikely, that the court will impose no sentence and simply place the Defendant on probation. In Maryland, the maximum period of probation is five years in Circuit Court and three years in District Court.

It is possible that the Defendant will be on both parole and probation at the same time. For example, the Defendant is convicted of robbery, and the trial court imposes a sentence of ten years, and suspend all but five years, with five years supervised probation upon release. Let's assume that the Defendant is paroled after three years. For the first two years after release, the Defendant is on supervision by a parole officer. For the first five years after release, the Defendant is on supervision by a probation agent. Those two supervising individuals are almost certainly the same person.

The Defendant is under supervision to the executive branch of government for parole and under supervision to the judicial branch of government for probation. If the Defendant is alleged to violate parole and/or probation, the following will happen. For the alleged violation of parole, a retake warrant will result in the Defendant being taken back to the Division of Correction (DOC), where the Defendant will be scheduled for a hearing before a parole commissioner who will serve as the judge for the parole violation hearing. For the alleged violation of probation, most likely a summons will issue, placing the Defendant before the judge who placed the Defendant on probation.

If the Defendant is found "guilty" of violation of parole, the Defendant (a) could be sent back to the DOC for all of his un-served time (two years in the hypothetical); (b) could lose some or all of his diminution credits; and (c) could face prison time if it was a criminal charge that resulted in the revocation of parole. If the Defendant is found "guilty" of violation of probation, the Defendant (a) could be sent back to the DOC for all of his un-served and suspended time (seven years in the hypothetical); and (b) could face prison time if it was a criminal charge that resulted in the violation or probation.

C. Concurrent sentences versus consecutive sentences

In Maryland, when the Defendant has been found guilty of multiple non-merging offenses, the trial court usually has discretion to permit multiple sentences to be served at the same time, i.e., the sentences are concurrent, or to require that multiple sentences to be served one after the other, i.e., the sentences are consecutive.

The purpose of consecutive versus concurrent sentences is to provide discretion to the trial court. A consecutive sentencing option ensures that a person who commits separate and distinct violations of the law may receive separate and distinct punishments. *See Kaylor v. State*, 285 Md. 66, 70 (1979) (citations omitted). Occasionally, the legislature takes the "consecutive-concurrent" sentencing decision away from the sentencing judge, and requires consecutive sentence. *See, e.g., Fleeger v. State*, 301

Md. 155, 166-67 (1984) (mandatory consecutive sentence for escape). *See* Md. Code Ann., Crim. Law § 9-407(1).

If, as in most cases, the sentencing court has discretion regarding concurrent or consecutive sentences, and if, when imposing sentence, the court is silent or ambiguous as to whether the sentences will be served concurrently or consecutively, the sentences are deemed to be concurrent, interpreting the silence or ambiguity most favorably to the Defendant. *Nash v. State*, 69 Md. App. 681, 691-92 (1987); *Nelson v. State*, 66 Md. App. 304, 314 (1986); *Dutton v. State*, 160 Md. App. 180, 188-92 (2004).

In *Parker v. State*, 193 Md. App. 469, 486-87 (2010), the Court of Special Appeals held that, even if the sentencing judge does not use the term consecutive, the sentences are consecutive if the judge announces the beginning date of one sentence as the same as the ending date of another sentence. *See Gatewood v. State*, 158 Md. App. 458, 479-82 (2004), *aff'd*, 388 Md. 526 (2005); *Collins v. State*, 69 Md. App. 173, 196-97 (1986).

In *Oregon v. Ice*, 555 U.S. 160, 163-64 (2009), the Supreme Court held that the Sixth Amendment right to trial by jury does not prohibit assigning to the judge, and not the jury, the power to make findings of fact necessary for the imposition of consecutive, rather than concurrent, sentences for multiple offenses. If a Defendant is given a sentence to run concurrent with his sentence in another jurisdiction, and is subsequently paroled in that other jurisdiction, he or she will have to serve the remaining portion of the Maryland sentence in Maryland. *State v. Parker*, 334 Md. 576, 595-96 (1994).

If the sentence contained in the docket entries is different than the sentence imposed during sentencing, the transcript will control the actual sentence. *Shade v. State*, 18 Md. App. 407, 411 (1973).

D. Paroleable sentences versus without parole sentences

Maryland and most states have a parole system. Federal law eliminated parole in 1987. 18 U.S.C. §§ 4201 to 4218. Even with a parole system, legislatures sometimes establish sentences that are not eligible for parole or establish sentences that have a certain period of non-parole eligibility.

It is not an inherent part of the judicial sentencing function to regulate the parole eligibility of an inmate. Except in those limited circumstances when the Legislature has expressly empowered the court, or mandate the court, to impose no-parole sentence, the parole function is exclusively within the control of the executive branch of government. *DeLeon v. State*, 102 Md. App. 58, 73 (1994). In *Simms v. State*, 65 Md. App. 685 (1986), the sentencing judge attempted to impose conditions on parole. The Court of Special Appeals held that the trial court may impose conditions on probation, which is within the inherent control of the judiciary, but not on parole, which is within the power of the legislature. *Id.* at 689-90.

E. Life sentence

In Maryland, the Defendant is eligible for a life sentence for first degree murder, first degree rape, first degree sex offense, and the inchoate offenses thereto, e.g., attempt, solicitation, conspiracy. Md. Code Ann., Crim. Law §§ 2-201, 3-303(d), & 3-305(d). For a life sentence, the Defendant is eligible for parole (1) after serving 15 years (less diminution credits), or (2) 25 years (less diminution credits) if first degree murder and State unsuccessfully sought the death penalty.

In *Richardson v. State*, 332 Md. 94, 101-07 (1993), the Court of Appeals held that the statutory 25-year parole eligibility requirement may be imposed only upon Defendants not eligible for the death penalty. Md. Code Ann., Crim. Law § 2-201(b). Since 1995, no Maryland "lifer" has been paroled, although some have had their sentences commuted to less than life.

In 2013, the Maryland General Assembly eliminated the death penalty as a sentencing option. Thus, for first degree murder, the sentence may be (1) life without parole (if the State placed the Defendant on notice of its intent to seek a life without parole; or (2) life with parole. Md. Code Ann., Crim. Law § 2-201. In *Johnson v. State*, 362 Md. 525, 534-35 (2001), the Court of Appeals held that life, without the possibility of parole. is an illegal sentence for conspiracy to commit first degree murder. In *Gary*, 341 Md. at 520, the Court of Appeals held that a sentence of life, with the possibility of parole, is a legal sentence for conspiracy to commit first degree murder.

F. Split sentence

The court may (1) impose a sentence for specified period of time and order that a portion of the sentence be served in confinement; (2) suspend the remainder of the sentence; and (3) order probation for a statutorily permitted period upon release from the unsuspended potion of the sentence. Md. Code Ann., Crim. Proc. § 6-222(a); *Benedict v. State*, 377 Md. 1, 7-8 (2003).

In *Cathcart v. State*, 397 Md. 320, 330 (2007), the Court of Appeals held that, if the court orders a split sentence, yet fails to impose a period of probation to be served subsequent to the Defendant serving the unsuspended portion of the split sentence, the sentence converts to a sentence equal to the unsuspended portion. For example, if a Defendant is convicted of first degree murder, and the court imposes a sentence of life, with all but 50 years suspended, but fails to place the Defendant on probation upon his release, the sentence of "life suspend all but 50 years" converts to a straight 50 years.

In *Greco v. State*, 427 Md. 477 (2012), the Court of Appeals overruled *Cathcart*, holding: "[The Defendant's] previously imposed sentence for first degree premeditated murder of life, suspend all but fifty years, was converted by operation of law into a term-of-years sentence of fifty years imprisonment. That converted sentence was not authorized by statute; therefore, it was illegal. On remand, the Circuit Court is limited by the maximum legal sentence that could have been imposed, with the illegality removed. That is, the Circuit Court must impose a sentence of life imprisonment, all but fifty years suspended, to be followed by some period of probation." 427 Md. at 512.

G. Sentences for conspiracy or attempt

The maximum sentence for conspiracy and attempt is generally the same as the maximum sentence for the crime to which conspired or attempted. Md. Code Ann., Crim. Law §§ 1-201 & 1-202. In *Hardy v. State*, 301 Md. 124, 132 (1984), the Court of Appeals held that the legislative intent was to limit the maximum potential sentence to the sentence for the consummated crime. *Accord Walker v. State*, 53 Md. App. 171, 187 n.5 (1982); *see Gary v. State*, 341 Md. 513, 520 (1996).

Life without the possibility of parole is the maximum sentence for first degree murder. However, a Defendant convicted of attempted first degree murder or conspiracy to commit first degree murder may be sentenced only to life and may not be sentenced to life without parole. *Johnson v. State*, 362 Md. 525, 534-35 (2001) (conspiracy); *Hardy*, 301 Md. at 139-40 (attempt).

If the Defendant is found guilty of conspiracy or attempt, as to two different crimes, the sentence for the crime with the greater sentence is also the maximum sentence for attempt or conspiracy. *See Campbell v. State*, 325 Md. 488, 508 n.11 (1992); *Henry v. State*, 324 Md. 204, 240 (1991); *Jordan v. State*, 323 Md. 151, 162 (1991); *Wilson v. State*, 148 Md. App. 601, 640-41 (2002).

H. Sentence for first degree murder—
life with or with out parole

Maryland, by statute, has abrogated the death penalty. 2013 Md. Laws ch. 156. Thus, for first degree murder, in Maryland, the State may seek life without parole or life with the possibility of parole. Md. Rule 4-342; *see Sucik*, 344 Md. at 615; *Woods v. State*, 315 Md. 591, 601 (1989). For a sentence of life without parole, the State must notify the Defendant of its intent to seek the enhanced sentence. Md. Code Ann., Crim. Law § 2-203(1). If the State does not seek life without parole, the sentence, if the Defendant is found guilty, must be life or life with all but a finite number of years suspended.

I. Methods of serving a sentence

1. Division of Correction (DOC)

To be incarcerated in the DOC, the Defendant must receive a sentence that exceeds 12 months, both imposed and executed. Md. Code Ann., Corr. Serv. § 9-104.

2. Local detention center

To be incarcerated in a local detention center, the Defendant must receive a sentence, as imposed and executed, that does not exceed 12 months. *Id.* § 9-105.

3. Home detention

For most offenses, the court may sentence the Defendant to home detention, with appropriate monitoring. *Id.* § 3-404.

4. In-patient drug or alcohol treatment

The trial court may place the Defendant in long-term, in-patient care in lieu of incarceration. This issue may be presented to the court at the original sentencing. It may be presented to the court through a motion for modification or reduction of sentence, which may be filed at any time. It may be presented to the Maryland Parole Commission at any time.

The burden is on the Defendant. The first step is to persuade the court, using testimony, medical records, and/or affidavits that the Defendant (a) is drug dependent, (b) is not violent; and (c) is amendable to drug rehabilitation through long-term in-patient treatment. If the Defendant is able to persuade the court of the legitimacy of the Defendant's proffer and/or evidence, the court will most likely refer the Defendant to the Department of Health & Mental Hygiene (DHMH) for its evaluation and recommendation to the court regarding whether the Defendant (a) is drug dependent; (b) is not violent; and (c) is amendable to long-term, in-patient drug rehabilitation. Md. Code Ann., Health Gen. § 8-507.

If the DHMH evaluation is favorable to the Defendant, the court, within its discretion, may order long-term, in-patient drug treatment in lieu of incarceration. If the court issues an order for such treatment, it may take three months to a year to "find a bed" for the Defendant in an approved facility. Once a placement is located, and the Defendant is assigned to it, if the Defendant cannot, though treatment, become drug free, the Defendant "fails out" and is returned to the DOC. If the Defendant does succeed in becoming drug free, through long-term, in-patient treatment, which usually takes six months to a year, the court typically places the Defendant on supervised probation, with long-term outpatient treatment. *Id.*

§ IX. Recidivism enhanced sentences

A. Enhancement sentencing applicable only if there is an enhancement statute applicable to the Defendant

The State may not seek, and the court may not impose, enhanced sentencing if the legislature has not provided statutory authority for an enhanced sentence. Even if there is a statutorily enhanced sentence, the Defendant may not be eligible for enhancement. Ambiguity in a sentencing statute must be interpreted in favor of the Defendant. *Cantine v. State*, 160 Md. App. 391, 413 (2004). Any ambiguity as to whether the legislature intended multiple punishments for the same act "will be resolved against turning a single transaction into multiple offenses." *Simpson v. United States*, 435 U.S. 6, 15 (1978).

In *Scott v. State*, 351 Md. 667, 676-77 (1998), the Court of Appeals held that, when there is an ambiguity as to whether two sentencing enhancements could apply together, the rule of lenity precludes applying both. In *Price v. State*, 405 Md. 10, 33-34 (2008), the Court of Appeals held that sentences on multiple counts, all stemming from the same transaction, cannot each be enhanced by the same enhancement statute under the rule of lenity. In *Gargliano v. State*, 334 Md. 428, 449 (1994), the Court of Appeals held that when it is unclear whether the legislature intended to authorize an enhanced sentence, the court must assume that the legislature did not intend to do so.

In *Harris v. State*, 169 Md. App. 98, 103-05, *cert. denied*, 394 Md. 481 (2006), the Court of Special Appeals held that the trial court could not impose a mandatory 25-year sentence, without parole, when the statute was ambiguous as to inclusion of conspiracy to distribute cocaine as a qualifying conviction.

In *Loveday*, 296 Md. 226, the Court of Appeals held that, if the Defendant can demonstrate that (a) the crimes are not qualifying crimes of violence, or (b) the proceeding is defective, e.g., that the Defendant unlawfully lacked counsel, there can be no enhanced sentence. *Id.* at 237; *see State v. Fincham*, 71 Md. App. 314, 315 (1987).

B. Enhancement sentencing for subsequent offenders

Subsequent offender statutes apply when prior convictions make the Defendant eligible for, or mandate, an enhanced sentence. Md. Rule 4-245(a). The decision to pursue a mandatory minimum sentence, when provided by a subsequent offender statute, is a matter of prosecutorial discretion. The court is not bound to impose a mandatory sentence if the prosecution does not provide, or provides but later withdraws, notice to the Defendant of its intent to pursue an enhanced sentencing and the supporting prior conviction(s). In *Beverly v. State*, 349 Md. 106, 127-28 (1998), the Court of Appeals upheld a plea agreement in which the State agreed not to treat the Defendant's conviction as a subsequent offense for enhancement purposes.

In *Shilling v. State*, 320 Md. 288, 296-97 (1990), the Court of Appeals held that a PBJ is a conviction for the purposes of sentence enhancement. In *Whack v. State*, 338 Md. 665, 678-79 (1995), the Court of Appeals held that a conviction on appeal is a predicate conviction for the purposes of enhancement. Two enhancement statutes may be applied in the same case to enhance sentences on different counts. However, in *Price v. State*, 405 Md. 10, 32-34 (2008), the Court of Appeals held that sentences on multiple counts, based on the same transaction, cannot each be enhanced by the same enhancement statute.

In *Muir v. State*, 308 Md. 208 (1986), the Court of Appeals held that the fact that the Defendant's prior convictions were for offenses he committed as a juvenile did not preclude them from serving as predicate felonies under the enhanced punishment statute: "Not to count such convictions as predicate crimes of violence would, we think, thwart the legislative purpose of protecting the public and deterring the commission of violent crimes." *Id.* at 218.

In *Teeter v. State*, 65 Md. App. 105, 120 (1985), *cert. denied*, 305 Md. 245 (1986), the Court of Special Appeals held that, if the prerequisites for imposing a mandatory minimum sentence have not been met, it is illegal to impose such a sentence. In *Stevenson v. State*, 180 Md. App. 440, 447 (2008), the Court of Special Appeals held that the Defendant was not a repeat offender, for purposes of enhanced sentencing, because the Defendant's pre-trial detention did not count as a "term of confinement" under the statute. In *State v. Green*, 367 Md. 61, 80 (2001), the Court of Appeals held that a mandatory sentence may not be modified by commitment to the Department of Health and Mental Hygiene.

C. Permissive enhancement versus mandatory enhancement

Sentencing enhancement statutes include permissive enhancement and mandatory enhancement. Md. Rule 4-245(c). In *Loveday v. State*, 296 Md. 226, 241 (1983), the Court of Appeals held that enhancement sentencing, based on prior convictions, is constitutional.

Pursuant to Md. Rule 4-245(c), in *State v. Montgomery*, 334 Md. 20 (1994), the Court of Appeals held that (a) if the sentencing enhancement statute is mandatory; (b) if the statutory requirements are satisfied; and (c) if the requisite notice is provided, the sentencing judge must impose the enhanced sentence. The Court stated: "[T]he rule precludes a Defendant from being able to evade the imposition of a mandatory penalty, which, if all the statutory requirements are met, must be imposed." *Id.* at 25 (citing *Loveday v. State*, 296 Md. 226, 236-37 (1983)).

D. Requirement for notice of intent to seek enhancement

1. Logistics of proving notice of enhancement

Both permissive enhancement and mandatory enhancement require the State to provide notice to the Defendant of its intent to seek enhancement sentencing. Pursuant to Md. Rule 4-245(b), the State must hand deliver to defense counsel, or must send via first class mail, mailed no later than 15 days prior to trial, its notice of intent to seek enhanced sentencing. *Lee v. State*, 332 Md. 654, 664 (1993).

2. Guilty pleas

In a guilty plea case, *State v. Armstrong*, 60 Md. App. 244, 249 (1984), *cert. denied*, 302 Md. 288 (1985), provides that the notice must be received prior to the entry of the plea, which may include the day of the plea. *See Oyler v. Boles*, 368 U.S. 448, 452-53 (1962). For permissive enhancement, if the case does not result in a plea, the State must provide notice at least 15 days prior to trial in Circuit Court and at least five days prior to trial in District Court. Md. Rule 4-245(b).

3. Mandatory enhancement

For mandatory enhancement, the State must provide notice at least 15 days prior to sentencing in Circuit Court and at least five days prior to sentencing in District Court. Md. Rule 4-245(c). The State's notice is valid, even if it cites the enhancement statute incorrectly, *Vines v. State*, 40 Md. App. 658, 661-62 (1978), *aff'd*, 285 Md. 369 (1979), or cited no enhancement section at all. *Ogunbowale v. State*, 120 Md. App. 648, 650 (1998).

The State's notice must indicate (a) the particular prior conviction(s) that the State intends to use for enhancement; (b) the date of the conviction(s); (c) the court in which the conviction(s) occurred; (d) the statute under which the conviction(s) resulted; and (e) the nature of the crime(s). Once the Defendant is given proper notice, the burden is on the State to prove, beyond a reasonable doubt, the existence of the statutory conditions required to impose an enhanced sentence. *Sutton v. State*, 128 Md. App. 308, 327 (1999) (quoting *Beverly v. State*, 349 Md. 106 (1998)).

In *King v. State*, 55 Md. 672, 687 (1983), *aff'd*, 300 Md. 218 (1984), the Court of Special Appeals held that the State's failure to provide proper notice to the Defendant regarding the prior conviction was harmless error, when defense counsel admitted that he knew the conviction on which the State was relying when he received notice. In *Carter v. State*, 319 Md. 618, 621-22 (1990), the Court of Appeals held that if the Defendant was convicted in District Court, and appealed to Circuit Court, the State may not seek an enhanced sentence in Circuit Court if the State failed to give notice prior to trial in District Court. On remand, the State is not required to file a new notice. *Gantt v. State*, 73 Md. App. 701, 703-04 (1988).

In *Booze v. State*, 140 Md. App. 402, 406-07 (2001), the Court of Special Appeals held that enhanced drug penalty provisions were applicable even if the Defendant did not receive notice of the consequences of a subsequent conviction at the time his guilty plea was accepted. In *State v. Purcell*, 342 Md. 214, 222 (1996), the Court of Appeals held that the Defendant waived his right to notice by providing proof of his prior conviction and refusing the opportunity to withdraw his guilty plea and postpone proceedings.

4. Failure to provide notice

If the State fails to provide timely notice of a permissive enhancement, the sentencing judge may not enhance the sentence. In *Armstrong v. State*, 69 Md. App. 23, 35-36 (1986), the Court of Special Appeals stated that the reason that the notice of permissive sentencing enhancement must be provided timely pre-trial, and not pre-sentencing, is because the State's decision to seek enhancement is a factor for the Defendant in deciding whether to accept a plea or go to trial.

If State fails to provide timely notice of mandatory enhancement, the sentencing judge must postpone sentencing at least 15 days, unless the Defendant waives the notice requirement. Md. Rule 4-245(c). In *State v. Montgomery*, 334 Md. 20, 25-26 (1994), the Court of Appeals held that the State was entitled to a continuance after failure to provide timely notice of mandatory enhancement because of a mistake in captioning the notice. In *State v. Thurmond*, 73 Md. App. 686, 692, *cert. denied*, 312 Md. 602 (1988), the Court of Special Appeals remanded for re-sentencing when the trial court refused to postpone the sentencing, as required by Md. Rule 4-245(c), after the State failed to provide timely notice to the Defendant.

In 2011, the Maryland General Assembly amended Md. Code Ann., § 5-133, regarding possession of a regulated firearm by a person convicted of a disqualifying crime. There is a mandatory five-year minimum sentence for possession of a firearm by a person convicted of a disqualifying crime. However, under the amended law, imposition of the five-year minimum is within the discretion of the court if five years has elapsed since the Defendant completed his sentence, including parole, probation, and supervision. The Court may not impose the mandatory minimum unless the State provides the Defendant with notice that it intends to seek the mandatory minimum.

E. Non-disclosure to the jury of enhancement sentencing

The Defendant's subsequent offender status may not be disclosed to the jury without the Defendant's consent, except as otherwise permissible, e.g., impeachment by prior conviction. Md. Rule 4-245(d). In *State v. Giddens*, 335 Md. 205, 217 (1994), the Court of Appeals held that the Defendant's prior conviction for cocaine distribution was relevant to his credibility and was thus admissible for impeachment purposes.

F. State has the burden of persuasion as to the Defendant's prior convictions & incarceration

In *Cunningham v. California*, 549 U.S. 275 (2007), the Supreme Court held that a sentencing enhancement statute violates the right to trial by jury if the judge finds the facts, other than a prior conviction, that result in a greater sentence, instead of having the jury make findings beyond a reasonable doubt. *See Deville v. State*, 383 Md.

217, 232 (2004). In *Jones v. State*, 324 Md. 32 (1991), the Court of Appeals held that both the permissive and mandatory enhanced sentencing statutes place the burden on the State, beyond a reasonable doubt, to prove all statutory conditions precedent to imposition of an enhanced sentence. *Id.* at 37 (citing *Bowman v. State*, 314 Md. 725, 733 (1989)); *see Sullivan v. State*, 29 Md. App. 622, 631 (1976).

The State must offer formal proof of the Defendant's prior convictions. In *Ford v. State*, 73 Md. App. 391, 402-03 (1988), the Court of Special Appeals held that it was insufficient, for subsequent offender enhancement, for the State to argue the existence of a certified copy of a prior conviction, yet fail to offer it into evidence. In *Irby v. State*, 66 Md. App. 580, 588 (1986), *cert. denied*, 308 Md. 270 (1987), the Court of Special Appeals held that the evidence in the court file was sufficient to prove the predicate convictions beyond a reasonable doubt. The PSI report and/or the Defendant's testimony may show prior convictions and incarceration for enhanced sentence purposes.

In *Sutton v. State*, 128 Md. App. 308, 330 (1999), the Court of Special Appeals held that an unchallenged PSI report satisfied the State's burden of proving prior a qualifying conviction beyond a reasonable doubt. *Accord Collins v. State*, 89 Md. App. 273, 286 (1991) (PSI report of prior convictions and Defendant's admission to them at trial); *Hall v. State*, 69 Md. App. 37, 63 (1986) (PSI report that attributed prior convictions to police records sufficient for enhanced sentence).

G. Predicate conviction may not be challenged in enhancement sentencing proceeding

In *State v. McGhee*, 331 Md. 494, 495 (1993), the Court of Appeals held that, even though the burden is on the State, the Defendant may not challenge a facially valid prior conviction during a recidivist sentencing proceeding. In *Fairbanks v. State*, 331 Md. 482, 493-94 (1993), the Court of Appeals held:

> Allowing a Defendant to mount any constitutionally based challenge to a predicate conviction at a recidivist (or other) sentencing proceeding would present significant procedural difficulties. Our rules do not establish a specific procedure for such challenges. Although the State is required to serve notice of predicate convictions on the Defendant before sentencing, there is no requirement that the Defendant give notice of any proposed challenge to those convictions. On the other hand, there exists a statutory procedure for the orderly bringing of a collateral challenge against prior convictions resulting in continued confinement, parole, or probation. Common law actions, including the writ of error *coram nobis*, may be available for collateral attacks on prior convictions that no longer impose restraints on a Defendant.

Id. at 486 (internal citations & quotations omitted).

The State must offer formal proof of the Defendant's prior convictions. In *Ford v. State*, 73 Md. App. 391, 402-03 (1988), the Court of Special Appeals held that it was insufficient, for subsequent offender enhancement, for the State to argue the existence of a certified copy of a prior conviction, yet fail to offer it into evidence. In *Irby v. State*, 66 Md. App. 580, 588 (1986), *cert. denied*, 308 Md. 270 (1987), the Court of Special Appeals held that the evidence in the court file was sufficient to prove the predicate convictions beyond a reasonable doubt. The PSI report and/or the Defendant's testimony may show prior convictions and incarceration for enhanced sentence purposes.

In *Sutton v. State*, 128 Md. App. 308, 330 (1999), the Court of Special Appeals held that an unchallenged PSI report satisfied the State's burden of proving prior a qualifying conviction beyond a reasonable doubt. *Accord Collins v. State*, 89 Md. App. 273, 286 (1991) (PSI report of prior convictions and Defendant's admission to them at trial); *Hall v. State*, 69 Md. App. 37, 63 (1986) (PSI report that attributed prior convictions to police records sufficient for enhanced sentence).

H. Sentencing factor for sentencing judge versus element for the fact finder

In *McMillan v. Pennsylvania*, 477 U.S. 79 (1986), the Defendant was sentenced to a mandatory five-year sentence based on a statute that imposed that sentence if the trial judge found, by a preponderance of the evidence, that the Defendant visibly possessed a firearm. The Defendant argued the statute violated due process by allowing the mandatory minimum to be imposed based on an element not proven beyond a reasonable doubt. The Supreme Court disagreed, holding that possession of a firearm was a "sentencing consideration rather than an element of a particular offense" and need not be proven beyond a reasonable doubt. *Id.* at 91.

In *Almendarez-Torres v. United States*, 523 U.S. 224 (1998), the Supreme Court held that recidivism based on the commission of a prior crime was a sentencing factor and not an element of a crime. The Court noted that the issue was controlled by *McMillan*. The *McMillan* Court pointed out that (1) the statute plainly does not transgress the limits set out in *Specht v. Patterson*, 386 U.S. 605 (1967); (2) the Defendant did not face a differential in sentencing ranging from a nominal fine to a mandatory life sentence; (3) the statute did not alter the maximum penalty for the crime but operates solely to limit the sentencing court's discretion in selecting a penalty within the range available; (4) the stature did not create a separate offense calling for a separate penalty; and (5) the statute gave no impression of having been tailored to permit the visible possession finding to be "a tail that wags the dog" of the substantive offense but, to the contrary, simply took one factor that has always been considered by sentencing courts to bear on punishment and dictated the precise weight to be given that factor. *Id.* at 235.

In *Almendarez-Torres*, the Court stated:

This case resembles *McMillan* in respect to most of these factors. But it is different in respect to the third factor, for it does alter the maximum penalty for the crime, and it also creates a wider range of appropriate punishments than did the statute in *McMillan*. We nonetheless conclude that these basic differences do not change the constitutional outcome for several basic reasons.

First, the sentencing factor at issue here—recidivism—is a traditional, if not the most traditional, basis for a sentencing court's increasing an offender's sentence.

. . .

Second, the major difference between this case and *McMillan* consists of the circumstance that the sentencing factor at issue here (the prior conviction) triggers an increase in the maximum permissive sentence, while the sentencing factor in *McMillan* triggered a mandatory minimum sentence.

. . .

Third, the statute's broad permissive sentencing range does not itself create significantly greater unfairness.

. . .

Finally, the remaining *McMillan* factors support the conclusion that Congress has the constitutional power to treat the feature before us—prior conviction of an aggravated felony—as a sentencing factor for this particular offense . . .

. . .

For these reasons, we cannot find in *McMillan* (a case holding that the Constitution *permits* a legislature to *require* a longer sentence for gun possession) significant support for the proposition that the Constitution *forbids* as legislature to *authorize* a longer sentence for recidivism.

Id. at 242-46 (internal citations, quotations, & alterations omitted).

In *State v. Stewart*, 368 Md. 26 (2002), the Court of Appeals held that prior incarceration, like conviction for a prior crime, is not an element of an offense and that "the *Almendarez-Torres* exception covers questions related to recidivism [and] recidivism is a question that has traditionally been reserved for the sentencing court." *Id.* at 41.

In *Jones v. United States*, 526 U.S. 227 (1999), the Defendant was convicted of carjacking, and his sentence was enhanced by the sentencing judge, based on the conclusion that the Defendant had caused "serious bodily injury" to the victim. The Supreme Court held that the "serious bodily harm" requirement for an increased sentence was an element of the crime and, therefore, had to be proven beyond a reasonable doubt. *Id.* at 235.

In *Apprendi v. New Jersey*, 530 U.S. 466 (2000), the Defendant entered a guilty plea to possession of a firearm for an unlawful purpose and unlawful possession of a prohibited weapon. Under a hate crime statute, the sentencing judge increased the sentence after finding, by a preponderance of the evidence, that the Defendant was motivated by racial animus. The Supreme Court held that the enhancement was unconstitutional because, other than the fact of a prior conviction, any fact that increases the penalty beyond the prescribed statutory maximum must be submitted to the jury and proven beyond a reasonable doubt. The Court stated:

> Our answer to [the holding] was foreshadowed by our opinion in *Jones v. United States*, 526 U.S. 227 (1999), construing a federal statute. We there noted that "under the Due Process Clause of the Fifth Amendment and the notice and jury trial guarantees of the Sixth Amendment, any fact (other than prior conviction) that increases the maximum penalty for a crime must be charged in the indictment, submitted to a jury, and proven beyond a reasonable doubt." *Id.* at 243 n.6. The Fourteenth Amendment commands the same answer in this case involving a state statute.

Id. at 476; *see Blakely v. Washington*, 542 U.S. 296, 301 (2004) ("Other than the fact of a prior conviction, any fact that increases the penalty for a crime beyond the prescribed statutory maximum must be submitted to a jury, and proven beyond a reasonable doubt.").

In *Harris v. United States*, 536 U.S. 545 (2002), the Supreme Court answered the question of "whether *McMillan* stands after *Apprendi*." *Id.* at 550. The Court answered that question in the affirmative:

> [The reasoning of *McMillan*] still controls. If the facts the judges consider when exercising their discretion within the statutory range are not elements, they do not become as much merely because legislatures require the judge to impose a minimum sentence when those facts are found—as sentence the judge could have imposed absent the finding.

Id. at 560.

In *Booker & Fanfan*, 543 U.S. 220, the Defendant was convicted of possession of crack cocaine with intent to distribute. The maximum punishment for this crime was ten years to life. However, the judge held a post-trial hearing, in which he found, by a preponderance of the evidence, that the Defendant possessed an additional quantity of drugs beyond the amount found by the jury and that the Defendant had obstructed justice. This finding led to a sentence greater than the maximum allowable absent the judge's findings. The Supreme Court reversed:

[W]e reaffirm our holding in *Apprendi*: Any fact (other than a prior conviction) which is necessary to support a sentence exceeding the maximum authorized by the facts established by a plea of guilty or a jury verdict must be admitted by the Defendant or proved to a jury beyond a reasonable doubt."

Id. at 244.

In *Wadlow v. State*, 335 Md. 122 (1994), the Court of Appeals held:

In Maryland . . . we have generally drawn a distinction between sentencing enhancement provisions that depend upon prior conduct of the offender and those that depend upon the circumstances of the offense. In the former situation, involving recidivism, we have made it clear that determination of the requisite predicate facts is for the sentencing judge.

. . .

In the latter case, however, where the legislature has prescribed different sentences for the same offense, depending upon the particular circumstance of the offense, we have held that the presence of that circumstance must be alleged in the charging document, and must be determined by the trier of fact applying the reasonable doubt standard.

Id. at 128-29.

In *Parker v. State*, 185 Md. App. 399 (2009), the Defendant was charged with witness intimidation, which provides for a five-year sentence, unless the testimony or official complaint of the witness related to a crime of violence or drug crime, in which case the sentence was 20 years. The jury was instructed as to the applicable law of witness intimidation, but was not instructed that it needed to find, beyond a reasonable doubt, that the witness's testimony or complaint related to a drug crime. The Defendant was sentenced to 20 years. The Court of Special Appeals reversed, holding:

Complaints of illegal drug activity are . . . the functional equivalent of an element of a greater offense, because this was the basis on which [the Defendant] was exposed to a punishment greater than that otherwise legally prescribed. Yet, the jury was not asked to determine whether the evidence proved those facts. Rather, it was only instructed "the State must prove [that the Defendant retaliated] because the victim or witness either gave evidence in an official proceeding or reported a crime or delinquent act." Therefore, the jury returned a guilty verdict for retaliation, without deciding whether [the witness]'s complaints concerned drug activity.

Id. at 420 (internal citations, alterations, & quotations omitted).

I. Recidivist sentencing statutes

1. Enhanced sentence based on multiple crimes of violence

Md. Code Ann., Crim. Law § 14-101 enumerates 24 crimes that qualify as crimes of violence. Section 14-101 provides mandatory sentences, sometimes non-paroleable, for individuals convicted, on multiple occasions, of a crime of violence. *See Jones v. State*, 336 Md. 255, 265 (1994); *Temoney v. State*, 290 Md. 251, 263 (1981).

Consecutive sentences from the same incident qualify as only one predicate conviction for purposes of enhancement. *Montone v. State*, 308 Md. 599, 615 (1987). In *Stanley v. State*, 390 Md. 175, 177, 183 (2005), the Court of Appeals held that the predicate offense for enhancement required a crime of violence and a felony, and second degree assault, even though a crime of violence, was not a felony.

2. Enhanced sentence for a Defendant with a second crime of violence

If the Defendant is convicted for a second time of a crime of violence, the Defendant may receive the statutory sentence, but must receive a sentence of at least ten years, none of which may be suspended. Md. Code Ann., Crim. Law, § 14-101(e). This is contingent on the Defendant having served a "term of confinement in a correctional facility for that conviction." *Id.* § 14-101(e)(1)(ii).

In *Stevenson v. State*, 180 Md. App. 440, 451 (2008), the Court of Special Appeals held that pre-trial detention is not a term of confinement. In *Simpkins v. State*, 70 Md. App. 687, 698 (1989) the Court of Special Appeals held that the fact that a federal court imposed a sentence that was concurrent with a sentence imposed six years earlier did not preclude that "term of confinement" from being separate for purpose of enhancement.

3. Enhanced sentence for a Defendant with a third crime of violence

If the Defendant is convicted for a third time of a crime of violence, the Defendant may receive the statutory sentence, but must receive a sentence of at least 25 years, none of which may be suspended, and the Defendant is not eligible for parole. Md. Code Ann., Crim. Law § 14-101(d). This is contingent on (a) the two prior convictions arising from separate incidents; (b) the second crime occurring after the filing of a charging document for the first crime; and (c) the Defendant having served one term of confinement in a correctional facility for a crime of violence. *Id.* § 14-101(d)(1)(i).

In *McGlone v. State*, 406 Md. 545, 558 (2008), the Court of Appeals held that the sentence enhancement does not require the predicate convictions be imposed sequentially. In *Creighton v. State*, 70 Md. App. 124, 142 (1987), the Court of Special Appeals held that, for the statute to apply, the current offense must post-date the two predicate convictions. *See Garrett v. State*, 59 Md. App. 97, 112 (1984). In *Taylor v. State*, 333 Md. 229, 237 (1994), the Court of Appeals held that the statutory limitations on suspended sentence and parole eligibility apply only to the first 25 years of a life sentence.

4. Enhanced sentence for a Defendant with a fourth crime of violence

If the Defendant is convicted for a fourth crime of violence, the Defendant must receive a sentence of life without parole. Md. Code Ann., Crim. Law § 14-101(c). This is contingent on three separate terms of confinement in a correctional facility for the three separate crimes of violence. *Id.* In *Creighton v. State*, 70 Md. App. 124, 145 (1987), the Court of Special Appeals held that the Defendant must have served some portion of each of the three predicate sentences before being sentenced to life without parole under the four-time loser statute.

In *Gerald v. State*, 137 Md. App. 295, 313, *cert. denied*, 364 Md. 462 (2001), the Court of Special Appeals held that the State must prove that the that the Defendant was convicted of three distinct and unrelated crimes of violence resulting from different events, and the Defendant served separate terms of incarceration for those convictions.

If a Defendant is released on parole, after serving a term of confinement, and is convicted of a crime while on parole, the Defendant is subject to enhancement, using the offense for which he was paroled as a predicate crime, notwithstanding that the Defendant could have been sent back to prison for violation of parole. Thus, for a Defendant on parole, the conviction for which he was paroled can serve as a predicate for enhancement, even though the Defendant did not serve the entire term. *Davis v. State*, 56 Md. App. 694, 705 (1983), *cert. denied*, 299 Md. 425 (1984); *accord McLee v. State*, 46 Md. App. 472, 476 (1980), *cert. denied*, 289 Md. 738 (1981).

5. Using convictions for crimes of violence from other jurisdictions as predicates for Maryland enhancement

Determining whether an out-of-state conviction qualifies as a predicate conviction for a crime of violence is a two-step process. First, the court must determine whether the Maryland counterpart to the out-of-state crime is a "crime of violence." Second, the court must ensure that the elements of the out-of-state crime are sufficiently limited to the elements of the Maryland offense. In *DiBarolomeo v. State*, 61 Md. App. 302 (1985), the Court of Special Appeals held that a conviction for sodomy is not a crime of violence for enhancement sentencing.

In *Bowman v. State*, 314 Md. 725, 733-34 (1989), the State submitted certified docket entries from the District of Columbia showing convictions for armed robbery and robbery to satisfy the two predicate convictions. The Court of Appeals invalidated the sentence because, even though robbery in the District of Columbia could qualify as a crime of violence, the docket entries, without more, were insufficient to prove, beyond a reasonable doubt, that the Defendant had two prior convictions of crimes of violence.

In *Temoney v. State*, 290 Md. 251, 263-64 (1981), the Court of Appeals held that a robbery conviction from the District of Columbia did not qualify as a predicate for enhancement in Maryland because, in the District of Columbia, robbery included crimes that may only be theft in Maryland, e.g., pickpocketing. Although the Defendant's District of Columbia convictions may have been crimes of violence, that was not discernible from the docket entries admitted into evidence.

In *Powell v. State*, 56 Md. App. 351, 374 (1983), *cert. denied*, 298 Md. 540 (1984), an enhanced sentence was invalid because, under District of Columbia law, one modality of bank robbery would not qualify as a crime of violence in Maryland. *Accord Myers v. State*, 48 Md. App. 420, 422, *cert. denied*, 290 Md. 719 (1981) (District of Columbia robbery could not enhance the Maryland sentence); *Butler v. State*, 46 Md. App. 317, 322-23 (1980). In *Mitchell v. State*, 56 Md. App. 162, 183 (1983), the Court of Special Appeals held that statutory rape, under Missouri law, was insufficient for enhancement, because there was no evidence that the victim was under age 14, which was necessary as a predicate in Maryland.

In *Brown v. State*, 311 Md. 426, 440 (1988), the Court of Appeals held that police testimony about the Defendant's conduct was insufficient because a prior conviction for a crime of violence requires a prior "conviction" and not merely the Defendant's "act." In *Muir v. State*, 308 Md. 208, 217 (1986), the Court of Appeals held that a court martial conviction for robbery and attempted robbery qualified as a "crime of violence" for sentencing enhancement.

In *Hubbard v. State*, 76 Md. App. 228, 247, *cert. denied*, 313 Md. 688 (1988), the Court of Special Appeals held that a conviction for robbery or attempted robbery in any state that defines robbery substantially as Maryland does is a crime of violence for purposes of enhancement. In *Hall v. State*, 69 Md. App. 37, 63 (1986), the Court of Special Appeals held that daytime housebreaking, in a foreign jurisdiction, may qualify as a predicate conviction for enhancement.

6. Crimes that are not "crimes of violence" when committed, but which later qualify as a "crime of violence"

In *Hawkins v. State*, 302 Md. 143, 148 (1985), the trial court used, as a predicate conviction, the Defendant's prior conviction for daytime housebreaking even though, at the time it was committed, daytime housebreaking did not qualify as a crime of violence. The statute was amended, to include daytime housebreaking as a crime of violence, prior to the Defendant's third conviction. The Court of Appeals held that the Defendant's mandatory minimum sentence was proper, noting that the sentence under the statute is only for the new crime, and inclusion of predicate offenses committed before the new statute's effective date does not render the statute retrospective in application. *See Muir v. State*, 308 Md. 208, 217 (1986).

7. Prior invalid convictions used for enhancement

In *Raiford v. State*, 296 Md. 289, 291, 299 (1983), the Court of Appeals held that the State could not use, for enhancement purposes, the Defendant's prior "adult" conviction from when the Defendant was age 17, when Baltimore City was exempt from the juvenile age limit of 18. In *Long v. Robinson*, 316 F. Supp. 22, 30 (D. Md. 1970), *aff'd*, 436 F.2d 1116 (4th Cir. 1971), the Fourth Circuit held that Baltimore City's exemption from the juvenile age limit violated the Equal Protection Clause. *See Wiggins v. State*, 275 Md. 689, 691 (1975); *State v. Loveday*, 48 Md. App. 478, 483-84 (1981) (unconstitutionally obtained conviction may not be used for enhancement).

8. Accessory to a crime of violence is itself a crime of violence

In *Sanders v. State*, 57 Md. App. 156, 177, *cert. denied*, 299 Md. 656 (1984), the Court of Special Appeals held that a conviction as an accessory to robbery qualified as a robbery conviction and could serve as a predicate conviction for sentencing enhancement.

9. Conviction used as predicate conviction on appeal

In *Butler v. State*, 46 Md. App. 317, 322, *cert. denied*, 288 Md. 743 (1980), the Court of Special Appeals held that a conviction on appeal was not a final conviction and could not be used as a predicate for enhancement. However, in *Whack v. State*, 338 Md. 665, 675 (1995), the Court of Appeals held that a conviction on appeal could be used as a predicate for enhancement because the legislative intent to require finality of a prior convictions for the purposes of enhancement.

10. Parole eligibility for Defendants with an enhanced sentence based on a third or fourth crime of violence

A Defendant sentenced to an enhanced penalty, as a three-time loser or four-time loser for violent crimes is eligible for parole if the Defendant (a) is at least age 65; and (b) has served at least 15 years of that sentence. *Id.* §14-101(g).

11. Enhanced sentence for a Defendant with a second drug conviction

A Defendant convicted of a Schedule I or Schedule II drug offense is guilty of a felony and may be sentenced to 20 years. *Id.* § 5-608(a). A Defendant convicted of a second enumerated drug offense must receive a sentence of at least ten years without parole.

Id. § 5-608(b). In *Gargliano v. State*, 334 Md. 428, 432 (1994), the Court of Appeals held that, to qualify for sentence enhancement, the prior conviction must precede the commission of (but not the conviction for) the principal offense.

In *Veney v. State*, 130 Md. App. 135, 149, *cert. denied*, 358 Md. 610 (2000), the Court of Special Appeals held that, under the rule of lenity, only one enhanced penalty may be imposed when there are multiple convictions arising from a single incident. *See Lett v. State*, 51 Md. App. 668 (1982).

12. Enhanced sentence for a Defendant with a third drug conviction

A Defendant convicted of a third enumerated drug offense must receive a sentence of at least 25 years without parole, provided the (a) other two convictions arose from separate occasions; and (b) the Defendant has served at least one term of confinement of at least 180 days in a correctional facility. *Id.* § 5-608(c). In *Deville v. State*, 383 Md. 217, 230 (2004), the Court of Appeals held that confinement in a "correctional institution" does not include home detention for purposes of enhanced penalty statute for recidivist drug offenders.

In *Taylor v. State*, 175 Md. App. 153, 162-63, *cert. denied*, 401 Md. 174 (2007), the Court of Special Appeals held that a Defendant who has not served 180 days on the second conviction may not receive a 25-year sentence for the third offense, but may be sentenced to the mandatory ten-year minimum sentence for the second offense. In *Melgar v. State*, 355 Md. 339, 348 (1999), the Court of Appeals held that the 180-day confinement does not include time spent in pre-trial detention or time awaiting trial. In *State v. Polley*, 97 Md. App. 192, 195, 201 (1993), the Court of Special Appeals held that the 180-day confinement must be served before committing the third offense to qualify for enhancement as a three-time drug offender.

In *Nelson v. State*, 187 Md. App. 1, 22-24 (2009), the Court of Special Appeals held that the sentence as a two-time loser is not a prerequisite to imposing a three-time loser sentence. In *Briggs v. State*, 413 Md. 265, 272 (2010), the Court of Appeals held that the requirement that the Defendant receive a "charging document" for the first offense before receiving an enhanced sentence for subsequent offenses was satisfied by the Defendant's receipt of a statement of charges. For a drug crime enhancement, the Defendant's period of incarceration for those crimes must be served in Maryland. *Cantine v. State*, 160 Md. App. 391, 412 (2004), *cert. denied*, 386 Md. 181 (2005) (Virginia conviction could not serve as a predicate for enhancement).

13. Enhanced sentence for a Defendant with a fourth drug conviction

A Defendant convicted of a fourth enumerated drug offense must receive a sentence of at least 40 years without parole, provided the Defendant has served at least three separate terms of confinement. *Id.* § 5-608(d).

14. Volume drug dealer

A Defendant convicted of possessing or distributing large amounts of drugs, as set forth in Md. Code Ann., Crim. Law § 5-612(a), is subject to a sentence of a mandatory minimum of five years. *Id.* § 5-612.

15. Drug kingpin

A drug kingpin is "an organizer, supervisor, financier, or manager who acts as a co-conspirator in a conspiracy to manufacture, distribute, dispense, transport, or bring into the state a controlled dangerous substance," and is subject to a mandatory 20-year sentence. *Id.* § 5-613. *See Williams v. State*, 89 Md. App. 685, 692 (1991), *rev'd on other grounds*, 329 Md. 1 (1992) (there may be more than one "kingpin" in a given drug organization or conspiracy).

§ X. Patuxent Institution

Patuxent Institution treats and provides programs and services to (a) youthful offenders; (b) other "eligible persons"; and (c) mentally ill inmates. Md. Code Ann., Corr. Serv. § 4-202. To be eligible for Patuxent Institution, the Defendant must be (a) under age 21; (b) have at least three years remaining on his sentence; (c) have intellectual impairment or emotional imbalance; (d) be likely to respond favorably to Patuxent programs and services; and (e) meet eligibility criteria that the Secretary of Department of Public Safety & Correctional Services establishes. *Id.* §§ 4-101 & 4-208(a) & (b).

To be eligible for Patuxent Institution, the Defendant cannot be serving a life sentence, or be convicted of life offense, i.e., first degree murder, first degree rape, or first degree sexual offense, unless the sentencing judge specifically recommends Patuxent. *Id.* A three-judge sentence review panel has the authority to review a recommendation that a Defendant be evaluated at Patuxent Institution. In *Resper v. State*, 354 Md. 611, 619-21 (1999), the Court of Appeals held that a three-judge panel may review the trial court's recommendation that the Defendant be evaluated for the Patuxent Institution, and the three-judge panel may adopt that recommendation or reject it. *See Watson v. State*, 289 Md. 300, 301-02 (1979).

Patuxent Institution must maintain a record for each Defendant sent to Patuxent for treatment, including (a) police reports and information concerning the offense(s) for which convicted; (b) the Defendant's criminal and juvenile history; (c) the PSI report and DPP reports; (d) school records; (e) medical and mental health history; and (f) other relevant information. Md. Code Ann., Corr. Serv. § 4-209(b). A Defendant under supervision at Patuxent is released on mandatory supervision under the same conditions and in same manner as Defendants released from the DOC. A Defendant may be released on mandatory supervision at any time after one year. *Id.* §§ 7-101(g) (1) & (2) & § 7-501(a)(1)-(3).

Under Md. Code Ann., Corr. Serv. § 4-213(b)-(e), the Director decides release from Patuxent. In calculating release, diminution credits are awarded in Patuxent in the same manner as in the DOC. The Director may restore diminution credits that the Defendant lost because of violation(s) of institutional disciplinary rules. The Director may make the Defendant's release on mandatory supervision subject to special terms and conditions. A Defendant in Patuxent is eligible for work release and other leave. *Id.* §§ 3-806 to 3-811.

A Defendant's eligibility for work release is determined by the Patuxent Board of Review. Prior to granting work release, the Board of Review must provide written notice to the victim and allow the victim reasonable opportunity to provide written or oral input. *Id.* § 4-303(b)(1)-(2). Upon reaching a decision regarding work release, the Board of Review must promptly notify the victim. *Id.* § 4-303(b)(3). Prior to allowing the Defendant access to the victim's written statement, the Board of Review must delete the victim's name, address, and phone number. *Id.* § 4-303(b)(5).

If not previously released on parole or mandatory supervision, a Defendant in Patuxent must be released upon expiration of sentence. Following transfer to Patuxent for treatment as an "eligible person," but prior to expiration of sentence, the Board of Review may grant parole from Patuxent for up to one year if the Board finds that (a) parole will not impose unreasonable risk to society; and (b) parole will assist in remediation of eligible person. See *Gluckstern v. Sutton*, 319 Md. 634, 642 (1990). After 1982, the Board's decision as to inmates sentenced to life in Patuxent after 1982, just like the MPC's decision as to DOC inmates serving life, are only release recommendations to the Governor, who retains exclusive authority over release. *Id.* at 643-44 (the 1982 statutory changes to then Md. Ann. Code art. 31B, § 11(b)(2), granting the Governor sole authority over release could not be applied retroactively to inmates convicted prior to 1982 without violating ex post facto).

The Board of Review may (a) attach reasonable conditions to parole from Patuxent; (b) make appropriate modifications to parole conditions; and (c) revoke parole if the Board of Review finds violation(s) of parole condition. Md. Code Ann., Corr. Serv. § 4-305(c)(1). If there is evidence that a parolee violated parole, the Board of Review conducts a preliminary hearing to determine whether there is "probable cause" to revoke parole. If probable cause is found, within 90 days after the preliminary hearing, the Board of Review must provide notice of a revocation hearing. At both the preliminary hearing and the revocation hearing, the parolee has right to call witnesses, present evidence, and question adverse witnesses.

The Board must provide written notice to the victim of the parole hearing and must grant the victim an opportunity to be heard regarding parole, either orally or in writing. *Pollock v. Patuxent Institution Board of Review*, 358 Md. 656, 659-60 (2000); Md. Code Ann., Corr. Serv. § 4-305(c) & (d). Following the revocation hearing, the Board of Review may revoke parole or continue parole. The Board must provide written notice to the victim(s) of its decision regarding parole. *Id.* § 4-305(d). If the Board determines to continue parole, the Secretary must approve the decision. *Id.* § 4-305(e). Prior to deciding whether to grant parole, the Board must grant the inmate's victim the opportunity to be heard, either orally or in writing. *Id.* § 4-305(d)(2).

§ XI. Credit for time served

A. Entitled to credit for time served

The Defendant receives credit against an imposed sentence for time served in custody on that offense, both pre-trial and post-trial. Md. Rule 4-342(h); Md. Code Ann., Crim. Proc. § 6-218; *Fleeger v. State*, 301 Md. 155, 165 (1984). In *Roberts v. State*, 56 Md. App. 562, 566 (1983), *cert. denied*, 299 Md. 426 (1984), the Court of Special Appeals held that, if a Defendant is incarcerated pre-trial on charge #1, and while incarcerated, charge #2 is filed, if the Defendant is acquitted on charge #1, the time spent in custody is credited toward the sentence for charge #2.

In *Gilmer v. State*, 389 Md. 656, 664 (2005), the Court of Appeals held that a nolle prosequi on charge #2, prior to sentencing on charge #1, constitutes a dismissal of charge #2, for purposes of the statute requiring credit for pre-trial custody on an unrelated charge that results in "dismissal or acquittal." *See Roberts v. State*, 56 Md. App. 562, 565-66 (1983), *cert. denied*, 299 Md. 426 (1984); *Magrogan v. State*, 56 Md. App. 289, 293 (1983). If a sentence or multiple sentences is (are) vacated on direct appeal or collateral attack, the Defendant receives credit for time served if serving time on other sentence. Md. Code Ann., Crim. Proc. § 6-218(c) & (d).

If a Defendant is convicted of escape from a place of confinement, the custody requirement is met. In *Toney v. State*, 140 Md. App. 690, 695 (2001), the Court of Special Appeals held that a home detention agreement does not have to expressly inform the Defendant that he will be eligible for prosecution for escape if he leaves home, as a predicate for being in custody for purposes of determining credit for time served.

In *Dedo v. State*, 343 Md. 2, 4 (1996), the Court of Appeals held that the Defendant is entitled to credit for time served on home detention pre-trial, *Jones v. State*, 138 Md. App. 12, 22, *cert. denied*, 364 Md. 535 (2001), and between the finding of guilt and the sentencing. *See Kang v. State*, 163 Md. App. 22, 46-47 (2005). In *Spriggs v. State*, 152 Md. App. 62, 69 (2003), the Court of Special Appeals held that the Defendant was entitled to credit for privately monitored home detention when the Defendant could have been prosecuted for escape if he left his home during that period.

B. Not entitled to credit for time served

In *Gasque v. State*, 45 Md. App. 471, 475 (1980), the Court of Special Appeals held that the Defendant is not entitled to credit against a sentence for escape for the time in custody awaiting trial on escape charges. In *Lawson v. State*, 187 Md. App. 101, 107 (2009), the Court of Special Appeals held that the Defendant is not entitled to credit for time in custody awaiting trial when already incarcerated on an unrelated charge. In *Roberts v. State*, 56 Md. App. 562, 566-67 (1983), *cert. denied*, 299 Md. 426 (1984), the Court of Special Appeals held that the Defendant is not entitled to credit when a charge is stetted because the charge is still viable.

In *Blankenship v. State*, 135 Md. App. 615, 623 (2000), the Court of Special Appeals held that the Defendant was entitled to credit for time served on only one of the nine consecutive sentences because, to receive credit on the other eight counts, would be duplicative credit. The Defendant was not entitled to credit for time served at a private residential treatment facility, *Maus v. State*, 311 Md. 85, 107 (1987); in voluntary home confinement, as a condition of probation, when the Defendant was free to leave home, *Balderston v. State*, 93 Md. App. 364, 370 (1992); or in a state mental facility.

C. Separate federal & state sentences

If a Defendant is sentenced to two separate terms of imprisonment—one federal and one in Maryland—and the Maryland sentence is concurrent, the Defendant may be entitled to credit on the Maryland sentence for time served in federal prison. *See State v. Parker*, 334 Md. 576, 596 (1994).

D. Failure to object to judge's failure to award credit for time served

If the sentencing judge fails to give credit for time served, and the Defendant does not object, because it is an illegal sentence, it may be challenged at any time under Md. Rule 4-345. *Smitley v. State*, 61 Md. App. 477, 481 (1985).

§ XII. Merger doctrine & the rule of lenity

A. Merger

Merger is a mechanism to determine whether it is permissible to impose separate consecutive sentences for criminal offenses arising from a single criminal transaction. Regarding each criminal transaction, if the Defendant is found guilty, the issue is how many times may the Defendant be punished or sentenced. This requires a determination of whether multiple offenses, arising out of one criminal transaction, constitute separate offenses for sentencing purposes or are deemed to be same offense. In *Jones v. State*, 357 Md. 141, 157 (1999), the Court of Appeals stated: "We determine first whether the charges arose out of the same act or transaction, and second, whether the crimes charged are the same offense."

If the offenses arising from one transaction are separate offenses, they may be sentenced separately and consecutively. If the offenses are deemed to be the same offense, they may be sentenced separately, but the sentence for lesser included offense(s) merge into the sentence for the greater offense.

In *Washington v. State*, 200 Md. App. 641 (2011), the Court of Special Appeals stated: "In a single prosecution, the Double Jeopardy Clause of the Fifth Amendment to the United States Constitution and the Maryland common law of double jeopardy prohibit the imposition of multiple penalties for the same offense." *Id.* at 647 (citing *Taylor v. State*, 381 Md. 602, 610 (2004)). Thus, because merger is a sentencing issue, a jury may return guilty verdicts for both the lesser and greater offenses, but the sentences on those verdicts are subject to merger. *Harris v. State*, 160 Md. App. 78, 103 (2004).

Moreover, in one transaction, one law may be violated multiple times. In crimes against persons, each person is a separate unit of criminality. Thus, if there are multiple victims of crimes against persons, during one criminal transaction, the number of victims determines the units of criminality.

In *Harris v. State*, 42 Md. App. 248, 259 (1979), *superseded by Md. Rule 4-246, as recognized in Walker v. State*, 406 Md. 369, 379 n.3 (2008), the Court of Special Appeals held that there were two units of criminality when the Defendant shot at two police officers. In *Savoy v. State*, 67 Md. App. 590 (1986), the Court of Special Appeals stated: "[W]e have held that where a single criminal indictment results in multiple victims, the number of victims can determine the number of violations." *Id.* at 594 (citing *Jackson v. State*, 63 Md. App. 149, 157-59 (1985); *Jones v. State*, 3 Md. App. 608 (1968)).

1. *Blockburger* required evidence test

The *Blockburger* required evidence test is used to determine whether two offenses, arising from one criminal transaction, are separate offenses or are deemed to be same offense. *Snowden v. State*, 321 Md. 612, 616-17 (1991); *Monoker v. State*, 321 Md. 214, 217 n.2 (1990); *Gianiny v. State*, 320 Md. 337, 342 (1990); *Middleton v. State*, 318 Md. 749, 757 (1990); *White v. State*, 318 Md. 740, 742-43 (1990); *Hagans v. State*, 316 Md. 429, 449 (1989); *State v. Ferrell*, 313 Md. 291, 295 (1988); *Nightingale v. State*, 312 Md. 699, 702-03 (1988); *State v. Jenkins*, 307 Md. 501, 517 (1986); *Simms v. State*, 288 Md. 712, 718-19 (1980); *Brooks v. State*, 284 Md. 416, 420-22 (1979); *Thomas v. State*, 277 Md. 257, 262-67 (1976); *Flannigan v. State*, 232 Md. 13, 19 (1963); *Veney v. State*, 227 Md. 608, 611-14 (1962).

For the *Blockburger* required evidence test to apply, and for crimes to be subject to merger, the crimes must have occurred in one criminal transaction. Merger is never an issue if the crimes occurred in multiple criminal transactions.

2. No merger when "actual evidence" is the same but "required evidence" is different

The *Blockburger* required evidence test examines only the law of the elements of each offense and ignores the facts. This is accomplished by determining what elements are required, as a matter of law, in order to establish a prima facie case for each offense arising from one criminal transaction and what evidence is required to support those elements. *See Brooks*, 284 Md. at 421-24; *Newton v. State*, 280 Md. 260, 268 (1977). When the actual evidence establishing a prima facie case is identical for two offenses, it may appear that the offenses merge. However, the two offenses do not merge if the required evidence is different, even when the actual evidence is the same.

3. Merger under the required evidence test

Any offense that must, of necessity, be established in the process of establishing another offense in the same transaction is a lesser included offense of that greater offense. This occurs if every element of lesser included offense is also an element of the greater offense. *Hagans*, 316 Md. at 449 n.8. Therefore, one offense is a lesser included offense if it is impossible to commit the greater offense without also committing the lesser offense. *Id.* at 449 (citing *Gov't of Virgin Islands v. Parrilla*, 550 F.2d 879, 881 (3d Cir. 1977); *State v. Lovelace*, 322 N.W.2d 673 (Neb. 1982)).

As such, a lesser included offense is deemed to be the same offense as the greater offense. Because they are deemed to be the same offense, and the Defendant may be punished only one time for one offense, the lesser included offense merges into the greater offense and, thus, the sentence for the lesser included offense merges into the sentence for the greater offense.

4. No merger under the required evidence test

Offenses are separate offenses if each offense has at least one element that the other offense does not have. If so, neither offense merges into the other offense. If, under the required evidence test, two offenses are separate offenses, not only can they be prosecuted separately, even though they arose from one criminal transaction, they can be sentenced separately and consecutively whether or not they are prosecuted together or separately. In *Williams v. State*, 187 Md. App. 470, 478-79, *cert. denied*, 411 Md. 602 (2009), the Court of Special Appeals held that first degree assault and robbery do not merge.

The aggravating factors necessary to make a second degree assault become first degree may be proven disjunctively, by actual or intended serious physical injury, or by a firearm, neither of which is a required element of robbery. Moreover, robbery requires a taking, which is not a required element of assault. In *Burkett v. State*, 98 Md. App. 459, 473-74 (1993), the Court of Special Appeals held that assault and weapons offenses do not merge.

5. Disjunctive methods of proving an offense & the required evidence test

When an offense can be committed in alternative or disjunctive ways, a Defendant cannot be convicted twice based on the same conduct, even if the conduct establishes a prima facie case under multiple methods of proof. *Illinois v. Vitale*, 447 U.S. 410, 421 (1980); *Biggus v. State*, 323 Md. 339, 348-49 (1991). Whether a given offense is proven one way or proven multiple ways, it is still only one offense.

Furthermore, when applying the required evidence test to offenses with alternative elements for merger purposes, regardless of whether the disjunctive offense is the greater offense or the lesser offense, the court must analyze the required evidence test by using only the method or methods for which there was a prima facie case, and for which the finder of fact found guilt. *Nightingale v. State*, 312 Md. 699, 705 (1988), *superseded by statute, as recognized in Fisher v. State*, 367 Md. 218, 242 (2001); *State v. Ferrell*, 313 Md. 291, 298 (1988); *Adams v. State*, 86 Md. App. 377, 389 (1991) (citing *Vogel v. State*, 76 Md. App. 56, 61 (1988), *aff'd*, 315 Md. 458 (1989)).

If crime #1 requires element A and either element B or element C, a Defendant cannot be convicted twice for that crime based on conduct that satisfies elements A, B, and C. Element B and element C are merely alternative ways to arrive at the same place. In *Ferrell*, the Court of Appeals stated: "[W]hen a common law offense or a criminal statute is multi-purpose, embracing different matters in the disjunctive, a court applying the required evidence test must examine 'the alternative element relevant to the case at hand.'" 313 Md. at 298 (quoting *Nightingale*, 312 Md. at 705); *see Newton v. State*, 280 Md. 260, 265-66 (1977); *Thomas*, 277 Md. at 267-68.

In *Washington*, 200 Md. App. 641, the Court of Special Appeals held that the Defendant could not be sentenced twice for fleeing and eluding police by vehicle and then on foot. The Court stated: "[The Defendant] committed one crime of fleeing or eluding the police. The fact that he committed that crime first by driving and not stopping does not mean that he committed two crimes." *Id.* at 664.

In *Eldridge v. State*, 329 Md. 307, 315 (1993), the Court of Appeals held that the crime of carrying a deadly weapon can be established by carrying a deadly weapon openly with intent to injure or by carrying a deadly weapon concealed and, if established both ways, it is still only one crime of carrying a deadly weapon.

In *Wagner v. State*, 160 Md. App. 531, 566 (2005), the Court of Special Appeals held that the crime of murder can be established by premeditated murder or by felony murder, and if established both ways, against one murder victim, it is still only one crime of murder. The Court stated: "'[I]f one willfully, with deliberation and premeditation, kills a person in the course of an armed robbery, [the killer] cannot receive both a sentence for deliberate and premeditated murder . . . and a separate sentence for felony murder.'" *Id.* at 566 (quoting *Williams v. State*, 323 Md. 312, 325 (1991)).

Moreover, if the trial court fails to instruct the jury to identify, on the verdict sheet, whether it finds premeditated murder, felony murder, or both, then, for merger purposes, the verdict sheet must be construed most favorably to the Defendant. *See Nightingale*, 312 Md. at 709; *Dixon v. State*, 364 Md. 209, 248-49 (2001). This means that, if the Defendant is charged with murder and robbery, and the verdict sheet is silent as to the method of murder, a guilty verdict for murder, without identification of the method of malice found by the jury, results in the murder being deemed to be felony murder, with robbery merging, and be deemed not to be premeditated murder, for which robbery would not merge. *Id.*

In *Dixon*, 364 Md. at 240-41, the Court of Appeals held that first degree assault, when established by actual or intended deadly force, merges into attempted voluntary manslaughter, but first degree assault, when established by a firearm, does not merge into attempted voluntary manslaughter.

6. Merger & conspiracy

Convictions for conspiracy and the crime(s) to which conspired do not merge. Conspiracy is the crime of entering an agreement to commit a crime. It has no substantive offense, but it does have an agreement. The substantive offense to which agreed has no agreement, but it does have the substantive offense. *Kelly v. State*, 195 Md. App. 403, 441-42 (2010). In *Murray v. State*, 89 Md. App. 626, 634-35 (1991), the Court of Special Appeals held that conspiracy to distribute cocaine and distribution of cocaine do not merge.

As for the unit of criminality, one agreement to commit multiple offenses is one conspiracy. Thus, only one sentence can be imposed for one conspiracy no matter how many criminal acts the conspirators agreed to commit. *Jordan v. State*, 323 Md. 151, 161-62 (1991). In *Tracy v. State*, 319 Md. 452 (1990), the Court of Appeals stated: "It is well settled in Maryland that only one sentence can be imposed for a single common law conspiracy no matter how many criminal acts the conspirators have agreed to commit. The unit of prosecution is the agreement or combination rather than each of its criminal objectives." *Id.* at 459.

In *Mason v. State*, 302 Md. 434, 445 (1985), the Court of Appeals held: "Ordinarily, a single agreement to engage in criminal activity does not become several conspiracies because it has as its purpose the commission of several offenses." *See Somers v. State*, 156 Md. App. 279, 317 (2004); *Wilson v. State*, 148 Md. App. 601, 640-41 (2002); *Simpson v. State*, 121 Md. App. 263, 291 (1998); *Allen v. State*, 89 Md. App. 25, 53-54 (1991); *Vandegrift v. State*, 82 Md. App. 617, 645 (1990).

In *Manuel v. State*, 85 Md. App. 1, 10-12 (1990), the Court of Special Appeals held that multiple heroin agreements, arising from one conspiracy, constitutes one agreement. However, if there are two agreements—one to distribute heroin and to distribute cocaine—there are two conspiracies.

7. General offenses merge into specific offenses

When there is a general version and a specific version of the same offense, the specific version is the greater offense and the general version is the lesser included offense, with the general offense merging into the specific offense. The specific offense is the greater offense because the specific offense contains all of the elements of the general offense, plus the additional element that makes the specific offense more specific. Involuntary manslaughter is the general offense and motor vehicle manslaughter is the specific offense because motor vehicle manslaughter requires all of the elements of involuntary manslaughter, plus the additional element of a motor vehicle. Md. Code Ann., Crim. Law §§ 2-207 & 2-209.

8. The elements & not the sentence determine which offense is the greater offense & which offense is the lesser included offense

Offense #1 is the lesser included offense, consisting of elements A, B, and C. Offense #2 is the greater offense, consisting of elements A, B, C, and D. The greater offense is the offense with the greater elements and not the offense with the greater penalty. Thus, if the sentence for the lesser included offense #1, with elements A, B, and C, is ten years, and the sentence for the greater offense #2, with elements A, B, C, and D, is five years, the ten-year sentence will merge into the five-year sentence.

In *Spitzinger v. State*, 340 Md. 114 (1995), the Court of Appeals stated: "Where there is a merger of a lesser included offense into a greater offense, we are not concerned with penalties—the lesser included offense generally merges into and is subsumed by the greater offense regardless of penalties." *Id.* at 125 (citing *Simms v. State*, 288 Md. 712 (1980)).

In *State v. Lancaster*, 332 Md. 385, 404-07 (1993), the Court of Appeals held that unnatural or perverted sexual practice merges into fourth degree sex offense, even though the sentence for unnatural or perverted sexual practice was greater than the sentence for fourth degree sex offense. *See Simms*, 288 Md. at 718-19; *Johnson v. State*, 283 Md. 196, 203-04 (1978); *Flannigan v. State*, 232 Md. 13, 19 (1963); *Cortez v. State*, 104 Md. App. 358, 368-69 (1995).

In *Slye v. State*, 42 Md. App. 520 (1979), the Court of Special Appeals stated: "When a merger is necessitated, the 'lesser' crime is merged into the 'greater' crime and the judgment of conviction and the sentence on the lesser offense are vacated." *Id.* at 526 (citing *Stewart v. Warden*, 243 Md. 697, 699 (1966)).

9. Impermissible for the State to nol pros the greater offense, when it has a lesser maximum sentence, after jeopardy attaches & the maximum sentence is the sentence for the greater offense, which is the lesser sentence

Let's assume that offense #1 is a greater offense and offense #2 is a lesser included offense of offense #1. Let's assume that, even though offense #2 is the lesser included offense, offense #2 has a greater maximum statutory penalty. If the Defendant is found guilty of both offense #1 and offense #2, then offense #2 (and its sentence) merges into offense #1 (and its sentence). Thus, the maximum sentence is the sentence for the greater offense, which is the lesser sentence.

Moreover, if the Defendant is found not guilty of offense #1 (the greater offense with the lesser sentence) and found guilty of offense #2 (the lesser included offense with the greater maximum sentence), the result is the same. This means that the maximum potential sentence is the sentence for the greatest offense charged, which is offense #1, with its lesser sentence.

In *Dixon v. State*, 364 Md. 209 (2001), in the first trial, the Defendant was convicted of (1) first degree assault and sentenced to 20 years, and (2) attempted voluntary manslaughter and sentenced to a concurrent ten years. The Court of Special Appeals reversed and held that assault, as the lesser included offense, merged into attempted voluntary manslaughter, as the greater offense. On remand, the State nol prossed attempted voluntary manslaughter, and the Defendant was convicted of first degree assault and sentenced to 20 years.

The Court of Appeals vacated the 20-year sentence, holding that, when the Defendant is charged with a greater offense and a lesser included offense, and jeopardy has attached, if the Defendant is convicted of the lesser included offense and acquitted on the greater offense, or the greater offense is nol prossed, the Defendant cannot receive a sentence for the lesser included offense that exceeds the maximum sentence for the greater offense. *Id.* at 223-26; *accord Johnson v. State*, 310 Md. 681, 690-91 (1987); *Gerald v. State*, 299 Md. 138, 145-46 (1984); *Simms v. State*, 288 Md. 712, 724 (1980). These cases were superseded by Md. Code Ann., Crim. Law § 3-202, as recognized in *Robinson v. State*, 353 Md. 683, 693 n.6 (1999).

In *Matthews v. State*, 68 Md. App. 282, 303 (1986), the Court of Special Appeals held that this limitation does not apply when the greater offense and the lesser offense arise from different criminal transactions.

Prosecutors have discretion in charging. A Defendant may be convicted of, and sentenced for, a lesser included offense that exceeds the penalty for the greater offense, if the greater offense is not charged. *Turner v. State*, 45 Md. App. 168, 170 (1980).

10. Merger examples

The following are examples of lesser included offenses that, as a matter of law, must be established in the process of producing a prima facie case of the greater offense. Thus, the lesser included offense is the same offense as the greater offense, and the sentence for the lesser included offense merges into the sentence for the greater offense.

Crime(s)	Merger	Authority
Solicitation & conspiracy	Solicitation merges into conspiracy.	*Monoker v. State*, 321 Md. 214, 223-24 (1990).
	Solicitation to commit murder merges into accessory before the fact to murder.	*Lewis v. State*, 285 Md. 705, 723 (1979).
Larceny & shoplifting	Larceny merges into shoplifting.	*Slye v. State*, 42 Md. App. 520, 525 (1979).
Burglary & attempted rape	First degree burglary merges into first degree attempted rape.	*Utter v. State*, 139 Md. App. 43, 54 (2001).
Assault & robbery; assault & murder	Assault merges into robbery.	*Snowden v. State*, 321 Md. 612, 619 (1991).
	First degree assault merges into robbery with dangerous weapon.	*Thompson v. State*, 119 Md. App. 606, 611-12 (1998).
	First degree assault merges into second degree murder.	*Sifrit, B. v. State*, 383 Md. 116, 137-38 (2004).
	Assault merges into second degree rape.	*State v. Allewalt*, 308 Md. 89, 110 (1986).
	First degree assault, when based on actual or intended serious bodily harm, and not based on firearm, merges into attempted voluntary manslaughter.	*Dixon v. State*, 364 Md. 209, 225 (2001).
Robbery & murder; robbery & robbery with a dangerous weapon	Attempted robbery merges into felony murder.	*Newton v. State*, 280 Md. 260, 268 (1977).
	Robbery merges into robbery with a dangerous weapon.	*White v. State*, 300 Md. 719, 726 (1984).

Crime(s)	Merger	Authority
Robbery with a dangerous weapon & murder	Robbery with a dangerous weapon merges into felony murder.	*State v. Rivenbank*, 311 Md. 147, 161 n.5 (1987); *State v. Frye*, 283 Md. 709, 722 (1978); *Carlton v. State*, 111 Md. App. 436, 445-46 (1996).
	Attempted robbery with a dangerous weapon merges into felony murder.	*Higginbotham v. State*, 104 Md. App. 145, 166 (1995).
False imprisonment & rape	False imprisonment merges into rape when the victim is detained only long enough to effectuate the rape.	*Testerman v. State*, 61 Md. App. 257, 270-71 (1985); *Hawkins v. State*, 34 Md. App. 82, 92 (1976).
Unlawfully transporting a handgun in a vehicle & use of a handgun in the commission of a felony or crime of violence	Unlawfully transporting handgun in a vehicle merges into use of a handgun in the commission of a felony or crime of violence.	*Hunt v. State*, 312 Md. 494, 510 (1988).
Sex offenses & unnatural & perverted practice	Unnatural or perverted practice merges into fourth degree sex offense when the act is the same for both.	*State v. Lancaster*, 332 Md. 385, 401 (1993).
Second degree murder & first degree murder	Second degree murder merges into first degree murder.	*Harris v. State*, 160 Md. App. 78, 102-03 (2004); *Moore v. State*, 84 Md. App. 165, 180-81 (1990).
Motor vehicle theft & theft	Motor vehicle theft merges into theft of over $1,000.	*Rudder v. State*, 181 Md. App. 426, 467 (2008); Md. Code Ann., Crim. Law § 7-105(d).
Battery & robbery; battery & false imprisonment; battery & murder; battery & assault with intent to prevent lawful apprehension	Battery merges into robbery when force used is only the force necessary to complete the robbery.	*Adams v. State*, 86 Md. App. 377, 390 (1991).
	Battery merges into false imprisonment.	*Lamb v. State*, 93 Md. App. 422, 474 (1992).
	Battery merges into murder.	*Souffie v. State*, 50 Md. App. 547, 566 (1982).

Crime(s)	Merger	Authority
	Battery merges into assault with intent to prevent lawful apprehension.	*Claggett v. State*, 108 Md. App. 32, 53 (1996).
Theft & burglary	Theft under $1,000 merges into fourth degree burglary.	*Goines v. State*, 89 Md. App. 104, 113 (1992); *Warfield v. State*, 76 Md. App. 141, 149 (1988).
	Theft over $1,000 merges into robbery.	*Rudder v. State*, 181 Md. App. 426, 469-70 (2008).
	Misdemeanor theft under $1,000 merges into felony theft (but theft under $100 does not merge).	*Younger v. State*, 94 Md. App. 644, 648 (1993).
Unauthorized use of a vehicle & theft	Unauthorized use of a vehicle merges into theft over $1,000.	*Allen v. State*, 157 Md. App. 177, 196-97 (2004).
False pretenses & welfare fraud	False pretenses merges into welfare fraud.	*Johnson v. State*, 283 Md. 196, 204 (1978).
Wearing & carrying a handgun & use of a handgun in the commission of a felony or crime of violence	Wearing & carrying a handgun merges into use of a handgun in the commission of a felony or crime of violence.	*Wilkins v. State*, 343 Md. 444, 446-47 (1996); *Hunt v. State*, 312 Md. 494, 510-11 (1988).
Possession with intent to distribute & distribution	Possession of cocaine with intent to distribute merges into distribution of cocaine.	*Hankins v. State*, 80 Md. App. 647, 658-59 (1989).
	Possession of heroin with intent to distribute merges into distribution of heroin.	*Manuel v. State*, 85 Md. App. 1, 8 (1990).
Reckless driving & vehicular manslaughter	Reckless driving merges into motor vehicle manslaughter.	*Pineta v. State*, 98 Md. App. 614, 622 (1993).
Engaging in a speed contest & reckless driving	Engaging in a speed contest merges into reckless driving.	*Pineta v. State*, 98 Md. App. 614, 621 (1993)
Driving while suspended & driving while revoked	Driving with a suspended license merges into driving with a revoked license.	*Tederick v. State*, 125 Md. App. 37, 41 (1999)

11. Non-merger examples

If offense #1 consists of elements A, B, and C (but not element D), and offense #2 consists of elements A, B, and D (but not element C), neither offense is a lesser included offense of other offense, nor a greater offense to the other. Each offense has at least one element that the other offense does not have and, thus, each is separate offense. As such, the trial court may sentence separately and consecutively for each offense, even if they arose from the same criminal transaction.

The following are examples of offenses in which neither offense is a lesser included offense of the other offense. Thus, as a matter of law, each offense requires a different prima facie case than the other offense. As such, the two offenses are not the same offense as each other. Instead, each offense is a different offense, and each offense may be sentenced separately and consecutively.

Crime(s)	No Merger	Authority
Certain thefts; theft & carjacking	Theft & carjacking do not merge.	*Price v. State*, 111 Md. App. 487, 502 (1996).
	Theft under $100, by statute, does not merge into theft under $1,000 or theft over $1,000.	*Stubbs v. State*, 406 Md. 34 (2008).
Burglary & rape	Fourth degree burglary & second degree rape do not merge.	*Fenwick v. State*, 135 Md. App. 167, 176 (2000).
Malicious destruction of property & burglary	Malicious destruction of property & burglary do not merge.	*Christian v. State*, 65 Md. App. 303, 308-09 (1985)
Arson & reckless endangerment	First degree arson & reckless endangerment do not merge.	*Holbrook v. State*, 364 Md. 354, 371 (2001).
Wearing or carrying a dangerous weapon openly with intent to injure & robbery with a dangerous weapon &/or sex offense	Wearing or carrying a dangerous weapon openly with intent to injure & robbery with a dangerous weapon do not merge.	*Selby v. State*, 76 Md. App. 201, 218-19 (1988).
	Wearing or carrying a dangerous weapon openly with intent to injure & sex offense do not merge.	*Burkett v. State*, 98 Md. App. 459, 473-75 (1993); *Nance v. State*, 77 Md. App. 256, 265-67 (1988).
Use of a firearm in the commission of a felony or crime of violence	Use of a firearm in the commission of a felony or crime of violence & the felony or crime of violence do not merge.	*Godwin v. State*, 41 Md. App. 233, 235-37 (1977); *Robeson v. State*, 39 Md. App. 365, 383 (1978), *aff'd*, 285 Md. 498 (1979).

Crime(s)	No-Merger	Authority
Rape & child sex abuse	Rape & child sex abuse do not merge.	*Rutherford v. State*, 160 Md. App. 311, 327-29 (2004).
Child sex abuse & sex offense	Child sex abuse & sex offense do not merge.	*Rutherford v. State*, 160 Md. App. 311, 327-29 (2004).
Murder & use of a handgun in the commission of a felony or crime of violence	First degree premeditated murder & use of a handgun in the commission of a felony or crime of violence do not merge.	*Robeson v. State*, 39 Md. App. 365, 382 (1978).
First degree assault & robbery; first degree assault & burglary	First degree assault & robbery (with or without a dangerous weapon) do not merge.	*Williams v. State*, 187 Md. App. 470, 478-79, *cert. denied*, 411 Md. 602 (2009); *Garcia-Perlera v. State*, 197 Md. App. 534, 559-60 (2011).
	First degree assault & first degree burglary do not merge under rule of lenity	*Pryor v. State*, 195 Md. App. 311, 338-39 (2010).
False imprisonment & sex offense; false imprisonment & robbery	False imprisonment & second degree sex offense do not merge.	*Jones-Harris v. State*, 179 Md. App. 72, 99-101 (2008).
	False imprisonment & robbery do not merge when the victim is imprisoned longer than necessary to accomplish the robbery.	*Garcia-Perlera v. State*, 197 Md. App. 534, 558-59 (2011).
DUI, DUI per se, & DWI	DUI, DUI per se, & driving while impaired do not merge.	*Turner v. State*, 181 Md. App. 477, 488-50 (2008).
Unlawful possession of a firearm by a convicted felon & unlawful wearing, carrying, or transporting a firearm	Unlawful possession of a firearm by convicted felon & unlawful wearing, carrying, or transporting a firearm do not merge.	*Pye v. State*, 397 Md. 626, 636-37 (2007).
Conspiracy & substantive crime	Conspiracy & the crime to which conspired do not merge.	*Kelly v. State*, 195 Md. App. 403, 442 (2010).
	Conspiracy to distribute cocaine & possession of cocaine with intent to distribute do not merge.	*Wadlow v. State*, 335 Md. 122, 127 n.2 (1994).

Crime(s)	No-Merger	Authority
Possession with intent to distribute & manufacturing	Possession with intent to distribute & manufacturing do not merge.	*Spiering v. State*, 58 Md. App. 1, 13 (1984).
Rape & incest; rape & battery	Rape & incest do not merge. Rape & battery do not merge when the battery is a separate battery than the battery effectuating the rape.	*Smith v. State*, 62 Md. App. 670, 684-85 (1985). *Thomas v. State*, 39 Md. App. 217, 229-30 (1978), *aff'd*, 285 Md. 458 (1979).
Use of a firearm in relation to a drug trafficking offense & wearing, carrying, or transporting a firearm	Use of firearm in relation to drug trafficking offense & wearing, carrying, or transporting a firearm do not merge.	*Johnson v. State*, 154 Md. App. 286, 311 (2003).
Speeding & engaging in a speeding contest	Speeding & engaging in a speeding contest do not merge.	*Pineta v. State*, 98 Md. App. 614, 620-21 (1993).
Assault & resisting arrest	Assault & resisting arrest do not merge.	Md. Code Ann., Crim. Law § 3-203(c).
Unauthorized use of a credit card & obtaining property with a stolen credit card	Unauthorized use of a credit card or disclosure of a credit card number do not merge with obtaining property by use of a stolen credit card.	*Montgomery v. State*, 206 Md. App. 357, 411-12 (2012).

B. Statutory construction

Beginning in 1932, under federal law, under *Blockburger*, the Double Jeopardy Clause of the Fifth Amendment prohibited separate consecutive sentences for lesser included offenses arising from the same criminal transaction. In *Benton v. Maryland*, 395 U.S. 784, 794-96 (1969), the Double Jeopardy Clause was made applicable to states through the Due Process Clause of the Fourteenth Amendment. Although many cases still speak in terms of double jeopardy, that has not been the correct analysis since 1983.

In four decisions, beginning with *Simpson*, 435 U.S. 6, and ending with *Missouri v. Hunter*, 459 U.S. 359 (1983), the Supreme Court gradually replaced the double jeopardy analysis, under *Blockburger*, with a statutory construction, non-constitutional analysis to determine when it is permissible to impose separate and consecutive sentences.

Under the statutory construction approach, if the legislature expressly authorizes separate and consecutive sentences for lesser included offense(s), the trial court may impose and execute on separate consecutive sentences for lesser included offenses. *Hunter*, 459 U.S. at 368-69; *Albernaz v. United States*, 450 U.S. 333, 340 (1981); *Rutherford v. State*, 160 Md. App. 311, 329 (2004). However, legislatures are usually silent as to whether separate and consecutive sentences are authorized. When the legislature is silent, or even ambiguous, the Supreme Court assumes that the legislature intended the *Blockburger* analysis. If there is ambiguity, the law is construed most favorably to the Defendant under the rule of lenity. Thus, in the vast majority of situations, even post-1983, *Blockburger* controls, but it controls under a statutory construction approach and not under a double jeopardy approach. In *Hunter*, the Supreme Court stated:

> Where, as here, a legislature specifically authorizes cumulative punishment under two statutes, regardless of whether those two statutes proscribe the same conduct under *Blockburger*, a court's task is at an end and the prosecutor may seek and the trial court or jury may impose cumulative punishment under such statutes in a single trial.

459 U.S. at 368-69.

In *Albernaz*, the Supreme Court stated: "[T]he question of what punishments are constitutionally permissible is not different from the question of what punishments the Legislative Branch intended to be imposed. Where Congress intended, as it did here, to impose multiple punishments, imposition of such sentences does not violate the Constitution." 450 U.S. at 344. In *Brown v. Ohio*, 432 U.S. 161, 165 (1977), the Supreme Court stated: "Where consecutive sentences are imposed at a single criminal trial, the role of the constitutional guarantee is limited to assuring that the court does not exceed its legislative authorization by imposing multiple punishments for the same offense."

1. Offenses that merge under *Blockburger* & there is legislative silence or ambiguity as to separate & consecutive sentences under *Blockburger* or under the rule of lenity

If offenses merge under the *Blockburger* required evidence test, and there is legislative silence or legislative ambiguity as to separate and consecutive sentences, separate sentences are not permissible. This is because, under statutory construction, they merge under *Blockburger* if the legislature is silent, or they merge under the rule of lenity, if there is ambiguity and, thus, uncertainty as to whether they should merge. The offenses are deemed to be the same offense under *Blockburger*, and the legislature is deemed to understand and apply *Blockburger* as a principle of statutory construction and, thus, deemed to have intended that the Defendant be sentenced only once for the same offense.

In *Moore v. State*, 163 Md. App. 305, 320-21 (2005), the Court of Special Appeals held that theft under $1,000 merges into receiving stolen credit cards because there was no indication that the legislature intended separate sentences. In *Jones v. State*, 357 Md. 141, 167 (1999), the Court of Appeals held that multiple subsections of Md. Code Ann., Transp. Art., merge, under the rule of lenity, because of legislative ambiguity. *Spitzinger v. State*, 340 Md. 114, 124 (1995). On the other hand, in *DePierre v. United States*, 131 S. Ct. 2225 (2011), the Supreme Court held that, because it did not have to "guess at what Congress intended," the rule of lenity did not apply. *Id.* at 2237 (quoting *Reno v. Koray*, 515 U.S. 50, 65 (1995)). *See United States v. Santos*, 553 U.S. 507, 514 (2008); *Smith v. United States*, 508 U.S. 223, 239 (1993).

2. Offenses that merge under *Blockburger*, but there is express legislative intent for separate & consecutive sentences

Usually, if offenses merge under the *Blockburger* required evidence test, separate sentences are not permissible because the offenses are deemed to be the same offense. However, separate and consecutive sentences are permissible, even when the offenses are the same offense under the *Blockburger* required evidence test, if the legislature, pursuant to *Missouri v. Hunter*, expressly authorizes separate and consecutive sentences.

In *Nightingale v. State*, 312 Md. 699, 708-09 (1988), the Court of Appeals held that the underlying sex offense merged into child sex abuse, stating that, when an offense, such as child abuse, contains multiple alternatives, the court must look to the alternative elements relevant to that case. In *White v. State*, 318 Md. 740 (1990), the Court of Appeals applied this same rationale to merge child physical abuse into first degree murder: "We conclude that, in the absence of express statutory language to the contrary, a child abuse conviction merges into a homicide conviction when both are based on the same acts." *Id.* at 748.

In response, the legislature enacted Md. Code. Ann., Crim. Law § 3-601(e), authorizing separate and consecutive sentences for child abuse and the underlying offense(s). In *Rutherford v. State*, 160 Md. App. 311, 329 (2004), the Court of Special Appeals held that concurrent sentences for rape and sex offense and consecutive sentences for child abuse do not merge because the legislature expressly authorized multiple punishments for child abuse and the sex offense(s) that constitute the child abuse.

3. Offenses that do not merge under *Blockburger* & there is legislative silence or ambiguity as to separate & consecutive sentences

No "legislative merger" under the rule of lenity

Separate and consecutive sentences are permissible for offenses that are separate offenses under the *Blockburger* required evidence test. Because the legislature is deemed to know the law of *Blockburger*, legislative silence or ambiguity usually means no merger. In *Albernaz*, the Supreme Court stated:

> Congress cannot be expected to specifically address each issue of statutory construction. But, as we have previously noted, Congress is predominantly a lawyer's body, and it is appropriate for us to assume that our elected representatives know the law. As a result, if anything can be assumed from . . . congressional silence . . . it is that Congress was aware of the *Blockburger* rule and legislated with it in mind.

450 U.S. at 341 (internal citations, quotations, & alterations omitted). Unless there is some clear legislative intent not to apply the law of *Blockburger*, non-merging offenses are deemed to be separate offenses and, thus, separate and consecutive sentences are permissible.

In *Biggus*, 323 Md. at 356-57, the Court of Appeals held that carrying a weapon openly or concealed does not merge into a third degree sex offense because they are separate offenses, and the legislature appears to have intended that the rule of lenity should not apply. In *Wooten-Bey v. State*, 76 Md. App. 603, 628-30 (1988), *aff'd*, 318 Md. 301 (1990), the Court of Special Appeals held that conspiracy to commit robbery and attempted robbery with a dangerous weapon do not merge because they are separate offenses for which the legislature provided distinct punishments.

In *Brooks v. State*, 284 Md. 416, 422-23 (1979), the Court of Appeals held that carrying a weapon openly with intent to injure does not merge into assault with intent to murder.

"Legislative merger" under the rule of lenity

Sometimes, even when offenses are separate offenses under the *Blockburger* required evidence test, courts apply the rule of lenity, often called "legislative merger," when there is legislative silence or ambiguity, construing silence or ambiguity most favorably to the Defendant, and merging the offenses. In *Monoker v. State*, 321 Md. 214 (1990), the Court of Appeals held:

> Even though two offenses do not merge under the required evidence test, there are nevertheless times when the offenses will not be punished separately. Two crimes created by legislative enactment may not be punished sepa-

rately if the legislature intended the offenses to be punished by one sentence. It is when we are uncertain whether the legislature intended one or more than one sentence that we make use of an aid to statutory interpretation known as the "rule of lenity." Under that rule, if we are unsure of the legislative intent in punishing offenses as a single merged crime or distinct offenses, we, in effect, give the Defendant the benefit of the doubt and hold that the crimes do merge.

Id. at 222 (citing *White v. State*, 318 Md. 740, 744-45 (1990); *Hunt v. State*, 312 Md. 494, 510 (1988); *Dillsworth v. State*, 308 Md. 354, 361-67 (1987); *State v. Jenkins*, 307 Md. 501, 518-19 (1986); *Whack v. State*, 288 Md. 137, 143 (1980)). In *Quansah v. State*, 207 Md. App. 636 (2012), the Court of Appeals stated: "[M]erger may be necessary if the Legislature did not intend to authorize multiple punishments based on a single act . . . or there is uncertainty as to whether the Legislature intended to do so." *Id.* at 653 (citations omitted). This is particularly true if, for other offenses, the legislature has expressly authorized separate and consecutive sentences, and the court deems the expression of one to be the exclusion of others.

Under the rule of lenity, although the law would permit non-merged separate and consecutive sentences, because it is unclear whether the legislature intended to do that which it had the power to do, the Defendant may be punished only once and not twice. Based on legislative silence or ambiguity, the legislature may not have meant to punish the Defendant twice, even though double punishment would be permissible.

In *Sifrit, B. v. State*, 383 Md. 116, 138-39 (2004), the Court of Appeals held that first degree assault by firearm merges, under the rule of lenity, into second degree murder. In *McGrath v. State*, 356 Md. 20, 28 (1999), the Court of Appeals held that unlawful taking of a motor vehicle merges, under the rule of lenity, into theft under $1,000. In *Eldridge v. State*, 329 Md. 307, 320 (1993), the Court of Appeals held that carrying a dangerous weapon merges, under the rule of lenity, into robbery with a dangerous weapon.

In *Dickerson v. State*, 324 Md. 163 (1991), the Court of Appeals held that the legislature intended merger for drug possession with intent to distribute and possession of drug paraphernalia when the paraphernalia possessed was the vial that contained the drugs. In *State v. Burroughs*, 333 Md. 614, 626 (1994), the Court of Appeals held that the legislative history indicated an intent for only one punishment for embezzlement and theft by deception.

In *Hunt*, 312 Md. at 510-11, the Court of Appeals held that carrying, wearing, or transporting a handgun merges, under the rule of lenity, into use of handgun in the commission of a felony or crime of violence. *Accord Tilghman v. State*, 117 Md. App. 542, 571-72 (1997). In *Washington, E. v. State*, 190 Md. App. 168, 178 (2010), the Court of Special Appeals held that DUI merges into DUI per se, under the rule of lenity, when the offenses arise from one act of driving. In *Marlin v. State*, 192 Md. App. 134, *cert. denied*, 415 Md. 339 (2010), the Court of Special Appeals held that reckless endangerment merges, under the rule of lenity, into first degree assault by firearm. In *Abeokuto v. State*, 391 Md. 289, 359 (2006), the Court of Appeals held that child kidnapping merges, under the rule of lenity, into kidnapping.

In *Somers v. State*, 156 Md. App. 279, 316-17 (2004), the Court of Special Appeals held that carrying a dangerous weapon openly with intent to injure merges, under the rule of lenity, into robbery with a dangerous weapon. *Accord Eldridge v. State*, 329 Md. 307, 316-21 (1993). In *Jenkins v. State*, 146 Md. App. 83, 135 (2002), *rev'd on other grounds*, 375 Md. 284 (2003), the Court of Special Appeals held that first degree assault by firearm merges, under the rule of lenity, into first degree murder.

In *Jackson v. State*, 141 Md. App. 175, 198 (2001), the Court of Special Appeals held that felony theft merges, under the rule of lenity, into robbery or into robbery with a dangerous weapon. *Accord Bellamy v. State*, 119 Md. App. 296, 307 (1998). In *White v. State*, 100 Md. App. 1, 11-12 (1994), the Court of Special Appeals held that misappropriation by a fiduciary merges, under the rule of lenity, into theft.

In *State v. Jenkins*, 307 Md. 501, 521 (1986), the Court of Appeals held that assault with intent to maim, disfigure, or disable merges, under the rule of lenity, into assault with intent to murder. In *Moore v. State*, 198 Md. App. 655, 703-04 (2011), the Court of Special Appeals held that uttering merges, under the rule of lenity, into attempted theft over $500. In *Moore v. State*, 153 Md. App. 305, 316 (2005), the Court of Special Appeals held that theft under $500 merges, under the rule of lenity, into receiving a stolen credit card. In *Marquardt v. State*, 164 Md. App. 95, 152-53 (2005), the Court of Special Appeals held that fundamental fairness requires that malicious destruction of property merge into burglary.

When offenses merge, under the rule of lenity, the offense with the lesser sentence merges into the offense with the greater sentence. In *Miles v. State*, 349 Md. 215 (1998), the Court of Appeals held:

> [W]here two offenses are separate under the required evidence test, there still may be merger for sentencing purposes based on consideration such as the rule of lenity, historical treatment, judicial decisions which generally hold that the offenses merge, and fairness. When merger is not based upon the required evidence test, and therefore neither offence is the greater in terms of elements, the offense carrying the highest maximum authorized sentence is ordinarily considered to be the greater offense. Thus, the offense carrying the lesser maximum penalty merges into the offense carrying the greater penalty.

Id. at 221 (internal citations & quotations omitted). *See State v. Jenkins*, 307 Md. 501, 521 (1986).

4. Common law offenses that do not merge under *Blockburger* may merge under fundamental fairness

The rule of lenity is a principle of statutory construction and applies only to statutory offenses. In *Carroll v. State*, 428 Md. 679 (2012), the Court of Appeals stated: "Rare are the circumstances in which fundamental fairness requires merger of separate convictions or sentences." *Id.* at 695. The Court held that fundamental fairness did not require merger of conspiracy to commit armed robbery and attempted armed robbery. *Id.* at 698-99.

In *Monoker v. State*, 321 Md. 214, 223-24 (1990), the Court of Appeals held that the common law crimes of solicitation and conspiracy, even though not the same offense under the required evidence test, merge under fundamental fairness when the solicitation is an "integral component" of the conspiracy.

5. Offenses that do not merge under *Blockburger* & there is express legislative intent for separate sentences & no rule of lenity

Courts may impose separate sentences when the legislature expressly authorizes separate sentences for non-merging offenses. In *Missouri v. Hunter*, 459 U.S. 359 (1983), the Supreme Court held: "With respect to cumulative sentences imposed in a single trial, the Double Jeopardy Clause does no more than prevent the sentencing court from prescribing greater punishment than the legislature intended." *Id.* at 678.

In *Khalifa v. State*, 382 Md. 400, 435-37 (2004), the Court of Appeals held that (a) convictions for child abduction and child detention do not merge under the *Blockburger* required evidence test, because each offense has a separate element, and they do not merge under the rule of lenity, because the legislature unambiguously intended to create separate categories of prohibited conduct with abduction and detention; and (b) conspiracy to commit child detention did not merge into child detention because conspiracy does not merge into the substantive crime. However, child detention outside Maryland merged, as a lesser included offense, into child detention outside the United States under the Blockburger required evidence test. *Id.* at 437-38.

In *State v. Lancaster*, 332 Md. 385 (1993), the Court of Appeals held: "The only exception to the principle that merger follows as a matter of course if one offense is included within the other under the required evidence test, is where, under some circumstances, the General Assembly has specifically or expressly authorized multiple punishments." *Id.* at 394. *See Frazier v. State*, 318 Md. 597, 614-15 (1990).

Robbery with a dangerous weapon and use of a handgun in the commission of a felony or a crime of violence do not merge. The offense of robbery with a dangerous weapon has the additional element of "robbery." Robbery, which is both a felony and a crime of violence, is a permissible way of establishing a prima facie case of the element of "felony or crime of violence" for the offense of use of a handgun in the commission of a felony or crime of violence, but robbery is not required.

Similarly, the offense of use of a handgun in the commission of a felony or crime of violence has the additional element of a "handgun." A handgun, which is a dangerous weapon, is a permissible way of establishing a prima facie case of the element of "with a dangerous weapon" for the offense of robbery with a dangerous weapon" but a handgun is not required.

In *Whack v. State*, 288 Md. 137 (1980), the Court of Appeals held that the legislature intended separate sentences for robbery with a dangerous weapon and use of a handgun in the commission of a felony or crime of violence and stated:

> The legislature's concern about the use of a weapon to intimidate a robbery victim, and its additional concern when that weapon is a handgun, is certainly not unreasonable. When it expressly shows an intent to punish, under two separate statutory provisions, conduct involving those aggravating factors, the Fifth Amendment's double jeopardy prohibition has not heretofore been regarded as a bar.

Id. at 150. *See Clark v. State*, 188 Md. App. 185, 208 (2009) (no merger when the statute contained an anti-merger provision); *Johnson v. State*, 67 Md. App. 347, 378 n.5 (1986); *Stevenson v. State*, 43 Md. App. 120, 131-32 (1979), *aff'd*, 287 Md. 504 (1980).

6. When two statutes apply two different penalties to the same conduct, the rule of lenity does not apply

If two statutes unambiguously apply two different penalties for the same conduct, the rule of lenity does not apply. In *United States v. Batchelder*, 442 U.S. 114 (1979), the Supreme Court held:

> This Court has long recognized that when an act violates more than one criminal statute, the Government may prosecute under either so long as it does not discriminate against any class of Defendants. Whether to prosecute and what charge to file or bring before a grand jury are decisions that generally rest in the prosecutor's discretion.

Id. at 123 (internal citations omitted); *Alston v. State*, 159 Md. App. 253, 271 (2004). In *Brack v. Wells*, 184 Md. 86, 90 (1944), the Court of Appeals stated: "As a general rule, whether the State's Attorney does or does not institute a particular prosecution is a matter which rests in his [or her] discretion." In *State v. Lee*, 178 Md. App. 478, 489-90 (2008), the Court of Special Appeals held that the rule of lenity does not permit the trial court, at sentencing, to substitute a lesser offense, with a lesser sentence, over the objection of the State.

7. Examples of "legislative merger" under the rule of lenity

The following are examples of offenses that Maryland holds are subject to "legislative merger" under the rule of lenity.

Crime(s)	Legislative merger under "Rule of Lenity"	Authority
Assault & murder	First degree assault, based on a firearm, merges into second degree murder.	*Sifrit, B. v. State*, 383 Md. 116, 138-39 (2004).
	First degree assault, based on a firearm, merges into attempted first degree murder.	*Jenkins v. State*, 146 Md. App. 83, 135 (2002), *rev'd on other grounds*, 375 Md. 284 (2003).
	Assault with intent to maim, disfigure, or disable merges into assault with the intent to murder.	*State v. Jenkins*, 307 Md. 501, 521-22 (1986).
	Assault with intent to murder merges into attempted first degree murder.	*Green v. State*, 79 Md. App. 506, 511-12 (1989).
	Common law assault merges into attempted first degree rape.	*Walker v. State*, 53 Md. App. 171, 200-02 (1982).
Unauthorized use of a motor vehicle & theft	Unlawful use of a motor vehicle merges into theft under $1,000.	*McGrath v. State*, 356 Md. 20, 28-29 (1999).
Embezzlement & theft by deception	Embezzlement merges into theft by deception.	*State v. Burroughs*, 333 Md. 614, 624-27 (1994).
Theft & robbery	Felony theft merges into robbery.	*Jackson v. State*, 141 Md. App. 175, 197-98 (2001).
	Theft merges into robbery or robbery with a dangerous weapon.	*Bellamy v. State*, 119 Md. App. 296, 307 (1998).
Theft & receiving stolen credit cards	Theft under $1,000 merges into receiving a stolen credit card.	*Moore v. State*. 163 Md. App. 305, 321 (2005).
Theft & misappropriation by a fiduciary	Misappropriation by a fiduciary merges into theft.	*White v. State*, 100 Md. App. 1, 11-12 (1994).
Carrying a dangerous weapon & robbery with a dangerous weapon	Carrying a dangerous weapon merges into robbery with a dangerous weapon.	*Eldridge v. State*, 329 Md. 307, 314-15 (1993).

Crime(s)	Legislative merger under "Rule of Lenity"	Authority
Possession of drug paraphernalia & possession with intent to distribute	Possession of drug paraphernalia merges into possession with intent to distribute when paraphernalia was vial that contained drugs.	*Dickerson v. State*, 324 Md. 163, 172-73 (1991).
Carrying, wearing, or transporting a firearm & use of a handgun in commission of a felony or crime of violence	Carrying, wearing, or transporting a firearm merges into use of a firearm in the commission of a felony or crime of violence.	*Wilkins v. State*, 343 Md. 444, 446-47 (1996); *Hunt v. State*, 312 Md. 494, 510-11 (1988); *Tilghman v. State*, 117 Md. App. 542, 572 (1997).
Carrying a weapon openly with intent to injure & robbery with a dangerous weapon	Carrying a weapon openly with intent to injure merges into robbery with a dangerous weapon.	*Somers v. State*, 156 Md. App. 279, 317-18 (2004).
DUI & DUI per se	DUI merges into DUI per se merge when based on the same act of driving.	*Washington, E. v. State*, 190 Md. App. 168, 177 (2010).
Reckless endangerment & first degree assault	Reckless endangerment merges into first degree assault, based on a firearm.	*Marlin v. State*, 192 Md. App. 134, 169-71 (2010).
Child kidnapping & kidnapping	Child kidnapping merges into kidnapping.	*Abeokuto v. State*, 391 Md. 289, 359 (2006).
Uttering & theft	Uttering merges into theft over $1,000.	*Moore v. State*, 198 Md. App. 655, 703-04 (2011).
Aggressive panhandling & assault	Aggressive panhandling (ordinance) merges into second degree assault, even though general state offense is lesser included offense of local specific offense.	*Miles v. State*, 349 Md. 215, 228-29 (1998).
Violating peace order & assault	Violating a peace order merges into second degree assault.	*Quansah v. State*, 207 Md. App. 636, 656 (2012).

C. Appeal

In *Walzak v. State*, 302 Md. 422 (1985), the Court of Appeals held that the trial court's failure to merge, when required, resulted in an illegal sentence, which may be raised on appeal, even if not raised at trial. *Accord Tederick v. State*, 125 Md. App. 37, 40-41, *aff'd*, 357 Md. 141 (1999); *Lamb v. State*, 93 Md. App. 422 (1992). In *Campbell v. State*, 65 Md. App. 498, 510-11, *cert. denied*, 305 Md. 599 (1985), the Court of Special Appeals held that the failure to merge makes the sentence(s) illegal, even though the sentences ran concurrently.

In *Lamb*, 93 Md. App. 422, the Court of Special Appeals held: "Although the [Defendant] made no timely objection to the non-merger of convictions at the time of sentencing, it is clear that the issue of non-merger is reviewable by an appellate court even absent preservation of the issue by the [Defendant]." *Id.* at 427.

In a de novo appeal, the Defendant may be re-tried on any charge that merged into another charge in the first trial. *Lewis v. State*, 289 Md. 1, 6 (1980).

In *Snowden*, 321 Md. at 619, the Court of Appeals held that the record was unclear as to whether the robbery resulted from the lesser included assault or from a separate assault, and thus the assault must merge into the robbery. In *Gerald v. State*, 137 Md. App. 295, 312 (2001), the Court of Special Appeals held that when the indictment is ambiguous, and the trial court does not give jury instructions to resolve the ambiguity, the ambiguity must be resolved in favor of the Defendant and the sentences must merge.

In *Bayne v. State*, 98 Md. App. 149, 160-61 (1993), when the jury instructions failed to define sexual contact as excluding penile penetration, the Court of Special Appeals held that third degree sex offense merged into second degree rape because the record was unclear as to whether they were based on the same conduct.

If there is more than one disjunctive method of proof supporting a guilty verdict, but the jury instructions and/or verdict sheet do not permit the appellate court to determine, with reasonable certainty, which one or more disjunctive methods the jury found, the verdict must be construed most favorably to the Defendant.

In *State v. Frye*, 283 Md. 709, 723 (1978), the jury instructions and the verdict sheet failed to explain whether the jury's first degree murder verdict was based on (a) felony murder; (b) premeditated murder; or (c) both. If the basis was (b) or (c), a consecutive sentence for robbery was permissible. If the basis was (a) only, a consecutive sentence for robbery was not be permissible because robbery would be a lesser included offense of felony murder. The Court of Appeals construed that ambiguity in the record most favorably to the Defendant and merged the robbery into the murder.

In *Dixon v. State*, 364 Md. 209, 244-53 (2001), the Court of Appeals held that first degree assault merged into attempted voluntary manslaughter when the jury was instructed on the multiple modalities of first degree assault, and jury returned a general verdict without specifying which modality. In *Cortez v. State*, 104 Md. App. 358 (1995), the Court of Special Appeals held:

We are confronted with the same problem of ambiguity of verdict that confronted the Court of Appeals in *Snowden* . . . This merger problem continues to arise despite *Nightingale, Biggus, Snowden,* and *Lancaster.* We believe it can be avoided in a case in which separate convictions and sentences might be sustainable on the evidence. In a bench trial, the solution is simple: the trial judge need only articulate for the record the basis for the dual verdicts, stating the separate acts justifying both convictions.

In a jury trial, the solution, as suggested in *Snowden*, is the giving of an appropriate instruction. For example, the trial judge might instruct the jury that, if it found the Defendant guilty of robbery (or kidnapping, or other compound crimes in which force or the threat of force is an element), it could find the Defendant guilty of battery (or assault, or both) only if it found that there was a use of force (or threat of force) separate from and independent of the force (or threat of force) employed to effect the greater offense. If such an instruction were given, a conviction of battery or assault in addition to the conviction of the greater offense would not merge, and the only debatable issue would be the sufficiency of the evidence of a separate battery or assault to sustain the conviction.

Id. at 369-70.

XIII. Sentencing following appeal

On remand, following a successful appeal, the sentencing judge may not impose a more severe sentence than previously imposed, unless a greater sentence is based on additional objective information concerning identifiable bad conduct on the part of the Defendant since the last sentence, and the basis for the increased sentence appears on the record. Md. Code Ann., Cts. & Jud. Proc. § 12-702(b) & (c). In *Briggs v. State*, 289 Md. 23, 33 (1980), the Court of Appeals held that the Defendant's bad conduct must have occurred after the original sentence even if the Defendant has elected a *de novo* trial in the Circuit Court after a District Court trial. *Accord Jones v. State*, 307 Md. 449, 455-56 (1986); *Coley v. State*, 76 Md. App. 731, 735-36 (1988).

In *Nimon v. State*, 71 Md. App. 559, 735-37 (1987), the Court of Special Appeals held that, if restitution was not part of the original sentence, it cannot be part of sentence on remand, because that would constitute a sentence increase. *See Hill v. State*, 64 Md. App. 194, 200-01(1985). In *Willey v. State*, 90 Md. App. 349, 358-59 (1992), the Court of Appeals held that an increased sentence, in a VOP hearing, was permissible when, between the reversal of the first sentence and the VOP, the Defendant was convicted of murder. *See Davis v. State*, 312 Md. 172 (1988). Courts may not re-impose an illegal sentence.

In *Dixon v. State*, 364 Md. 209 (2001), the Defendant was sentenced to ten years for attempted voluntary manslaughter and 20 years for first degree assault. On appeal, the sentence for the lesser included first degree assault (20 years) was merged into the sentence for the greater attempted voluntary manslaughter (ten years). After reversal on a separate issue, the State entered a nol pros on the attempted voluntary manslaughter, and the Defendant was convicted of first degree assault and sentenced to 20 years. The Court of Appeals vacated the sentence, holding that the sentence was capped, not by the original sentence, which was illegal without the required merger, but by the post-merger sentence of ten years, regardless of the nol pros for attempted voluntary manslaughter at the second trial. *Id.* at 250-51.

In *Sweetwine v. State*, 288 Md. 199, 213-15 (1980), the Defendant was charged with, found guilty of, and sentenced for robbery, but the conviction was overturned on appeal. On remand, the Defendant was charged with, found guilty of, and sentenced for robbery with a dangerous weapon. Even though the sentence from the second trial was greater than the sentence from the first trial, the Court of Appeals upheld the second sentence, because it was based on a separate crime, with a higher statutory maximum sentence, and was not in retaliation for taking an appeal. *See Gardner v. State*, 420 Md. 1, 11-12 (2011) (sentence review panel's sentence, which increased the initial sentence, was the "sentence previously imposed" for the purposes of Md. Code Ann., Crim. Proc. § 12-702(b)).

XIV. Probation & probation before judgment (PBJ)

A. Probation options & conditions

The sentencing court may stay the judgment and permit the Defendant to serve his sentence not in prison, but in the community, either in an unsupervised status, or supervised by an agent of the Department of Parole & Probation (DPP). The more onerous of the two probation options is probation after judgment. This means that (1) the Defendant pleads guilty or is found guilty; (2) the judge usually sentences the Defendant and, if so, suspends the sentence; and (3) the judge places the Defendant on probation. Even if the Defendant successfully completes probation and serves no period of incarceration, the Defendant has a criminal record because his probation was after his judgment.

The less onerous of the two probation options is probation before judgment (PBJ). This means that (1) the Defendant pleads guilty or is found guilty; (2) the court strikes the finding of guilt; and (3) the court enters probation before judgment (PBJ). Unlike probation after judgment, which results in a criminal record, PBJ does not result in a criminal record.

Sometimes, the court will place the Defendant on probation and give the Defendant the opportunity to "earn" a PBJ by successfully completing probation, at which time the court would convert probation after judgment to a PBJ. If the Defendant either receives a PBJ at the outset or earns a PBJ while on probation, the Defendant has no criminal record and can obtain an expungement of his record. Md. Code Ann., Crim. Proc. § 6-220.

For both probation after judgment and PBJ, the court may (and usually does) impose reasonable conditions. Failure to comply with probation conditions may result in incarceration. Probation conditions may include (1) a monetary fine; (2) restitution; or (3) participation in a rehabilitation program, parks program, or voluntary hospital program, etc. *Id.* § 6-220(b)(2). By statute, PBJ is not available for certain enumerated crimes. *Id.* § 6-220(d).

B. Waiver of the right to appeal

In order to receive PBJ, the Defendant must waive the right to appeal. *Id.* § 6-220(e).

C. Violation of probation

If a Defendant who received a PBJ is found guilty of a PBJ condition, the court may enter judgment and proceed as if the stay had never been entered. *Id.* § 6-220(f).

D. Satisfaction of the PBJ conditions

Upon satisfactory fulfillment of the PBJ conditions, the court shall discharge the Defendant from probation. Discharge is a final disposition of the case, is without judgment, and is not a conviction for the purpose of any disqualification or disability imposed by law. *Id.* § 6-220(g). Thus, the Defendant is eligible to have the PBJ expunged. If the Defendant is not a U.S. citizen, federal immigration authorities consider a PBJ a conviction, making a lawful alien subject to deportation, depending on the offense.

§ XV. Sex offender registration

A. Sex offender registration is part of the sentence & the ex post facto clauses prohibit retroactive application

Sex offender registries came about in the mid-1990s. Originally, the statutory requirement to register as a sex offender was not considered part of the sentence. It was considered a mere regulatory requirement to provide the public with notice of who are sex offenders and where they live. *Young v. State*, 370 Md. 686, 716 (2002). In *Sweet v. State*, 371 Md. 1, 8-9 (2002), the Court of Appeals held that, because registration was not part of the sentence, there was no constitutional requirement for the jury to make any finding, including no requirement to find that the Defendant poses a risk of committing future sexual offenses as a predicate to sex offender registration. *See Connecticut Dep't of Pub. Safety v. Doe*, 538 U.S. 1, 7-8 (2003).

In *Doe v. Department of Public Safety & Correctional Services*, 430 Md. 535 (2013), the Court of Appeals held that the requirement to register as a sexual offender is part of the Defendant's sentence, and it is not merely a collateral consequence. Legislatures, having previously assumed that the sex offender registration was merely a collateral consequence, often made the registration requirements more onerous and applied them retroactively.

Because Maryland now considers sex offender registration to be punishment, when the legislature creates new registration requirements that are both (1) more onerous, and (2) apply retroactively, the legislation is ex post facto by retroactively applying more onerous sentencing to Defendants whose conduct pre-dates the new registration requirements.

In *Doe*, the Defendant was convicted in 2006 of child sexual abuse for an incident that took place while he was a teacher during the 1983-84 school year. In 2009 and 2010, the Maryland General Assembly amended the registration law and required registration of child sex offenders who committed offenses before 1995, but were convicted after 1995, who had not previously been required to register. Under the new law, the Defendant was required to register as a child sex offender for life. In *Doe*, a three-judge plurality held that the retroactive registration requirement violated Md. Decl. of Rights art. 17, which prohibits ex post facto laws. The Court held:

> Based on principles of fundamental fairness and the right to fair warning within the meaning of Article 17, retrospective application of the sex offender registration statute to [the Defendant] is unconstitutional. [The Defendant] committed his sex offense during the 1983-84 school year. The Maryland sex offender registration statute did not go into effect until a decade later in 1995. As a result of the 2009 and 2010 amendments to the statute, the registration requirements were applied retroactively to [the Defendant]. He could not have had fair warning that he would be required to register. In fact, during the 2010 trial court proceedings in the present case, the trial judge, who also presided over [the Defendant]'s original sentencing four years earlier, stated "no one could have anticipated, I certainly didn't in 2006, that in 2009, the law would change to require someone to register if an offense had occurred during the time period that it did occur in this particular case." If in 2006, "no one could have anticipated" that [the Defendant] would be required to register, he could hardly have had fair warning of the requirement two decades earlier. [The Defendant] could not have had fair warning of, and should not

face, legally imposed sanctions beyond those provided for at the time of the commission of the crime. Ensuring this protection is especially vital in this case because a sex offender registration statute imposes significant affirmative obligations and a severe stigma on every person to whom it applies.

Id. at 553.

B. Defendants to whom the sex offender registration applies

Maryland Defendants convicted of certain sex offenses in Maryland or in another jurisdiction are required to register as a sex offender if they (1) were found guilty; (2) pleaded guilty; (3) pleaded nolo contendere; (4) were granted PBJ with registration as a condition of probation; or (5) were found NCR.

1. Tier I sex offender

A Tier I sex offender is a Defendant who has been convicted of (a) fourth degree sex offense (or conspiracy or attempt); (b) visual surveillance of a minor with prurient intent (or conspiracy or attempt); (c) possession of visual representations of a child under age 16 engaged in sadomasochistic abuse, sexual conduct, or in a state of sexual excitement (or conspiracy or attempt); (d) a crime on a federal, military, tribal, or another state, which, if committed in Maryland, would constitute (a), (b), or (c) above; (e) a federal offense of sexual misuse of the Internet, illicit sexual conduct in a foreign country, transmitting information about a minor to further illicit sexual conduct, sex trafficking by force, fraud, or coercion, or foreign travel with intent to engage in illicit sexual conduct; or (f) sex offense on a military installation.

2. Tier II sex offender

In 2011, the Maryland General Assembly modified the registration requirements for Tier II offenders, making registration a requirement for offenders who committed an offense (or conspiracy or attempt) on or after October 1, 2010, if their crime was a felony. A Tier II sex offender is a Defendant who has been convicted of (a) soliciting an undercover officer, believing it to be a minor; (b) child pornography under Md. Code Ann., Crim. Law § 11-207; (c) hiring a minor for a prohibited purpose under Md. Code Ann., Crim. Law § 11-209; (d) pandering when the intended prostitute is a minor; (e) abduction of a minor for prostitution; (f) operating a house of prostitution with a minor prostitute; (g) sexual conduct between a correctional employee or juvenile services employee and a confined minor at least age 14; (h) sale of a minor at least age 14; or (i) a crime on a federal, military, tribal, or another state, which, if committed in Maryland, would constitute an enumerated crime.

3. Tier III sex offender

A Tier III sex offender is a Defendant who has been convicted of one or more of the following offenses (or conspiracy or attempt): (a) first degree murder committed while perpetrating or attempting to perpetrate rape, first or second degree sex offense, or sodomy; (b) actual or attempted first or second degree rape; (c) actual or attempted first or second degree sex offense; (d) third degree sex offense committed with a dangerous weapon or with infliction of serious injury; (e) a continuing course of rape or sex offenses with a minor at least age 14 over a 90-day or longer period; (f) incest; (g) kidnapping a minor (or adult if ordered by the court to register); (h) sex abuse of a minor; (i) sodomy committed by force or threat of force; (j) sexual contact with a minor under age 14 by a Defendant at least four years older; (k) sexual conduct between a correctional employee or juvenile services employee and a confined minor under age 14; (l) child kidnapping of a minor under age 14; (m) sex abuse of a minor under age 14; (n) false imprisonment of a minor; (n) conspiring to commit, attempting to commit, or committing Tier I or Tier II sex offense after already registered as a Tier II sex offender; or (o)a crime on a federal, military, tribal, or another state, which, if committed in Maryland, would constitute an enumerated crime.

4. Sexually violent predator

A sexually violent predator is a Defendant who is convicted of a predicate offense and found to be a sexually violent predator. A predicate offense is (a) actual or attempted first or second degree rape; or (b) first, second, or third degree sex offense. For the Defendant to be determined to be a sexually violent predator, the State must provide written notice, at least 30 days before trial, of intent to have the Defendant determined to be a sexually violent predator. If so, the court should make the sexually violent predator determination before or at sentencing, considering (a) the pre-sentence investigation (PSI) report; (b) the Defendant's institutional record; (c) evidence introduced by the Defendant; and (d) a victim impact statement (VIS).

5. Registration

Tier I, Tier II, and Tier III sex offenders must register. A sex offender from another jurisdiction, who enters Maryland to live, work, attend school, or as a transient, must register as a sex offender. Sex offender registry must include (a) full name and home address; (b) name and address of all employers and where employment duties are performed; (c) name and address of educational institution; (d) description of the crime requiring registration; (e) date of conviction; (f) venue and court where convicted; (g) list of aliases, former names, email addresses, computer log-in or screen name identities, instant-messaging identities, and electronic chat room identities; (h) date of birth and Social Security number; (i) physical description and identifying factors; (j) a copy of any passport and immigration papers; (k) professional licenses;

(l) license plate number, registration number, description, and location of all vehicles, boats, and aircraft; (m) all phone numbers; (n) a copy of any driver's license or ID card; (o) fingerprints and palm prints; (p) criminal history and parole, probation, and release status; and (q) signature and date.

6. Additional contents if registrant has been determined to be a sexually violent predator

Additional content includes (a) anticipated future residence, if known; and (b) documentation of treatment received for mental abnormality or personality disorder.

7. Term of registration

The term of registration is calculated from (a) the last date of release; (b) the date probation was granted; (c) the date that a suspended sentence was granted; or (d) the date that juvenile jurisdiction terminates. The term of the registration depends on the tier, as follows: (a) Tier I sex offender must register in person with a local law enforcement agency every six months for 15 years; (b) Tier II sex offender must register in person with a local law enforcement agency every six months for 25 years; and (c) Tier III sex offender must register in person with a local law enforcement agency every three months for life.

8. Failure to register

A Defendant who is required to register and who knowingly (a) fails to register; (b) fails to provide all required information; (c) fails to provide notice of change in circumstances; or (d) provides false information of a material fact, is subject to the following. The first offense is a misdemeanor, subject to three years and/or a $5,000 fine. A subsequent offense is a felony, subject to five years and/or a $10,000 fine.

9. Reduction in term of registration

The registration term for a Tier I sex offender is reduced to ten years, if during that time, the Defendant (a) is not convicted of an offense subject to more that one year; (b) is not convicted of any sex offense; (c) successfully completes any period of supervised release; and (d) successfully completes a sex offender treatment program.

10. Lifetime sex offender registry

Lifetime sex offender registry is required for (a) a Defendant found to be a sexually violent predator; (b) a Defendant convicted of actual or attempted first or second degree rape; (c) a Defendant convicted of actual or attempted first degree sex offense; (d) a Defendant convicted of actual or attempted second degree sex offense committed with force or threat of force if the victim is mentally defective, mentally incapacitated, or physically helpless, and the Defendant knew of the victim's status; (e) a Defendant convicted of sex abuse of a minor under age 12; and (f) a Defendant convicted more than once arising out of separate incidents of a crime that requires sex offender registry.

11. Terms of lifetime sex offender registration

The terms of lifetime sex offender registration are (a) GPS monitoring; (b) restriction on living near, or loitering near, schools, day care centers, child care centers, or places frequented by minors; (c) restriction on employment involving contact with minors; (d) sex offender treatment program; (e) prohibited from using drugs or alcohol; (e) access to the Defendant's personal computer to monitor for material relating to sexual relations with minors; (f) regular polygraph exams; (g) prohibited from contacting certain persons or groups of persons; and (h) other terms and conditions that the court deems appropriate.

12. Violation of terms of lifetime sex offender registration

A Defendant who is subject to lifetime sex offender registration, and who knowingly or willfully violates the terms and conditions is subject to the following: (a) the first offense is a misdemeanor, subject to three years and/or a $5,000 fine; and (b) a subsequent offenses is a felony, subject to ten years and/or a $10,000 fine.

13. Retroactive application:

In 1995, the Maryland General Assembly first enacted the Maryland sex offender registration statute. As enacted, the statute applied prospectively to sex offenders who committed sex crimes after on or after October 1, 1995.

In 2001, the sex offender registration statute was amended and was applied retrospectively to different groups of sex offenders, including "a child sex offender who committed [his or her] sexual offense before October 1, 1995 [if that offender was] under the custody and supervision of the supervising authority on October 1, 2001." Md. Code Ann., Crim. Proc. § 11-702.1.

In 2009, the retroactive application of the statute was once again amended and registration was required of a child sex offender who committed his or her crime before October 1, 1995, but was convicted on or after October 1, 1995, irrespective of when the offender was incarcerated or under supervision.

In 2010, the sex offender registration was amended again, and among other things, the amendment addressed the retroactive application of the statute. The 2010 amendment required retroactive registration of all persons who were already required to register on September 30, 2010, the day before the amendment went into effect. This language had the consequence of incorporating the retroactive application of the statute as amended in 2009.

It was these retroactive provisions that were held to violate the prohibition against ex post facto laws in *Doe*, 430 Md. 535.

§ XVI. Reporting in drug cases

If a Defendant who is convicted of certain drug offenses holds one or more of certain state-issued licenses, the court must report a drug conviction to the licensing authority if (a) the Defendant has a prior drug conviction after 1991; or (b) there is relationship between the current conviction and the license. Md. Rule 4-340; Md. Code Ann., Crim. Law § 5-810.

§ XVII. Community service

The court may require the Defendant to perform specified community service, without compensation, through a public agency or a non-profit organizations. *See State v. Duran*, 407 Md. 532, 546 n.7 (2009); *ABA Standards for Criminal Justice* Standard 18-3.17.

§ XVIII. Court costs & fines

A. Court costs

The court may assess court costs against the Defendant upon (1) a finding of guilt; (2) an entry of probation before judgment (PBJ); or (3) the acceptance of a plea of nolo contendere. Alternatively, the court may waive court costs or suspend a portion of the court costs, considering the Defendant's financial circumstances. Md. Rule 4-353. In *Medley v. State*, 386 Md. 3, 9-10 (2005), the Court of Appeals held that the Defendant may not be assessed jury costs. *See ABA Standards for Criminal Justice* Standard 18-3.22.

B. Fines

The court may impose a fine, which the court may stay. If the Defendant appeals a fine-only sentence, and court sets an appeal bond, the bond may not exceed the amount of the fine and the court costs. Md. Rule 4-348(c).

C. Money judgment

If the court orders the Defendant to pay money, in the form of a fine, court costs, or restitution, it is enforceable as a money judgment. Md. Rule 4-354.

D. Time allowed for payment

The court may order the Defendant to pay pursuant to a specific installment plan, and the court may make payment a condition of probation. Md. Code Ann., Cts. & Jud. Proc. § 7-503.

E. Failure to pay fines & court costs

If the Defendant fails to pay a fine, the court may order the Defendant incarcerated until payment is made, subject to the following limitations.

(1) Incarceration cannot exceed one day for each $10 of unpaid fine.

(2) If the offense is subject to incarceration, the period of incarceration for non-payment cannot exceed one-third of maximum sentence authorized or 90 days, whichever is less.

(3) If the offense is not subject to incarceration, the maximum period for non-payment is 15 days.

(4) The length of incarceration for non-payment, when added to the original sentence, cannot exceed the maximum sentence.

(5) Incarceration for non-payment of two or more fines must run concurrently. Md. Code Ann., Cts. & Jud. Proc. § 7-504. The Defendant may not be incarcerated for failure to pay a fine if non-payment was based solely on the inability to pay.

Because court costs cannot be part of the sentence, the Defendant cannot be incarcerated for failure to pay court costs. Unpaid court costs can be collected as a civil judgment. *Id.* § 7-505. Fines and court costs are paid to the venue where convicted and may not be paid to an informant. *Id.* §§ 7-506, 7-507.

F. Restitution

An order of restitution, as a condition of probation, is part of the sentence. As such, an illegal order of restitution may be challenged as an illegal sentence. *Goff v. State*, 387 Md. 327, 339-40 (2005). Restitution is a criminal sanction and not a civil remedy and, thus, restitution is not dischargeable in bankruptcy. *State v. Garnett*, 384 Md. 466, 478 (2004).

§ XIX. Nolle prosequi or stet with a requirement that the Defendant participate in drug or alcohol treatment

The State's Attorney, at the request of the Defendant or on the State's motion, may offer a Defendant, if qualifying for drug or alcohol treatment, a dismissal, by entering a nolle prosequi or indefinite stet, conditioned on successful completion of drug and alcohol treatment. Md. Code Ann., Crim. Proc. § 6-229(c)(4)(ii).

XX. Sentencing Motions

A. Application for review of sentence by a three-judge panel

1. Applicability

The Defendant may file an application for review of sentence by a three-judge panel if the sentence exceeds two years incarceration. Md. Code Ann., Crim. Proc. § 8-102; Md. Rule 4-344. Review of a sentence by three-judge panel is permitted following imposition of an original sentence or re-imposition of a previously suspended sentence. *Collins v. State*, 321 Md. 103, 110 (1990). The application must be signed by the Defendant in substantially the form provided in Md. Rule 4-344(b). Md. Code Ann., Crim. Proc. § 8-102; Md. Rule 4-344(a).

The Defendant must sign the pleading, and agree to this proceeding, because, unlike a motion for modification or reduction of sentence, for which there is no potential "downside," for an application for review of sentence, there is potential "downside" because the panel may increase the sentence. *See Rendelman v. State*, 73 Md. App. 329, 331 (1987). An indigent Defendant is entitled to counsel for a three-judge panel at State's expense. Md. Code Ann., Crim. Proc. § 8-103. A valid waiver of counsel at trial does not "carry over" to a sentence review proceeding. *Rendelman*, 73 Md. App. at 339.

2. Filing an application

The Defendant must file an application for review of sentence by three-judge panel no later than 30 days after imposition of sentence or re-imposition of a previously suspended sentence. Md. Rule 4-344(b); *Collins*, 321 Md. at 110. In *Mendes v. State*, 102 Md. App. 246, 253-54 (1994), the Court of Special Appeals held that the application for review of sentence must be filed within 30 days of imposition of sentence (and not final judgment, if those dates are different).

In *Green v. State*, 96 Md. App. 601, 607 (1993), the Court of Special Appeals held that the 30-day filing requirement is jurisdictional and, as such, the trial court lacks the authority to extend the time for filing. In *Tucker v. State*, 89 Md. App. 295, 299-300 (1991), the Court of Special Appeals held that, although there is a statutory deadline for filing an application, if the application is filed timely, there is no deadline for the three-judge panel to act on the application for review of sentence.

Filing an application for review of sentence (a) does not stay the sentence; (b) does not affect the time allowed to file an appeal or a motion for new trial; and (c) does not affect the power of the sentencing judge to modify or reduce the sentence. Md. Rule 4-344(a); Md. Code Ann., Crim. Proc. § 8-104(a). Although there is no right to have the sentence stayed, pending the resolution of a review by a three-judge panel, the sentencing judge may, within his or her discretion, grant a stay of execution of sentence pending the decision. Md. Rule 4-344(a); Md. Code Ann., Crim. Proc. § 8-104.

3. Withdrawing the application

The Defendant may withdraw the application for review of sentence at any time before receipt of the notice of a hearing and, thereafter, with permission of the three-judge panel. The application for review of sentence may not be withdrawn after the three-judge panel renders its decision. Md. Rule 4-344(c).

4. Three-judge panel

The three-judge panel consists of three judges of the judicial circuit in which the sentencing court is located. The three-judge panel may not include the sentencing judge. Md. Code Ann., Crim. Proc. § 8-105(a). However, the three-judge panel may consult with the sentencing judge, and the sentencing judge may sit with the three-judge panel as an advisor. *Id.* § 8-105(b); Md. Rule 4-344(d). In *Jackson & Glascoe v. State*, 408 Md. 231, 239-40 (2009), the Court of Appeals held that, if a three-judge panel hears the sentencing matter, and then one member of the panel dies before the decision is rendered, the remaining two judges may issue the decision if they are in agreement.

5. Procedure & decision

If the three-judge panel decides to grant a hearing, the panel may increase the sentence, may decrease the sentence, may keep sentence the same, or impose conditions which could have been lawfully imposed by the sentencing judge. Md. Code Ann., Crim. Proc. § 8-105(c)(3); Md. Rule 4-344(f); *see Robinson v. Warden, Maryland House of Correction*, 455 F.2d 1172, 1176 (4th Cir. 1972) (increase in sentence does not violate the Double Jeopardy Clause).

Under Md. Rule 4-342, if the three-judge panel decides to increase the sentence, the Defendant must be brought before the panel and be re-sentenced by the panel. If the three-judge panel decides not to grant a hearing, it becomes a denial, in that the three-judge panel must keep the sentence the same. Thus, the Defendant should always request a hearing because, without a hearing, the Defendant cannot succeed. Before the three-judge panel increases or decreases the sentence, both the Defendant and the State have an opportunity to be heard at the hearing. The three-judge panel renders its decision by majority vote. Md. Code Ann., Crim. Proc. § 8-107(a).

A three-judge panel may decrease a mandatory minimum sentence, but only if its decision is unanimous. Md. Code Ann., Crim. Proc. § 8-107(c). Although a three-judge panel is supposed to file a written decision within 30 days after the application is filed, that requirement is directory only. *Id.* § 8-107(b). In *Tucker*, 89 Md. App. at 299-300, the Court of Special Appeals held that, once the three-judge panel acquires jurisdiction, based on a timely filed application, the panel does not lose jurisdiction by failing to act within 30 days.

If the Defendant has filed an appeal and/or a motion for modification or reduction of sentence, the Defendant may request, and the three-judge panel may agree to, a stay of the three-judge panel proceeding until after the appeal or after a ruling on the motion for motion for reduction of sentence. The three-judge panel may require the DPP (a) to conduct an investigation; (b) to prepare a post-sentencing investigation report; and (c) to make a sentencing recommendation to the three-judge panel. Md. Code Ann., Crim. Proc. § 8-105(c)(2). If the three-judge panel orders a new sentence for the Defendant, the three-judge panel becomes the "re-sentencing judge." Id. §§ 8-105(c)-(d), 8-106(a)-(b), & 8-107 to 8-108; Md. Rule 4-344(e) & (f).

If the administrative judge enters an order, denying an application for review by a three-judge panel, that order is appealable. *Collins*, 321 Md. at 106-07. The sentence of a three-judge panel is appealable in the same manner that any other sentence is appealable, e.g., illegality because it is unconstitutional, is beyond the statutory limits, or is motivated by impermissible considerations. *Rendelman*, 73 Md. App. at 335.

6. The victim's right to be heard

If the victim requested notification of any sentencing proceeding, the three-judge panel may not rule on the application for review of sentence unless the victim is notified and is present, or the victim waives the right to be present. The victim may address the three-judge panel. Md. Code Ann., Crim. Proc. § 8-106.

7. Three-judge panel following a guilty plea

A three-party agreement with an agreed upon sentence

In *Dotson v. State*, 321 Md. 515, 522-23 (1991), the Court of Appeals held that if the sentence at trial was an agreed upon sentence, pursuant to three-party agreement (State, defense, and trial court), the three-judge panel may not increase or decrease the sentence unless all three parties agree, i.e., State, Defendant, and the three-judge panel.

A three-party agreement with an agreed upon sentence range

If the sentence at trial was a sentence within an agreed upon sentence range, pursuant to a three-party agreement, the three-judge panel is bound by the agreed upon sentence range, and any change in sentence must be within that range.

A two-party agreement

If the sentence at trial was pursuant to a two-party agreement, in which State bound itself to argue to "cap," the State is bound by that same "cap" before the three-judge panel.

B. Motion for modification or reduction of sentence

1. Applicability

Pursuant to Md. Rule 4-345(e), the Defendant may file a motion for modification or reduction of sentence, with the sentencing judge, within 90 days of the sentence. This is sometimes referred to as a motion to reduce sentence. A motion for modification or reduction of sentence may be filed even if the sentence did not result in incarceration. In *Greco v. State*, 347 Md. 423, 437 (1997), the Court of Appeals held that any modification of sentence is a new sentence, which entitles the Defendant to file a new motion for modification or reduction of sentence.

The judge's options are (a) deny a hearing (which precludes a modification or reduction of sentence); or (b) grant a hearing and (i) deny the motion for modification or reduction of sentence, or (ii) grant the motion for modification or reduction of sentence. The judge may leave the sentence unchanged or may make the sentence less onerous, but the judge may not make the sentence more onerous.

In *Coley v. State*, 74 Md. App. 151, 156 (1988), the Court of Special Appeals held that, if a new sentence is imposed, the 90-day time limit begins to run from the date that the new sentence is imposed. If the sentence is vacated, and the case is remanded for a new sentence, even if the court re-imposes exactly the same sentence, that is a new sentencing, which entitles the Defendant to file a new motion for modification or reduction of sentence. *McDonald v. State*, 314 Md. 271, 285 (1988); *Pitts v. State*, 155 Md. App. 346, 352-53 (2004). The filing of a motion for modification or reduction of sentence does not stay the sentence. Md. Code Ann., Crim. Proc. § 8-104; Md. Rule 4-345(e).

The 90-day (not three months) filing deadline is jurisdictional. Thus, if the motion is not filed timely, the sentencing court cannot retain jurisdiction over the sentence. Let's assume that the sentencing judge, at the time of sentencing, promised the Defendant the following: "If you satisfactorily complete probation, I promise that I will strike the guilty verdict, and I will enter a PBJ." Despite that promise, the court cannot strike the guilty verdict and enter a PBJ unless the court retains subject matter jurisdiction. The sentencing court will forever lose jurisdiction over the sentence unless the Defendant timely files a motion for modification or reduction of sentence.

2. Only one modification motion

If a motion for modification or reduction of sentence is denied, the Defendant may not file another motion for modification or reduction of sentence. *See State v. Karmand*, 183 Md. App. 480, 494-95 (2008).

3. Appeal pending

For a Circuit Court sentence, a motion for modification or reduction of sentence may be filed even if the Defendant filed an appeal. Md. Rule 4-345(c). However, for a District Court sentencing, a motion for modification or reduction of sentence may not be filed if the Defendant has filed an appeal, because the case will be tried de novo, on appeal, in the Circuit Court. *Id.*

4. Right to counsel

In *State v. Flansburg*, 345 Md. 694, 698 (1997), the Court of Appeals held that, in Maryland, by statute, an indigent Defendant is entitled to counsel at State's expense on a motion for modification or reduction of sentence. In *Collins v. State*, 69 Md. App. 173, 195 n.11 (1986), the Court of Special Appeals stated that the Defendant has no right to be present at a modification hearing, but does have a "right to be heard," through counsel, before the sentence is modified.

5. Trial court's jurisdiction over a pending motion for modification or reduction of sentence

A motion for modification or reduction of sentence is heard by the sentencing judge. *Tatem v. State*, 419 Md. 630, 642 n.2 (2011). In *Strickland v. State*, 407 Md. 344, 361 (2009), the Court of Appeals held that the Administrative Judge may assign a different judge, stating "'a motion for reduction of sentence should be heard or otherwise disposed of by the court which imposed the sentence,' refer[ing] to the sentencing court and not the sentencing *judge*." *Id.* at 361 (quoting *Duffin v. Warden*, 235 Md. 685, 686 (1964)).

6. Whether to grant or deny a hearing

Whether to conduct a hearing on the motion for modification or reduction of sentence is discretionary. Without a hearing, the sentencing judge cannot grant the motion and can only deny the motion. Thus, the Defendant should request a hearing because, without a hearing, the Defendant cannot succeed.

7. Court may hold the motion for modification or reduction of sentence sub curia

A sentencing judge may, either sua sponte or on the Defendant's motion, hold the motion for modification or reduction of sentence sub curia, without ruling, awaiting the Defendant to come forward with an amended motion for modification or reduction of sentence. There was an unlimited potential sub curia period for Defendants sentenced prior to July 1, 2004. However, by statute, the sub curia period is limited to five years from the date of sentencing for Defendants sentenced on July 1, 2004, or later. This does not mean that the Defendant needs a ruling within five years and not just a hearing date. Otherwise, the sentencing court will lose jurisdiction.

If the sentencing judge grants a hearing, the judge may decrease the sentence or leave the sentence the same, but the judge may not increase the sentence. Md. Rule 4-345(e); *Greco*, 347 Md. at 425. The Defendant should always file a motion for modification of reduction of sentence because there is no "down side" to such a pleading.

Moreover, if the sentence sought to be modified or reduced is a long sentence, e.g., ten years or more, the Defendant should always ask the court to hold the motion sub curia, pending the Defendant coming forward and requesting a hearing.

8. An illegal increase in sentence

If the sentencing court modifies the sentence by changing the sentence from concurrent to consecutive, that is an illegal sentence increase. *Collins*, 69 Md. App. 173, 189 (1987) ("when a concurrent sentence is made consecutive, there has been a modification upward"); *Wilson v. State*, 45 Md. App. 675, 676-77 (1980); *see Brown v. State*, 153 Md. App. 544, 584-85 (2003); *Hohensee v. State*, 42 Md. App. 329, 340 n.21 (1979) (increase in the term of probation is an illegal increase in the sentence). In *State v. Griswold*, 374 Md. 184, 197-98 (2003), the Court of Appeals held that a court may not retroactively change a judgment of conviction, so as to modify a sentence or avoid imposing a mandatory minimum sentence.

9. Not an illegal increase in sentence

In *McRoy v. State*, 54 Md. App. 516, 518-19 (1983), the Court of Special Appeals held that, because the sentencing was a re-sentencing, and not a motion for modification or reduction of sentence, the court did not err when ordering that the sentence for second degree rape be served consecutively after the sentence for first degree rape, which was originally to be served concurrently. The Court held that it was an "initial" sentencing and not a replacement sentence. In *Argabright v. State*, 76 Md. App. 706, 708 (1988), the Court of Special Appeals held that the court could increase the term of probation because the sentencing was for a violation of probation, and not a motion for modification or reduction of sentence.

10. The victim's right to be heard

If the victim requested notification of any sentencing proceeding, the sentencing judge may not hold a hearing and reduce or modify the sentence unless the victim is notified and is present, or the victim waives the right to be present. The victim may address the sentencing judge.

11. Filing a motion for modification or reduction of sentence, requesting long-term, in-patient drug treatment in lieu of incarceration

The Defendant may file, at any time and not limited by the 90-day deadline, a motion for modification or reduction of sentence, requesting that the court order a drug evaluation by the Department of Health & Mental Hygiene (DHMH) to determine if the Defendant is (a) addicted to drugs; (b) amenable to long-term in-patient drug treatment; and (c) non-violent. Md. Code Ann., Health-Gen. § 8-507. In *Fuller v. State*, 169 Md. App. 303 (2006), *aff'd*, 397 Md. 372 (2007), the Court of Special Appeals held:

As a result of the 2004 amendments to H-G § 8-507(b), the court in which the defendant/petitioner was sentenced retains jurisdiction to grant a post-sentence petition for commitment to ADAA even if Maryland Rule 4-345(e) no longer provides the sentencing judge with revisory power over the sentence, either because the defendant/petitioner never filed a timely motion for reconsideration, or because such a motion was denied.

The burden is on the Defendant. The first step is to persuade the court, using testimony, medical records, and/or affidavits that the Defendant (a) is drug dependent; (b) is not violent; and (c) is amendable to drug rehabilitation through long-term in-patient treatment. It is within the court's discretion whether to order a DHMH evaluation. If the Defendant persuades the court of the legitimacy of the Defendant's proffer and/or evidence, the court will likely refer the Defendant to the Department of Health & Mental Hygiene (DHMH) for its evaluation and recommendation to the court regarding whether the Defendant (a) is drug dependent; (b) is not violent; and (c) is amendable to long-term, in-patient drug rehabilitation.

If the court orders a DHMH evaluation, and the DHMH provides the court with an evaluation that the Defendant is (a) addicted to drugs; (b) amenable to long-term in-patient treatment; and (c) non-violent, the trial court may, within its discretion, but is not required to, place the Defendant in long-term, in-patient drug treatment in lieu of incarceration. If the court issues an order for such treatment, it may take three months to a year to "find a bed" for the Defendant in an approved facility.

Once a placement is located, and the Defendant is assigned to it, if the Defendant cannot, though treatment, become drug free, the Defendant "fails out" and is returned to the DOC. If the Defendant does succeed in becoming drug free, through long-term, in-patient treatment, which usually takes six months to a year, the court typically places the Defendant on supervised probation, with long-term outpatient treatment.

C. Motion to correct illegal sentence

Under Md. Rule 4-345, a sentence may be challenged as an illegal sentence at any time. An illegal sentence may also be raised on direct appeal or in collateral review. *See Evans v. State*, 382 Md. 248, 278-79 (2004); *Ridgeway v. State*, 369 Md. 165, 171 (2002); *Moosavi v. State*, 355 Md. 651, 662-63 (1999). Even if a Defendant consents to a sentence, it may still be challenged as illegal. *Holmes*, 362 Md. 190, 195-96 (2000); *White v. State*, 322 Md. 738, 749 (1991).

1. Filing a motion to correct illegal sentence

The Defendant may file a motion to correct an illegal sentence at any time because the sentencing court never loses jurisdiction to correct an illegal sentence. Md. Rule 4-345(a). The sentencing judge is the judge who rules on the motion to correct an illegal sentence.

2. Disposition of a motion to correct illegal sentence

The sentencing judge may (a) deny the motion to correct illegal sentence without a hearing; (b) conduct a hearing and hold that the sentence is legal; or (c) (i) grant a hearing, (ii) hold that the sentence is illegal, and (iii) re-sentence the Defendant in a manner that is legal, or (iv) schedule a new sentencing hearing. In *Scott v. State*, 379 Md. 170, 190 (2004), the Court of Appeals held that the correction of a commitment record is not a sentencing and does not require a hearing. The Defendant should request a hearing on a motion to correct illegal sentence because, without a hearing, the Defendant cannot succeed.

An illegal sentence may be challenged through a motion to correct illegal sentence. In *Johnson v. State*, 427 Md. 356 (2012), the Court of Appeals explained that what constitutes an illegal sentence is not always easy to define, stating:

> To constitute an illegal sentence under Rule 4-345(a), "the illegality must inhere in the sentence itself, rather than stem from trial court error during the sentencing proceeding." (quoting *Matthews v. State*, 424 Md. 503, 512 (2012)). Accordingly, "we have denied relief pursuant to Rule 4-345(a) because the sentences imposed were not inherently illegal, despite some form of error or alleged injustice." *Id.* at 513. For example, a motion alleging consideration of improper factors by the sentencing court or illegal conduct by the Parole Commission, without more, is not cognizable under Rule 4-345(a). *See Montgomery v. State*, 405 Md. 67, 74-75 (2008) ("[A] trial court error during the sentencing proceeding is not ordinarily cognizable under Rule 4-345(a) where the resulting sentence or sanction is not itself lawful." (citations & quotation marks omitted). There is no simple formula to determine which sentences are illegal within the meaning of Rule 4-345(a) . . .

427 Md. at 367-68. *See Taylor v. State*, 407 Md. 137, 141 n.4 (2009); *Chaney v. State*, 397 Md. 460, 466 (2007); *Pollard v. State*, 394 Md. 40, 42 (2006); *State v. Wilkins*, 393 Md. 269, 273 (2006); *Baker v. State*, 389 Md. 127, 133 (2005); *Evans v. State*, 389 Md. 456, 463 (2005); *Ridgeway v. State*, 369 Md. 165, 171 (2002); *State v. Kanaras*, 357 Md. 170, 185 (1999); *Moosavi v. State*, 355 Md. 651, 662 (1999); *Campbell v. State*, 325 Md. 488, 508-09 (1992); *Walczak v. State*, 302 Md. 422, 425-27 (1985).

3. Illegal sentences that may be corrected through a motion to correct illegal sentence

Sentence that imposes a cruel & unusual punishment

The Eighth Amendment to the United States Constitution provides that "[e]xcessive bail shall not be required, nor excessive fines imposed, nor cruel and unusual punishment inflicted" by the courts. *See Wilkerson v. Utah*, 99 U.S. 130 (1878); Md. Decl. of Rights art. 25 provides "[t]hat excessive bail ought not be required, nor excessive fines imposed, nor cruel and unusual punishment inflicted, by the Courts of Law." Md. Decl. of Rights art. 16 provides "[t]hat sanguinary Laws ought to be avoided as far as it is consistent with the safety of the State; and no Law to inflict cruel and unusual pains and penalties ought to be made in any case, or at any time, hereafter."

The Eighth Amendment prohibition against cruel and unusual punishment is applicable to the States through the Due Process Clause. *Robinson v. California*, 370 U.S. 660, 676 (1962). However it is not confined to barbarous punishment and instead it seeks to prohibit punishment that goes against civilized standards and human decency. *Estelle v. Gamble*, 429 U.S. 97, 102-03 (1976). In determining whether a punishment is cruel and unusual, based on disproportionality, a court will often look at the proportionality of the sentence compared to the offense. *See Walker v. State*, 53 Md. App 171, 183 (1982).

A sentence is cruel and unusual if it is grossly disproportionate in comparison with the facts surrounding the offense. *See Thomas v. State*, 333 Md. 84, 93 (1993); *Phipps v. State*, 39 Md. App. 206, 214 (1978) (sentence of life for first degree rape is not cruel and unusual). Any sentence that falls within the statutory limits is not cruel and unusual punishment. *Allen v. State*, 2 Md. App. 740, 745 (1968). Consecutive sentences are not "cruel and unusual" if the length of each sentence falls within the statutory limits. *Kaylor v. State*, 285 Md. 66, 69 (1979).

Sentence based on impermissible considerations

Although preservation is not necessary to argue the illegality of a sentence, a sentence based on impermissible considerations may require an objection to preserve the argument for appellate review. *Kamara v. State*, 184 Md. App. 59, 80-81 (2009); *Reiger v. State*, 170 Md. App. 693, 700-01 (2006). Impermissible considerations include ill will, race, gender, religion, and other impermissible considerations. *State v. Wilkins*, 393 Md. 269, 287 (2006).

In *Rudder v. State*, 181 Md. App. 426, 475 (2008), the Court of Special Appeals held that there is nothing illegal per se about impermissible considerations. Improper motivation on the part of a trial judge during sentencing may justify vacating a sentence, but it does not render the sentence illegal within the meaning of Md. Rule 4-345. In *Randall Book Corp. v. State*, 316 Md. 315, 331-32 (1989), the Court of Appeals stated that an error in sentencing, made by the trial court, does not ordinarily make the sentence illegal if the resulting sentence is lawful.

A sentencing court may not change its sentence, unless in open court, even if the sentence was illegal. *Mateen v. Saar*, 376 Md. 385, 398-99 (2003) (court erroneously sentenced the Defendant, who was convicted of first degree murder, to 50 years rather than life, suspending all but 50 years). A fine imposed as reimbursement for jury costs is an illegal sentence. *Medley v. State*, 386 Md. 3, 9-10 (2005) (trial judge imposed a fine stating, "because after all, the jury has to be paid").

Sentence that exceeds the statutory maximum

A sentence may not exceed the statutory maximum. *Boyd v. State*, 321 Md. 69, 74 n.2 (1990); *Rose v. State*, 74 Md. App. 644, 649 (1988) (five-year sentence for transporting a handgun exceeded the maximum sentence for first-time offenders); *Cook v. State*, 62 Md. App. 634, 642-43 (1985) (sentence exceeded the statutory maximum for possession of paraphernalia); *Hamilton v. State*, 62 Md. App. 603, 619 (1985).

Sentence when the court failed to sentence consistent with a three-party plea agreement

In *Cuffley v. State*, 416 Md. 568 (2010), the plea agreement called for a specific sentence, but the trial court sentenced the Defendant to a greater sentence, with all suspended, except for the amount of the agreed upon sentence. The Court of Appeals held that the sentence was illegal and could be challenged through a motion to correct illegal sentence. The Court held that the issue is resolved solely by examining the transcript of the guilty plea and the transcript of the sentencing hearing. If a reasonable lay person Defendant would not have believed that an agreed to sentence of X would result in a sentence of X plus Y, with Y suspended, the sentence was illegal. *Accord Matthews v. State*, 424 Md. 503, 524-25 (2012).

In *Soloranzo v. State*, 397 Md. 661, 667 (2007), the Court of Appeals held that when the trial court approves a three-party plea agreement, but fails to honor it, the Defendant is entitled to specific performance, and the sentence may be challenged through a motion to correct illegal sentence: "In *Santobello v. New York*, 404 U.S. 257 (1971), the Supreme Court noted two options available to a Defendant who has not received the benefit of a plea bargain. The Defendant can either (a) have the bargain specifically enforced; or (b) withdraw his plea of guilty.

Sentence placing the Defendant on home detention as a condition of probation

In *Holmes v. State*, 362 Md. 190, 195 (2000), the Court of Appeals held that, when the trial court imposed a sentence, and then suspended all of that sentence, with three years probation, it was an illegal sentence to place the Defendant on home detention as a condition of probation, and the sentence could be challenged through a motion to correct illegal sentence. Confinement as a condition of probation is permitted only in Allegany County, Calvert County, Charles County, Garrett County, Howard County, and St. Mary's County. *Id.*; *accord Bailey v. State*, 355 Md. 287, 300 (1999).

Sentence increase because of the Defendant's failure to attend sentencing, even though it was a three-party binding agreement that did not require the Defendant's attendance

In *Tweedy v. State*, 380 Md. 475 (2004), the Court of Appeals held that the trial court imposed an illegal sentence, when the court exceeded the sentence that had been agreed upon because the Defendant did not attend sentencing. The Court held that the plea agreement did not require the Defendant to attend the sentencing, and the sentence could be challenged through a motion to correct illegal sentence. *Id.* at 485 (citing *State v. Poole*, 321 Md. 482, 497 (1991)).

Sentence that stayed execution of the sentence for three years, promising to un-execute the three years if the Defendant's conduct was good

In *Montgomery v. State*, 405 Md. 67, 80-81 (2008), the Court of Appeals held that the sentence for violation of probation was illegal when the sentencing judge deferred incarceration for three years and promised to vacate the ten-year sentence if the Defendant remained on good behavior during the three-year deferment. An unauthorized suspension of part of an otherwise lawful sentence make the sentence illegal. *Benedict v. State*, 377 Md. 1, 11-12 (2003) (court had no authority to execute upon a portion of a sentence that was previously unsuspended); *Sonner v. Shearin*, 272 Md. 502, 519 (1974).

Sentence that imposed a fine imposed to reimburse the court system for the cost of the jury

In *Medley v. State*, 386 Md. 3, 9-10 (2005), the Court of Appeals held that a fine is an illegal sentence when assessed to reimburse the State the cost of the jury, and the sentence could be challenged through a motion to correct illegal sentence.

Sentence illegally requiring sex offender registration

In *Cain v. State*, 386 Md. 320, 340 (2005), the Court of Appeals held that a sentence is illegal when the trial court requires sex offender registration in violation of Maryland law, and the sentence could be challenged through a motion to correct illegal sentence.

Sentence illegally imposing recidivist enhancement

In *Stevenson v. State*, 180 Md. App. 440, 457 (2008), the Court of Special Appeals held that pre-trial confinement did not qualify as a term of confinement, for enhanced sentencing purposes, making the sentence illegal, and the sentence could be challenged through a motion to correct illegal sentence.

Sentence failing to merge sentences when required

In *Williams*, 187 Md. App. at 476-77, the Court of Special Appeals held that the sentence was illegal when the trial court imposed a permissible sentence on the lesser included offense, but failed to merge that sentence into the sentence for the "flagship" offense.

The failure to merge sentences that require merger make the unmerged sentence illegal. *Moore v. State*, 163 Md. App. 305, 316 (2005). In *Tederick v. State*, 125 Md. App.

37, 47 (1999), the Court of Special Appeals held that the failure to merge two offenses that are required to be merged is an illegal sentence, even when the court makes the two sentences run concurrently. *See Lamb*, 93 Md. App. at 427.

Sentence ordering NCR Defendant to pay restitution

In *State v. Garnett*, 172 Md. App. 558, 568 (2007), the Court of Special Appeals held that, because a Defendant who is found NCR cannot be punished, and restitution is punishment, the sentence was illegal and could be challenged through a motion to correct illegal sentence.

Sentence failing to credit time on pre-trial home detention

In *Toney v. State*, 140 Md. App. 690, 695 (2001), the Court of Special Appeals held that the failure to credit pre-trial home detention time rendered the sentence illegal, and the sentence could be challenged through a motion to correct illegal sentence.

Sentence when verdict not announced in court

In *Jones v. State*, 384 Md. 669, 672 (2005), the Court of Appeals held that a sentence was illegal, and could be challenged through a motion to correct illegal sentence, when the sentence was imposed following a guilty verdict that was not announced in open court.

Sentence promising reduction in sentence if the Defendant paid restitution

A court may not offer to suspend a part of the Defendant's sentence upon the payment of restitution. In *Reddick v. State*, 327 Md. 270, 273-74 (1992), the trial court's offer to suspend five years of the Defendant's sentence, if the Defendant paid $3,000 of the victim's expenses, was illegal because imprisonment for lack of financial resources is illegal. A court may order restitution only if it directly relates to the victim's financial loss; otherwise, it would be an unauthorized punishment. *Pete v. State*, 384 Md. 47, 56-57 (2004) (order of restitution illegal when imposed because of damages resulting from an unrelated act).

Sentence under an incorrect statute is an illegal sentence

A sentence that is imposed based on an incorrect statute is illegal. In *Moosavi*, 355 Md. at 663-67, the Court of Appeals held that, because the Defendant's conduct was not prohibited under the statute with which he was charged, the sentence was illegal. *See Campbell v. State*, 325 Md. 488, 508-09 (1992) (sentence under an inapplicable statute is illegal sentence and may be challenged at any time).

In *Alston v. State*, 425 Md. 326, 342 (2012), the Defendant's petition for post conviction relief was granted and a new trial was ordered. Forty-four days later, the State filed a motion for reconsideration, which, after a hearing, the court granted and resentenced the Defendant. The Court of Appeals held that the re-imposition of the Defendant's sentence was illegal because the State failed to file an application for leave to appeal within 30 days.

Sentence of life without parole for conspiracy to commit murder

In *Johnson v. State*, 362 Md. 525, 534 (2001), the Court of Appeals held that life imprisonment without the possibility of parole is an illegal sentence for the crime of conspiracy to commit first degree murder. Life without parole is permissible for first degree murder but not for conspiracy.

4. Illegal sentences that may not be corrected through a motion to correct illegal sentence

Sentence imposed improperly but State failed to timely appeal

In *Alston v. State*, 425 Md. 326 (2012), the Defendant filed for post conviction relief and a new trial was granted based on ineffective assistance of counsel. Forty-four days after the new trial was granted trial Circuit Court granted the State's motion for reconsideration, arguing that the basis for granting relief had been finally litigated. *Id.* at 330-31. The court granted the motion and re-imposed the Defendant's sentence. The Court of Special Appeals held that even though the re-imposed sentence was illegal, the post conviction relief became a final judgment, which was not timely appealed.

In *Alston*, the Court of Appeals held: "There is one type of illegal sentence which this Court has consistently held should not be corrected under Rule 4-345(a)[, i.e., when] the trial court imposes a sentence [when] no sentence or sanction should have been imposed . . ." *Id.* at 339. *See Johnson v. State*, 427 Md. 356, 377-78 (2012) (sentence illegal when the Defendant not charged with that crime); *Ridgeway v. State*, 369 Md. 165, 171 (2002) (sentence illegal when Defendant acquitted); *Moosavi v. State*, 355 Md. 651, 662 (1999) (sentence illegal when Defendant convicted under inapplicable statute).

Sentence in which the judge failed to exercise discretion given by the legislature or case law

A motion to correct illegal sentence is not a proper method to challenge a sentence when the trial court failed to exercise discretion afforded by the legislature. *Pollard v. State*, 394 Md. 40, 47 (2006); *State v. Wilkins*, 393 Md. 269, 284 (2006) (judge's failure to use discretion in sentencing does not render the sentence illegal under Md. Rule 4-435(a)).

Challenging sentence on underlying conviction based on double jeopardy

In *Ingram v. State*, 179 Md. App. 485 (2008), the Court of Special Appeals held that a motion to correct illegal sentence is not a proper method to challenge the underlying conviction, as barred by double jeopardy, even if the double jeopardy claim would have succeeded on direct appeal. The Court stated: "Because the claim . . . arises out of [the Defendant's] prosecution, rather than the sentence itself, the issue is not properly raised by way of a motion to correct an illegal sentence." *Id.* at 489.

Cannot challenge sentence after fully served

In *Barnes v. State*, 423 Md. 75 (2011), the Court of Appeals held that a Defendant, ordered to register as a sex offender, could not challenge the registry requirement under Md. Rule 4-345(a) after being released from incarceration. The Court stated: "As Rule 4-345(a) simply permits a court to revise an illegal sentence, rather than to modify or overturn the underlying conviction, it follows that a court can no longer provide relief under that rule once a Defendant has completed his or her sentence." *Id.* at 86.

Cannot challenge procedural errors during &/or after sentencing

In *Tshiwala v. State*, 424 Md. 612 (2012) (internal citations omitted), the Defendant was sentenced to 60 years, which was subsequently reduced to 39 years by a three judge panel. The Defendant filed a motion for modification or reduction of sentence, which was denied by the three-judge panel. The Defendant filed a motion to correct illegal sentence, arguing that the panel lacked authority to rule on his motion for modification or reduction of sentence. The Court of Appeals held:

> [W]here the sentence imposed is not inherently illegal, and where the matter complained of is a procedural error, the complaint does not concern an illegal sentence for purposes of Rule 4-345(a). A sentence does not become an illegal sentence because of some arguable procedural flaw in the sentencing procedure. . . . A motion to correct an illegal sentence ordinarily can be granted only where there is some illegality in the sentence itself or where no sentence should have been imposed. [A] trial court error during the sentencing proceeding is not ordinarily cognizable under Rule 4-345(a) where the resulting sentence or sanction is itself lawful.

Id. at 619. The Court continued: "[The Defendant's] complaint is not that the sentences totaling 39 years, imposed by the review panel, are in any manner illegal. [His] complaint is aimed at a procedural matter occurring after the imposition of the 39-year sentences, namely that . . . the motion should not have been assigned to [the three-judge panel]. Assuming *arguendo* that this assignment was improper, a sentence does not become illegal because of some arguable procedural flaw. This is particularly true when the alleged "procedural flaw occurred after sentencing and related to a motion for reconsideration." *Id.* at 620.

Appeal

If an illegal sentence issue is litigated at trial or in a motion to correct illegal sentence, an unfavorable ruling is directly appealable to the Court of Special Appeals. If an illegal sentence issue is litigated in a petition for post conviction relief, an unfavorable ruling is not directly appealable, and the Defendant must file an application for leave to appeal. *See State v. Kanaras*, 357 Md. 170, 184 (1999); *Herrera v. State*, 357 Md. 186, 189 (1999).

D. Sentencing motion based on fraud, mistake, or irregularity

A sentencing judge has revisory power over a sentence in case of fraud, mistake, or irregularity. Md. Rule 4-345(b). These three terms all have the same meaning in a criminal case as in a civil case. *Minger v. State*, 157 Md. App. 157, 172 (2004). "Irregularity" is the doing or not doing of that [which] ought or ought not to be done. Moreover, irregularity as a ground for revising an enrolled judgment usually contemplates an irregularity of process or procedure but not an error, which in legal parlance, generally connotes a departure from truth or accuracy of which a Defendant had notice and could have challenged. *Id.* In the civil context, "mistake" is limited to a jurisdictional error, i.e., when the court has no power to enter judgment. *Id.*

Chapter 31

New Trial Motions

§ I. Post-verdict & post-sentencing release

A. Overview

Both post-verdict release (with sentencing pending) and post-sentencing release (with appeal pending) are discretionary because there is no longer a presumption of innocence. Md. Rules 4-342(j) & 4-349. Because release is discretionary, there is no right to bail and no right to a de novo hearing for habeas corpus relief. *Hurley v. State*, 59 Md. App. 323, 327-28 (1984).

For Defendants who were incarcerated pre-trial, the trial court almost never releases them post-verdict and/or post-sentencing. If during the pre-trial phase, when the presumption of innocence was still applicable, the Defendant could not be trusted to attend trial and/or could not be trusted not to pose danger, courts almost never release the Defendant post-verdict and/or post-sentencing.

On the other hand, for Defendants who were released pre-trial, the court may permit continued release for about two months pending sentencing. However, even for Defendants who were released pre-trial, if they were not released post-verdict, they are almost never released post-sentencing for about 18 months pending appeal. *See Bigley v. Warden, Maryland Correctional Institution for Women*, 16 Md. App. 1 (1972) (discussing release pending appeal).

B. Post-verdict &/or post-sentencing release options

In the event that the trial court elects to grant post-verdict release, the options include (1) continuing the pre-trial release conditions; (2) making the post-verdict release conditions more onerous than the prior pre-trial release conditions, e.g., increasing the amount of bail and/or imposing additional requirements; and/or (3) placing the Defendant in the custody of a designated person(s), a designated organization, or personnel of the Division of Parole and Probation. Md. Rule 4-349(c) & (d).

C. Predicates to post-verdict release &/or post-sentencing release

To be eligible for post-verdict release and/or post-sentencing release, the Defendant has the burden of establishing that the Defendant (1) will not flee; (2) will not pose a danger to the victim; (3) will not pose a danger to the community; and (4) will not intimidate the victim(s) or witness(es). Md. Rule 4-349(b)-(d) & 4-216(e). The court must ensure that the conditions of post-verdict release and/or post-sentencing release will reasonably ensure the appearance of the Defendant at sentencing and/or after appeal, if the appellate court affirms. *Id.*

It is very rare for the Defendant to be released post-sentencing, pending an appeal. Md. Code Ann., Crim. Proc. § 5-207; Md. Rule 4-349(b). When the Defendant is sentenced, any bond on which the Defendant was released, post-verdict, pending sentencing, is terminated. If, while an appeal is pending, the trial court grants an appeal bond, the Defendant must post a new bond. Md. Code Ann., Crim. Proc. § 5-207.

D. Factors for deciding whether to release the Defendant post-verdict &/or post-sentencing &, if released, the terms & conditions

The factors used to determine whether to release the Defendant post-verdict and/or post-sentencing are (1) the (a) nature of the offense(s) charged, (b) the strength of the State's case, and (c) the potential sentence; (2) the Defendant's prior record for appearance at court proceedings versus flight, and the risk of willful non-appearance; (3) the Defendant's (a) family ties, (b) employment status and history, (c) financial resources, (d) reputation and character, (e) mental condition, and (f) length of residence in the community and the State; (4) recommendation(s) for release by (a) an appropriate agency, or (b) the State's Attorney; (5) the danger that the Defendant poses to (a) the victim, (b) the community, and/or the Defendant; (6) information presented by the Defendant or defense counsel; and (7) prior convictions and/or delinquency adjudications within three years.

§ II. Post-verdict & post-sentencing motions for a new trial

A. Form of motion

Post-verdict motions for a new trial and post-sentencing motions for a new trial must be in writing and must provide grounds sufficient to place the State on notice. Md. Rule 4-331(e); *Jeffries v. State*, 113 Md. App. 322, 331 (1997).

B. Hearing

It is very difficult for the Defendant to prevail on a post-verdict or post-sentencing motion for a new trial. When filing a motion for a new trial, the Defendant should include a memorandum of law. Both the motion for a new trial and memorandum of law should be thorough, but concise, and should be compelling. Regardless of how compelling the pleading is, it is almost impossible to prevail on a motion for a new trial without a hearing. Thus, the Defendant should accompany the motion for a new trial and memorandum of law with a request for a hearing.

Granting a hearing is generally within the trial court's discretion. Md. Rule 4-331(b)(1). If a motion for a new trial is based on newly discovered evidence, and if it is properly pleaded, the court is required to conduct a hearing, if requested. Md. Rule 4-331(c) & (e); *State v. Matthews*, 415 Md. 286, 309 (2010); Md. Code Ann., Crim. Proc. § 8-301(e).

C. Trial court's jurisdiction over an order granting a new trial

A trial court retains jurisdiction over its order granting a new trial, which permits the court to vacate its order, if appropriate. *Alston v. State*, 92 Md. App. 117, 124 (1992). In *Christian v. State*, 65 Md. App. 303, 307 (1985), *aff'd*, 309 Md. 114 (1986), the Court of Special Appeals held that, in a criminal case, there is no final judgment until sentencing and, until that time, the court may reconsider its order granting a new trial. *Accord Williamson v. State*, 25 Md. App. 338, 348, *cert. denied*, 275 Md. 758 (1975).

D. Appellate review of denial of a motion for a new trial

The appellate standard of review for the denial of a motion for a new trial is usually abuse of discretion but, occasionally, the standard is incorrect, as a matter of law. *See Miller v. State*, 380 Md. 1, 28 (2004); *Jenkins v. State*, 375 Md. 284, 298-99 (2003); *Campbell v. State*, 373 Md. 637, 665-66 (2003). In *Merritt v. State*, 367 Md. 17, 25 (2001), the Court of Appeals rejected the State's argument that denial of a motion for a new trial is reviewable only when the trial court fails to exercise discretion. *See Jackson v. State*, 164 Md. App. 679, 703-04 (2005), *cert. denied*, 390 Md. 501 (2006).

§ III. Standard motion for a new trial

A motion for a new trial is filed in most cases, but it is rarely granted. A motion for a new trial is within the trial court's discretion and may be granted or denied, with or without a hearing, and with or without reasons provided. In *Argyrou v. State*, 349 Md. 587 (1998), the Court of Appeals stated:

[T]he breadth of the trial court's discretion to grant or deny a new trial is not fixed and immutable, it will expand or contract depending upon the nature of the factors being considered, and the extent to which its exercise depends upon the opportunity the trial judge had to feel the pulse of the trial, and to rely on his or her own impression in determining the questions of fairness and justice.

Id. at 600.

A. Timely filing of a motion for a new trial & steps for the defense to take

The Defendant must file a motion for a new trial no later than ten days after the verdict. Md. Rule 4-331(a). In most Circuit Court cases, if the jury renders a verdict of guilty, the trial court orders a pre-sentence investigation (PSI) report and schedules sentencing for about two months later. Within ten days after the verdict, defense counsel usually files a motion for a new trial. Most typically, the motion is a generic motion, arguing that the verdict went against the weight of the evidence. Also most typically, the court does not rule on the motion, and does not schedule a hearing on the motion. Instead, the court treats the motion for a new trial as the first item of business at the sentencing. A motion for a new trial is almost always denied.

The chance of having a motion for a new trial granted is increased if defense counsel is able to persuade the court to (1) grant a continuance to enable the Defendant to obtain and evaluate the transcript of the trial and any pre-trial motions; and (2) schedule a hearing on the motion for a new trial on a day other than the day of sentencing, and rescheduling the sentencing for a later date, if the motion for a new trial is denied. The continuance motion should request time to (1) obtain the transcript; (2) research, prepare, and file an amended motion for a new trial and memorandum of law in support of the amended motion for a new trial; and (3) permit the State time to respond to the motion and memorandum.

If the court grants the continuance motion, when the Defendant files the amended motion and memorandum, if the court has not yet ruled on moving the sentencing to a later date, defense counsel should re-request that the previously scheduled sentencing date be used solely for a hearing on the amended motion for a new trial, with a later new sentencing date if the motion for a new trial is denied.

B. Untimely filing of a motion for a new trial or amended motion for a new trial

If the Defendant files (1) an untimely motion for a new trial; or (2) an untimely amendment to a timely filed motion for a new trial, the trial court is precluded from considering the untimely filed motion or untimely filed amendment under Md. Rule 4-331(a).

See Ramirez v. State, 178 Md. App. 257, 279 (2008), *cert. denied*, 410 Md. 561 (2009); *Ware v. State*, 3 Md. App. 62, 65-66 (1968). However, the court may, within its discretion, in the interest of justice, treat the Defendant's untimely motion for a new trial or untimely amendment as a prematurely filed motion for new trial based on newly discovered evidence. *See Campbell*, 373 Md. at 665.

C. Filing a notice of appeal prior to filing a motion for a new trial

A motion for a new trial is filed within ten days after the verdict. An appeal is noted within 30 days after sentencing. Thus, usually, the motion for a new trial is ruled on before an appeal could be noted. However, if the Circuit Court sentences the Defendant at the time of the verdict, it is possible to have a timely filed appeal that is filed earlier than a timely filed motion for a new trial. If so, the trial court retains jurisdiction over the motion for a new trial. *Folk v. State*, 142 Md. App. 590, 596-97 (2002).

D. Bases for granting a new trial

The bases for granting a new trial are open-ended. In *Ruth v. State*, 133 Md. App. 358, *cert. denied*, 361 Md. 435 (2000), the Court of Special Appeals stated: "A trial court has wide latitude in considering a motion for a new trial and may consider many factors, including the weighing of evidence and the credibility of witnesses." *Id.* at 366. *See Jackson*, 164 Md. App. at 715; *Giddens v. State*, 148 Md. App. 407, 413 (2002) (new expert testimony available prior to trial is not grounds for a new trial); *Love*, 95 Md. App. at 427.

In *Love v. State*, 95 Md. App. 420, *cert. denied*, 331 Md. 480 (1993), the Court of Special Appeals stated: "The list of possible grounds for granting a new trial by the trial judge within ten days of the verdict is virtually open-ended." *Id.* at 427. Typical grounds for granting a motion for a new trial include (1) the verdict being contrary to the weight of the evidence; (2) newly discovered evidence; (3) prosecutorial misconduct in failing to disclose exculpatory evidence; (4) juror misconduct; and (5) reversible error on the part of the judge. *See Argyrou*, 349 Md. at 599; *State v. Devers*, 260 Md. 360, 374 (1971), *overruled on other grounds, In re Petition for Writ of Prohibition*, 312 Md. 280 (1988).

1. Reversible error

If a trial court recognizes that it committed reversible error, the court may grant a new trial, which will save the time and expense of an appeal, only to reach the same result. *See ALI-ABA Trial & Post-Trial Proceedings* 280-81 (5th ed. 1989); Md. Rule 4-331(f).

2. Verdict against the weight of the evidence

The trial court may act as the "13th juror" and grant a new trial because the trial court believes that, although the State met its burden of production, and produced a prima facie case, the State did not satisfy its burden of persuasion, i.e., the verdict went against the weight of the evidence. *Id.* at 279-80.

3. Ineffective assistance of counsel

Defense counsel may have provided ineffective assistance of counsel by committing serious attorney error that resulted in prejudice to the Defendant. Trial counsel cannot post convict himself or herself. An ineffective assistance of counsel, in almost all cases, must be raised in a post conviction petition and not on direct appeal. *See Massaro v. United States*, 538 U.S. 500 (2003). However, if the Defendant changed counsel after the verdict, new counsel may file a motion for a new trial and argue ineffective assistance of counsel.

E. "Interest of justice" is the standard for granting a new trial

The standard for determining whether to grant a new trial is the "interest of justice." Md. Rule 4-331(a). If the trial court grants a new trial, it must state the reason(s) on the record. Md. Rule 4-331(e). In *Jackson*, the Court of Special Appeals stated:

> New trial motions almost invariably (if not invariably) are based on events that happen in the course of a trial; such as, e.g., ruling on admissibility, potential trial error that may or may not be recognized at the time of the occurrence, jury instructions, jury behavior, etc. These events are of a type that will ordinarily happen under the direct eye of the trial judge. For that reason, [Md. Rule 4-331(a)] expressly provides that the trial judge may order a new trial "in the interest of justice" for it is he who has his thumb on the pulse of the trial and is in a unique position to assess the significance of such events.

164 Md. App. at 699.

§ IV. Motion for a new trial based on the trial court's revisory power

Even rarer than the trial court granting a ten-day motion for a new trial is the trial court granting a new trial based on its revisory power after sentencing. Even if the Defendant failed to file a ten-day motion for a new trial, or filed such motion and it was denied, the Defendant may file a motion for a new trial, under the court's revisory power, based on an unjust or improper verdict, if filed within 90 days after sentencing. Md. Rule 4-331(b).

§ V. Motion for a new trial based on newly discovered evidence

Even rarer than the trial court granting a 90-day motion for a new trial is the trial court granting a new trial based on newly discovered evidence. Md. Rule 4-331(c); *see ALI-ABA Trial & Post-Trial Proceedings* at 281-82. If a post-verdict motion is based on newly discovered evidence, it must describe the newly discovered evidence.

A. When filed

A motion for a new trial, based on newly discovered evidence, must be filed within one year of sentencing, if no appeal was taken, or within one year after the mandate from the Court of Special Appeals or Court of Appeals. Md. Rule 4-331(c)(1).

B. Due diligence requirement

A motion for a new trial, based on newly discovered evidence, requires evidence that was not discovered, and could not have been discovered through due diligence, in time to file a 10-day or a 90-day motion for a new trial. Md. Rule 4-331(c); *Furda v. State*, 194 Md. App. 1, 72 (2010) ("Motion for a New Trial is not a vehicle to obtain the proverbial 'second bite at the apple.'"); *Love*, 95 Md. App. 420; *Bloodsworth*, 76 Md. App. 23, 45, *cert. denied*, 313 Md. 688 (1988); *Brittingham v. State*, 63 Md. App. 164, 184-85 (1985).

Due diligence requires the Defendant to act reasonably and in good faith to obtain newly discovered evidence. *See Campbell*, 373 Md. 637. Thus, even if the evidence is material, if it could have been discovered through due diligence, the Defendant's motion for a new trial based on newly discovered evidence will be denied. *Mack v. State*, 166 Md. App. 670, 681-82 (2006).

C. DNA evidence

A motion for a new trial based on newly discovered evidence may be filed at any time, based on DNA testing or other generally accepted scientific techniques, if the results could prove that the Defendant is innocent. Md. Rule 4-331(c)(3).

D. Standard of review

A motion for a new trial based on newly discovered evidence requires a substantial or significant possibility that verdict would have been different had the newly discovered evidence been available. *Yorke v. State*, 315 Md. 578, 587 (1989); *cf. Evans v. State*, 382 Md. 248, 264-65 (2004) (no substantial or significant possibility of a different verdict because no newly discovered evidence that the Defendant was not the "triggerman"); *see Argyrou*, 349 Md. at 599-600 (court may consider the credibility of witnesses on a motion for a new trial because the court has "wide latitude").

E. Materiality

For a motion for new trial based on newly discovered evidence, the threshold issue is materiality. *Stevenson v. State*, 299 Md. 297, 301-02 (1984). Evidence that is merely cumulative or impeaching is not material. *Campbell*, 373 Md. at 669; *Jackson*, 164 Md. App. at 696.

F. Examples of evidence that is not newly discovered

In *Argyrou*, 349 Md. at 608-09, the Court of Appeals held that the confession of a third party, which lacked credibility, was not newly discovered evidence. In *Mack*, 166 Md. App. at 694-95, the Court of Special Appeals held that there was no newly discovered evidence because the Defendant intentionally concealed his mental illness to avoid long-term incarceration. In *Miller*, 380 Md. at 20, the Court of Appeals held that a non-disclosed promise of leniency for testimony was not newly discovered evidence. *Giddens*, 148 Md. App. at 414-15, the Court of Special Appeals held that a new expert witness was not newly discovered evidence.

In *Bloodsworth*, 76 Md. App. at 45, the Court of Special Appeals held that it was not newly discovered evidence when the evidence was discovered during trial. In *Tibbs v. State*, 72 Md. App. 239, 257 (1987), the Court of Special Appeals held that evidence that a witness may have testified in exchange for a reduction in his bail is not newly discovered evidence. In *Bright v. State*, 68 Md. App. 41, 56 (1986), the Court of Special Appeals held that cumulative impeachment evidence was not newly discovered evidence. In *Harker v. State*, 55 Md. App. 460, 475 (1983), the Court of Special Appeals held that discovery, after trial, that a key witness had been diagnosed as mentally ill was not material.

G. Example of evidence that is newly discovered

In *Newman v. State*, 156 Md. App. 20, *rev'd on other grounds*, 384 Md. 285 (2004), the Court of Special Appeals held that a non-testifying co-conspirator's post-trial statement was newly discovered evidence. *Id.* at 72.

§ VI. Motion for a new trial based on newly discovered evidence of actual innocence

Even rarer than the trial court granting a one-year motion for a new trial, based on newly discovered evidence, is the trial court granting a new trial based on newly discovered evidence of actual innocence. *ALI-ABA Trial & Post-Trial Proceedings* at 281-82. In *Jackson*, 164 Md. App. 679, the Court of Special Appeals stated:

> There is . . . a fundamental difference in kind between a new trial motion pursuant to subsection (a), dealing with what happens in the course of the trial and essentially under the eye of the trial judge, and a new trial motion pursuant to subsection (c), based on allegedly newly discovered evidence. The latter, by definition, deals with things outside the course of the trial, with evidence that was not introduced because it could not, with due diligence, have been discovered in time to be introduced. The litigation of a new trial motion pursuant to subsection (c) deals with phenomena, such as due diligence, that do not occur under the direct eye of the trial judge. In contrast to subsection (a), subsection (c) significantly does not contain the language "in the interest of justice" to be assessed by the trial judge.

Id. at 700.

A motion for a new trial, based on newly discovered evidence of actual innocence, is the same as a motion for a new trial based on newly discovered evidence, except (a) there is no time deadline for filing a motion for a new trial, based on newly discovered evidence of actual innocence; (b) there must be evidence of a significant possibility or a substantial probability of actual innocence; and (c) the newly discovered evidence of actual innocence could not have been discovered, through due diligence, in time to file a one-year motion for a new trial based on newly discovered evidence.

§ VII. Motion for a new trial based on fraud, mistake, or irregularity

Even rarer than granting a motion for a new trial, based on newly discovered evidence of actual innocence, is the trial court granting a new trial based on fraud, mistake, or irregularity. A motion for a new trial, based on fraud, mistake, or irregularity, may be filed at any time. Md. Rule 4-331(b); *see, e.g., Gorman v. State*, 67 Md. App. 398, 407 (1986) (failure to obtain a witness because of a lack of funding is not an irregularity invoking the court's revisory power when the witness is merely cumulative). The fraud required for this motion is extrinsic fraud and not intrinsic fraud. In *Tandra S. v. Tyrone W.*, 336 Md. 303 (1994), the Court of Appeals held:

> Intrinsic fraud is defined as "[t]hat which pertains to issues in the original action or where acts constituting fraud were, or could have been, litigated therein." Extrinsic fraud, on the other hand, is "fraud which is collateral to the issues tried in the case where the judgment is rendered." Fraud is extrin-

sic when it actually prevents an adversarial trial. In determining whether or not extrinsic fraud exists, the question is not whether the fraud operated to cause the trier of fact to reach an unjust conclusion, but whether the fraud prevented the actual dispute from being submitted to the fact finder at all.

Id. at 315 (citations omitted); *see State v. Rodriguez*, 125 Md. App. 428, 449-50 (1999).

Chapter 32

Appeals

§ I. History of the federal & state court systems & appellate review

Since *Marbury v. Madison*, 5 U.S. (1 Cranch) 137 (1803), under the principle of judicial review, in an actual case or controversy, the judicial branch controls the legislative branch by issuing decisions and orders that interpret acts of Congress, including voiding, as unconstitutional, acts of Congress. The judicial branch controls the executive branch by issuing decisions and orders regarding (a) the authority of the executive branch to act and the lawfulness and constitutionality of its conduct; and (b) interpretation of administrative rules and regulations promulgated by the executive branch. Thus, *Marbury v. Madison* established the principle of judicial review.

A. Federal

1. Supreme Court trial jurisdiction versus appellate jurisdiction

The Constitution

U.S. Const. art. III, § 2, provides:

> The judicial Power shall extend to all Cases, in Law and Equity, arising under this Constitution, the Laws of the United States, and Treaties made, or which shall be made, under their authority. In all Cases affecting Ambassadors, other public Ministers and Counsuls, and those in which a State shall be a Party, the supreme Court shall have original Jurisdiction. In all the other Cases before mentioned, the supreme Court shall have appellate Jurisdiction.

Marbury v. Madison

In *Marbury v. Madison*, the Supreme Court interpreted its trial and appellate jurisdiction, as set forth in U.S. Const. art. III, § 2, and applied the Supremacy Clause, as set forth in U.S. Const. art. VI, to hold that the Judiciary Act of 1789 was unconstitutional, to the extent that it gave the Supreme Court original jurisdiction over petitions for writ of mandamus.

The Court held that the framers gave original jurisdiction to the Supreme Court in cases affecting ambassadors, public ministers and counsuls, while giving the Court appellate jurisdiction in all the other cases. This was the first time that the Supreme Court struck down, as unconstitutional, a statute of Congress. In *Little v. Barreme*, 6 U.S. (2 Cranch) 170 (1804), the Supreme Court, for the first time, declared an executive branch action to be unconstitutional.

Marbury v. Madison established the principle of judicial review, making the judicial branch "first among equals." The legislative branch enacts the laws, the executive branch enforces the laws, and the judicial branch determines what those laws mean and whether they are constitutional. Thus, after *Marbury v. Madison*, the judiciary speaks last among the three branches and, within the judiciary, the appellate court speaks last.

2. Supreme Court appellate jurisdiction "of right" versus "discretionary"

Supreme Court evolved from appeals of right to discretionary appeals

From 1789 to 1891, the Supreme Court was the federal appellate court of right. The Judiciary Act of 1891, which created the United States Courts of Appeal, made a small portion of the Supreme Court's docket discretionary, including appellate cases in diversity, patent, revenue, criminal, and admiralty. However, the Supreme Court still had direct appellate authority over the vast majority of appeals, and very little of its jurisdiction was discretionary.

The Judiciary Act of 1925 (referred to as the Certiorari Act) made the majority of the Supreme Court's docket discretionary. Annually, the Supreme Court receives about 8,000 petitions for a writ of certiorari. The Court grants certiorari, and issues signed opinions, in about 75 cases. Each "term of the court" commences on the first Monday in October. The Court hears oral argument between October and April, and the term of the Court ends by July 1.

Supreme Court certiorari process

A party that loses in a state court of last resort or in a federal circuit court may file a petition for writ of certiorari in the Supreme Court. A certiorari petition focuses more on why the case presents an important issue and less on why the lower court was incorrect. The Supreme Court grants certiorari to address important questions of (a) interpretation of the United States Constitution, federal statutes, federal regulations, federal rules of court, and treaties; and (b) a conflict among the federal circuits and/ or among state courts of last resort.

The Supreme Court accepts a case if four justices vote to issue a writ of certiorari. Eight of the nine justices (excluding Justice Alito) have created a "cert. pool," meaning that each of the eight justices reads only one-eighth of the certiorari petitions, and the other seven "cert. pool" justices adopt the position of that justice.

If the Supreme Court is seriously considering a petition for writ of certiorari, the Court will issue a "call for response," asking for a brief in opposition to the petition for a writ of certiorari. The Court requests about 200 briefs in opposition annually. This represents less than 3% of all petitions for a writ of certiorari. Of course, that party may have already filed a brief in opposition to the certiorari petition.

If the Supreme Court is still seriously considering the case, it will "conference" the case (about 250 cases are "conferenced" annually). Then the justices vote whether to grant certiorari. About 75 petitions are granted annually. Although overall, the chance that certiorari will be granted in any given case is 0.9%, that chance increases to 8.6% for cases for which the Court called for a response. *See* David C. Thompson & Melanie F. Waddell, *An Empirical Analysis of Supreme Court Certiorari Procedures: The Call for Response and the Call for the Views of the Solicitor General*, 16:2 Geo. Mason L. Rev. 238, 245-50 (2009) (analyzing statistics from the 2001 term through the 2004 term).

3. Supreme Court appeals after certiorari is granted

After issuing a writ of certiorari, the Supreme Court establishes a briefing schedule for the Brief of Petitioner, Brief of Respondent, and discretionary Reply Brief of Petitioner. The Brief of Petitioner explains why the lower court was incorrect and why, when the law is applied to the record in this case, the Court should reverse the lower court. The Brief of Petitioner often asks the Supreme Court to declare a statute unconstitutional, either on its face or as applied, and/or asks the Court to set policy and/or make new law. If Congress has "already spoken," the Court's task, under *Marbury v. Madison*, is limited to interpretation of the law.

The Brief of Respondent explains why the lower court was correct and why, when the law is applied to the record in this case, the Court should affirm the lower court. The Reply Brief of Petitioner explains why the Respondent is incorrect in its belief that the lower correct did not commit legal error.

After the briefs are filed, the Supreme Court hears oral argument en banc, meaning all nine justices hear the argument (although six justices constitute a quorum). In the vast majority of cases, each side is granted 30 minutes to present oral argument. The Petitioner may present rebuttal oral argument if the Petitioner reserved time from its 30 minutes for rebuttal.

After oral argument, the Supreme Court discusses the case. Prior to the Roberts' Court, discussion began with the "baby justice" and worked toward seniority. The Roberts' Court begins with the Chief Justice and works toward the least senior. No justice may speak a second time until all justices have spoken once. After discussion, the justices vote.

If the Chief Justice is in the majority, the Chief Justice assigns a justice to write the Court's opinion. If the Chief Justice is not in the majority, the senior justice (Justice Scalia) assigns a justice to write the Court's opinion. Justices in the majority may file a concurring opinion, which agrees with the Court's disposition of the case, but either disagrees with the Court's reasoning or believes that the Court's reasoning does not go far enough. Justices in the minority may file a dissenting opinion that disagrees with the Court's disposition of the case and its reasoning. The Court files a written opinion in all cases heard that term prior to the end of the term. The Court's opinions are "published" or "reported."

4. Number of justices, presidential appointment, & Senate confirmation

Justices are nominated by the President, who may nominate any person to the Supreme Court because the Constitution provides no requirements for appointment. The Constitution provides for "advice and consent" by the Senate, meaning that confirmation requires a majority vote of the Senate. Justices serve for life "during good behavior," meaning that justices are subject to impeachment. The only Supreme Court Justice to be impeached was Justice Samuel Chase, a Maryland signer of the Declaration of Independence, who was impeached by the House of Representatives for his conduct in several "political trials." He was acquitted by the Senate.

The Constitution is silent on the number of justices. The Court has had between six and ten justices at any given time, and has had nine justices since 1869. In 1937, President Franklin Roosevelt tried to change the number of justices, from nine to 15, in an unsuccessful attempt to "pack the Court."

There have been 112 Supreme Court justices. From 1789 to 1836, every justice was white, male, Christian, and Protestant, and 89 of the 112 justices are in that category. There have been 23 justices who were not white, male, Christian, and Protestant, which is slightly more than 20%. These 23 justices make up 28 categories of justices who are not white, male, Christian, and Protestants, explained by the fact that Justice Sotomayor is female, Latino, and Catholic; Justice Thomas is African-American and Catholic; Justice Ginsburg is female and Jewish; and Justice Kagan is female and Jewish.

Since the confirmation of Justice Kagan in 2010, for the first time, no justice is white, male, Christian, and Protestant, meaning that more than 40% of the all justices, in 224 years, who were not white, male, Christian, and Protestant, currently sit on the Court.

There have been 13 Catholic justices, including six sitting today. There have been eight Jewish justices, including three sitting today. There have been two African-American justices, including one sitting today. There have been four female justices, including three sitting today. There have been six foreign born justices.

All 112 justices have been attorneys. However, many early justices did not attend law school, and some did not even attend college or high school. For its first 57 years, the Supreme Court had no justice with a law degree. From 1789 to 1957, the Court always had at least one justice who did not graduate from law school.

There have been six justices from Maryland, including Chief Justice Taney (the first Catholic justice and author of the *Dred Scott* decision), Justice Chase (the only impeached justice (but acquitted)), and Justice Marshall (the first African-American justice and one of the counsel in *Brown v. Board of Education*). Of the current members of the Court, five graduated from Harvard Law School, three graduated from Yale Law School, and one graduated from Columbia Law School.

5. The Supreme Court has been located in three cities, but always in the nation's capital

Although the early Government made arrangement for the Executive Branch, i.e., the White House, and the Legislative Branch, i.e., the Capitol, initially, it failed to make arrangements for the Judicial Branch. In 1790, the court sat in New York City, which was the nation's capital, using the Merchants' Exchange Building. Later in 1790, the Court moved to Philadelphia (the nation's new capital), where the Court sat in Independence Hall for one term, before moving to Old City Hall from 1791 to 1800.

Since 1800, the Court has sat in Washington, D.C. (the nation's new capital). From 1800 to 1810, the Court sat in homes, in taverns, and in rooms in the Capitol. From 1810 to 1860, the Court sat on the first floor of the Capitol. From 1860 to 1935, the Court sat on the second floor of the Capitol. On the first Monday of October, 1935, the Court moved into its permanent location, where it has sat ever since.

6. Congressionally created "inferior courts"

The Constitution provides for one Supreme Court and "such inferior Courts as the Congress may from time to time ordain and establish." U.S. Const. art. III, § 1. Congress created the federal trial court system through the Judiciary Act of 1789. There are 94 District Courts. There are 951 District Judges, including senior judges. There are 635 federal magistrate judges, including part-time, clerk/magistrate judges, and recalled judges. There are 371 bankruptcy judges, including recalled judges. There are 33 judges on the Tax Court, including senior and special judges. There are 14 judges on the Court of International Trade, including senior judges. There are 16 judges on the Court of Federal Claims. There are 14 judges on the Court of Appeals for Veterans Claims, including senior judges.

Congress started the process of creating the federal appellate court system through the Judiciary Act of 1891. There are 13 Courts of Appeal, including the First Circuit through the Eleventh Circuit, the District of Columbia Circuit, and the Federal Circuit. Maryland's federal appellate court is the United States Court of Appeals for the Fourth Circuit. There are 246 federal circuit judges, counting both active and senior status. Each Supreme Court justice serves as the Circuit Justice for one or two of the 13 circuits, limited to emergencies, extensions, and stays. Maryland's Circuit Justice is Chief Justice Roberts.

7. Supreme Court expansion of individual rights & liberties

The following are examples of the Supreme Court finding constitutional, or striking down, as unconstitutional, acts of the executive branch and/or laws of Congress.

The *Dred Scott* case

In the *Dred Scott v. Sanford*, 60 U.S. 393 (1857), the Supreme Court upheld, as constitutional, laws that made slaves personal property of their owner, precluding them from being persons entitled to constitutional protections.

Plessey v. Ferguson

In *Plessey v. Ferguson*, 163 U.S. 537 (1896), the Supreme Court upheld, as constitutional, laws that enforced segregation in public accommodations, notwithstanding the Fourteenth Amendment Equal Protection Clause, so long as the difference in racial treatment was "fair," establishing the "separate but equal" doctrine.

Brown v. Board of Education

In *Brown v. Board of Education*, 347 U.S. 483 (1954) (and four other consolidated cases), by a vote of 9-0, the Supreme Court held that segregation of public schools denied African-American children their rights under the Fourteenth Amendment Equal Protection Clause. The Court held that it did not matter whether the physical facilities for white and black schools were equal, because separate educational facilities, based on race, are inherently unequal. If a State provides public school education, it must provide it equally to all.

The criminal justice system

For 170 years, from 1791 to 1961, Supreme Court interpreted the Bill of Rights as a limitation only on the federal government, and not as a limitation on state and local governments.

Incorporation of the Fourth Amendment against the states

Mapp v. Ohio, 367 U.S. 643 (1961), was the first in a decade-long series of cases in which the Supreme Court incorporated, under the Due Process Claus of the Fourteenth Amendment, the individual liberties provided in the Bill of Rights in criminal cases, as limitations on state and local governments, and not just limitations on the federal government. In *Mapp*, the Court incorporated, against the states, the Fourth

Amendment remedy of exclusion of evidence when obtained in violation of the Fourth Amendment.

Incorporation of the Fifth Amendment privilege against compelled self-incrimination against the states

In *Malloy v. Hogan*, 378 U.S. 1 (1964), the Supreme Court incorporated the Fifth Amendment privilege against compelled self-incrimination against the states. In *Miranda v. Arizona*, 384 U.S. 436 (1966), the Court interpreted the Fifth Amendment privilege against compelled self-incrimination to require the giving of what are known as "*Miranda* warnings" and obtaining a waiver prior to custodial interrogation.

The Court held that custodial confessions violate the Fifth Amendment privilege against compelled self-incrimination when the Defendant is not advised of the right to remain silent and the right to an attorney present during interrogation. Custodial interrogation requires advice (a) of the right to remain silent; (b) that any statement given will be used against him; (c) of the right to have an attorney present during questioning; and (d) that an attorney will be appointed if he cannot afford one. *Id.* at 444.

Incorporation of the Fifth Amendment prohibition against double jeopardy against the states

Benton v. Maryland, 395 U.S. 784 (1969), was the last in a decade-long series of cases in which the Supreme Court incorporated, under the Due Process Claus of the Fourteenth Amendment, limitations against the federal government as also being limitations against state and local governments. In *Benton*, the Court incorporated the prohibition against double jeopardy.

Incorporation of the Sixth Amendment right to appointed counsel, if indigent, against the states

In *Gideon v. Wainwright*, 372 U.S. 335 (1963), the Supreme Court incorporated the right to counsel against the states, entitling indigent Defendants to counsel, at government expense, when charged with a felony. On remand, when represented by counsel, Gideon was acquitted.

Incorporation of the Sixth Amendment right to confrontation against the states

In *Pointer v. Texas*, 380 U.S. 400 (1965), the Supreme Court incorporated the Sixth Amendment right to confrontation against the states.

Incorporation of the Sixth Amendment right to speedy trial against the states

In *Klopfer v. North Carolina*, 386 U.S. 213 (1967), the Supreme Court incorporated the Sixth Amendment right to speedy trial against the states.

Incorporation of the Sixth Amendment
right to compulsory process against the states

In *Washington v. Texas*, 388 U.S. 14 (1967), the Supreme Court incorporated the Sixth Amendment right to compulsory process against the states.

Incorporation of the Sixth Amendment
right to trial by jury against the states

In *Duncan v. Louisiana*, 391 U.S. 145 (1968), the Supreme Court incorporated the Sixth Amendment right to trial by jury against the states, but did not incorporate the unanimity requirement.

Incorporation of the Eighth Amendment prohibition
against cruel & unusual punishment against the states

In *Robinson v. California*, 370 U.S. 660 (1962), the Supreme Court incorporated the Eighth Amendment prohibition against cruel and unusual punishment against the states.

Fourteenth Amendment due process right of privacy

In *Griswold v. Connecticut*, 381 U.S. 479 (1965), the Warren Court interpreted the Fourteenth Amendment Due Process Clause to contain a right of privacy, which was violated by a law that prohibited the distribution of contraceptive information to unmarried women.

In *Roe v. Wade*, 410 U.S. 113 (1973), the Burger Court interpreted the right of privacy to protect, from state interference, a woman's (and her doctor's) reproductive decision regarding abortion during the first trimester.

In *Lawrence v. Texas*, 539 U.S. 558 (2003), the Rehnquist Court held that the Fourteenth Amendment Due Process Clause protects consensual homosexual conduct. The *Lawrence* Court held that convictions for homosexual conduct violated a liberty and privacy interest because (a) the statute impermissibly sought to control personal relationships between two individuals; (b) the stigma imposed by the statute was significant; and (c) the statute did not further a legitimate state interest that could justify this severe intrusion into personal and private lives.

The right of privacy protects all sexual conduct that that is (a) consensual; (b) private; (c) among adults; (d) non-commercial; and (e) non-incestial. The Court noted that *Bowers* was overruled, in part, because of the emerging recognition that individuals are protected in their determination of how to conduct private matters pertaining to sex.

In *Gonzales v. Carhart*, 550 U.S. 124, 157 (2007), the Roberts Court upheld the Partial-Birth Abortion Ban Act of 2003, ruling that the statute was not void for vagueness and did not impose an undue burden on women. The Court noted the state's interest in maintaining respect for human life and protecting the integrity and ethics of the medical profession.

8. The Supreme Court has power to "make" or "break" a President

"Breaking" a President

A grand jury indicted individuals with offenses, including conspiracy to obstruct justice, naming President Nixon as an un-indicted co-conspirator. The special prosecutor subpoenaed audiotapes and documents of conversations between President Nixon and his staff. The President Nixon moved to quash the subpoena, citing executive privilege.

In *United States v. Nixon*, 418 U.S. 683 (1974), the Supreme Court held that (a) it had jurisdiction; (b) the District Court subpoena was appealable and presented a justiciable controversy; (c) presidential assertion of "intra-branch dispute" in the executive branch did not defeat federal jurisdiction; (d) the subpoena satisfied the requirements of the Fed. R. Crim. P.; and (e) a mere claim of executive privilege, without a specific assertion of the privilege against disclosure of particular diplomatic or military secrets, cannot trump due process, requiring disclosure of all relevant evidence in a criminal case.

Under separation of powers, the President lacked the power to terminate the Watergate special prosecutor and was required to turn over the audiotapes that were made in the Oval Office. The Supreme Court holding had the net effect of ending the Nixon presidency.

"Making" a President

In the 2000 presidential election, Florida reported that George Bush received 1,784 more votes than Vice-President Al Gore. Because this constituted less than .5% of the votes cast, by statute, an automatic machine recount was ordered. After the recount, Bush was 327 votes ahead. Gore requested, under Florida law, a manual recount, in four counties, and the counties agreed. However, with a seven-day deadline to conduct the manual recount and certify the results, no county believed it could complete the recount within seven days.

On the seventh day, a Florida state court ruled that the deadline was not waivable, but that the counties could amend their returns later, and that it was within the discretion of the Secretary of State to include late returns in the final Florida vote count. Only one county submitted certified results by the deadline. The other three counties requested extensions, which were denied. Gore and Palm Beach County filed suit to compel the Florida Secretary of State to accept the amended returns.

The Florida Supreme Court issued an injunction, preventing certification of the election until a final ruling from the trial court and ordering acceptance of results submitted by November 26. Miami-Dade County stopped the recount, contending that it could not finish by November 26. Florida declared Bush the winner by 537 votes.

Gore filed suit to contest the election results, and the Florida Supreme Court ordered a manual recount in Miami-Dade and ordered that all manual recounts from the three other counties be included in the final tally. Bush appealed to the Supreme Court.

In *Bush v. Gore*, 531 U.S. 98 (2000), the Supreme Court held (5-4) that the recount must stop. The Court held (7-2) that the Fourteenth Amendment prohibited a recount because there was no uniform procedure across counties for counting the votes, such that votes would be treated differently depending on their county of origin. The holding of the Supreme Court had the net effect of creating the Bush presidency.

B. Maryland

1. Structure of the Maryland judiciary

In Maryland, the judicial branch of government is a $452 million enterprise. Maryland's judicial branch of government has four courts, 289 judges (up from 172 judges 35 years ago), and 2.1 million filings annually (up from one million 30 years ago).

Court of Appeals of Maryland

In Maryland, the state supreme court or court of last resort is the Court of Appeals, which consists of seven judges, hearing cases en banc.

Court of Special Appeals of Maryland

The State's intermediate appellate court is the Court of Special Appeals, which consists of 15 judges, hearing cases in three-judge panels.

Circuit Courts

The State's trial court system of general jurisdiction is the 24 Circuit Courts (one per county), which consist of 157 judges.

District Court of Maryland

The State's trial court system of limited jurisdiction is the District Court of Maryland, which consists of 112 judges in 12 districts.

Other courts & other judges

In addition to the 289 judges, all of whom are appointed by the Governor, there are 470 other judicial officers in Maryland. These include 69 Circuit Court masters; 66 Orphans' Court judges; 61 administrative law judges in the Office of Administrative Hearings; 240 court commissioners; 14 United States District Judges, including senior judges; nine United States magistrate judges, including one part-time magistrate judge; nine United States bankruptcy judges, including senior judges; and two United States Circuit Judges.

2. History & structure of the Court of Appeals

In 1637, Cecilius Calvert, having been granted the Charter by Charles the First, appointed Leonard Calvert (his brother) as Chief Judge of the Court of Appeals and named three others to the Court. Written opinions date to 1637. Reported opinions were published as early as 1658 in the Maryland Reports, which predates the second oldest reports (Virginia) by 72 years. The reported opinions from 1658 to 1776 cover a little more than one volume.

In Maryland's 1776 Constitution, judges were appointed by the Governor based on "integrity and sound judgment in the Law." In 1778, the legislature made the Court of Appeals a five-judge court. The Honorable Benjamin Rumsey was named the first post-colonial Chief Judge of the Court of Appeals, serving for 28 years. In 1801, the Court of Appeals was changed from five judges to three judges. In 1806, the Court of Appeals was changed from three judges to six judges, and the Honorable Jeremiah Chase became the second Chief Judge of the Court of Appeals, serving for 18 years.

In 1824, the Honorable John Buchanan, who had been on the Court of Appeals for 18 years, became the third Chief Judge of the Court of Appeals, serving for an additional 20 years. Oral argument time was not limited until 1826, when a six-hour limit was placed on oral argument. In 1844, the Honorable Stephenson Archer became the fourth Chief Judge of the Court of Appeals, serving for four years. In 1848, the Honorable Thomas Dorsey became the fifth Chief Judge of the Court of Appeals, serving for three years. Until 1851, the Court of Appeals was required to sit on both the Eastern Shore and the Western Shore.

In the 1851 Constitution, the Court of Appeals was changed to four judges, who were elected in contested elections, to serve a ten-year term and were required to retire at age 70. The Governor was required to select the Chief Judge from among the four elected judges, subject to approval by the Senate. In 1851, the Honorable John LeGrand became the sixth Chief Judge of the Court of Appeals, serving for ten years. By 1852, the oral argument time was limited to two and a half hours and later was limited to one hour. In 1861, the Honorable Richard Bowie became the seventh Chief Judge of the Court of Appeals, serving for six years. The 1864 Constitution changed the Court of Appeals from four judges to five judges.

The 1867 Constitution changed the Court of Appeals from five judges to eight judges. In 1867, the Honorable James Bartol became the eighth Chief Judge of the Court of Appeals, serving for 16 years. In 1883, the Honorable Richard Alvey became the ninth Chief Judge of the Court of Appeals, serving for ten years. In 1893, the Honorable John Robinson became the tenth Chief Judge of the Court of Appeals, serving for three years.

In 1943, the Court of Appeals was changed from eight judges to five judges, and the term for succeeding in the contested election was changed from ten years to 15 years. In 1960, the Court of Appeals was changed from five judges to seven judges. In

1967, when the Court of Special Appeals was created, and became the appellate court of right for criminal cases, the Court of Appeals was the appellate court of right for civil cases and became the discretionary, certiorari appellate court for criminal cases.

In 1975, when the Court of Special Appeals became the appellate court of right for almost all cases appealed from the Circuit Court, the Court of Appeals became almost exclusively a certiorari court. In 1996, the Honorable Robert Bell became the 23rd Chief Judge of the Court of Appeals, and the first African-American Chief Judge. In 2013, the Honorable Mary Ellen Barbera became the 24th Chief Judge of the Court of Appeals, the first female Chief Judge, and the first Chief Judge to preside over a majority female Court of Appeals.

3. Caseload of the Court of Appeals

In FY 2011, there were 766 cases filed in the Court of Appeals. The vast majority of these cases came to the Court of Appeals by way of a petition for a writ of certiorari. Cases in which the Court of Appeals is the appellate court of right—and not a certiorari court—include (a) "by-pass" cases that the Court of Appeals takes away from the Court of Special Appeals; (b) death penalty cases (the death penalty was repealed in 2013); (c) legislative redistricting cases; (d) election law cases; (e) cases involving the removal of certain officers; (f) certified questions from the United States District Court; and (g) bar admission and discipline cases.

The Court of Appeals hears about 160 cases annually, which is about four cases a day, four days a month, ten months of the year. In FY 2011, the Court of Appeals accepted 104 cases, which was 17% of the cases filed (19% of the civil cases and 15% of the criminal cases). The Court of Appeals hears oral argument en banc and files an opinion in virtually every case in which it grants certiorari (about 55% civil cases and about 45% criminal cases), except for about ten cases annually that are dismissed as "certiorari improvidently granted."

Unlike the Supreme Court, which typically grants certiorari to reverse, meaning the certiorari petitioner prevails about 70% of the time, the Court of Appeals does not, and Petitioners and Respondents prevail about equally.

4. History & structure of the Court of Special Appeals

In 1967, the legislature created the Court of Special Appeals as a five-judge intermediate appellate court, which heard only criminal appeals and heard them en banc. In 1970, the Court of Special Appeals became the appellate court of right for almost all cases appealed from Circuit Court. At that time, the number of judges was changed from five to nine, and the Court began hearing appeals in three-judge panels, like the federal circuits. In 1972, the Court went from nine judges to ten judges. In 1974, the Court went from ten judges to 12 judges. In 1977, the Court went from 12 judges to 13 judges. In 2013, the Court went from 13 judges to 15 judges.

About once every two years, after hearing a case in a three-judge panel, the Court elects to re-hear that case en banc before all 15 judges.

In criminal cases, there is no appeal of right (a) from a guilty plea; (b) from denial of a petition for post conviction relief or motion to reopen a closed post conviction proceeding; (c) from denial of a state habeas corpus petition; (d) from a conviction for violation of probation; or (d) from denial of relief before the Inmate Grievance Commission. In those cases, there is only the right of file an application for leave to appeal. If the application is granted, it usually results in the case being placed on the regular appellate docket. The Court of Special Appeals grants about 5% of the applications filed. The sixth Chief Judge of the Court of Special Appeals is the Honorable Peter Krauser.

5. Case load of the Court of Special Appeals

In FY 2011, there were 2,116 cases filed in the Court of Special Appeals. About 85% of those cases were direct appeals (about 55% were civil cases and 45% were criminal cases), and about 15% were applications for leave to appeal. The Court of Special Appeals grants oral argument in about two-thirds of its direct appeals. Although the Court of Special Appeals files opinions in about 1,300 cases annually, it files a "reported opinion" in only one time out of eight among the cases in which it files an opinion. Only reported opinions are precedent and may be cited as authority. Md. Rule 8-605.1. The Appellant prevails, in whole or in part, in about 13% of criminal appeals and about 12% of civil appeals.

6. History & structure of the Circuit Courts

In 1776, 24 Circuit Courts were established (one Circuit Court for each of 23 counties and one for Baltimore City). The 24 Circuit Courts are divided into eight judicial circuits. There are 157 Circuit Court judges, ranging from seven one-judge counties (Caroline County, Dorchester County, Garrett County, Kent County, Queen Anne's County, Somerset County, and Talbot County) to 33 judges in Baltimore City. Because Circuit Court judges sit on 24 separate courts, there is no statewide Circuit Court Chief Judge. Each county has a Chief Judge, each county has an administrative judge, and each judicial circuit has an administrative judge.

The First Circuit (eight judges) consists of Dorchester County, Somerset County, Wicomico County, and Worcester County. The Second Circuit (eight judges) consists of Caroline County, Cecil County, Kent County, Queen Anne's County, and Talbot County. The Third Circuit (23 judges) consists of Baltimore County and Harford County. The Fourth Circuit (eight judges) consists of Allegany County, Garrett County, and Washington County. The Fifth Circuit (21 judges) consists of Anne Arundel County, Carroll County, and Howard County. The Sixth Circuit (27 judges) consists of Frederick County and Montgomery County. The Seventh Circuit (33 judges) consists of Calvert County, Charles County, Prince George's County, and St. Mary's County. The Eighth Circuit (33 judges) consists of Baltimore City.

Circuit Courts are courts of general jurisdiction, sitting as both jury trial courts and non-jury trial courts, with some concurrent jurisdiction with the District Court. Circuit Courts also sit as de novo (criminal and civil) and "on the record" (civil only) appellate courts for cases appealed from District Court and from certain administrative agencies.

7. Case load of the Circuit Courts

In FY 2011, there were 315,000 cases filed in the 24 Circuit Courts (99,000 family law cases, 85,000 criminal cases, 91,000 civil cases, and 40,000 juvenile cases).

8. The history & structure of the District Court of Maryland

In 1971, the legislature created the District Court of Maryland. It is a non-jury trial court of limited jurisdiction, with some concurrent jurisdiction with Circuit Courts. The 24 counties are divided into 12 districts. The First District (28 judges) consists of Baltimore City. The Second District (six judges) consists of Dorchester County, Somerset County, Wicomico County, and Worcester County. The Third District (six judges) consists of Caroline County, Cecil County, Kent County, Queen Anne's County, and Talbot County.

The Fourth District (six judges) consists of Calvert County, Charles County, and St. Mary's County. The Fifth District (16 judges) consists of Prince George's County. The Sixth District (12 judges) consists of Montgomery County. The Seventh District (nine judges) consists of Anne Arundel County. The Eighth District (13 judges) consists of Baltimore County. The Ninth District (four judges) consists of Harford County.

The Tenth District (seven judges) consists of Carroll County and Howard County. The Eleventh District (five judges) consists of Frederick County and Washington County. The Twelfth District (three judges) consists of Allegany County and Garrett County. Starting with 78 judges in 1971, the District Court now has 112 judges (111 associate judges and the Chief Judge), hearing cases in 34 locations. The fourth Chief Judge of District Court, who is appointed by the Chief Judge of the Court of Appeals, is the Honorable Ben C. Clyburn.

9. Case load of the District Court of Maryland

In FY 2011, there were 1.8 million cases filed in the District Court. This is more than three times the number of cases filed in 1971. More than one-half of the cases are filed in Baltimore City, Prince George's County, and Baltimore County. The number of filings represents one case annually for every three men, women, and children in Maryland. In FY 2011, there were 650,000 motor vehicle cases, 640,000 landlord-tenant cases, 340,000 civil cases, and 184,000 criminal cases. More than 40% of the criminal cases were filed in Baltimore City and Prince George's County.

10. Judicial selection & retention in Maryland

Maryland's adoption of the modified "Missouri Plan" for judicial selection & retention

In 1937, Missouri became the first state to adopt a system of (a) judicial nominating commissions for screening judicial candidates based on merit; and (b) non-competitive "yes/no" retention elections. In 1970, Maryland adopted a modified version of the "Missouri Plan" when Governor Mandel created, by Executive Order, multiple Trial Court Judicial Nominating Commissions (TCJNCs) and one Appellate Judicial Nominating Commission (AJNC). The Executive Order has been amended numerous times.

In 2007, Governor O'Malley issued Executive Order 01.01.2007.08, which established a 17-member AJNC, with 12 members appointed by the Governor and five members appointed by the Maryland State Bar Association. The Executive Order also established 16 regional TCJNCs. In 2008, Governor O'Malley issued Executive Order 01.01.2008.04, rescinding Executive Orders 01.01.2007.08 and 01.01.2007.11, but making only minor changes to the TCJNC.

Selection of judges for appellate courts

There is one AJNC. The AJNC has 17 at-large members (ten is a quorum), including 12 members appointed by the Governor and five members appointed by the Maryland State Bar Association. If the MSBA fails to submit five persons for appointment within 60 days of the date of the Executive Order, or submits fewer than five persons, the Governor makes the additional appointments.

For selection to Maryland's appellate courts (Court of Appeals and Court of Special Appeals), (a) the AJNC nominates by recommending qualified candidates to the Governor; (b) the Governor makes judicial appointments; (c) the Maryland Senate confirms appointments for a ten-year term; and (d) the judges enter a "yes/no" non-competitive retention election for that ten-year term. The Governor selects the Chief Judge of the Court of Appeals and the Chief Judge of the Court of Special Appeals from among the judges on the Court of Appeals and Court of Special Appeals. There are seven appellate judicial circuits (AJC).

The First AJC consists of Caroline County, Cecil County, Dorchester County, Kent County, Queen Anne's County, Somerset County, Talbot County, Wicomico County, and Worcester County. The Second AJC consists of Baltimore County and Harford County. The Third AJC consists of Allegany County, Carroll County, Frederick County, Garrett County, Howard County, and Washington County. The Fourth AJC consists of Prince George's County. The Fifth AJC consists of Anne Arundel County, Calvert County, Charles County, and St. Mary's county. The Sixth AJC consists of Baltimore City. The Seventh AJC consists of Montgomery County. The Court of Appeals consists of seven judges—one from each AJC. The Court of Special Appeals consists of 15 judges—one from each AJC and eight at large.

Selection of judges for trial courts

There are 16 TCJNCs (11 one-county TCJNC districts and five multi-county TCJNC districts). Maryland trial court selection process is different for Circuit Court and District Court. For the Circuit Court, (a) the appropriate TCJNC nominates by recommending qualified candidates to the Governor; (b) the Governor makes judicial appointments; and (c) the judge competes for a 15-year term through a competitive election in which attorneys may "run against" sitting judges in a non-partisan election, i.e., all candidates are automatically cross-filed in the Democratic and Republican primaries.

Judges on the Circuit Court are elected to 15-year terms in contested elections that often "pit" judges appointed by the Governor against (a) attorneys who "made the list" but were not appointed by the Governor; (b) attorneys who failed to make the "qualified" list; or (c) attorneys who never applied for a judicial vacancy. Judges on the District Court are appointed by the Governor and confirmed by the Senate for a ten-year term, but do not stand for election.

For the District Court, (a) the appropriate TCJNC nominates by recommending qualified candidates to the Governor; (b) the Governor makes judicial appointments; and (c) the Maryland Senate confirms the appointment for a ten-year term.

Each of the 16 TCJNCs has 13 members (nine is a quorum), including (a) nine persons appointed by the Governor; and (b) four persons submitted for appointment by presidents of the bar associations in the political subdivisions for which the Commission is responsible. If the presidents of the bar associations do not submit names for appointment within 60 days of the date of the Executive Order, or submit fewer than four persons, additional members of the commission are appointed by the Governor. No more than one lawyer from the same firm or legal office may serve on the commission at any time. No member of the TCJNC may simultaneously serve on the ACJNC. No elected official or active or senior member of state or federal judiciary may serve on the TCJNC.

Judicial qualification

To be constitutionally eligible to be a state judge in Maryland, a candidate must be (a) at least 30 years old; (b) a United States citizen; (c) a licensed attorney in Maryland in good standing with the Court of Appeals and the Client Protection Fund; (d) a Maryland resident for at least five years; (e) a resident of the AJC or county in which trial court is located for at least six months; and (f) not a member of a JNC. All judges must, by Constitution, retire on the day that he or she turns 70. However, once the judge reaches mandatory retirement, if the judge would like to hear cases, the Chief Judge may call that judge into part-time service not to exceed 90 days annually.

The constitutional standard for appointment to the bench is "most distinguished for integrity, wisdom, and sound legal knowledge." Other criteria include outstanding and extensive legal experience, judicial temperament of fairness and open-mindedness, excellent performance under pressure, strong interpersonal skills, commitment to public service, and a reputation for integrity and good character. No member of a JNC may attend or participate in deliberations of certain relatives or co-workers and must disclose substantial personal, business, professional, or political relationship to any judicial applicant.

Judicial application process

Attorneys seeking a judicial appointment and judges seeking elevation to a higher court may apply, when an opening occurs, to the appropriate TCJNC and/or to the AJNC. A judicial applicant must submit (a) a completed questionnaire, including academic, legal, and community experience (when applying for any court); and (b) two writing samples (when applying for the Court of Appeals, Court of Special Appeals, or a Circuit Court).

Members of the appropriate JNC (a) review the questionnaires and writing samples, if applicable; (b) obtain input from various sources, e.g., Attorney Grievance Commission; Commission on Judicial Disabilities, if applicable; interested individuals and groups; and state and local bar association ratings of "highly qualified," "qualified," and "not qualified"; and (c) interview the candidates to determine character, personality, temperament, judicial philosophy, and analytical ability.

§ II. Right to Appeal

A. Defendant's right to appeal

1. No federal constitutional right to appeal

There is no federal constitutional right to appeal. In *McKane v. Durston*, 153 U.S. 684 (1894), the Defendant was convicted of a crime relating to elections and voter registration. He was denied an appeal bond. On appeal, the Defendant argued that the United States Constitution guaranteed his right to have bail pending appeal. The Supreme Court held:

> An appeal from a judgment of conviction is not a matter of absolute right, independent of constitutional or statutory provisions allowing such an appeal. A review by an appellate court of the final judgment is a criminal case, however grave the offense of which the accused was convicted, was not at common law, and is not now, a necessary element of due process of law. It is wholly within the discretion of the state to allow or not to allow such a review.

Id. at 687-88; *see Griffin v. Illinois*, 351 U.S. 12, 18 (1956) (no constitutional right to appeal).

In *Jones v. Barnes*, 463 U.S. 745 (1983), Justice Brennan, in dissent, stated:

> If the question were to come before us in a proper case, I have little doubt that
> the passage of nearly 30 years since *Griffin* and some 90 years since *McKane*
> *v. Durston*, 153 U.S. 684 (1894), upon which Justice Frankfurter relied, would
> lead us to reassess the significance of the factor upon which Justice Frank-
> furter based his conclusion. I also have little doubt that we would decide
> that a State must afford at least some opportunity for review of convictions,
> whether through the familiar mechanism of appeal or through some form
> of collateral proceeding. There are few, if any, situations in our system of
> justice in which a single judge is given unreviewable discretion over matters
> concerning a person's liberty or property, and the reversal rate on mandatory
> appeals in the state courts, while not overwhelming, is certainly high enough
> to suggest that depriving Defendants of their right to appeal would expose
> them to an unacceptable risk of erroneous conviction.

Id. at 756 n.1 (Brennan, J., dissenting) (citation omitted).

If a state elects to provide for an appeal, that right may not be restricted in a manner that violates the Equal Protection Clause. *Griffin*, 351 U.S. at 18. In *Griffin*, the
Defendants were convicted of armed robbery and filed for appeal pursuant to Illinois
Law, which provided for writs of error in all criminal cases. However, neither Defendant could afford to have the transcript created and filed a motion with the trial court
seeking a waiver of the cost associated with preparing the transcript. The motion was
denied. The Supreme Court held that this denial violated the Equal Protection Clause,
stating:

> There is no meaningful distinction between a rule which would deny the
> poor the right to defend themselves in a trial court and one which effectively
> denies the poor an adequate appellate review accorded to all who have money
> enough to pay the costs in advance. It is true that a State is not required by the
> Federal Constitution to provide appellate courts or a right to appellate review
> at all. But that is not to say that a State that does grant appellate review can
> do so in a way that discriminates against some convicted Defendants on
> account of their poverty. Appellate review has not become an integral part
> of the Illinois trial system for finally adjudicating the guilt or innocence of
> a Defendant. Consequently at all stages of the proceedings the Due Process
> and Equal Protection Clauses protect persons like petitioners from invidious
> discriminations.

Id. (internal citations omitted). *See Lane v. Brown*, 372 U.S 477, 485 (1963) (Defendant
could not be denied appellate review of denial of his writ of coram nobis based solely
on his indigency); *Draper v. Washington*, 372 U.S. 487, 493 (1963) (free transcript

for an indigent Defendant cannot be denied under theory that appeal is "patently frivolous"); *Rinaldi v. Yeager*, 384 U.S. 305, 309-10 (1966) (statute imposing costs for transcript production for appeal violated the Equal Protection Clause when applied to indigent Defendant).

2. One appeal of right under Maryland law in most cases

In Maryland, a Defendant who has been convicted of a crime is entitled, by both Constitution and statute, to one appeal of right from a final judgment in most situations. *See* Md. Const. art. IV, §§ 14, 14A, & 22; Md. Code Ann., Cts. & Jud. Proc. §§ 12-301, 12-303, 12-305, & 12-307; *Bienkowski v. Brooks*, 386 Md. 516, 543-44 (2005). In a criminal case, a final judgment occurs when the Defendant is sentenced. The Defendant cannot appeal from a probation before judgment, but can appeal from a probation after judgment. *See Warren v. State*, 281 Md. 179, 187-88 (1977).

In some situations, the Defendant's appellate right is limited to filing an application for leave to appeal, seeking an order granting the right to appeal. The Defendant also has a limited right to take appeals from judgments that are not final, i.e., from interlocutory orders and judgments.

A Defendant who is found guilty in District Court has the right to an appeal in Circuit Court in the form of a trial de novo jury trial or court trial. *Stone v. State*, 344 Md. 97, 105 (1996). Neither the District Court, nor the Circuit Court, may suggest to the Defendant that the sentence will be harsher in Circuit Court than in District Court. In *Tellington v. State*, 336 Md. 567, 586 (1994), the Court of Appeals vacated the conviction when the Circuit Court judge indicated that if the Defendant elected trial by jury, and the verdict was guilty, he would be sentenced to incarceration rather than afforded probation or a suspended sentence. *Hardy v. State*, 279 Md. 489, 492-93 (1977).

3. Waiver of the right to appeal

A Defendant may knowingly and voluntarily waive the right to appeal. *Thanos v. State*, 332 Md. 511, 520 (1993) (Public Defender had no authority to file an appeal on behalf of a Defendant who waived the right to appeal); *Cubbage v. State*, 304 Md. 237, 247-48 (1985) (Defendant waived the right to appeal after being found guilty, but before sentencing, when he negotiated a lower sentence in return for waiving his appeal).

4. Fugitive forfeiture of the right to appeal

A fugitive Defendant forfeits the right to appeal his conviction while "on the run" during the pendency of an appeal. *See Ortega-Rodriguez v. United States*, 507 U.S. 234, 139 (1993) (appellate court may dismiss an appeal if the Defendant becomes a fugitive from justice during the appeal); *Estelle v. Dorrough*, 420 U.S. 534, 539-41 (1975); *Allen v. Georgia*, 166 U.S. 138, 141 (1897) (by escaping legal custody, the Defendant abandoned the right to pursue his appeal).

B. State's right to appeal

1. No common law right for the State to appeal

The State does not have a common law right to appeal, which must derive, if at all, from the legislature. *See Carroll v. United States*, 354 U.S. 394, 407 (1957); *United States v. Sanges*, 144 U.S. 310 (1892); *State v. Green*, 367 Md. 61, 79 (2001) (no common law right of appeal under Maryland law); *Jones v. State*, 298 Md. 634, 637 (1984); *see* Md. Code Ann., Cts. & Jud. Proc. §§ 12-401(b) & 12-302(c). The provisions of any statute granting the State the right to appeal a decision in a criminal case will be strictly construed. *Arizona v. Maypenny*, 451 U.S. 232, 247 (1981).

2. No right to appeal a "not guilty" verdict or the granting of an MJOA

Double jeopardy prohibits the State from appealing an acquittal or the granting of an MJOA, even when based on judicial error. *Shilling v. State*, 320 Md. 288, 291 (1990) (State has no right of appeal when Defendant is tried & acquitted); *State v. Adams*, 196 Md. 341, 349 (1950); *State v. Levitt*, 48 Md. App. 1, 18 (1981) (State has no right to appeal grant of MJOA). The State has no right to appeal the granting of a writ of habeas corpus. *State v. Thornton*, 84 Md. App. 312, 316 (1990).

3. State may appeal the granting of a motion to suppress

The State has a right to appeal the granting of a motion to suppress, subject to statutory requirements. Md. Code Ann., Cts. & Jud. Proc. § 12-302(c)(3); *State v. James*, 87 Md. App. 39 (1991). The State does not have to object in the trial court to a suppression ruling to be entitled to appeal that ruling. *State v. Coley*, 145 Md. App. 502, 516-17 (2002). To the contrary, the Defendant does not have a right to an immediate appeal from the trial court's denial of a motion to suppress. *Rush v. State*, 403 Md. 68, 103-04 (2008). The State may not appeal an order suppressing evidence for a violation of the Wiretapping & Electronic Surveillance Act. *Derry v. State*, 358 Md. 325, 345-46 (2000).

An appeal of a grant of a motion to suppress must be made before jeopardy attaches and within 15 days of the suppression order. Md. Code Ann., Cts. & Jud. Proc. § 12-302(c)(3)(ii). The Court of Special Appeals must decide the appeal within 120 days from the time that the record is filed in that court. *Id.* § 12-302(c)(3)(iii). Before appealing the grant of a motion to dismiss, the State must certify that (a) the appeal is not being prosecuted for purposes of delay; and (b) the evidence that is the subject of the appeal is substantial proof of a material fact in the proceeding. *Id.* § 12-302(c)(3)(iii).

Case must be dismissed if the State loses the appeal (except in murder cases)

Except in murder cases, if the State appeals the granting of a motion to suppress, and the trial court is affirmed, the charges are dismissed, and the State is barred from pursuing those charges or other related charges arising from the same incident. *Id.* § 12-302(c)(3)(iv). In *McNeil v. State*, 112 Md. App. 434 (1996), the Court of Special Appeals stated: "By imposing the harsh consequences of mandatory dismissal, the Legislature made clear its intent that the State should pursue appeals under the statute only in a limited number of cases, when the suppressed evidence is important to the prosecution and the State truly believes that the trial court erred." *Id.* at 452-53.

The State may withdraw the appeal, if done in good faith. *Id.* at 466 (1996) (Defendant entitled to a hearing to determine whether the State acted in bad faith in noting and subsequently withdrawing the appeal of the trial court's decision to suppress the Defendant's confession).

Appellate court lacks jurisdiction to hear "cross-appeal" of the Defendant when the State files an interlocutory appeal from a grant of a motion to suppress

In *Rush*, 403 Md. at 103-04, the Court of Appeals held that the Defendant did not have the right to a "cross-appeal" when the State noted an interlocutory appeal from the grant of a motion to suppress. However, the Defendant may advance alternate grounds for upholding the trial court's ruling.

4. State may appeal a court's failure to impose a mandatory sentence

The State may appeal if the sentencing court fails to impose a sentence that is mandated by law. Md. Code Ann., Cts. & Jud. Proc. § 12-302(c)(2). The purpose of the State's statutory right to appeal when a court fails to impose a mandatory sentence is to ensure that courts follow legislative policy mandating or prohibiting certain sentences.

In *State v. Griswold*, 374 Md. 184, 197 (2003), the Court of Appeals held that the State could appeal a trial court's reduction of sentence when the sentence had been imposed as part of a three-party binding agreement. The State may appeal a sentence imposed in violation of a statute or a court rule. Md. Code Ann., Cts. & Jud. Proc. § 12-302(c)(2)(ii); *see State v. Karmand*, 183 Md. App. 480, 489-90 (2008).

In *Mateen v. Saar*, 376 Md. 385, 399-400 (2003), the Court of Appeals held that a sentence that may be suspended is not a mandatory sentence, and thus the State may not appeal. In *State v. Green*, 367 Md. 61, 83-84 (2001), the Court of Appeals held that the State could appeal a modification of the Defendant's sentence, which committed the Defendant to DHMH, when the sentence was mandatory and could not be modified by an order of commitment.

In *State v. Purcell*, 342 Md. 214, 220 (1996), the Court of Appeals held that the State could appeal, arguing that the court lacked authority to grant a PBJ for a second DUI within five years of a first DUI. In *Shilling v. State*, 320 Md. 288, 293 (1990), the Court of Appeals held that a statute prohibiting PBJ is a mandatory sentencing statute.

In *State v. Montgomery*, 334 Md. 20, 21-22 (1994), the Court of Appeals held that the State could appeal the trial court's denial of postponement, requested by the State, so that it could serve notice of intent to seek a mandatory sentence. In *State v. Hannah*, 307 Md. 390, 392 (1986), the Court of Appeals held that the State could appeal the trial court's failure to impose the mandatory minimum sentence required by the handgun statute.

5. State may appeal the granting of a motion to dismiss a charging document

In *State v. Monroe*, 82 Md. App. 65, 71 (1990), the Court of Special Appeals held that Md. Code Ann., Cts. & Jud. Proc. § 12-302(c)(1), permits the State to appeal from the dismissal of an indictment or information. *See Kendall v. State*, 429 Md. 476, 483 n.7 (2012); *State v. Pike*, 287 Md. 120, 123-24 (1980). In *Purohit v. State*, 99 Md. App. 566, 582 (1994), the Court of Special Appeals held that the State may appeal a dismissal of case for discriminatory prosecution.

In *State v. Armstrong*, 46 Md. App. 641, 651 (1980), the Court of Special Appeals held that the State may appeal from the dismissal of a case based on the denial of the right to speedy trial. *Accord State v. Becker*, 24 Md. App. 549, 560 (1975). In *Jones v. State*, 298 Md. 634, 638 (1984), the Court of Appeals held that if a court dismisses one count of an indictment, the State cannot appeal until the final judgment on the entire indictment. In *Nnoli v. Nnoli*, 389 Md. 315, 324 (2005), the Court of Appeals held that the denial of a motion to quash an arrest warrant is not appealable without a specific statutory authority.

§ III. Right to counsel on appeal

To ensure meaningful access to the appellate process, the Constitution requires that indigent Defendants be provided with counsel for the first appeal. *Douglas v. California*, 372 U.S. 353, 357-58 (1963). However, a Defendant does not have a right to counsel for a discretionary state appeal or discretionary review by the Supreme Court. *Ross v. Moffitt*, 417 U.S. 600, 616 (1974) ("duty of the State . . . is not to duplicate the legal arsenal that may be privately retained . . . but only to assure the indigent defendant an adequate opportunity to present his claims fairly in the context of the State's appellate process").

In *Halbert v. Michigan*, 545 U.S. 605 (2005), the Defendant pleaded nolo contendere. Under state law, he was not entitled to a direct appeal, and was required to file an application for leave to appeal. Even though the Defendant was indigent, he was denied appellate counsel.

The Supreme Court held that regardless of whether the Defendant is filing a direct appeal or an application for leave to appeal, he is entitled to appellate counsel. The State argued that review of a guilty plea, through application for leave to appeal, is a discretionary appeal and, thus, under *Ross*, the Defendant is not entitled to counsel. The Supreme Court disagreed, stating that the appellate court's "ruling on a plea-convicted Defendant's claim provides the first, and likely the only, direct review the Defendant's conviction and sentence will receive." *Id.* at 607.

§ IV. Appeal from District Court to Circuit Court

A. Securing appellate review

In criminal cases, appeals from District Court to Circuit Court are always tried de novo. Thus, the appeal is always in the form of a new trial and is never heard on the record. To obtain appellate review in Circuit Court, appealing from District Court, the Defendant must file a notice of appeal and the filing fee (waived with an affidavit of indigency) with clerk of the District Court within 30 days after sentencing. Md. Code Ann., Cts. & Jud. Proc. § 12-401(e); Md. Rules 1-325(a) & 7-104; *see State v. Armstrong*, 60 Md. App. 244, 252 (1984).

Filing a motion for a new trial does not change the 30-day deadline for filing the notice of appeal. *Kirsner v. State*, 296 Md. 567, 570-72 (1983). The District Court has the power to rule pre-trial issues, such as the constitutionality of a search or seizure, a confession, the right to counsel, confrontation, compulsory process, and any other constitutional trial right. *White v. State*, 89 Md. App. 590, 595-96 (1991). A District Court ruling on such issues is not immediately appealable to Circuit Court, but upon conviction, any such issues can be reviewed in the Defendant's trial de novo appeal in Circuit Court. *Id.*

B. Entry of appearance of counsel

Even if counsel in Circuit Court is the same person who was counsel in District Court, counsel must enter his or her appearance in Circuit Court because the entry of appearance is not transferred from District Court. Md. Rule 7-107(a)(2).

C. District Court record

The Clerk of the District Court shall transmit the record to Circuit Court within 60 days after the notice of appeal is filed. Md. Rule 7-108(a). The record includes a certified copy of the docket entries and all original papers, unless omitted by stipulation of the parties. Md. Rule 7-109(a). On motion by a party, or by the Circuit Court sua sponte, the Circuit Court may, by court order, correct any error or omission in the record. Md. Rule 7-109(d).

D. Format of appeal is a trial de novo

Criminal appeals to Circuit Court are in the form of a trial de novo, regardless of whether the District Court case was a trial, a guilty plea, or a plea of nolo contendere. Md. Rule 7-102(b); *Garrison v. State*, 350 Md. 128, 138-39 (1998); *State v. Jefferson*, 319 Md. 674, 681-83 (1990); *McDonald v. State*, 314 Md. 271, 274 (1988) (trial de novo appeal from a VOP); *Harper v. State*, 312 Md. 396, 400 (1988); *Hardy v. State*, 279 Md. 489, 496 (1977). The District Court judgment (the finding of guilt and the sentence) remains in effect until the Circuit Court disposition of the trial de novo appeal. Md. Rule 7-112 (b).

1. District Court charging document becomes the Circuit Court charging document

Under Md. Rule 4-201(c)(3), the Circuit Court may use or amend the District Court charging document as the charging document on the appeal de novo, unless precluded by double jeopardy. *See* Md. Rule 7-112(d)(1). In *Pinkett v. State*, 30 Md. App. 458, 469-70 (1976), the Court of Appeals held:

> [W]e find plain intent from the statute and rules that a trial de novo in a criminal case on appeal to the circuit court from a final judgment of the District Court shall proceed only on the same charging document which was the basis of the original trial. A trial on appeal under any other charging document is void. The de novo trial washes out the trial in the District Court but not the basis for it. Thus, the requirement that the appeal be tried under the same charging document may not be obviated by agreement, nor may it be waived, either expressly or by the failure to object.

Id. at 469-70; *see Lewis v. State*, 289 Md. 1, 4-5 (1980).

2. De novo appeal of nol prossed or stetted charges

In *LaFaivre v. State*, 338 Md. 151, 154-55 (1995), the Court of Appeals held that, unless a new charging document is filed in Circuit Court, a de novo trial of nol prossed charges is improper. However, a de novo trial of stetted charges is permissible. *See Ward v. State*, 290 Md. 76, 101 (1981) (nolle prosequi precludes further prosecution on the nol prossed charging document or count, but does not prevent a new charging document).

3. Sentencing upon a guilty verdict in a trial de novo

Md. Code Ann., Cts. & Jud. Proc. § 12-702(c), provides: "If a Defendant who appeals from a conviction in the District Court is convicted after a trial de novo on appeal, the appellate court may impose a more severe sentence than that imposed in the District Court . . ." Although a harsher sentence may be imposed following a conviction in a trial de novo, the basis for the harsher sentence cannot be the Defendant's assertion of his right to appeal. *Abdul-Maleek v. State*, 426 Md. 59, 73 (2012).

4. Evidence presented

Generally, the parties to a de novo appeal are neither limited to the evidence they presented in District Court, nor are they required to present the same evidence. *Garrison v. State*, 350 Md. 128, 136 (1998). However, pursuant to Md. Rule 7-102(b) and Md. Code Ann., Cts. & Jud. Proc. § 12-401(f), the parties may consent to an "on the record" appeal, as opposed to a de novo trial appeal.

5. Original judge is prohibited from being the trial de novo judge

The judge that presided over the original trial in District Court may not also preside over the trial de novo appeal in Circuit Court. *Brooks v. State*, 312 Md. 115, 116 (1988) (per curiam).

6. Effect of appeal

Entry of a notice of appeal in District Court, to have the case heard de novo in Circuit Court, does not extinguish the District Court judgment for all purposes. *Stanton v. State*, 290 Md. 245, 246-47 (1981). The District Court conviction remains in place until the trial de novo is concluded. *Id.* at 249-50; Md. Rule 7-112(b). Until the trial de novo is resolved, a court may impose a sentence to run consecutively to the District Court conviction then on appeal. *Id.* at 248-50.

7. Right to trial by jury

On a trial de novo appeal, the Defendant is entitled to trial by jury if subject to jail time. Md. Code Ann., Cts. & Jud. Proc. § 12-401(g)(1). *See Harper v. State*, 312 Md. 396, 400 (1988) (entitled to a trial de novo jury trial on appeal from a District Court contempt order).

§ V. Standard of review by appellate courts hearing appeals on the record

A law review article, by Professor Amy E. Sloan, titled *Appellate Fruit Salad & Other Concepts: A Short Course in Appellate Process*, 35 U. Balt. L. Rev. 45 (2005), explains the three standards that appellate courts employ when reviewing a case on appeal. Professor Sloan wrote:

> Appellate courts generally apply one of three standards of review: de novo, clearly erroneous, or abuse of discretion. De novo review gives no deference to the decision below, allowing the appellate court to reevaluate an issue on its own. It applies primarily to questions of law. Two reasons are usually

advanced for this searching degree of review. First, a trial court may have to make decisions quickly, in the heat of trial, whereas the appellate court can take as much time as it needs to consider and resolve the issue. Second, one of the functions of appellate court is to clarify ambiguities in the law or even make new legal rules when necessary, and appellate decisions have precedential value affecting the resolution of future cases. Giving appellate courts plenary review of questions of law is consistent with this function.

Clearly erroneous is the standard applied to review questions of fact decided by the judge. This is a more deferential standard than de novo review. According to the Supreme Court, "[a] finding is 'clearly erroneous' when although there is evidence to support it, the reviewing court on the entire evidence is left with the definite and firm conviction that a mistake has been committed." The appellate court will not substitute its judgment for that of the trial court, even if the appellate court might have ruled differently if it had been the trier of fact.

The justifications for this deferential standard also turn on the respective functions of trial and appellate courts. Trial courts find facts. Appellate courts will not encroach on that function in the absence of clear error. In addition, trial courts viewing live testimony are better positioned to assess the credibility of witnesses than are appellate courts that review only transcripts of the testimony. The paper record does not allow the appellate court to get the same sense of the credibility of a witness that the trial court's actual observation provides. Although credibility determinations are one justification for the clear error standard, the same standard applies to all factual findings, regardless of whether they are based on the testimony of witnesses or other forms of evidence.

The third standard of review is abuse of discretion. This standard is also deferential to the trial court. Discretion is the authority to make a reasoned choice. Many matters within the course of litigation are committed to the trial court's discretion. That is, the trial judge has the authority to choose from among a range of options. If the trial judge could legitimately have chosen one course of action over another, the appellate court will not substitute its judgment for that of the trial judge.

A judge can commit an abuse of discretion in three ways: (1) by failing to consider a factor relevant to the decision; (2) by considering and giving significant weight to an irrelevant or improper factor; or (3) by making a clear error of judgment. Challenging a discretionary decision on the ground that the judge made a clear error of judgment is possible, but is an uphill climb because trial judges do not often make decisions entirely outside the range of the appropriate options. Arguments based on the other two forms of error are more likely to be successful because they focus on the decision-making process. For example, if a statute requires a judge to consider specific factors in making child custody decisions, the judge may abuse her discretion by failing to consider one of the factors. The error in the result stems from error in the decisional process, not the judge's error in judgment.

Id. at 62-64 (internal citations & footnotes omitted). Cases that demonstrate the three standards of appellate review are as follows:

De novo review cases include *Salve Regina College v. Russell*, 499 U.S. 225, 238 (1991); *Blickenstaff v. State*, 393 Md. 680, 683 (2001) ("[O]ur Court must determine whether the lower court's conclusions are legally correct under a de novo standard of review."); *Gray v. State*, 388 Md. 366, 374-75 (2005) ("When trial court's order includes an interpretation and application of Maryland law, our Court must determine whether the lower court's conclusions are legally correct under a de novo standard of review.").

Clearly erroneous cases include *Anderson v. City of Bessemer*, 470 U.S. 564 (1985); *United States v. U.S. Gypsum Co.*, 333 U.S. 364, 395 (1948); *Jones v. State*, 410 Md. 681, 699 (2009) (applying clearly erroneous standard of review to fact finding); *Bailey v. State*, 84 Md. App. 323, 328-29 (1990) (Defendant must show that trial judge's fact finding was clearly erroneous).

Abuse of discretion cases include *Aventis Pasteur, Inc. v. Skevofilax*, 396 Md. 405, 443 (2007) (abuse of discretion standard of review is premised "on the concept that matters within the discretion of the trial court are much better decided by the trial judges than by appellate courts[, and] an appellate court should not reverse a decision vested in the trial court's discretion merely because the appellate court reaches a different conclusion"); *University of Maryland Medical System Corp. v. Gholston*, 203 Md. App. 321, 329 (2012) (abuse of discretion standard of review applies to the denial of a motion for a new trial); *Collins v. National Railroad Passenger Corp.*, 417 Md. 217, 228 (2010) (abuse of discretion standard of review applies to the denial of a proposed jury instruction); *State v. Walker*, 345 Md. 293, 325 (1997) (however, there are limits on judicial discretion).

§ VI. Appeals in the Court of Special Appeals

A. Overview

An appeal from District Court to Circuit Court, in a criminal case, is always tried de novo and is never tried on the record. It is exactly the opposite for an appeal from Circuit Court to the Court of Special Appeals and Court of Appeals, i.e., the appeal is never in the form of a trial de novo, and is always an appeal on the record.

In the Court of Special Appeals, the Defendant prevails about one time in eight. The good news for the Defendant is that, if there are, for example, five appellate issues, the Defendant can lose on four issues and still win the appeal. Thus, the bad news for the State is that if it loses on any one issue, it loses the appeal.

Even though the State is required to prevail on appeal on each issue, the good news for the State is that it has three ways for the State to prevail on each issue. The State's first argument may be that the issue is not before the appellate court because the Defendant failed to preserve that issue for appellate review, and thus there is no appeal. Moreover, there is no reason for the Court to recognize "plain error" when the Defendant failed to preserve the issue.

The State's second argument is that, even if the Defendant did preserve the issue for appeal, the trial court ruled correctly and committed no legal error. The State's third argument is "so what?' This argument is that, even if the Defendant preserved the issue, and even if the trial court committed reversible error, it can be stated, beyond a reasonable doubt, that the error in no way contributed to the finding of guilt.

Appellate defense counsel, even if successful on appeal, can rarely take the Defendant to a place called "not guilty." Almost always, the best that appellate counsel can accomplish is having the appellate court reverse the conviction and remand the case for a new trial. This is not so if the Defendant prevails on appeal on the issue of insufficiency of the evidence as to all counts. Prevailing on insufficiency of the evidence on appeal is the same as prevailing on an MJOA at trial, i.e., the Defendant is not guilty as a matter of law and may not be re-tried.

Moreover, even if the Defendant prevails on appeal, the State may elect to go forward, and not go backward. This means that instead of the State going back to Circuit Court to retry the case, the State may take the case forward by filing a petition for a writ of certiorari in the Court of Appeals.

The party appealing to the Court of Special Appeals is the Appellant, and the adverse party is the Appellee. If the Appellee also appeals, the Appellee is the Appellee/Cross-Appellant, and the Appellant is the Appellant/Cross-Appellee. Md. Rule 8-111(a). For appeals from juvenile court, the appeal is captioned "In re _____," using the juvenile's first name and first initial of last name. For appeals from a grand jury investigation, the appeal is captioned "In re: Criminal Investigation No. _____ in Circuit Court for _____." In juvenile cases and grand jury cases, secrecy of the last name and content of the record is required. Md. Rule 8-121.

B. Counsel

Unless appearance is stricken, a lower court appearance of counsel continues in the Court of Special Appeals and in Court of Appeals. Md. Rule 8-402(a).

C. Trial court jurisdiction while appeal is pending

The trial court retains fundamental jurisdiction over a case even while the case in pending on appeal. In *Jackson v. State*, 358 Md. 612, 620 (2000), the Court of Appeals stated: "[A] circuit court is not divested of fundamental jurisdiction to take post-judgment action in a case merely because an appeal is pending from the judgment." In *State v. Peterson*, 315 Md. 73, 84-85 (1989), the Court of Appeals held that the Circuit Court retained jurisdiction over a violation of probation hearing after the Court of Appeals granted certiorari. *See Pulley v. State*, 287 Md. 406, 414 (1980).

However, in Jackson, the Court stated that the trial court may not exercise the "jurisdiction in a manner that affects either the subject matter of the appeal or appellate proceeding itself—that, in effect, precludes or hampers the appellate court from acting on the matter before it." 358 Md. at 620; *see In re Emileigh F.* 355 Md. 198, 204 (1999) (closing case and terminating jurisdiction improper when appeal is pending).

D. Scope of appellate review

In a criminal case in Maryland, the only "on-the-record" appellate court of right is the Court of Special Appeals, which hears appeals on the record from the Circuit Court. The Court of Special Appeals must dispose of the case, but it does not necessarily have to dispose of every issue. For example, if the Defendant raises five issues on appeal, and the State prevails on every issue, the Court of Special Appeals must address all five issues in order to dispose of the appeal.

If, however, the Defendant raises five issues on appeal and prevails on appeal, the Court of Special Appeals has options. If the Defendant prevails on one or more issues, the disposition of the Court of Special Appeals will be a reversal and remand for a new trial. The Court of Special Appeals may (1) address all five issues; (2) address one issue with no mention of the other issues; or (3) address one issue and provide guidance for the lower court, on remand, by way of dicta, on one of more other issues.

1. No appeal prior to sentencing

A Defendant may not appeal a conviction, unless and until the lower court imposes a sentence or sanction. *See Webster v. State*, 359 Md. 465, 474 (2000); *Johnson v. State*, 142 Md. App. 172, 202 (2002) (with no sentence or other disposition, the case is not appealable). As long as the lower court imposed a sentence, the Defendant may appeal, even if imposition and/or or execution of the sentence was suspended. Md. Code Ann., Cts. & Jud. Proc. § 12-301.

2. Presumption that the trial court knows the law and applies it properly

Appellate courts start with the presumption that the lower courts know the law and apply it properly. *State v. Chaney*, 375 Md. 168, 184 (2003) ("error is never presumed by a reviewing court, and we shall not draw negative inferences from this silent record"). The burden of establishing error is on the party alleging error. *Wooddy v. Mudd*, 258 Md. 234, 237 (1970).

§ VII. Appeals in the Court of Appeals

When there has already been appeal in the Court of Special Appeals, and the losing party seeks review by the Court of Appeals, that party is the Petitioner, and the adverse party is the Respondent. If the Respondent cross-appeals, the Respondent is the Respondent/Cross-Petitioner, and the Petitioner is the Petitioner/Cross-Respondent. Md. Rule 8-412(b). If the appeal has "bypassed" the Court of Special Appeals, the moving party is the Appellant and the adverse party is the Appellee. In the non-bypass scenario, it is a discretionary appeal. In the bypass scenario, it is an appeal of right, with the Court of Appeals replacing the Court of Special Appeals as the appellate court of right.

A. Securing appeal in the Court of Appeals

The Court of Appeals is a discretionary appellate court, meaning there is no appeal of right. In an attempt to secure an appeal in the Court of Appeals, the Defendant must file a petition for a writ of certiorari, asking the Court of Appeals to take the appeal. Typically, the case comes from the Court of Special Appeals, and certiorari must be sought no later than 15 days after the mandate of the Court of Special Appeals, which is 30 days after the opinion of the Court of Special Appeals. Although this is the deadline for filing a petition for a writ of certiorari from the Court of Special Appeals, a petition may be filed as early as the date of the final judgment in the Circuit Court, which is the date of sentencing.

The Defendant may file a petition for a writ of certiorari in the Court of Appeals, seeking discretionary appellate review from the Circuit Court, but only when the Circuit Court was sitting as an appellate court, hearing a trial de novo appeal from the District Court (and not when the Circuit Court was sitting as a trial court). The petition for a writ of certiorari must be filed no later than 30 days after the final judgment in the Circuit Court, i.e., 30 days after sentencing, or 30 days after the denial or withdrawal of a motion for a new trial.

The Court of Appeals grants certiorari in cases of public importance. The Court is most likely to deem a case to be of public importance if the petition for a writ of certiorari present the Court with (1) a case of first impression; (2) an important issue (perhaps, a controversial issue), particularly if that issue has not been revisited in ten or 20 years; (3) an issue that the legislature has avoided or has addressed on multiple occasions, but no legislation has resulted; or (4) an issue of federal or state constitutional law.

B. Contents of a petition for a writ of certiorari

A petition for a writ of certiorari must be filed in eight copies, not to exceed 25 pages. Md. Rule 8-303(a) & (b). The petition must contain (1) the procedural history of the case; (2) the question(s) presented; (3) the reasons why this case presents an issue of public importance and certiorari should be granted; (4) legal authority; (5) a statement of facts; (6) argument; (7) docket entries; and (8) the opinion of the Court of Special Appeals and/or the Circuit Court, as applicable. Md. Rule 8-303(b).

The more issues that are presented, the less likely that certiorari will be granted. The recommended maximum number of issues is two. The odds that certiorari will be granted is one in seven. The Court of Appeals is not a "right-wrong" court. It does not care whether the Court of Special Appeals was correct or incorrect. The Court cares about the policy issues and the importance of the issues presented.

C. Optional response to a petition for a writ of certiorari

After a petition for a writ of certiorari is filed, (1) another party, within 15 days after service, may file a petition for a writ of certiorari; (2) the opposing party may file an answer, explaining why the petition should be denied; or (3) the opposing party may file a cross-petition for a writ of certiorari or a conditional cross-petition, i.e., the Court should not grant the petition but, if it does, it should also grant a petition on the following issue or issues. Md. Rules 8-302(c) & 8-303(d)).

D. Disposition of the petition for a writ of certiorari

The Court of Appeals grants 17% of the petitions for a writ of certiorari that are filed, including 15% of the petitions in criminal cases. The Court of Appeals may (1) deny the petition; (2) grant the petition and place the case on the regular appellate docket; (3) grant the petition as to less than all the issues petitioned; and/or (4) grant of deny a cross-petition.

§ VIII. Logistics & mechanics of appeals in the Court of Special Appeals & Court of Appeals

A. Appellate jurisdiction of right

To obtain appellate review in the Court of Special Appeals, the Defendant must file a notice of appeal and the filing fee (waived if indigent) with the clerk of the Circuit Court in which convicted. Md. Rule 8-201; *see Crippen v. State*, 207 Md. App. 236, 248-49 (2012). The notice of appeal must be filed within 30 days after sentencing or the denial or withdrawal of a motion for new trial. A notice of a cross-appeal may be filed within ten days after the notice of appeal is filed. Md. Rule 8-202(a), (b) & (e). *But see Keys v. State*, 195 Md. App. 19, 29-31 (2010) (30-day period for noting an appeal of a restitution order begins to run on the date the order is entered and not on the date of the judgment in the underlying criminal matter).

B. Discretionary appellate jurisdiction

There is no appeal of right from (1) a guilty plea (traditional plea or *Alford* plea, *see Ward v. State*, 83 Md. App. 474, 479-80 (1990); (2) a denial of a petition for post conviction relief or motion to reopen a closed post conviction proceeding; (3) a state habeas corpus proceeding; (4) a guilty verdict from a violation of probation proceeding; and (5) a denial of bail or bail set too high.

When there is no right to an appeal from Circuit Court, sitting as trial court, to the Court of Special Appeals, the Defendant may file an application for leave to appeal in the Court of Special Appeals. Md. Rule 8-204. The application for leave to appeal must be filed within 30 days, except that denial of bail must be filed within ten days. The Court of Special Appeals grants about 5% of applications for leave to appeal that are filed. *See State v. Hernandez*, 344 Md. 721, 728-29 (1997).

Although a direct appeal of right requires only a mere notice of appeal, an application for leave to appeal must contain concise statement of errors committed and reasons why judgment should be reversed or modified. Md. Rule 8-204(b)(2). *See Hernandez v. State*, 108 Md. App. 354, 362-63 (1996) (applications may be denied as untimely, lacking reason why judgment should be reversed, or lacking specificity in describing errors committed); *Boone v. State*, 56 Md. App. 8, 10 (1983) ("[B]ald allegations, made without adequate specification, afford no grounds for relief"). The Court of Special Appeals may (1) deny the application; (2) grant the application and affirm or reverse; (3) remand with directions; or (d) place the case on the regular appellate docket.

C. Trial transcript for appeal

Within ten days after filing a notice of appeal, the Defendant must order the trial transcript, in writing, from court reporter. Md. Rule 8-411. Under *Griffin v. Illinois*, 351 U.S. 12 (1956), the State is required to provide the trial transcript, at no cost to an indigent Defendant, but transcript need not be provided if the State can "find other means for affording adequate and effective appellate review to the Defendant." *Id.* at 20. *But see State v. Miller*, 337 Md. 71, 75-76 (1995) (indigent Defendant is entitled to a free transcript only when represented by the Office of the Public Defender).

In order for a new trial to be granted on the basis of errors or omissions in the trial transcript, the errors must be prejudicial to the Defendant and not trivial or inconsequential. *Wilson v. State*, 334 Md. 469, 477 (1994). The Defendant must be diligent in his attempt to reconstruct the missing testimony. *Smith v. State*, 291 Md. 125, 138 (1981) (Defendant "has the responsibility to make a sincere effort to perfect the record").

D. The record to the Court of Special Appeals

The clerk of the Circuit Court must transmit the record to the Court of Special Appeals within 60 days after the notice of appeal is filed, unless the time is shortened or extended by the Court of Special Appeals. Md. Rule 8-412(a) & (d); *see Mora v. State*, 355 Md. 639, 650 (1999) ("It is incumbent upon the appellant claiming error to produce a sufficient factual record for the appellate court to determine whether error was committed . . .").

E. The record to the Court of Appeals

Within 15 days after the Court of Appeals issues a writ of certiorari to the Court of Special Appeals, the clerk of the Court of Special Appeals must transmit the record to the Court of Appeals. Within 60 days after the Court of Appeals issues a writ of certiorari to the Circuit Court, the clerk of the Circuit Court must transmit record to the Court of Appeals.

The Court of Appeals may shorten or extend the time for transmittal of record. Md. Rule 8-412(d). The record includes certified copies of the docket entries, transcripts, original papers, cover page, and table of contents. Md. Rule 8-413. A party may file motions in appellate courts, alleging record omissions or errors, supported by affidavit, if necessary.

F. Motions

A party may file a motion and a proposed order, with eight copies in the Court of Appeals and five copies in the Court of Special Appeals, stating facts (accompanied by affidavit, if necessary) and authority on which the motion is based. Any response must be filed within five days after service of the motion. Md. Rule 8-431. Motion and response may not exceed 15 pages in the Court of Special Appeals and 25 pages in the Court of Appeals. Md. Rule 8-503(d).

G. Record extract

A record extract is not filed in criminal appeal in the Court of Special Appeals. A record extract is required to be filed with the Appellant's brief in the Court of Appeals. Md. Rule 8-501(a) & (b). Although parties and the Court of Appeals may rely on material not included in the record extract, the record extract must include (1) the judgment appealed from; (2) the applicable jury instructions, if a jury trial; (3) the lower court opinion(s), if any; (4) parts of record reasonably necessary to address the questions presented; and (5) a table of contents. Md. Rule 8-501(c) & (h).

The parties should agree on the content of the record extract, which shall be filed with the Appellant's brief. The Appellee may include, as an appendix to the Appellee's brief, parts of record not included in the record extract, but which the Appellee believes are material. The Appellant may include, as an appendix to the Reply Brief, parts of record that are material in light of the Appellee's brief. Md. Rule 8-501(d)-(f).

H. Briefs

1. Brief of Appellant in the Court of Special Appeals

In the Court of Special Appeals, the Brief of Appellant must be filed within 40 days after the record is filed. The Brief of Appellant may not exceed 35 pages and must have a yellow cover. Md. Rule 8-503(c)(1)(A) & (d).

2. Brief of Petitioner in the Court of Appeals

In the Court of Appeals, the Brief of Petitioner must be filed within 40 days after the record is filed. The Brief of Petitioner may not exceed 50 pages and must have a white cover. Md. Rule 8-503(c)(2)(A) & (d). If the case is in the Court of Appeals, having "by-passed" the Court of Special Appeals, the parties are Appellant and Appellee and not Petitioner and Respondent.

3. Brief of Appellee or Appellee/Cross-Appellant in the Court of Special Appeals

In the Court of Special Appeals, the Brief of Appellee or the Brief of Appellee/Cross-Appellant must be filed within 30 days after the filing of the Brief of Appellant. The Brief may not exceed 50 pages and must have a green cover. Md. Rule 8-503(c)(1)(B) & (e).

4. Brief of Respondent or Respondent/Cross-Petitioner in the Court of Appeals

In the Court of Appeals, the Brief of Respondent or the Brief of Respondent/Cross-Petitioner must be filed within 30 days after the filing of the Brief of Petitioner. The Brief may not exceed 50 pages and must have a blue cover. Md. Rule 8-503(c)(2)(B) & (e).

5. Reply Brief of Appellant or Reply Brief of Appellant/Cross-Appellee in the Court of Special Appeals

Assuming that there is no "cross-briefing" in the Court of Special Appeals, there is one remaining brief, which is the optional Reply Brief of Appellant, which must be filed within 20 days after the filing of Brief of Appellee, but no later than ten days prior to oral argument. The brief may not exceed 15 pages and must have a light red cover. Md. Rule 8-503(c)(1)(C). If Appellant is also the Cross-Appellee, the Reply Brief of Appellant/Brief of Cross-Appellee must be filed within 30 days after the filing of the Brief of Appellee/Cross-Appellant. The brief may not exceed 50 pages, if it includes a

Reply Brief of Appellant and 35 pages if it does not include a Reply Brief of Appellant and must have a green cover. Md. Rule 8-503(c)(1)(B) & (e).

6. Reply Brief of Petitioner or Reply Brief of Petitioner/ Cross-Respondent in the Court of Appeals

Assuming that there is no "cross-briefing" in the Court of Appeals, there is one remaining brief, which is the optional Reply Brief of Petitioner, which must be filed within 20 days after the filing of the Brief of Respondent, but no later than ten days prior to oral argument. This brief may not exceed 25 pages and must have a tan cover. Md. Rule 8-503(c)(2)(C). If the Respondent is also the Cross-Petitioner, the Reply Brief of Petitioner/Brief of Cross-Respondent must be filed within 30 days after the filing of the Brief of Respondent/Cross-Petitioner. The brief may not exceed 50 pages and must have a blue cover. Md. Rule 8-503(c)(2)(C).

7. Cross-Appellant's Reply Brief in the Court of Special Appeals

If the Appellee in the Court of Special Appeals is also the Cross-Appellant, the optional Reply Brief of Cross-Appellant must be filed within 20 days after the filing of Brief of Cross-Appellee. This brief may not exceed 15 pages and must have a light red cover.

8. Cross-Petitioner's Reply Brief in the Court of Appeals

If the Respondent in the Court of Appeals is also the Cross-Petitioner, the optional Reply Brief of Cross-Petitioner must be filed within 20 days after the filing of Brief of Cross-Respondent. This brief may not exceed 25 pages and must have a tan cover.

9. Amicus briefs

Individuals or entities wishing to participate as amicus curiae, i.e., friends of the court, must file a motion, (a) identifying the interest of the amicus curiae; (b) stating the reasons why an amicus curiae brief is desirable; and (c) indentifying the issue(s) to be briefed. If the motion is granted, the briefing rules are the same as for a party the amicus is supporting, except that amicus curiae briefs are gray in both the Court of Appeals and the Court of Special Appeals. Md. Rule 8-503(c)(1)(D) & (2)(D).

10. Extension of time

The time for filing briefs may be extended by court order or by stipulation of parties, provided briefs are filed at least 30 days before oral argument and reply briefs are filed at least ten days before oral argument.

11. Number of briefs to be filed

In the Court of Appeals, the parties must file 20 briefs. In the Court of Special Appeals, the parties must file 15 briefs. Md. Rule 8-502(c).

12. Brief references

References in briefs are R. for record, T. for transcript, E. for record extract, App. for appendix to the Brief of Appellant, Apx. for appendix to the Brief of Appellee, and Rep. App. for appendix to a reply brief. Md. Rule 8-503(b).

13. Contents of a brief

Briefs must contain (a) a cover (including the name of the appellate court; the case number on appeal; the name, address, phone number, and e-mail address of the attorney; and the court and judge whose ruling is on appeal); (b) a table of contents; (c) a table of authorities; (d) a statement of the case (including the disposition of the lower court); (e) questions presented; (f) a statement of facts (including record references); (g) standard of review for each issue; (h) argument; (i) a conclusion setting forth the relief sought; (j) relevant jury instructions; (k) the Circuit Court opinion(s), if any; and (l) the text of pertinent non-case authority. Md. Rules 8-503 & 8-504(a).

I. Oral argument

Oral argument may be presented by one or two counsel per side. Md. Rule 8-522(c). Oral argument is limited to the issues presented in the brief. Md. Rule 8-522(f). In the Court of Special Appeals, oral argument is 20 minutes per side. In the Court of Appeals, oral argument is 30 minutes per side. A party may request additional time for oral argument, filed no later than ten days prior to oral argument, but this is rarely granted.

The Appellant or the Petitioner may reserve time for rebuttal (which is subtracted from the 30 minutes or 20 minutes), but the substance of the appeal should be completely presented during the original argument. Amicus curiae do not participate in oral argument, except with permission of the court, which is almost never granted. Md. Rules 8-511(c), 8-522(a)-(c).

J. Oral argument on motions

Unless directed by the court, oral argument on a motion to dismiss is not heard in advance of oral argument on the merits of the appeal. If the court does direct oral argument on a motion to dismiss, it is limited to 15 minutes per side. The court may permit briefs on the motion, which may not exceed 25 pages in the Court of Appeals and ten pages in the Court of Special Appeals. Md. Rule 8-603(e) & (f).

K. Consideration on brief with no oral argument

In the Court of Appeals, there is a presumption against submission on brief, which requires permission of the court, following written request, submitted at least 15 days prior to oral argument. In the Court of Special Appeals, there is no presumption against submission on brief, but the court may require oral argument. In the Court of

Special Appeals, if all three judges assigned to the panel that will hear a particular case determine that they would not be assisted by oral argument, they may direct the case to be submitted on brief. In such case, a party may file a request for oral argument. Md. Rule 8-523(b).

L. Dismissal of appeal

In the Court of Special Appeals, the Appellant may file a notice of dismissal at any time prior to the court filing its opinion. Dismissal of an appeal does not dismiss a cross-appeal. Md. Rule 8-601. On the court's own initiative, or a motion of a party (including affidavits), filed within ten days after (a) the record is not filed; (b) the Brief of Appellant is not filed; or (c) the case becomes moot, the court may dismiss the appeal. Md. Rule 8-602(a). An appeal from a violation of probation is not moot simply because the Defendant served the sentence.

Bases for dismissal of an appeal also include (1) the appeal not allowed by law; (2) the notice of appeal not filed timely, *see Preston v. State*, 57 Md. App. 403, 406, *cert. denied*, 300 Md. 89 (1984); *McCoy v. Warden*, 1 Md. App. 108, 121 (1967); (3) the record inadequate or filed untimely (if the Appellant's fault); and (4) briefs or record extract inadequate or filed untimely. *See Adkins v. State*, 324 Md. 641, 646-47 (1991); *United States v. Juvenile Male*, 131 S. Ct. 2860, 2864 (2011). The Office of the Public Defender lacks standing to bring an appeal on its own on behalf of a Defendant. *Thanos v. State*, 332 Md. 511, 520 (1993).

M. Disposition of the appeal

The appellate court has multiple ways to dispose of an appeal. Md. Rule 8-604; *see Deloso v. State*, 37 Md. App. 101, 107 (1977). Once an appellate court has ruled on an issue presented on appeal, the parties to the case and the lower courts are bound by the ruling under the "law of the case doctrine." *Scott v. State*, 379 Md. 170, 183-84 (2004); *Trimble v. State*, 157 Md. App. 73, 77 (2004). In *State v. Garnett*, 172 Md. App. 558, 562-63 (2007), the Court of Special Appeals held that the "law of the case" doctrine did not preclude the Defendant from challenging an illegal sentence on remand, even though she did not challenge the sentence as illegal on appeal. The law of the case doctrine does not bind the Court of Appeals. In *Loveday v. State*, 296 Md. 226 (1983), the Court of Appeals held:

> [W]e hold that the failure of [the Defendant] to petition for a writ of certiorari to review the first judgment of the Court of Special Appeals does not preclude this court, upon granting a writ from the second judgment of that court, from reviewing the entire record and rendering any judgment and making any order which it deems appropriate in the circumstances.

Id. at 234.

The appellate court's disposition options include (1) dismiss the appeal; (2) affirm all or part of the judgment; (3) vacate or reverse all or part of judgment; (4) modify all or part of the judgment; and/or (5) remand the case to the lower court for further proceedings consistent with court's opinion or order. *See Southern v. State*, 371 Md. 93, 104 (2002); *McMillian v. State*, 325 Md. 272, 296-97 (1992); *Deloso*, 37 Md. App. at 112.

N. Death of the Defendant

If the Defendant dies while his case is on appeal, Md. Rules 8-401 and 2-241 provide for naming a substitute party to continue the appeal. Md. Rule 1-203(d) suspends all time requirements applicable to the deceased party from the date of death to the earlier of 60 days after death or 15 days after the appointment of a substitute party by the court. *See Surland v. State*, 392 Md. 17, 35-36 (2006). If a substitute party elects to pursue the appeal, counsel of record will remain in the case unless the substitute party obtains other counsel.

If no substitute party comes forward, the appeal will be dismissed for lack of prosecution (rather than for mootness), and the conviction and judgment against the deceased Defendant will remain intact. The substitute party and not the defense counsel has the authority to note an appeal on behalf of the deceased Defendant. *Chmurny v. State*, 392 Md. 159, 164 (2006). If Defendant dies after a guilty verdict, but prior to sentencing, there is no conviction and the verdicts and indictment are vacated. *Id.*; *see United States v. Green*, 507 U.S. 545 (1993) (dismissing a petition for a writ of certiorari upon the Defendant's death); *accord Mintzes v. Buchanon*, 471 U.S. 154 (1985); *Warden v. Palermo*, 431 U.S. 911 (1977); *Dove v. United States*, 423 U.S. 325 (1976).

O. Motion for reconsideration

A party may file a motion for reconsideration, not to exceed 15 pages, within 30 days after the court files its opinion. No answer to the motion is permitted, unless requested by the court, and there is no oral argument on a motion for reconsideration.

P. Mandate

The appellate mandate is judgment of the court. Md. Rule 8-606(a) & (b). Upon voluntary dismissal, the court's mandate issues immediately. In cases in which no motion for reconsideration is filed, the mandate issues 30 days after the court's opinion or order. If a motion for reconsideration is filed, the court's mandate may not issue until the court rules on the motion for reconsideration. Md. Rule 8-605.

§ IX. Preservation of issues for appeal

In *Basoff v. State*, 208 Md. 643, 650 (1956), the Court of Appeals held the following:

> When a party has the option either to object or not to object, his failure
> to exercise the option while it is still within the power of the trial court to
> correct the error is regarded as waiver of it estopping him from obtaining a
> review of the point or question on appeal. [This Court] adopted this rule to
> ensure fairness for all parties to cases and to promote the orderly adminis-
> tration of the law.

Id. at 650 (citing *Banks v. State*, 203 Md. 488 (1954)).

A. Issue must be raised in, & decided by, the trial court, or it is not preserved for appeal

The appellate courts usually do not address an issue unless that issue was raised in,
and decided by, the trial court. Without preservation, an issue is waived for appellate
review. Md. Rule 8-131(a); *see, e.g., Robinson v. State*, 410 Md. 91, 103-05 (2009) (failure to preserve denial of public trial was waiver); *Klauenberg v. State*, 355 Md. 528,
544 (1999); *Graham v. State*, 325 Md. 398, 411 (1992) (failure to object was waiver);
White v. State, 324 Md. 626, 640 (1991) (failure to preserve denial of right to compulsory process was waiver); *Morgan v. State*, 299 Md. 480, 483 (1984) (failure to object
to trial not commencing within 180 days was waiver); *Squire v. State*, 280 Md. 132,
134 (1977); *Rose v. State*, 240 Md. 65, 69 (1965) (failure to object to hearsay testimony
was waiver); *Lauder v. State*, 233 Md. 142, 144-45 (1963) (no objection to question,
no motion to strike answer, and no cross-examination was waiver); *Stone v. State*,
178 Md. App. 428, 444-45 (2008) (failure to object to whether cell phone tracking
violated Maryland Wiretap Act was waived); *Ramirez v. State*, 178 Md. App. 257, 274-
76 (2008), *cert. denied*, 410 Md. 561 (2009); *Cantine v. State*, 160 Md. App. 391, 407
(2004), *cert. denied*, 386 Md. 181 (2005) (failure to object to prosecutor in jury room to
teach jurors how to use playback equipment was waiver); *Lee v. State*, 193 Md. App.
45, 65-66 (2010) (failure to object to medical examiner's opinion as to whether victim
was under influence of PCP was waiver); *Schlossman v. State*, 105 Md. App. 277, 298
(1995) (failure to move for testimony to be stricken was waiver); *York v. State*, 56 Md.
App. 222, 232-33 (1983), *cert. denied*, 299 Md. 137 (1984) (proffer as to what witness
would have testified to had he not invoked his privilege against compelled self-incrimination insufficient to preserve issue); *Jorgensen v. State*, 80 Md. App. 595, 601 (1989)
(no proffer necessary to preserve issue when questions objected to clearly indicate
thrust of argument); *Jackson-El v. State*, 45 Md. App. 678, 680 (1980) (failure to raise
Sixth Amendment speedy trial issue was waiver); *Mitchell v. State*, 51 Md. App. 347,
357-58, *cert. denied*, 293 Md. 617, *cert. denied*, 459 U.S. 915, *reh'g denied*, 459 U.S.
1024 (1982); *Walker v. State*, 21 Md. App. 666, 672-73 (1974).

In *Acquah v. State*, 113 Md. App. 29 (1996), the Court of Appeals held that, in order to preserve an issue of the correctness of the trial court's ruling,

> the aggrieved party must (1) raise the issue during trial; (2) make a record with facts set forth in reasonable detail to show the purported bias of the court; (3) factual assertions supporting the claim must be made in the presence of the judge and opposing counsel; (4) the party must not be ambivalent in setting forth his or her position regarding the judge's actions; and (5) the specific relief sought must be stated with particularity.

Id. at 61.

If the argument, at trial, had a different basis than the argument on appeal, the issue is not preserved. *DeLeon v. State*, 407 Md. 16, 21 (2008); *State v. Bell*, 334 Md. 178, 188-89 (1994); *State v. Funkhouser*, 140 Md. App. 696, 719-20 (2001). In *Giordenello v. United States*, 357 U.S. 480, 488 (1958), the Supreme Court held that the Government could not inject a new theory into the case on appeal because that would deprive the Defendant of an opportunity to respond.

B. Whether to provide a basis for an objection

If defense counsel objects to evidence, he or she (1) may object, without offering a reason, if the court does not request a reason; (2) may object and offer a reason, even if the court does not request a reason; or (3) may object and must offer a reason, if the court requests a reason.

If the trial court does not request the basis for an objection, there is no need to offer a basis, and all correct bases may be argued on appeal. *Thomas v. State*, 413 Md. 247, 262-63 (2010); *Johnson v. State*, 408 Md. 204, 222-23 (2009).

If trial counsel gratuitously offers a basis for the objection, or if the trial court requests the basis for the objection, and one is given, appellate counsel will be limited to the basis given, and all other grounds are waived. Md. Rule 5-103; *State v. Funkhouser*, 140 Md. App. 696, 717-18 (2001).

In *Sifrit v. State*, 383 Md. 116 (2004), the Court of Appeals rejected the Defendant's argument that he was simply presenting a more detailed version of an argument that he presented to the trial court. The Court held: "To accept this argument . . . we would have to require trial courts to imagine all reasonable offshoots of the argument actually presented to them . . . We decline to place such a substantial burden on the trial court." *Id.* at 136.

In *von Lusch v. State*, 279 Md. 255 (1977), the Court of Appeals held that when the party "objecting to the admission of evidence, although not requested by the court to state his grounds, goes ahead and delineates the specific grounds for his objection, he will be bound by those grounds and will ordinarily be deemed to have waived other grounds not mentioned." *Id.* at 263. In *Anderson v. Litzenberg*, 115 Md. App. 549 (1997), the Court of Special Appeals held:

> [C]ounsel may state with particularity the grounds for an objection, either voluntarily or at the trial judge's request. If counsel provides the trial judge with specific grounds for an objection, the litigant may raise on appeal only those grounds actually presented to the trial judge. All other grounds for the objection . . . are deemed waived.

Id. at 569.

The grounds for the objection, whether offered gratuitously, or offered in response to the court's request, should be made with particularity. Appeal is usually limited to the ground provided at trial, and all other grounds are deemed waived. Md. Rule 4-323(a); *see, e.g., Starr v. State*, 405 Md. 293, 304 (2008); *Colvin-el v. State*, 332 Md. 144, 169 (1993).

If the court does not request the basis for the objection, and if counsel does not offer a basis to support the objection, all applicable grounds are preserved for appeal. *See Anderson v. Litzenberg*, 115 Md. App. 549, 569-70 (1997), *Johnson v. State*, 408 Md. 204, 222-223 (2009) (general objection to the admission of evidence preserved all grounds); *DeLeon v. State*, 407 Md. 16, 24-25 (2008); *Boyd v. State*, 399 Md. 457, 475-476 (2007).

If specific grounds are requested by the trial court, but not provided by counsel, the issue is not preserved for appeal. In *Bazzle v. State*, 426 Md. 541 (2012), the Court of Appeals stated: "[T]he trial court specifically offered to hear grounds for the objection, and said that without grounds, it would overrule. That was sufficient to put defense counsel on notice that the objection would not be preserved, under Rules 5-103(a) and 4-323, unless grounds were provided." *Id.* at 561-62.

In *Hall v. State*, 119 Md. App. 377, 390 (1998), the Court of Special Appeals held that, when a party objects on specific grounds, the party is bound to those grounds and is deemed to have waived other grounds. *Brecker v. State*, 304 Md. 36, 39-40 (1985); *Thomas v. State*, 301 Md. 294, 328 (1984), *cert. denied*, 470 U.S. 1088 (1985).

In *Boyd v. State*, 399 Md. 457, 473 (2007), the Court of Appeals rejected the State's argument that defense counsel's objection was a specific objection, and held that the Defendant's objection was "general," which was sufficient to preserve the issue for appeal on all bases.

In *Banks v. State*, 84 Md. App. 582, 587-88 (1990), the Court of Special Appeals held that, although normally a party is bound by the grounds asserted to support the objection, when that party makes an additional argument, prior to the evidence being shown to the jury, the issue is preserved. The Defendant does not waive an objection to inadmissible testimony by cross-examining the witness, but does waive the objection by offering testimony on the same matter. *See Peisner v. State*, 236

Md. 137, 144 (1964), *cert. denied*, 379 U.S. 1001 (1965); *Mills v. State*, 19 Md. App. 614, 616-17 (1974).

C. Continuing objections

A continuing objection may increase the Defendant's chance of successful appellate preservation. The Defendant may request, and a court may grant, within its discretion, a continuing objection. If a continuing objection is granted, it provides a continuing objection, without the need to re-object and re-raise the issue. However, a continuing objection only provides a continuing objection to questions clearly within its scope. Md. Rules 2-517 & 4-323. In *Johnson v. State*, 408 Md. 204, 222-23 (2009), the Defendant requested, and the trial court granted, a continuing objection to a K-9 officer's testimony related to the "currency contamination theory," which was preserved for appeal.

In *Wilson v. State*, 195 Md. App. 647, 693 (2010), a jury instruction was not requested, and the failure to give that instruction was not preserved for appeal. In *Brown v. State*, 90 Md. App. 220, 223-24, *cert. denied*, 326 Md. 661 (1992), defense counsel timely objected. However, later, the Defendant failed to object when the same evidence was again introduced, and he had not sought or obtained a continuing objection. The issue was not preserved for appeal. *Accord Ellerba v. State*, 41 Md. App. 712, 725 (1979).

If a continuing objection is granted, followed by a break in testimony, the objection must be renewed, or the appellate court may be unable to determine whether the trial court considered the continuing objection as remaining in effect. In *Sutton v. State*, 25 Md. App. 309 (1975), the Court of Appeals held that the failure to object to particular questions, after requesting and being denied a continuing objection, waives the issue for appellate review. *Id.* at 316.

In *Acquah*, 113 Md. App. at 61-62, the Court of Special Appeals held that, without a continuing objection, objections to specific instances of error do not preserve the issue as to other instances of the same error.

D. Examples of preservation satisfied

In *Braxton v. Faber*, 91 Md. App. 391, 407 (1991), the Court of Special Appeals held:

> We recognize that counsel is in a precarious position when he or she believes that the trial judge, by his actions, has caused harm to his or her client's case. The dilemma is he or she must choose between, on the one hand, remaining mute and not protecting a client's interest or, on the other hand, incurring the wrath of the trial judge in an effort to preserve a record on which the lower court's actions may be reviewed. Nevertheless, it is incumbent upon counsel to state with clarity the specific objection to the conduct of the proceedings and make known the relief sought.

Id. at 407. In *In re Ryan S.*, 369 Md. 26 (2002), the Court of Appeal stated that an objection is generally required to preserve an issue for review. The Court held that

> a party need not, in every circumstance, recite a specific litany to constitute an objection to a trial ruling or course of action . . . as long as the party . . . clearly makes the judge aware of the course of action he or she desires the court to take and the reasons for such course of action, the party shall have adequately preserved that issue for appellate review.

Id. at 34.

There is no need to cite the relevant section and subsection. In *In re Ryan S.*, the Court held that, even though counsel failed to cite the relevant subsection, citing that subsection was not necessary in order to preserve the issue for appeal. *Id.* at 35. Md. Rule 4-323(c) provides: "[I]t is sufficient that a party, at the time the ruling or order is made or sought, makes known to the court the action that the party desires the court to take or the objection to the action of the court."

1. Preservation of jury instruction issues

When the Defendant does not want a jury instruction, but the trial court gives an instruction, preservation requires objection to the instruction

To preserve, for appeal, an issue of a jury instruction that the trial court plans to give, but the Defendant does not want, defense counsel (a) should attempt to persuade the trial court not to give the instruction; and (b) must object on the record to the instruction being given immediately after jury instructions are given. Md. Rule 4-325(e). In *State v. Adams*, 406 Md. 240, 286 (2008), the Court of Appeals stated that, even a deficient reasonable doubt instruction can be waived by the failure to object at trial. In *Austin v. State*, 90 Md. App. 254 (1992), the Court of Special Appeals stated:

> The [Defendant] did not object to the instruction. Under the central thrust of Rule 4-325(e), therefore, he may not "assign as error the giving" of that instruction. The point, which would have been a very good one if properly preserved, has *not* been preserved for appellate review.
>
> . . .
>
> Many trial advocates seem to suffer the misapprehension that if the instructional error, even in the absence of an objection, is plain and is material to the rights of the accused, the appellate court is thereby divested of its discretion to consider the contention on its merits.

Id. at 261-62 (internal citations omitted); *see Walker v. State*, 343 Md. 629, 645 (1996) (failure to object to a jury instruction ordinarily constitutes a waiver of any later claim that the instruction was erroneous).

When the Defendant wants a jury instruction, but the trial court refuses to give that instruction, preservation requires evidence to generate the issue, a requested jury instruction, & an objection to the failure to so instruct

If the Defendant wants a jury instruction, the Defendant must (a) produce evidence to generate the issue for which the Defendant wants a jury instruction; (b) request the instruction, with specificity, offering a written instruction, placed on the record, proffering verbatim the desired instruction language, and/or identifying requested instruction by MPJI-Cr number; and (c) object on the record to the failure to give the requested instruction right after the jury instructions are given. Md. Rule 4-325(e); *Bowman v. State*, 337 Md. 65, 67-68 (1994); *Dykes v. State*, 319 Md. 206, 225 (1990); *Johnson v. State*, 310 Md. 681, 689 (1987) (Defendant must object immediately after the instructions are given); *Medley v. State*, 52 Md. App. 225, 229-30 (1982) (objection must be made prior to closing argument). *Bates v. State*, 127 Md. App. 678, 699-700 (1999).

Requesting a jury instruction that is rejected is insufficient to preserve the issue for appeal. The Defendant must object after the instructions are given. *Braboy v. State*, 130 Md. App. 220, 227, *cert. denied*, 358 Md. 609 (2000). However, in *Allen v. State*, 157 Md. App. 177, 183-84 (2004), the Court of Special Appeals held that the Defendant did not waive his right to appeal the trial court's instructions when defense counsel requested additional instructions, after stating that she had no exceptions to the instructions, and requesting the denied instruction twice.

In *Gore v. State*, 309 Md. 203 (1987), the Court of Appeals recognized that an objection may be preserved through "substantial compliance" with Md. Rule 4-325(e). The Court held:

> [When there] is an objection to the instruction; the objection . . . appears on the record; the objection [is] accompanied by a definite statement of the ground for objection unless the ground for the objection is immediately apparent from the record and the circumstances must be such that a renewal of the objection after the court instructs the jury would be futile or useless.

Id. at 209. *Accord Bowman v. State*, 337 Md. 65, 69 (1994) (recognizing the substantial compliance exception but holding it was not applicable in that case).

In *State v. Rich*, 415 Md. 567, 581 (2010), the Court of Appeals held that when a Defendant requests a voluntary manslaughter instruction, that request constitutes a waiver of the right to argue the evidence was insufficient to support a conviction for voluntary manslaughter.

Preserved without objection to jury instruction when the basis for objection was provided during a hearing on a motion in limine

In *Boyd v. State*, 399 Md. 457, 473-78 (2007), the trial court denied the Defendant's motion in limine to exclude prior bad acts evidence or a prior protective order. During trial, defense counsel asked for a continuing objection regarding events surrounding a previous protective order, but failed to state all of the grounds for the objection, but those grounds had been given during the hearing on the motion in limine. On appeal, the State argued that the hearsay issue was not preserved because of counsel's failure to state all the grounds. The Court of Appeals held that a general objection was sufficient.

Preservation by objection to supplemental jury instructions, even without earlier objection

If the jury requests a supplemental jury instruction, and the trial court gives that instruction again, or clarifies the original instruction, and the Defendant objects to that instruction, that preserves the issue for appeal, even if the Defendant failed to object to that instruction when originally given. *Dawkins v. State*, 313 Md. 638, 642 (1988).

2. Preservation of a denial of an MJOA

In a jury trial, preservation of sufficiency of evidence requires (a) an MJOA, made with particularity at the end of the State's case; and (b) an MJOA renewed at end of all the evidence. Md. Rule 4-324; *Ennis v. State*, 306 Md. 579, 585 (1986); *Fowler v. State*, 237 Md. 508, 515 (1965); *Brown v. State*, 182 Md. App. 138, 156-57 (2008); *Pugh v. State*, 103 Md. App. 624, 650 (1995) (MJOA untimely when made after court instructed the jury); *Ford v. State*, 90 Md. App. 673, 680-81 (1992); *Fraidin v. State*, 85 Md. App. 231, 245, *cert. denied*, 322 Md. 614 (1991).

The standard of review for evidentiary sufficiency "is whether any rational trier of fact could have found the essential elements of the crimes beyond a reasonable doubt." *Moye v. State*, 369 Md. 2, 5 (2002) (evidence insufficient to support actual or constructive drug possession); *Whiting v. State*, 160 Md. App. 285, 307 (2004), *aff'd on other grounds*, 389 Md. 334 (2005).

MJOA required at the close of State's case-in-chief, asserted with particularity

In a jury trial, the Defendant must make an MJOA, argued with particularity as to grounds supporting it, at the end of the State's case-in-chief. Md. Rule 4-324(a) & (b); *Polk v. State*, 378 Md. 1, 5 (2003); *Taylor v. State*, 175 Md. App. 153, 160 (2007), *cert. denied*, 401 Md. 174 (2007) (not preserved because MJOA failed to give particularized grounds); *Tarray v. State*, 410 Md. 594, 613-14 (2009).

In *Starr v. State*, 405 Md. 293, 302-03 (2008), the Court of Appeals held that the sufficiency of the evidence argument on appeal is limited to the grounds offered in support of the MJOA. *Berry v. State*, 155 Md. App. 144, 179-80 (2004). The Defendant may argue less than a "full" MJOA. *Brummell v. State*, 112 Md. App. 426, 428-29 (1996).

In *Price v. State*, 111 Md. App. 487, 493 (1996), the Court of Special Appeals held that the Defendant "only claimed that there had been presented no 'evidence of force or threat of force,' rather than that the evidence offered was insufficient. By failing to particularize his objection, he denied the trial court the opportunity to decide the merits of the claim[. C]onsequently, he has technically waived objection to the sufficiency claim."); *Dumornay v. State*, 106 Md. App. 361, 374-75 (1995), *cert. denied*, 341 Md. 172 (1996); *Garrison v. State*, 88 Md. App. 475, 478-79 (1991), *cert. denied*, 325 Md. 249 (1992); *Brooks v. State*, 68 Md. App. 604, 611-12 (1986).

If the court permits the State to re-open its case, following a defense MJOA, a new MJOA must be made at the close of the re-opened case. *Howell v. State*, 56 Md. App. 675, 678 (1983), *cert. denied*, 299 Md. 426, *cert. denied*, 469 U.S. 1039 (1984). A Defendant must argue an MJOA with specificity on all charges sought to be dismissed and all changes sought to be preserved for appeal. *Poe v. State*, 103 Md. App. 136, 142-43 (1995) (MJOA on attempted murder did not preserve sufficiency of the evidence on murder charge).

MJOA must be renewed at close of all the evidence, if the Defendant presents evidence

In a jury trial, if an MJOA is denied, and the Defendant introduces evidence, the MJOA is deemed withdrawn, and the Defendant must renew the MJOA at the close of all the evidence. Md. Rule 4-324(c).

In *Ennis v. State*, 306 Md. 579, 585 (1986), the Court of Appeals held: "[T]he statute and the rule have been construed to preclude appellate courts of this state from entertaining a review of the sufficiency of the evidence, in a criminal case tried before a jury, where the Defendant failed to move for judgment of acquittal at the close of all the evidence." *See Tetso v. State*, 205 Md. App. 334, 386-88 (2012); *Malarkey v. State*, 188 Md. App. 126, 155-56 (2009); *Ruth v. State*, 133 Md. App. 358, 364-65, *cert. denied*, 361 Md. 435 (2000); *Kenney v. State*, 62 Md. App. 555, 568-69 (1985); *Magness v. State*, 2 Md. App. 320, 324 (1967).

The motion must be renewed even when the Defendant called only one witness to answer a few questions. *Mitchell v. State*, 132 Md. App. 312, 361-62 (2000). The motion does not need to be renewed if, after denial of the MJOA, the Defendant rests without offering any evidence. *Simpson v. State*, 77 Md. App. 184, 189 (1988), *aff'd*, 318 Md. 194 (1989). In *Warfield v. State*, 315 Md. 474 (1989), the Court of Appeals explained that, although the MJOA must be renewed, if it is based on the same grounds as the earlier motion, it does not need to include the grounds with particularity if the Defendant incorporated the earlier grounds by reference. The Court stated:

> When a Defendant offers evidence on his own behalf after his motion for acquittal is denied, the motion is withdrawn and not subject to review. But the reasons given for the motion are still within the ambit of the trial; they are not erased. To strike them from the record so as to preclude their consid-

eration with respect to the second motion is against sound reason, common sense, and the legislative intent.

. . .

When a party makes a new motion for judgment at the conclusion of all the evidence and states that the motion is based upon the same reasons given at the time the original motion was made, or when a party "renews" a motion for judgment and thereby implicitly incorporates by reference the reasons previously given, the reasons supporting the motion are before the trial judge. If, for any reason, the judge desires that the reasons be restated, the judge may simply say so, and the moving party must then state the reasons with particularity. . . . Obviously, when the moving party wished to advance new or different reasons at the time the second motion is made, the party may do so, but should be careful to state whether the reasons being advanced are in lieu of or in addition to the reasons previously given.

We caution, however, that it would be far better for the Defendant to place on the record that his reasons are the same as previously stated, and set out such further reasons he may have, but we do not think the intent of the rule is that he must be denied a review of the evidence for failure to do so. There is a sharp distinction to be drawn between cases in which reasons have not been particularized in either motion, and cases in which adequate reasons were given to support the first motion but not expressly set out for the second motion. In short, the withdrawal of a motion by the offering of evidence by the Defendant does not kill it. It may be resurrected by renewing it, and the renewal will usually incorporate the reasons previously given.

Id. at 487-88.

Argument on appeal is limited to MJOA argument

The issue of sufficiency of the evidence is not preserved when the grounds for appeal are different than the grounds argued in the MJOA at trial. *Graham v. State*, 325 Md. 398, 416-17 (1992). In *Reeves v. State*, 192 Md. App. 277, 306 (2010), the Court of Special Appeals held that, on appeal, sufficiency of the evidence is limited to the specific grounds argued at the MJOA. In *Reeves*, defense counsel made an MJOA at the close of the State's case, offering specific arguments challenging various aspects of the charged against appellant. However, the Defendant did not make the argument advanced on appeal. *Accord Anthony v. State*, 117 Md. App. 119, 126, *cert. denied*, 348 Md. 205 (1997).

MJOA not required in a court trial

Md. Rule 8-131(c) provides: "When an action has been tried without a jury, the appellate court will review the case on both the law and the evidence." Thus, there is no requirement to preserve sufficiency of the evidence in a court trial, because the appellate court must, if requested, evaluate sufficiency of the evidence in a court trial. Md. Rule 8-131(c). *See Ennis v. State*, 306 Md. 579, 583-84 (1986); *Nicholson v. State*, 229 Md. 123, 125 (1962); *Stephens v. State*, 198 Md. App. 551, 557 (2011); *Slick v. Reinecker*, 154 Md. App. 312, 348-49 (2003). *In re Antoine M.*, 394 Md. 491, 501 (2006) (no MJOA required in a juvenile adjudication).

3. Preservation by objection to evidence

Objection to hearsay evidence that is raised outside the jury's presence need not be renewed in the jury's presence to preserve the issue for appeal. *Standifur v. State*, 64 Md. App. 570, 579 (1985).

An objection made after a question has been answered does not properly preserve the issue for appeal. Objection must be made before the answer is given unless the grounds for objection arise unexpectedly from the response to an unobjectionable question. Md. Rule 4-323(a) provides: "An objection shall be made at the time the evidence if offered or as soon thereafter as the grounds for objection become apparent. Otherwise, the objection is waived." *See Bruce v. State*, 328 Md. 594, 627-28 (1992), *cert. denied*, 508 U.S. 963 (1993).

In *Fowlkes v. State*, 117 Md. App. 573 (1997), *cert. denied*, 348 Md. 523 (1998), the Court of Special Appeals stated: "Counsel cannot wait to see whether the answer is favorable before deciding whether to object." *Id.* at 587. In *Williams v. State*, 99 Md. App. 711 (1994), the Court of Special Appeals stated: "It is only when an objectionable answer is given unexpectedly in response to an unobjectionable question that the offended party has slightly more leeway. Even in such a circumstance, however, it is required that the offended party move immediately to strike the objectionable answer." *Id.* at 717.

In *Byrd v. State*, 98 Md. App. 627 (1993), the Court of Special Appeals stated: "Surely, [the Defendant's] counsel knew of the basis for the objection as soon as the question was asked. Since there was not objection before the answer was given, it was waived. The issue is not preserved." *Id.* at 631.

In *Everhart v. State*, 274 Md. 459, 482-83 (1975), the trial court denied a motion to suppress. The Court of Appeals held that the Defendant preserved the issue because he adequately conveyed to the court the main thrust of his argument that the search was illegal because the warrant was tainted.

In *Pitt v. State*, 152 Md. App. 442 (2003), *aff'd on other grounds*, 390 Md. 697 (2006), the Court of Special Appeals held that "although counsel did not specifically use the word 'hearsay' in his objection, the substance of his objection is sufficient to preserve the issue for our review." *Id.* at 464.

4. Preservation of denial of a motion in limine

Motion in limine, by itself, is generally insufficient to preserve the issue for appeal

If the trial judge admits evidence that is the subject of a motion in limine, the party which sought to exclude the evidence must object contemporaneously with its introduction at trial. In *Klauenberg*, 355 Md. 528, the Court of Appeals held: "When a motion in limine to exclude evidence is denied, the issue of the admissibility of the evidence that was the subject of the motion is not preserved for appellate review unless a contemporaneous objection is made at the time the evidence is later introduced at trial." *Id.* at 539-40; *see Simons v. State*, 159 Md. App. 562, 568 (2004).

Preservation of denial of motion in limine when trial court renewed its ruling on motion, eliminating need for "re-objection"

In *Watson v. State*, 311 Md. 370, 372 (1988), the Defendant moved in limine to exclude a prior rape conviction as impeachment evidence. The trial court denied the motion. During trial, the State informed the trial court that it planned to impeach the Defendant with his prior conviction. The trial court affirmed its pre-trial ruling, and the State impeached the Defendant. The Court of Appeals held that, because the trial court reiterated its previous ruling, the Defendant was not required to make contemporaneous objection to preserve the issue for appeal.

5. Preservation of denial of mistrial even though made after the jury retired

In *Hill v. State*, 355 Md. 206, 219 (1999), the State made improper remarks regarding the Defendant's race and the danger that he posed. Throughout trial, defense counsel objected to the prosecutor's statements that jurors had a duty to keep the community safe from people like the Defendant. After the jury retired to deliberate, but before its verdict, the Defendant unsuccessfully moved for a mistrial. The Court of Appeals held that the issue was preserved because (a) the motion was not unduly delayed; (b) the timeliness was not raised at trial; and (c) the trial court did not consider timeliness as ground when denying the motion. Moreover, the Court held that there was no prejudice to the court or either party.

6. Preservation of denial of a *Batson* challenge against the use of peremptory strikes

In *Bundy v. State*, 334 Md. 131, 147 (1994), Co-Defendants were tried jointly, and one Defendant timely objected, on *Batson* grounds, when the State made its fifth peremptory challenge, but the trial court overruled the objection. Counsel for other Co-Defendant did not object until just prior to the trial court seating the jury. The Court of Appeals held that both Defendants preserved the issues because, when the trial court overruled the objection, it was ruling as to the number of peremptory challenges the State had used as against both Defendants, despite the fact that the second Co-Defendant did not object until just prior to seating the jury.

7. Preservation of a double jeopardy claim

Preservation of a double jeopardy issue, following the grant of a mistrial, at defense request or sua sponte, requires (a) objection to denial of the motion to dismiss the re-trial on double jeopardy grounds; and (b) denial of that motion; and/or (c) an objection to starting the re-trial. Md. Rule 4-525(a)(1). In *Taylor v. State*, 381 Md. 602, 610, 626-27 (2004), the Defendant did not raise the issue of double jeopardy, but only questioned whether the mistrial may have violated double jeopardy as an "appellate afterthought." *Id.* at 626-27.

8. Miscellaneous preservation issues

In *Dallas v. State*, 413 Md. 569 (2010), the Court of Appeals held that the trial court did not abuse its discretion in declining to rule on the admissibility of the Defendant's prior convictions until after he had testified. Nonetheless, the Court stated: "That said, trial courts should rule on motions in limine as early as practicable, which is often before the Defendant elects whether to testify or remain silent." *Id.* at 584-85 (citations omitted).

In *Clemons v. State*, 392 Md. 339, 362-63 (2006), the Defendant objected to the admissibility of scientific evidence. The trial court did not rule on the objection, but permitted the State to voir dire the witness, which the court qualified as an expert. The Court of Appeals held that defense objection to evidence was preserved, stating that, when the trial court ruled that the witness was an expert, the court implicitly ruled on the outstanding objection, which Defendant had not withdrawn.

In *Hood v. State*, 334 Md. 52, 56 (1994), during trial, the presiding judge was admitted to the hospital. When confronted with the fact that the original judge would be replaced with a substitute judge, the Defendant moved for a mistrial, which was denied. The Court of Appeals held that the general objection was sufficient to preserve the issue because the objection demonstrated non-consent to a mid-trial substitution of the judge: "While not a model of clarity, the Defendant's objection [was] sufficient to preserve this issue for review." *Id.*

A motion for mistrial based on an improper prosecutorial remark should be made before the jury retires. *Grier v. State*, 351 Md. 241, 261-62 (1998). However, in *Hill v. State*, 355 Md. 206, 219 (1999), the Court of Appeals held that the Defendant did not waive his claim that improper prosecutorial remarks should have resulted in a mistrial when defense counsel failed to move for a mistrial before the jury retired, but did so afterward.

E. Examples of preservation not required

1. No preservation required if the court denies a motion in limine & instructs counsel not to argue the issue at trial

If the trial judge rules on a motion in limine to exclude evidence, and instructs the party seeking to introduce the evidence not to proffer it during trial, the issue is preserved without further action. *Prout v. State*, 311 Md. 348, 356 (1988). In *Berry v. State*, 155 Md. App. 144, 169, *cert. denied*, 381 Md. 674 (2004), the Court of Special Appeals stated:

> *Prout* teaches that, absent both a clear statement by the court when ruling on a motion in limine that the evidence will be excluded, *and* an objection at that time by the proponent of the excluded evidence, the proponent has waived the right to complain on appeal about the in limine ruling unless, following that ruling, the proponent makes some effort to introduce the evidence.

Id. at 169; *see Maslin v. State*, 124 Md. App. 535, 540-41 (1999) (issue preserved when judge instructed the Defendant not to proffer the excluded evidence at trial); *Reed v. State*, 353 Md. 628, 643 (1999). To preserve issues contained in a motion in limine for appeal, counsel should provide a precise argument. *Reynolds v. State*, 327 Md. 494, 502-03 (1992); see *Williams v. State*, 110 Md. App. 1, 33 (1996); *Jordan v. State*, 323 Md. 151, 156 (1991).

2. No preservation required for an issue of subject matter jurisdiction &/or failure to charge an offense

The Defendant may raise, at any time, the issue of whether the trial court has or had subject matter jurisdiction, whether or not raised in, and decided by, the trial court. Md. Rule 4-252(d) provides: "A motion asserting failure of the charging document to show jurisdiction in the court or to charge an offense may be raised at any time." *See Cordovi v. State*, 63 Md. App. 455, 468 (1985) (charging document so defective it deprived court of jurisdiction); *Campbell v. State*, 86 Md. App. 158, 161 (1991); *Williams v. State*, 302 Md. 787, 792 (1985).

In *Pfeiffer v. State*, 44 Md. App. 49 (1979), the Court of Special Appeals stated: "Inasmuch as the failure to allege a crime is jurisdictional, the question may be raised at any time even though it was neither raised below nor in the appellant's brief." *Id.* at 58-59.

3. No preservation required for an illegal sentence

An illegal sentence may be challenged at any time, even if not preserved at trial. Md. Rule 4-345(a); *Moosavi v. State*, 355 Md. 651, 662-63 (1999); *Bowman v. State*, 314 Md. 725, 738 (1989); *Walczak v. State*, 302 Md. 422, 427 (1985); *Sutton v. State*, 128 Md. App. 308, 328 (1999); *Savoy v. State*, 67 Md. App. 590, 592 (1986). In *Jordan v. State*,

323 Md. 151, 161 (1991), the Defendant was sentenced separately for two conspiracies when State proved only one conspiracy. Recognizing plain error, the Court of Appeals vacated one conspiracy.

4. No preservation required if the Defendant has a reasonable basis for not objecting

In *Suggs v. State*, 87 Md. App. 250, 259 (1991), the Court of Special Appeals held that there was no need for defense counsel to object believing that objecting would harm the Defendant's case. In *Suggs*, the trial court prohibited defense counsel from continuing to question a witness and threatened to hold him in contempt if he attempted to continue questioning the witness and/or objected.

5. No preservation required when the record makes clear there was ineffective assistance of counsel in failing to make an MJOA

In *Testerman v. State*, 170 Md. App. 324, 341-42 (2006), the Court of Special Appeals recognized plain error when the Defendant made an MJOA on sufficiency of the evidence grounds, but failed to argue the MJOA with particularity. The Court held that the Defendant was denied effective assistance of counsel because, had trial counsel properly made the MJOA, it would have been granted. In *Covington v. State*, 282 Md. 540, 541 (1978), the Court of Appeals held that failure to object to being denied the opportunity to argue sufficiency of the evidence is reviewable on post conviction.

6. No preservation required for a violation of probation conviction based on an uncharged violation

In *Baldwin v. State*, 324 Md. 676, 684 (1991), the Court of Appeals, citing Md. Rule 8-131(a), held that the Defendant did not waive his right to review of his challenge of his revocation of probation on an uncharged count when it appeared from the record that the Defendant had minimal opportunity to object at the hearing.

F. Examples of issues not preserved for appeal

1. Preservation of denial of documentary or physical evidence requires objection & proffer or introduction of evidence for identification purposes

Preservation of the denial of admission of documentary or physical evidence requires introduction of that evidence for identification purposes, and, if necessary, a proffer of the relevance of the evidence and the non-harmless nature of exclusion. Md. Rule 5-103. However, if the trial judge clearly decides not to admit the evidence and instructs the party seeking to introduce of the evidence not to proffer it at trial, the issue is preserved with no further action. *Prout v. State*, 311 Md. 348, 356-57 (1988).

2. Preservation of improper closing argument requires objection & may require a requested curative instruction &/or a motion for mistrial

Preservation of prejudicial improper closing argument requires objection and may require a request for a curative instruction and/or a motion for mistrial. *Grandison v. State*, 341 Md. 175, 224 (1995). In *Hairston v. State*, 68 Md. App. 230 (1986), the Court of Special Appeals held: "[N]othing further is needed to preserve the issue for appellate review where an objection to counsel's argument is overruled. Only where an objection is sustained need specific relief be requested to preserve the issue for review." *Id.* at 237. *See Conner v. State*, 34 Md. App. 124, 135 (1976); *White v. State*, 23 Md. App. 151, 166-67 (1975).

3. In Circuit Court, the following matters must be raised by motion in conformity with Md. Rule 4-252 &, if not, are generally waived for appeal

In Circuit Court, Md. Rule 4-252 requires that the Defendant raise certain issues, by way of a pre-trial motion, which must be filed (a) within 30 days after the first appearance of the Defendant in Circuit Court or first appearance of defense counsel in Circuit Court; (b) within five days after the State provides discovery, if later; or (c) when permitted by the court, if later. Although the timing deadline is not jurisdictional, if the defense fails to comply timely, no 4-252 issue may be litigated at trial, and no such issue is preserved for appeal.

Defect in the institution of the prosecution

Under Md. Rule 4-252(a)(1), there is a rebuttable presumption that venue is proper, and the Defendant must generate the issue of improper venue in order to litigate the issue at trial and preserve the issue for appeal. *Smith v. State*, 116 Md. App. 43, 53-54, *cert. denied*, 347 Md. 254 (1997). Preservation of a venue issue requires a motion to dismiss or a motion to transfer for lack of proper venue and a denial of that motion and/or objection to commencement of the trial in that venue. *See Vernon v. State*, 12 Md. App. 157, 161 (1971); *Presley v. State*, 6 Md. App. 419, 428 (1969).

Defect in the charging document other than lack of subject matter jurisdiction or the failure to charge an offense

Under Md. Rule 4-252(a)(2), the Defendant bears the burden of timely raising most defects in the charging document through a pre-trial motion. *Spector v. State*, 289 Md. 407, 417 (1981). However, if the defect is the failure to charge a crime or a lack of subject matter jurisdiction, those defects may be raised at any time, including for the first time on appeal. *Accord Gardner v. Board of County Commissioners*, 320 Md. 63, 71 (1990).

Unlawful search & seizure

Under Md. Rule 4-252(a)(3), the Defendant bears the burden of timely raising an issue of illegal search and seizure issue, illegal interception of wire or oral communication through a pre-trial suppression motion. Failure to file a pre-trial suppression motion fails to raise the illegal search and seizure issue, and precludes litigating the issue at trial and fails to preserve the issue for appeal. As to interception of wire or oral communication, in *Perry v. State*, 357 Md. 37, 75 (1999), the Court of Appeals noted, but did not resolve, the apparent conflict between Md. Rule 4-252(a)(3), requiring a pre-trial motion, and Md. Code Ann., Cts. & Jud. Proc. § 10-408, permitting an objection at trial without a pre-trial filing.

Unlawfully obtained admission, statement, or confession

Under Md. Rule 4-252(a)(4), the Defendant bears the burden of timely raising an issue of illegally obtained admissions, statements, or confessions. Failure to file a pre-trial suppression motion fails to raise the illegal statement issue, and precludes litigating the issue at trial and fails to preserve the issue for appeal.

Unlawfully obtained eyewitness identification

Under Md. Rule 4-252(a)(3), the Defendant bears the burden of timely raising issue of unlawfully obtained eyewitness identifications. Failure to file a pre-trial suppression motion fails to raise the illegally obtained identification, and precludes litigating the issue at trial and fails to preserve the issue for appeal.

Request for separate trials by severing the trials of offenders or offenses

Under Md. Rule 4-252(a)(5), the Defendant bears the burden of timely raising the issue of separate trials through the severance of multiple offenders and/or multiple offenses. Failure to timely file a severance motion precludes severance and fails to preserve the issue for appeal. *See Carter v. State*, 374 Md. 693, 709 (2003). Preservation of prejudicial joinder requires a motion to sever based on improper joinder and/or an objection to the commencement of the non-severed trial. *Davenport v. State* 7 Md. App. 89, 98 (1969).

Need to generate issue by evidence to counter rebuttably presumed elements of the offense & affirmative defense not included within Md. Rule 4-252

For (a) elements rebuttably presumed to exist; and (b) affirmative defenses, which are all rebuttably presumed not to exist, the Defendant is only entitled to a jury instruction if the Defendant produces evidence to generate the issue and rebut the presumption. In *Outmezguine v. State*, 335 Md. 20, 51-52 (1994), the Court of Appeals held that, in a child pornography case, the Defendant failed to produce any evidence to generate the issue of whether knowledge of the age of the minor is an element in possession of child pornography.

Mental state element of malice for offenses of murder & attempted murder

In a case of murder or attempted murder, if there is direct or circumstantial evidence of the Defendant's intent to kill or intent to do serious bodily harm, then justifiers and excusers, e.g., perfect self-defense, and mitigators, e.g., imperfect self-defense, are rebuttably presumed not to exist. Unless the Defendant generates the issue of justification, excuse, or mitigation, (a) the rebuttable presumption becomes a conclusive presumption; (b) the Defendant is not entitled to a jury instruction on a perfect or imperfect necessity-based defense; and (c) the issue is not preserved for appeal. *Cunningham v. State*, 58 Md. App. 249, 255-56 (1984); *Evans*, 28 Md. App. at 702-03.

Mental state element of lack of permission or authorization for the offense of fourth degree burglary of the breaking & entering variety

In a case of fourth degree burglary of the breaking and entering variety, if there is direct or circumstantial evidence of the Defendant's breaking and entering the victim's dwelling or storehouse, the mental state of lack of permission and lack of authorization is rebuttably presumed to exist. Unless the Defendant generates the issue of permission or authorization to enter, (a) the rebuttable presumption no permission or authorization become a conclusive presumption; (b) the Defendant is not entitled to a jury instruction on permission or authorization to enter; and (c) the issue is not preserved for appeal. *Herd v. State*, 125 Md. App. 77, 93 (1999).

Lack of alibi

If there is direct or circumstantial evidence of the Defendant's criminal agency, lack of alibi is rebuttably presumed. Unless the Defendant generates an alibi issue, (a) the rebuttable presumption of lack of alibi becomes a conclusive presumption; (b) the Defendant is not entitled to a jury instruction on alibi; and (c) the issue is not preserved for appeal. *See State v. Grady*, 276 Md. 178, 181-82 (1975); *Jackson v. State*, 22 Md. App. 257, 262-63 (1974); *Robinson v. State*, 20 Md. App. 450, 463 (1974).

Voluntariness of criminal act

If there is direct or circumstantial evidence of the Defendant's actus reus, the voluntariness of the act is rebuttably presumed. Unless the Defendant generates the issue of the voluntariness of the actus reus, (a) the rebuttable presumption of the voluntariness of the actus reus becomes a conclusive presumption; (b) the Defendant is not entitled to a jury instruction on the voluntariness of the act; and (c) the issue is not preserved for appeal.

Lack of affirmative defenses

If there is direct or circumstantial evidence of the Defendant's criminal agency and actus reus, all affirmative defenses are rebuttably presumed not to exist. Unless the Defendant generates an issue of an affirmative defense, e.g., voluntary intoxication, entrapment, a necessity-based defense for a crime other than murder or attempted murder, (a) the rebuttable presumption of no affirmative defenses becomes a conclusive presumption; (b) the Defendant is not entitled to a jury instruction on any affirmative defense; and (c) the issue is not preserved for appeal. *Mackall v. State*, 283 Md. 100 (1978).

Sanity/NCR

If there is direct or circumstantial evidence of the Defendant's criminal agency and actus reus, the Defendant's sanity and lack of NCR is rebuttably presumed. Unless the Defendant pleads the issue of NCR and generates evidence of NCR, (a) the rebuttable presumption of no NCR and the rebuttable presumption of the Defendant's sanity at the time of the actus reus become a conclusive presumption; (b) the Defendant is not entitled to a jury instruction on NCR; and (c) the issue of NCR is not preserved for appeal. Md. Code Ann., Health-Gen. § 12-109(b); *Hyde v. State*, 228 Md. 209, 214 (1962).

Statute of limitations

Unless the Defendant generates an issue of statute of limitations, (a) the Defendant is not entitled to a jury instruction on statute of limitations; and (b) the issue is not preserved for appeal. Counsel's statement that "statute of limitations or something like that might come into play" was not particular enough to preserve a statute of limitations issue for appeal. *Harmony v. State*, 88 Md. App. 306, 316 (1991).

Speedy trial

Unless the Defendant files a motion to dismiss for lack of speedy trial and/or makes an objection to the commencement of the trial, the issue is not preserved for appeal. *See Klauenberg v. State*, 355 Md. at 556-57; *Kirby v. State*, 222 Md. 421, 424-25 (1960).

Pre-trial motion in limine generally not preserved unless the Defendant objects at trial

In *Eiler v. State*, 63 Md. App. 439 (1985), the Court of Special Appeals stated: "A motion in limine is not a ruling on the evidence. It is a 'procedural step prior to the offer of evidence,' which serves the purpose of pointing out, before trial, certain evidentiary rulings that the court may be called upon to make," thus, the motion, by itself, is not enough to preserve the issue." *Id* at 445. In *Franklin v. State*, 60 Md. App. 277, 286-87 (1984), the Court of Special Appeals held that the pre-trial motion in limine, by itself, was not enough to preserve the issue for review. See *Lapelosa v. Cruze*, 44 Md. App. 202, 207 (1979).

Preservation of whether expert testimony meets the *Frye/Reed* standards requires a request for a *Frye/Reed* hearing

Preservation of the issue of whether expert testimony meets the *Frye/Reed* standards requires defense counsel to request a *Frye/Reed* hearing. *Addison v. State*, 188 Md. App. 165, 180-81 (2009), *cert. denied*, 412 Md. 255 (2010).

Objection to amount of restitution does not preserve ability to pay issue

In *Brecker v. State*, 304 Md. 36, 40 (1985), the Court of Appeals held when trial counsel objected to the amount of restitution, that did not preserve the issue of the trial court's failure to inquire regarding the ability to pay.

Preservation of a constitutional challenge to a statute, as applied, requires an objection at trial

Preservation of an issue of the unconstitutionality of a statute requires an objection at trial. *Robinson v. State*, 404 Md. 208, 210 (2008); *Passamichali v. State*, 81 Md. App. 731, 737 (1990); *Hall v. State*, 22 Md. App. 240, 245-46 (1974).

Preservation of denial of an opportunity to cross-examine a witness requires attempt to cross-examine & objection to denial & may require a proffer

Preservation of the denial of the right to cross-examine a witness (a) requires an attempt to cross-examine the witness; (b) requires an objection to the denial of the right to cross-examine the witness; and (c) may require a proffer of what would be obtained through cross-examination. *von Lusch*, 279 Md. at 263.

Preservation of legally inconsistent verdicts

If a jury renders legally inconsistent verdicts, that inconsistency must be preserved for appeal prior to the verdict becoming final through polling or hearkening and prior to the jury being discharged. If the issue is not preserved, the claim is waived. The Defendant's silence is acceptance to a legally inconsistent verdict. Upon timely objection to legally inconsistent verdicts, the trial court should instruct or re-instruct the jury on the need for consistency and the permissible verdicts, and the jury should resume deliberations. Preservation of legally inconsistent verdicts requires an objection or request for the jury to be sent back to resolve the inconsistencies. *Price v. State*, 405 Md. 10 (2008); *see Tate v. State*, 182 Md. App. 114, 136-37 (2008); *Acquah v. State*, 113 Md. App. 29, 42-43 (1996) (legally inconsistent verdicts must be raised at trial).

"Un-preserving" preserved issue by subsequent conduct

Even though counsel objected to admission of the Defendant's confession, the issue was subsequently waived when counsel made statements that the confession was voluntary. *Stevens v. State*, 232 Md. 33, 37-38 (1963); *Kidd v. State*, 33 Md. App. 445, 456 (1976); *Hall v. State*, 6 Md. App. 356, 361 (1969). *See Brown v. State*, 373 Md. 234, 241 (2003) (Defendant waived right to appeal ruling that his conviction was admissible for impeachment purposes, when the Defendant introduced the prior conviction when testifying on direct).

Both Co-Defendants must preserve an issue

If one Defendant objects, and preserve an issue for appeal, that does not preserve the issue of a Co-Defendant, unless that Defendant also preserves the issue for appeal. *See Holt v. State*, 129 Md. App. 194, 210 (1999).

Preserve not just the issue but the remedy

If the Defendant objects, and the court sustains the objection, that precludes the evidence objected to from being admitted, but it does nothing else. Thus, if the Defendant needs additional relief, e.g., a curative instruction, the striking of evidence already admitted, a mistrial, the Defendant must explicitly and timely request such relief, or it is waived. *Lamb v. State*, 141 Md. App. 610, 644 (2001).

Failure to raise an issue in a brief or petition for a writ of certiorari

If an argument is not raised in a brief, a reviewing court will generally decline to address it. Md. Rule 8-504(a)(5). However, if an appellate court elects to address an unpreserved issue, and rules in favor of the Defendant, the Defendant receives the benefit of that ruling even though he failed to preserve the issue. *Moosavi v. State*, 355 Md. 651, 661 (1999); *DiPino v. Davis*, 354 Md. 18, 55 (1999).

In *McCray v. State*, 305 Md. 126, 136-37 (1985), the Court of Appeals noted that it will not normally decide an issue that is not presented in the petition for a writ of certiorari or in a cross-petition. In *Robeson v. State*, 285 Md. 498 (1979), *cert. denied*, 444 U.S. 1021 (1980), the Court of Appeals stated that when a party fails to raise an issue at trial, on brief in the Court of Special Appeals, or in a petition for a writ of certiorari, it is not preserved for appeal. Nonetheless, the Court stated:

> [When] the record in [the] case adequately demonstrates that the decision of the trial court was correct, although on a ground not relied upon by the trial court . . . an appellate court will affirm. In other words, a trial court's decision may be correct although for a different reason than relied upon by the court.

Id. at 502.

In *County Council of Prince George's County v. Ofen*, 334 Md. 499 (1994), the Court of Appeals stated:

> [A]n appellate court might raise an issue sua sponte in a situation in which a lower court decided a case correctly but reached such a result through faulty

analysis. . . . It must be kept in mind, however, that these examples represent exceptions to the general rule that an appellate court will not address matters that were not raised and decided in the trial court; as such, they are not to be applied haphazardly.

Id. at 509.

§ X. Interlocutory appeals

A. The three-part test for the collateral order doctrine

In a limited number of situations, even through the criminal case has not yet resulted in a final judgment, the Defendant may be permitted to take an interlocutory under the collateral order doctrine. The three-factor test includes (1) the matter to be reviewed must have been finally disposed of by the trial court; (2) the matter must be separate from merits of the case; and (3) there must be a risk of important loss if the limited review is not presently available. In *United States v. Yellow Freight System, Inc.*, 637 F.2d 1248, 1251 (9th Cir. 1980), the Ninth Circuit held:

> As applied to criminal pretrial orders, [the collateral order doctrine applies when], 1. The pretrial order fully disposed of appellant's claim; 2. The appellant's claim is collateral to, and separable from, the principal issue of guilt or innocence; and 3. The order involves an important right that would be lost if review had to await final judgment.

Id. at 1250-51.

B. Supreme Court cases

The Supreme Court has applied the collateral order doctrine in very limited circumstances. In *Cohen v. Beneficial Industrial Loan Corp.*, 337 U.S. 541 (1949), the Supreme Court held the "order [is] appealable because it is a final disposition of a claimed right which is not an ingredient of the cause of action and does not require consideration with it." *Id.* at 546-47.

In *Coopers & Lybrand v. Livesay*, 437 U.S. 463 (1978), the Supreme Court held: "To come within the 'small class' of decisions excepted from the final-judgment rule by *Cohen*, the order must conclusively determine the disputed question, resolve an important issue completely separate from the merits of the action, and be effectively unreviewable on appeal from final judgment." *Id.* at 469. *Compare Sell v. United States*, 539 U.S. 166, 176-77 (2003) (order to forcibly medicate the Defendant to make him competent to stand trial was immediately appealable); *Abney v. United States*, 431 U.S. 651, 659 (1977) (denial of a pre-trial motion to dismiss based on double jeopardy was immediately appealable); *Stack v. Boyle*, 342 U.S. 1 (1951) (order setting unreasonable bail was immediately appealable), *with Midland Asphalt Corp. v. United States*, 489 U.S. 794, 799-802 (1989) (the denial of a motion to dismiss an indictment based on the Government's violation of the federal rules was not immediately appealable); *Flanagan v. United States*, 465 U.S. 259, 260 (1984) (pre-trial disqualification of defense counsel on conflict grounds was not immediately appealable); *United States v. Hollywood Motor Car Co.*, 458 U.S. 263, 269-70 (1982) (order dismissing a vindictive prosecution claim was not immediately appealable); *United States v. MacDonald*, 435 U.S. 850, 861 (1978) (denial of a speedy trial claim was not immediately appealable).

In *Carroll v. United States*, 354 U.S. 394 (1957), the Supreme Court held that, in the criminal context, the collateral order doctrine applies in only very limited circumstances. In that case, the Defendant's motion to suppress evidence was granted and the Government appealed. The Supreme Court, granting certiorari only to consider whether that order was appealable, held that the suppression order was not appealable, stating: "If there is a serious need for appeals by the Government from suppression orders, or unfairness to the interests of effective criminal law enforcement . . . , it is the function of the Congress to decide whether to initiate a departure from the historical pattern of restricted appellate jurisdiction in criminal cases." *Id.* at 407.

C. Normally no appeal unless there is a final judgment in the entire case

Normally, there can be no appeal unless there is a final judgment in the entire case. In *Sigma Reproductive Health Center v. State*, 297 Md. 660 (1983), the Court of Appeals stated that requiring a final judgment, in most cases, before appealing is intended "to prevent piecemeal appeals and to prevent the interruptions of ongoing judicial proceedings." 297 Md. at 665.

In *Raimondi v. State*, 8 Md. App. 468 (1970), the Court of Special Appeals stated: "If the [Defendant] in a criminal case could deprive the trial judge of jurisdiction to try and determine his case by taking an appeal from a non-appealable interlocutory order, then he would be vested with the power to 'paralyze the administration of justice in the [courts] by the simple expedient of doing what the law does not allow him to do, i.e., taking an appeal from an order which is not appealable.'" *Id.* at 476 (citations omitted).

1. Not a final judgment & thus not appealable

Body attachment order is not a final judgment

In *Broadway v. State*, 202 Md. App. 464, 481 (2011), the Court of Special Appeals held that a body attachment order is not a final judgment and not appealable.

Speedy trial

A motion to dismiss based on denial of speedy trial is not immediately appealable. *United States v. MacDonald*, 435 U.S. 850, 861 (1978); *Stewart v. State*, 282 Md. 557, 564 (1978).

Transfer under the Interstate Agreement on Detainers

In *Bunting v. State*, 312 Md. 472 (1988), the Court of Appeals held that a ruling on the single transfer rule of the Interstate Agreement on Detainers is not an immediately appealable. The Court stated: "[T]he idea that an issue is not effectively reviewable after the termination of the trial because it involves a 'right' to avoid the trial itself, should be limited to double jeopardy claims and a very few other extraordinary situations." *Id.* at 481-82.

Motions regarding pre-trial discovery orders

Motions regarding pre-trial discovery orders are not immediately appealable. In *Harris v. State*, 420 Md. 300 (2011), the Court of Appeals held that the denial of a protective order attempting to shield the Defendant's medical records was not immediately appealable. The Court stated: "Post-trial, as with any other potential discovery order . . . if he is convicted, he may appeal the issue of the trial judge's exercise of discretion or failure to exercise discretion in denying his motion for a protective order." *Id.* at 330 (citations omitted). In *Sigma Reproductive Health Center*, 297 Md. at 675, the Court of Appeals held that a motion to quash a subpoena duces tecum is not immediately appealable.

Defendant's motion to suppress

The denial of a motion to suppress is not immediately appealable. *See id.* at 667.

Order of removal

An order of removal is not immediately appealable. *Parrot v. State*, 301 Md. 411, 426 (1984).

Evidentiary issues

Evidentiary questions, including constitutional questions, are not immediately appealable. *Waugh v. State*, 38 Md. App. 637, 643 (1978); *Williams v. State*, 17 Md. App. 110 (1973).

Order granting or denying a new trial

The State may not bring an immediate appeal from an order granting a new trial. *Dean v. State*, 302 Md. 493, 499 (1985).

Trial judge's decision to recuse himself

A trial judge's decision to recuse himself is not subject to an immediate appeal. *See Doering v. Fader*, 316 Md. 351, 360 (1989).

Denial of ex parte hearing

The denial of an ex parte hearing is not immediately appealable. *Addison v. State*, 173 Md. App. 138, 157 (2007).

2. Final judgment & thus appealable

Order denying a motion to dismiss

In *Buzbee v. State*, 199 Md. App. 678 (2011), the Court of Special Appeals held that an order denying a motion to dismiss is a final appealable order. The Court stated that, in order to come within the class of orders that are immediately appealable, the order must "be effectively unreviewable on appeal from final judgment." *Id.* at 687. *See Kacour v. State*, 70 Md. App. 625, 628 (1987) (quoting *Mann v. State's Attorney for Montgomery County*, 298 Md. 160 (1983)).

Competency to stand trial

A determination of competency to stand trial is immediately appealable. *Jolley v. State*, 282 Md. 353, 356-57 (1978).

Double jeopardy

A motion to dismiss based on double jeopardy is immediately appealable. *Block v. State*, 286 Md. 266, 267-68 (1979); *Neal v. State*, 272 Md. 323 (1974); *see Evans v. State*, 301 Md. 45, 50 (1984); *Bowling v. State*, 298 Md. 396 (1984); *White v. State*, 109 Md. App. 350, *cert. denied*, 343 Md. 565 (1996); *Lee v. State*, 62 Md. App. 341 (1985); *Mitchell v. State*, 44 Md. App. 451 (1979), *cert. denied*, 287 Md. 749 (1980); *Gray v. State*, 36 Md. App. 708, 714 (1977) (denial of a claim of double jeopardy is immediately appealable but it must be raised on the record prior at the start of trial or waived).

Contempt

A contempt order is immediately appealable. Md. Cts. & Jud. Proc. Code Ann. § 12-304.

Plea agreements

A court's refusal to enforce a term in a plea agreement is reviewable under the collateral order doctrine. *Jackson v. State*, 358 Md. 259, 270-71 (2000); *Courtney v. Harford County*, 98 Md. App. 649, 659 (1994). A ruling on whether the Defendant and the State reached a plea agreement is reviewable under the collateral order doctrine. *Rios v. State*, 186 Md. App. 354, 366 (2009). In *Jackson v. State*, 358 Md. 259, 268 (2000), the Court of Appeals held that the collateral order doctrine permitted review of State's refusal to dismiss an indictment after agreeing it would do so if DNA testing excluded the Defendant.

Denial of motion to dismiss for violation of the Full Faith & Credit Clause

The denial of a motion to dismiss charges under the Full Faith and Credit Clause is immediately appealable. *Gillis v. State*, 333 Md. 69, 71-72 (1993).

D. Trial court jurisdiction

The trial court retains fundamental jurisdiction to hear and decide a case even if an interlocutory appeal has been filed and is pending. In *McNeil v. State*, 112 Md. App. 434, 460-61 (1996), the Court of Special Appeals held that the trial court may continue with trial while the State's appeal is pending, although it may not be advisable. *Accord Pulley v. State*, 287 Md. 406, 418 (1980).

E. Consent is irrelevant

If an issue is not appealable, the parties may not confer jurisdiction on an appellate court by consent. *Sigma Reproductive Health Center*, 297 Md. at 664.

§ XI. Plain error

A. General considerations

1. Plain error is within the appellate court's discretion

Under the "plain error doctrine," appellate courts recognize plain error only in circumstances that are "compelling, extraordinary, exceptional, or fundamental to assure the Defendant a fair trial." Md. Rule 4-325(e); *State v. Hutchinson*, 287 Md. 198, 203 (1980); *Perry v. State*, 150 Md. App. 403, 436 (2002), *cert. denied*, 376 Md. 545 (2003); *Cook v. State*, 118 Md. App. 404, 411-12 (1997), *cert. denied*, 349 Md. 234 (1998).

It is always within an appellate court's discretion to address an issue that was not preserved for appellate review. There is a presumption against the recognition of plain error because, otherwise, the preservation requirement would be rendered meaningless. Defense counsel should zealously protect the record. Both the Court of Special Appeals and the Court of Appeals have discretion to recognize plain error and excuse the failure to preserve an issue. *See Squire*, 280 Md. at 134. An appellate court does not have to explain its reasons for recognizing or declining to recognize plain error. *Harris v. State*, 169 Md. App. 98, 108 (2006).

In *Austin v. State*, 90 Md. App. 254 (1992), the Court of Special Appeals stated that counsel "must never be lulled into the sense of false security that the notice of 'plain error' is routinely available to pull neglected chestnuts out of the fire." *Id.* at 271. *See Burris v. State*, 206 Md. App. 89, 140 (2012).

2. No precedential value in the recognition of plain error

Due to the discretionary nature of the plain error doctrine, it difficult to predict when an appellate court will recognize plain error. In the words of Judge Moylan, "[w]hen all is said and done about an appellate court's discretionary option to indulge in the 'plain error' exemption from the preservation requirement, the only hard and fast rule is that there are no hard and fast rules." *Morris v. State*, 153 Md. App. 480, 524 (2003), *cert. denied*, 380 Md. 618 (2004). In *Jones v. State*, 379 Md. 704 (2004), the Court of Appeals similarly acknowledged that "[t]here is no fixed formula for the determination of when discretion should be exercised, and there is no bright line rule to conclude that discretion has been abused." *Id.* at 713.

Simply because an appellate court recognizes plain error in one case does not mean that the court will recognize plain error in another case, even if identical or substantially similar. In fact, the earlier recognition of plain error may even be a factor against recognizing plain error in the latter scenario. In *Stockton v. State*, 107 Md. App. 395 (1995), the Court of Special Appeals rejected plain error, stating:

> On the appellate shore . . . there is, with each passing year, noticeable erosion of the preservation requirement and the dike is in need of constant repair.
>
> The [Defendant] leans heavily on *Himple v. State*, 101 Md. App. 579 (1994), an occasion on which we opted to notice plain error with respect to an instruction on the subject of reasonable doubt. An exercise of discretion by an appellate court, however, unlike a ruling of law, is unique and unreviewable and is not, therefore, precedent for the next occasion when an exercise of discretion is requested, even on the same subject matter under similar circumstances. Indeed, an earlier discretionary notice of plain error actually argues against its repetition. One of the reasons we sometimes elect to overlook non-preservation has nothing to do with the fortunes of the [Defendant]. We may choose to notice plain error simply to seize the occasion as a vehicle to communicate a desired message to bench and bar that might otherwise go unsent. Once having delivered a message . . . there is self-evidently less urgency to send it again, by way of redundant repetition.

Id. at 396-97 (citations omitted). In *Morris v. State*, 153 Md. App. 480 (2003), the Court of Special Appeals stated:

> [T]he discretionary decision of an appellate panel to notice plain error is totally ad hoc and a decision by one particular panel on one particular occasion to notice plain error is by no means precedentially binding on subsequent panels on subsequent occasions, even when similar subject matter seems to be involved. . . . An exercise of discretion, by its very nature, does not establish a precedent.

Id. at 517-18.

3. When is an appellate court more likely to recognize plain error?

Appellate courts are more likely to recognize plain error if (a) it is a close question as to whether the issue was preserved; (b) it is an issue of first impression; (c) it is an issue that the appellate court has not re-visited in years; (d) the case is being reversed and remanded for other reasons, and the appellate court believes that guidance should be provided to the trial court for remand; (e) the unpreserved issue was very thoroughly briefed by both sides; (f) the Defendant's right to effective assistance of counsel was so egregiously denied that a new trial will likely be granted if the Defendant seeks post conviction relief; (g) the Defendant's right to a fair trial was severely denied; or (h) addressing the issue to promote the orderly administration of justice. Md. Rule 8-131(a); *Robinson v. State*, 410 Md. 91, 111 (2009); *Jones v. State*, 379 Md. 704, 714 (2004); *Conyers v. State*, 354 Md. 132, 151 (1999); *Squire v. State*, 280 Md. 132, 134 (1977); *Stockton v. State*, 107 Md. App. 395, 398 (1995), *cert. denied*, 342 Md. 116 (1996). *Rubin v. State*, 325 Md. 552, 588 (1992); *State v. Hutchinson*, 287 Md. 198, 203 (1980); *Olson v. State*, 208 Md. App. 309, 363 (2012); *Claggett v. State*, 108 Md. App. 32, 40 (1996).

4. Prejudice to the Defendant is a factor

In determining whether a "plain error" was prejudicial, the error must be viewed in the context of the entire record. In *Lawson v. State*, 389 Md. 570 (2005), the Court of Appeals stated:

> Once error is determined during a "plain error" review, prejudice can only be determined by a consideration of the error in the context of the entire case including the cumulative effect of all errors on the ability of the jury to render a fair and impartial verdict in the context of the entire case.

Id. at 604-05. However, in *Sine v. State*, 40 Md. App. 628 (1978), *cert. denied*, 284 Md. 748 (1979), the Court of Special Appeals stated: "The mere fact that the alleged error may have resulted in some prejudice to [the Defendant] does not, in itself, justify the invocation of the plain error rule." *Id.* at 632.

5. Recognizing plain error to give the appellate court an opportunity to clarify the law

In rare cases, plain error may be invoked by appellate courts to provide guidance in an area of the law that is unclear. In *Austin*, 90 Md. App. 254, the Court of Special Appeals stated:

> On rarer occasions, we might even be influenced by the opportunity which the notice of "plain error" might afford to illuminate some murky recess of the law. The interpreting and molding of the law is as weighty as consideration in appellate councils as is the correction of error in individual cases.

Id. at 271; *see Evans v. State*, 28 Md. App. 640, 650-51 (1975), *aff'd*, 278 Md. 197 (1976). In *Morris*, 153 Md. App. 480, the Court of Special Appeals stated:

We explained in *Austin*, that sometimes an appellate court is motivated to take notice of some unpreserved plain error not because of the possible impact of the error on a particular defendant but because of the opportunity to use the contention as a desired vehicle for exploring some hitherto unexplored area of the law.

Id. at 518.

In *United States v. Olano*, 507 U.S. 725, 732-33 (1993), the Supreme Court stated that federal courts should recognize plain error when needed to "illuminate some murky recess of the law." *Id.* at 732-33.

6. Appellate court may decide an unpreserved issue that will necessarily arise on remand

In *Wieland v. State*, 101 Md. App. 1, 34-35 (1994), the Court of Special Appeals addressed an unpreserved jury instruction issue because the issue would inevitably arise on remand. Md. Rule 8-131 provides that the appellate "may decide such an issue if necessary or desirable to guide the trial court or to avoid the expense and delay of another appeal."

7. Plain error when error is egregious &/or extraordinary

An appellate court may recognize plain error if the error in giving the instruction is egregious. In *Williams v. State*, 34 Md. App. 206 (1976), the Court of Special Appeals stated: "Where error is flagrant and outrageous, we retain the residual option to notice it and to intervene. It is the extraordinary error and not the routine error that will cause us to exercise the extraordinary prerogative." *Id.* at 211.

8. Plain error based on law that was decided after trial, but prior to appeal

Interpreting Fed. R. Crim. P. 52(b), which is the federal "plain error" exception to preservation, the Supreme Court, in *Henderson v. United States*, 133 S. Ct. 1121 (2013), held that an error may be plain even though an appellate decision making an error "plain" was not decided until after the trial court made the ruling in question. The Court stated:

> The case before us concerns a District Court's decision on a substantive legal question that was unsettled at the time the trial court acted, thus foreclosing the possibility that any error could have been "plain" *then*. Before the case was final and at the time of direct appellate review, however, the question had become settled in the Defendant's favor, making the trial court's error "plain"—but not until a later time. In our view, as long as the error was plain as of that later time—the time of appellate review—the error is "plain" within the meaning of [Fed. R. Crim. P. 52(b)].

Id. at 1124-25. In *Teves v. State*, 33 Md. App. 195, 197 (1976), the Court of Special Appeals recognized plain error, when trial counsel failed to object. *Mullaney v. Wilbur*, which held that the burden of persuasion was unconstitutionally placed on the Defendant, was decided prior to appeal but after the trial.

9. Plain error in federal court

In *Johnson v. United States*, 520 U.S. 461, 466-67 (1997), the Supreme Court stated that plain error, when recognized by the federal judiciary, requires

> (1) error, (2) that it is plain, and (3) that affects substantial rights. If all three conditions are met, an appellate court may then exercise its discretion to notice a forfeited error, but only if (4) the error seriously affects the fairness, integrity, or public reputation of judicial proceedings.

Id. at 466-67 (internal citations & quotation omitted).

B. Examples of errors that have been deemed to be plain error

1. Plain error in jury instructions

Under Md. Rule 4-325, the Defendant must object to (a) the improper giving; or (b) the improper failure to give a jury instruction, in order to preserve the issue for appeal. In *Parker v. State*, 4 Md. App. 62 (1968), the Court of Special Appeals stated:

> The reason for the rule requiring objection as a prerequisite to appellate review is a salutary one, being designed to afford the trial judge an opportunity to correct inadvertent omissions or inaccuracies in his instructions, where the alleged error is one that might have been readily corrected if it had been called to the trial judge's attention.

Id. at 67 (citations omitted). However, the rule permits the appellate court, in its discretion, to take cognizance of plain error in jury instructions that are material to the rights of the Defendant, despite the failure to object. Md. Rule 4-325(e); *State v. Hutchinson*, 287 Md. 198, 203 (1980); *Squire*, 280 Md. at 134-35.

Even if an error is obvious, appellate consideration of that error is not a matter of right. In *Squire v. State*, 32 Md. App. 307 (1976), *rev'd on other grounds*, 280 Md. 132 (1977), the Court of Special Appeals stated: "[E]ven if an error in jury instructions is plain, its consideration on appeal is not a matter of right; the rule is couched in permissive terms and necessarily leaves its exercise to the discretion of the appellate court." *Id.* at 309.

Courts are highly unlikely to recognize plain error when it appears that defense counsel made a strategic decision to not correct an error by the trial judge in the giving or failing to give jury instructions. *Brown v. State*, 169 Md. App. 442, 459, *cert.*

denied, 395 Md. 56 (2006). In *Parker*, the Court of Special Appeals held that plain error "should not be invoked to cure bad guesses by counsel whether or not to object to the court's instructions, nor was it designed to alleviate consequences unfortunate to the [Defendant] resulting from his counsel's choice of trial tactics." 4 Md. App. at 67; *accord Madison v. State*, 200 Md. 1, 10 (1952).

Jury instructions should be considered as a whole. *Butler v. State*, 335 Md. 238, 261 (1994); *Wills v. State*, 329 Md. 370, 384 (1993); *State v. Daughton*, 321 Md. 206, 212 (1990); no confusion in jury instructions when read as a whole); *Denson v. State*, 331 Md. 324, 330 (1993) (jury instructions should not be read out of context); *see Green v. State*, 127 Md. App. 758, 771 (1999) (jury instructions not misleading).

Jury instruction errors of commission

In *Brown v. State*, 14 Md. App. 415, 422 (1972), the Court of Special Appeals explained that when an error in jury instructions is plain and material to rights of the Defendant, it is more likely to be reviewed on appeal if it is error of commission, rather than merely error of omission.

Jury instruction on reasonable doubt

In *Savoy v. State*, 420 Md. 232, 256 (2011), the Court of Appeals recognized plain error in the reasonable doubt instruction. In *Hutchinson v. State*, 41 Md. App. 569 (1979), the Court of Special Appeals recognized plain error when the trial judge did not instruct the jury that it could find the Defendant not guilty and made erroneous statements as to what was on the verdict sheet. *See State v. Daughton*, 321 Md. 206, 209-10 (1990). Even a constitutionally deficient reasonable doubt instruction requires an objection to preserve the issue for appeal. *State v. Rose*, 345 Md. 238, 250 (1997); *Morris v. State*, 153 Md. App. 480, 520-21 (2003) (refusing to recognize plain error in the giving of a reasonable doubt instruction).

Jury instruction on the mental state of willfully

In *Dziekonski v. State*, 127 Md. App. 191, 201 (1999), the Court of Special Appeals recognized plain error when the trial court failed to instruct the jury that the Defendant must have acted "willfully" to be convicted of disorderly conduct.

Jury instruction on the mental state of transferred intent

In *State v. Brady*, 393 Md. 502, 512-13 (2006), the Court of Appeals recognized plain error when the trial court, responding to a jury question, incorrectly told the jury that law of transferred intent applies to attempted murder cases. The Court held that it was an error of commission that "conveyed some prejudicial or confusing message" that impacted the Defendant's right to a fair and impartial trial, especially because the error occurred in response to a jury inquiry. *Accord Garrett v. State*, 394 Md. 217, 225 (2006).

However, in *Dionas v. State*, 199 Md. App. 483, 537 (2011), the Court of Special Appeals rejected plain error for an error regarding transferred intent and concurrent intent jury instructions, when the Defendant did not attempt to show how the instruction negatively affected the outcome, and the instructions at issue were given for offenses for which the Defendant was acquitted.

Jury instruction on specific intent

In *Richmond v. State*, 330 Md. 223 (1993), *overruled on separate grounds by Christian v. State*, 405 Md. 306 (2008), the Court of Appeals held that the trial court's failure to instruct the jury that the State was required to prove specific intent to disable to establish malicious wounding with an intent to disable was plain error. The Court stated:

> This is not a case . . . in which we must speculate as to the effect of an erroneous instruction; rather, here we can say with reasonable certainty that the error in the instruction resulted in a guilty verdict that otherwise would not have been rendered. That type of error "vitally affects a Defendant's right to a fair trial," and is therefore plain error of which we will take cognizance.

Id. at 236-37.

Jury instruction on the burden of persuasion as to alibi

In *Daniels v. State*, 24 Md. App. 1 (1974), the Court of Special Appeals recognized plain error when the trial court incorrectly instructed the jury that the Defendant had the burden of persuasion as to alibi. *Id.* at 6-7. However, in *Martin v. State*, 165 Md. App. 189, 206 (2005), *cert. denied*, 391 Md. 115 (2006), the Court of Special Appeals held that the trial court's failure to give an alibi instruction was not plain error, noting that the court gave an instruction that the State was required to prove the Defendant's presence at the scene.

Jury instruction on the "*Allen* charge"

In *Taylor v. State*, 17 Md. App. 41 (1973), the Court of Special Appeals recognized plain error. After the jury foreperson informed the trial court that the jury was divided, 11-to-1, the court stated, "it's up to the one to change," and the Court of Special Appeals found that remark "patently coercive" in violation of Defendant's right to fair and impartial jury. The Court stated:

> It is a well known fact that jurors are usually responsive to any suggestion made by the presiding judge regarding their conduct as a member of the panel. When the trial judge, in the course of urging the jury to agree, remarked "(i)t's up to the one to change" without any admonition whatever that the minority juror should vote in accordance with his conscientious beliefs, he clearly exerted undue pressure and coercion upon the minority juror.

Id. at 48.

In *Pinder v. State*, 31 Md. App. 126, 136-37 (1976), and in *Fletcher v. State*, 8 Md. App. 153, 159-60 (1969), the Court of Special Appeals recognized plain error in an *Allen* charge and reversed the Defendants' convictions. In *Pinder*, the trial court impermissibly told the jury: "For many reasons which I would think would be self evident to you, the court could like to avoid a retrial of this case[.]" 31 Md. App. at 134.

Jury instruction on unanimity

In *Danna v. State*, 91 Md. App. 443, 448-51, *cert. denied*, 327 Md. 627 (1992), the Court of Special Appeals held that the trial court's failure to instruct the jury that its verdict must be unanimous was plain error. *See* Md. Rules 4-325(e) & 8-131(a); *Stambaugh v. State*, 30 Md. App. 707, 710, *cert. denied*, 278 Md. 734 (1976); *Vernon*, 12 Md. App. at 162-63.

Jury instruction on the element of "firearm"

In *Walker v. State*, 192 Md. App. 678, 691-93 (2010), the Court of Special Appeals held that the trial judge committed plain error when he told the jury that a "starter pistol" is a firearm. The Defendant was convicted of possession of a regulated firearm by a felon. Had the jury believed the Defendant's testimony regarding the starter pistol, the jury would have acquitted.

Jury instruction on the burden of persuasion in murder cases

In *Stambaugh v. State*, 30 Md. App. 707, 710-1, *cert. denied*, 278 Md. 734 (1976), the Court of Special Appeals recognized plain error, regarding an unconstitutional jury instruction that homicide is presumed to be second degree murder. However, appellate courts will not always recognize plain error in unconstitutional jury instructions. *See Squire*, 32 Md. App. at 309-10.

Jury instruction on the limited use of impeachment testimony

In *McCracken v. State*, 150 Md. App. 330, 345 (2003), the Court of Special Appeals held that it was plain error for the trial court to fail to give a limiting instruction, explaining that the Defendant's impeachment testimony could be used only to measure his credibility as a witness and not to determine whether he is guilt. *But see Hall v. State*, 292 Md. 683, 689-92 (1982) (failure to give such a limiting instruction not plain error).

2. Other plain errors

Plain error for the judge to make improper remarks to the jury

In *Elmer v. State*, 239 Md. 1 (1965), the Court of Appeals held that the trial judge, declaring a witness hostile, in front of the jury, was plain error when the outcome of the trial hinged on the credibility of the witnesses. The Court stated:

As the case developed, its outcome depended almost entirely upon the credibility which the jury would accord the witnesses . . . When the trial judge declared [the witness] hostile to the State, after he had been called by the State and had given testimony favorable to the defense, the judge's remark clearly indicated his disbelief of the witness and unquestionably influenced the jury's appraisal of the credibility of the witness. It was, of course, the function of the jury alone, as the triers of facts, to weigh and determine that factor.

Id. at 10; *see Wolfe v. State*, 218 Md. 449, 455 (1958).

Plain error based on illegal restitution order

In *Chaney v. State*, 397 Md. 460 (2007), the Court of Appeals recognized plain error. The trial court ordered $5,000 in restitution as condition of probation, even though no evidence was admitted to support restitution, and the conviction did not warrant restitution. The Court stated:

In this case, we shall exercise discretion to consider [the defendant's] challenge to the restitution order . . . We shall consider the restitution because (a) it constitutes plain error, and (b) it transcends this case; it is one that may affect hundreds of cases that flow through our criminal and juvenile courts and that implicates Constitutional and statutory rights, and guidance is needed.

Id. at 468.

Plain error based on ineffective assistance of counsel

An appellate court's decision whether to recognize plain error may be influenced by evidence of ineffective assistance of counsel, particularly if counsel continually fails to object when the State succeeds in introducing inadmissible evidence. *Morris v. State*, 153 Md. App. 480, 523-24 (2003), *cert. denied*, 380 Md. 618 (2004). This may also occur when the Defendant's counsel does not know the law. In *Squire*, 280 Md. at 135-36, the Court of Appeals recognized plain error when counsel failed to object to a jury instruction that had been rendered unconstitutional by the Supreme Court four days before trial.

Plain error when the Defendant was wrongfully convicted

An appellate court may recognize plain error if it appears that a Defendant was wrongfully convicted. In *Morris v. State*, 153 Md. App. 480 (2003), the Court of Special Appeals stated:

If in a rare case an appellate court would actually be troubled by the "gut feeling" that substantive, as opposed to merely procedural, miscarriage of justice had occurred, to wit, that a factually innocent person had been erroneously convicted, that court would bend over backwards to find some way to reverse the conviction. That would include a decision to notice plain error.

Id. at 521. In *Perry v. State*, 150 Md. App. 403 (2002), the Court of Special Appeals stated: "[T]here is a moral distinction between an erroneous conviction of one who is almost certainly guilty and an erroneous conviction of one who is quite possibly truly innocent. Such moral, even if extralegal, distinctions do influence the exercise of discretion." *Id.* at 437. In *Jeffries v. State*, 113 Md. App. 322 (1997), the Court of Special Appeals stated: "[O]nly instances of truly outraged innocence call for the act of grace of extending gratuitous process." *Id.* at 326.

In *Austin*, 90 Md. App. at 269-70, the Court of Special Appeals stated: "We would be inhuman if we would not be more moved to intervene in the case of a probably erroneous conviction of a true innocent than in a case where the error only facilitated the conviction of a clear miscreant."

However, in *Martin v. State*, 165 Md. App. 189, 200 (2005), even though was a complete failure to instruct the jury on an offense, the Court of Special Appeals rejected plain error because the evidence of guilt was overwhelming.

Plain error when the judge acts as a co-prosecutor

In *Diggs v. State*, 409 Md. 260, 293-94 (2009), the Court of Appeals reversed the convictions of two Defendants because the judge in both cases acted as a co-prosecutor and departed from a neutral judicial role. The judge laid the foundation for State's evidence, established a chain of custody for State's evidence, cross-examined witnesses, questioned the accuracy of defense witness's testimony, and rehabilitated State's witnesses. The Court held that the trial judge created an atmosphere so flawed, that under a plain error analysis, the convictions had to be reversed.

Plain error when the sentence is based on impermissible considerations

In *Abdul-Maleek*, 426 Md. at 70, the Court of Appeals addressed whether the trial court improperly considered the Defendant's exercise of the right to a *de novo* appeal to the Circuit Court, stating that, by "addressing the issue presented, we are able to comment on the sentencing issue in the context of de novo appeal and thereby promote the orderly administration of justice."

3. Plain error based on the cumulative effect of multiple unpreserved errors

In *Lawson v. State*, 389 Md. 570, 593-94 (2005), the Court of Appeals recognized plain error based on the prejudicial effect of cumulative errors. The Court held that the trial court erred in permitting the State to (a) make numerous inflammatory remarks during closing argument; (b) make remarks not supported by the evidence; (c) make a "golden rule" argument; (d) vouch for witnesses; and (e) argue that a conviction would prevent future harm to children.

C. Examples of errors that are not plain error

1. No plain error solely because error is of constitutional dimension

An unpreserved error of constitutional dimension does not automatically invoke the plain error analysis. *See, e.g.*, *Robinson v. State*, 410 Md. 91, 106 (2009) (Sixth Amendment requires the right to a public trial); *Taylor v. State*, 381 Md. 602, 614 (2004); *Walker v. State*, 338 Md. 253, 263 (1995) (Due Process Clause & Sixth Amendment claims).

2. No plain error when jury instruction error is merely one of omission & not commission

In *Tull v. State*, 230 Md. 152, 156 (1962), the Court of Appeals rejected plain error when the trial court failed to instruct on self-defense. In *Carter v. State*, 15 Md. App. 242, 248-49, *cert. denied*, 266 Md. 734 (1972), the Court of Special Appeals held that there was no plain error in failing to instruct on less serious of the two crimes for which the Defendant was on trial.

In *Wilson v. State*, 44 Md. App. 318, 324 (1979), the Court of Special Appeals rejected plain error when the court gave a "beyond a reasonable doubt" instruction prior to the trial, but failed to repeat that instruction at the close of the trial. *See Lewis v. State*, 2 Md. App. 678, 686-87, *cert. denied*, 250 Md. 732 (1968) (no plain error in refusing requested jury instructions); *Bates v. State*, 127 Md. App. 678, 679 (1999) (failure to instruct on attempt not plain error); *Mazer v. State*, 231 Md. 40, 47 (1963); *Jones v. State*, 229 Md. 472, 474 (1962); *Harris v. State*, 169 Md. App. 98, 108 (2006); *West v. State*, 124 Md. App. 147, 159-160 (1998); *Hall v. State*, 57 Md. App. 1, 4 (1983); *Erman v. State*, 49 Md. App. 605, 631 (1981); *Lang v. State*, 6 Md. App. 128, 133 (1969); *White v. State*, 3 Md. App. 167, 171 (1968); *Law v. State*, 21 Md. App. 13, 32 (1974); *but see Danna*, 91 Md. App. at 452-53 (failure to instruct that jury must reach a unanimous verdict was plain error).

In *State v. Daughton*, 321 Md. 206, 213-14 (1990), the Court of Appeals held that jury instructions not expressly explaining the verdict in terms of "guilty" and "not guilty" was not plain error. In *Morris v. State*, 153 Md. App. 480 (2003), *cert. denied*, 380 Md. 618 (2004), the Court of Special Appeals held that the judge's "slip of the tongue" when describing the State's burden of persuasion was not plain error.

§ XII. Harmless error

If the trial court committed reversible error, and the Defendant preserved the issue for appeal, the court will reverse the conviction, unless the appellate court finds, beyond reasonable doubt, that the error in no way contributed to the verdict. Thus, the appellate court does not reverse the judgment below if the error was "harmless." *Chapman v. California*, 386 U.S. 18, 24 (1967); *State v. Logan*, 394 Md. 378, 387-88 (2006). In *Ross v. State*, 276 Md. 664 (1976), the Court of Appeals stated:

> The essence of this test is the determination whether the cumulative effect of the properly admitted evidence so outweighs the prejudicial nature of the evidence erroneously admitted that there is no reasonable possibility that the decision of the finder of fact would have been different had the tainted evidence been excluded.

Id. at 674. In *Dorsey v. State*, 276 Md. 638 (1976), the Court of Appeals held:

> When [the Defendant], in a criminal case, establishes error, unless a reviewing court, upon its own independent review of the record, is able to declare a belief, beyond a reasonable doubt, that the error in no way influenced the verdict, such error cannot be deemed "harmless" and thus reversal is mandated. Such review court must thus be satisfied that there is no reasonable possibility that the evidence complained of—whether erroneously admitted or excluded—may have contributed to the rendition of the guilty verdict.

Id. at 659. *See Joyner v. State*, 208 Md. App. 500, 522-23 (2012); *Davis v. State*, 207 Md. App. 298, 317 (2012); *Ray v. State*, 206 Md. App. 309, 355 (2012); *Samba v. State*, 206 Md. App. 508, 534-35 (2012); *Henry v. State*, 204 Md. App. 509, 542-43 (2012). If the Defendant establishes that there has been legal error, the burden is on the State to show that the error was harmless beyond a reasonable doubt. *Morris v. State*, 418 Md. 194, 221-22 (2011); *Dorsey*, 276 Md. at 658-59.

A. Examples of harmless errors

1. Improper vouching for witness credibility

In *Spain v. State*, 386 Md. 145, 154 (2005), the Court of Appeals held that, although the State made improper remarks that could have caused the jury to believe a police witness is more credible than other witnesses, the error was harmless, and the statements did not mislead or influence the jury.

2. Failure to swear the jury at the start of the trial, but sworn during trial

In *Harris v. State*, 406 Md. 115, 130-31 (2008), the Court of Appeals held that complete failure to swear the jury can never be harmless error and requires reversal of the conviction. However, when (a) the jury was sworn three days after the trial began; (b) there was no evidence of improper conversation or activities by the jury; and (c) the Defendant was not prejudiced by the delay, the late administration of the oath will be considered harmless error. *Alston v. State*, 414 Md. 92, 109 (2010).

3. Failure to change venue

In *Muhammad v. State*, 177 Md. App. 188, 304 (2007), the Court of Special Appeals recognized plain error and addressed whether there should have been a change of venue based on the extremely high profile of the case that received national publicity. However, Court affirmed because failure to remove the case was harmless error.

4. Erroneous admission of hearsay evidence

In *Hudson v. State*, 152 Md. App. 488, 508-09 (2003), the Court of Special Appeals held that, although the trial court erred in admitting hearsay within hearsay, admitting statements made by the victim to his mother, as later relayed by an officer who interviewed his mother, the error was harmless because the Defendant's guilt was established, beyond a reasonable doubt, through other witnesses. In *Fields v. State*, 395 Md. 758 (2006), the Court of Appeals held that, even if the trial court erred in permitting the officer to testify as to the Defendant's nickname, the error was harmless because, based on DNA evidence and ballistics, there was guilt beyond reasonable doubt.

5. Erroneous admission of DNA evidence

In *Gross v. State*, 371 Md. 334 (2002), the Court of Appeals held that, although the trial court incorrectly denied the Defendant's motion in limine to exclude DNA evidence, the error was harmless, beyond reasonable doubt, because there was compelling evidence, consistent with the Defendant's testimony, that linked him to the victim at the time of her murder.

6. Erroneous admission of a voice stress test

In *Whittington v. State*, 147 Md. App. 496, 535-36 (2002), the Court of Special Appeals held that, even though the trial court erroneously admitted evidence that the Defendant failed a voice stress test, the error was harmless, beyond a reasonable doubt, when the trial court gave adequate curative instructions, and it was undisputed that the Defendant shot the victim.

7. Erroneous jury instruction regarding deliberations

In *Jones-Harris v. State*, 179 Md. App. 72, 92-93 (2008), the Court of Special Appeals held that when a jury instruction is given, but not required to be given, trial court's error in telling jury that it could not discuss the case until all jurors were "assembled," instead of saying when "deliberations began," was harmless error beyond a reasonable doubt.

8. Erroneous exclusion of evidence of another shooter

In *Bellamy v. State*, 403 Md. 308, 334-36 (2008), the Court of Appeals held that, although the trial court erred in excluding a statement identifying someone other than Defendant as the shooter, the error was harmless, beyond a reasonable doubt, when, under the law of aiding and abetting, the State was not required to prove who fired the fatal shot to convict the Defendant of first degree murder.

9. Erroneous limits on cross-examination of expert witness

In *Fleming v. State*, 194 Md. App. 76, 98-99 (2010), the Court of Special Appeals held that, even if the trial court erred in denying defense counsel's cross-examination of the State's ballistics expert about new methods of ballistics comparison, the error was harmless, beyond a reasonable doubt, because the Defendant conceded that he shot the victim.

10. Erroneously allowing un-admitted transcript of a tape-recorded interview into the jury room during deliberations when the actual tape of the interview had been played for the jury at trial and had been admitted into evidence

In *Imes v. State*, 158 Md. App. 176, 180-87, *cert. denied*, 384 Md. 158 (2004), the Court of Special Appeals held that it was harmless error when (a) the jury was allowed to bring a transcript of a recorded interview of the Defendant into the jury room; (b) the jury heard the tape at trial; (c) the jury was given a copy of the transcript when the tape was played; (d) defense counsel did not request the jury return the transcript after listening to the tape; and (e) the transcript only confirmed what the jury heard in open court.

11. Erroneous admission of evidence that violated the attorney-client privilege

In *Rubin v. State*, 325 Md. 552, 579 (1992), the trial court erroneously allowed a private investigator, hired by the defense, to testify that he obtained evidence from the Defendant, in violation of the rule that the State should not identify the Defendant as the source of physical evidence, when the evidence was obtained from defense counsel (or an agent of defense counsel), who in turn received the evidence from the Defendant. Although this was error, the Court of Appeals held that it was harmless error, beyond a reasonable doubt, in light of other, overwhelming evidence of guilt.

12. Violation of the Defendant's right to be present at all stages

In *Noble v. State*, 293 Md. 549, 569-73 (1982), the Court of Appeals held that the error was harmless beyond a reasonable doubt, when the Defendant was not present when a juror was dismissed.

13. Error in sentencing proceeding

In *King v. State*, 300 Md. 218, 231-32 (1984), the Court of Appeals held that the harmless error doctrine applied at sentencing proceedings, and the State's deficient notice of intent to seek enhanced punishment was harmless error.

14. Admission of statements obtained in violation of Sixth Amendment right to counsel

In *Bruno v. State*, 332 Md. 673, 694 (1993), the Court of Appeals held that admission of statements, obtained in violation of the Defendant's Sixth Amendment right to counsel, was harmless error when they provided only inferential support for the conclusion that the Defendant committed the rape. In *Milton v. Wainwright*, 407 U.S. 371, 377-78 (1972), the Supreme Court held that admission of a post-indictment confession obtained by police posing as a fellow inmate was harmless error.

15. Admission of evidence in violation of the Fourth Amendment

Admission of evidence obtained in violation of the Fourth Amendment may be harmless error. *Compare Chambers v. Maroney*, 399 U.S. 42, 52-53 (1970) (admission of evidence in violation of the Fourth Amendment was harmless error), *with Bumper v. North Carolina*, 391 U.S. 543, 550 (1968) (admission of such evidence not harmless and reversible).

16. Admission of statements made by a Co-Defendant in violation of the Confrontation Clause

The admission of statements by a Co-Defendant, admitted in violation of the Confrontation Clause, is harmless error when the evidence of guilt is overwhelming. *Schneble v. Florida*, 405 U.S. 427, 432 (1972); *Harrington v. California*, 395 U.S. 250, 253-54 (1969).

17. Admission of post-*Miranda* silence

Admission of the Defendant's silence subsequent to receiving *Miranda* warnings was harmless error. *See Brecht v. Abrahamson*, 507 U.S. 619, 635-36 (1993).

18. Error in failing to sustain objection to improper prosecutor arguments

In *Frazier v. State*, 197 Md. App. 264, 283-90 (2011), the Court of Special Appeals held that it was harmless error for the trial court to overrule the Defendant's objection to the prosecutor's improper comments regarding his decision to exercise his right to trial by jury.

B. Examples of errors that are reversible because they are not harmless beyond a reasonable doubt

1. Improper prosecutorial remarks

In *Wilhelm v. State*, 272 Md. 404, 416 (1974), the Court of Appeals provided factors for determining whether a prosecutor's improper remark was harmless error, including (a) the closeness of the case; (b) the centrality of the issue affected by the error; and (c) the steps taken by the trial court to mitigate the error.

In *Bryant v. State*, 129 Md. App. 150, 162 (1999), *cert. denied*, 358 Md. 164 (2000), the Defendant elected not to testify and State remarked to jury about the Defendant's demeanor during testimony of the State's witness. The Court of Special Appeals held that the State's remarks constituted reversible error. Even though the trial court gave a curative instruction, in light of closeness of case and centrality of the issue, the error was not harmless because there was significant chance that the remark influenced the jury.

In *Brown v. State*, 339 Md. 385, 396-97 (1995), the Court of Appeals held that a prosecutor's statement to a deadlocked jury, that they could recommend mercy to the sentencing judge if they were concerned about the consequences of a guilty verdict, was not harmless error and required reversal.

In *Anderson v. Nelson*, 390 U.S. 523 (1968), the Supreme Court stated: "[C]omment on a Defendant's failure to testify cannot be labeled harmless error in a case in which (a) such comment is extensive; (b) an inference of guilt from silence is stressed to the jury as a basis for conviction; and (c) the evidence could have supported acquittal. *Id.* at 523-24; *see Hill v. State*, 355 Md. 206, 225-26 (1999) (State's argument that the jury should convict the Defendant to preserve the safety of the community was reversible); *Holmes v. State*, 119 Md. App. 518, 527 (1998) (State's comments violated prohibition against the "golden rule" argument).

2. Admission of prejudicial evidence that lacked probative value

In *Pickett v. State*, 120 Md. App. 597, 607-09 (1998), in a murder trial, the State impeached its own witness (the Defendant's sister) and adduced inadmissible hearsay testimony that the Defendant confessed to his sister. The Court of Special Appeals reversed, holding that admission of hearsay was error because impeaching the Defendant's sister had no probative value, and the Defendant's sister did not provide testimony damaging to the State's case. The error was not harmless because it could not be said that the error in no way influenced the jury

3. Admission of involuntary confession

In *Wallace v. State*, 100 Md. App. 235, 239 (1994), the Defendant's confession, which was coerced by police, who threatened not to take photographs of his injuries unless he withdrew his request for counsel, was admitted. The Court of Special Appeals reversed, holding that, although there was abundant evidence of guilt, even without the confession, it could not state that the State's case was so overwhelming to render the error harmless. In *Akonom v. State*, 40 Md. App. 676 (1978), the Court of Special Appeals stated that "the introduction into evidence of a coerced confession requires automatic reversal, at least in part because of the theory that its origin renders it highly unreliable." *Id.* at 680 n.3.

4. Waiver of counsel

In *Moten v. State*, 339 Md. 407, 411 (1995), the trial court failed to inform a pro se Defendant of the maximum sentence for the offenses charged. The Court of Appeals held that failure to adhere to Md. Rule 4-215 cannot be harmless under *Parren v. State*, 309 Md. 260 (1987). *See Richardson v. State*, 381 Md. 348, 367 (2004).

5. Admission of improper hearsay evidence

In *Thompson v. State*, 156 Md. App. 238 (2004), the trial court admitted transcript testimony of two witnesses from the Defendant's prior trial. The Court of Special Appeals held that, although it was a VOP proceeding, with relaxed rules of evidence, the State did not satisfy the hearsay exception because it failed to even proffer that witnesses were unavailable, and it was not harmless.

In *Corbett v. State*, 130 Md. App. 408, 429-30, *cert. denied*, 359 Md. 31 (2000), the Court of Special Appeals held that it was not harmless error to admit a witness's written statement into evidence, based on past recollection recorded, when the writing was not offered by an adverse party and the document contained information that was not covered by the witness's testimony.

6. Ordering the Defendant to pay restitution to the victim's creditor's in violation of the restitution statute

In *Chilcoat v. State*, 155 Md. App. 394, 413-14 (2004), the trial court ordered the Defendant to pay restitution to the victim's medical providers. The statute permits the court to order restitution paid only to the victim, to the DHMH, to the Criminal Injuries Compensation Board (or other government unit), or to a third-party payer. The State argued that the error was harmless because it does not matter to the Defendant who is paid. The Court of Special Appeals held that the error was not harmless because the law does not authorize the court to order the Defendant to pay restitution to medical providers.

7. Admission of the Defendant's confession in violation of *Miranda*

In *State v. Logan*, 394 Md. 378, 388-89 (2006), trial court denied the Defendant's motion to suppress his confession that he killed two officers. The Court of Special Appeals held that any error was harmless because the Defendant admitted criminal agency. The Court of Appeals reversed, holding that the error was not harmless because the State could not show, beyond a reasonable doubt, that the improperly admitted confession did not contribute to the guilty verdict.

8. Ex parte communication with the jury

In *Winder v. State*, 362 Md. 275, 323-24 (2001), the trial court engaged in two ex parte communications with jurors without notifying the Defendant or defense counsel. The Defendant appealed, arguing that the court violated Md. Rules 4-326(c) & 4-231 and the constitutional right to be present. The Court of Appeals held that, because the rules are mandatory, and there was no record to review, the ex parte communications could not be harmless error. In *Stewart v. State*, 334 Md. 213 (1994), the judge urging a distraught juror to return to deliberations violated the Defendant's right to be present.

In *Denicolis v. State*, 378 Md. 646 (2003), when the trial court received a jury note, the lack of court response on the record cannot make the failure to notify the Defendant harmless. *See Perez v. State*, 420 Md. 57 (2011) (failure to notify parties about jury notes regarding witnesses was not harmless); *Ogundipe v. State*, 424 Md. 58 (2011), *cert. denied*, 132 S. Ct. 1977 (2012).

9. Admission of the Defendant's post-arrest silence

In *Grier v. State*, 351 Md. 241, 263 (1998), the State adduced, over objection, evidence of the Defendant's post-arrest silence. The Court of Special Appeals affirmed, holding that the Defendant's general objection was insufficient to preserve the issue for appeal. The Court of Appeals reversed, holding that (a) issue was preserved; (b) admission of post-arrest silence was not a "fair response" to the defense theory; and (c) the error was not harmless because a layperson views assertion of the Fifth Amendment as evidence of guilt.

10. Failure to advise the Defendant of the maximum penalties in violation of Md. Rule 4-215(a)(3)

In *Moten*, 339 Md. at 411, the trial court permitted the Defendant to discharge counsel and failed to inform the Defendant of the maximum penalties for the crimes charged, as required by Md. Rule 4-215(a)(3). The Court of Special Appeals held that the error was harmless because the Defendant received the charging document and was convicted of same offenses two months earlier. The Court of Appeals reversed, holding that the harmless error analysis is inapplicable to violations of Md. Rule 4-215(a)(3) because the rule protects the right to counsel and requires strict compliance.

In *State v. Camper*, 415 Md. 44, 58-59 (2010), the Court of Appeals held that failure to advise the Defendant, on the record, of the mandatory minimum sentence required a new trial, even though the Defendant had actual knowledge that he faced an enhanced sentence due to his status as a repeat offender.

In *Turner v. State*, 192 Md. App. 45, 75-79 (2010), the Defendant's receipt of a "Notice of Intent to Seek Enhanced Penalty" did not substitute for on-the-record notice of the possible penalties. In *Knox v. State*, 404 Md. 76, 91-92 (2008), the Court of Appeals held that Md. Rule 4-215 requires the Defendant be informed of any enhanced or mandatory punishment that could be imposed on the Defendant as a subsequent offender.

11. Failure to instruct on lesser included offenses

In *Malik v. State*, 152 Md. App. 305, 334-36 (2003), the trial court rejected the defense request to instruct the jury on second degree specific intent murder as a lesser included offense of first degree premeditated murder. The Defendant was convicted of premeditated murder and felony murder and was sentenced for first degree premeditated murder. The Court of Special Appeals held that error was not harmless. However, if the Defendant had been sentenced for felony murder, the failure to give the instruction for second degree murder would have been harmless.

12. Admission of the Defendant's prior convictions

In *State v. Westpoint*, 404 Md. 455, 543 (2008), the trial court permitted the State to impeach the Defendant with a prior conviction for third degree sex offense. The Court of Appeals held that (a) prior conviction for third degree sex offense may not be used to impeach because it is not relevant to credibility; and (b) the error was not harmless. In *Hurst v. State*, 400 Md. 397, 418-19 (2007), the trial court admitted testimony that the Defendant had been found guilty of rape in a prior case for the purpose of proving lack of consent in the present case. The Court of Appeals held that the evidence was inadmissible, and the error was not harmless.

13. Refusal to allow the jury to view exhibits in the jury room

In *Adams v. State*, 415 Md. 585, 602 (2010), the Court of Appeals held that the trial court's denial of the jury's request to take a videotape, admitted as an exhibit, into the jury room, without first making a good cause determination as to the appropriateness of taking the video into the jury room, was an abuse of discretion and not harmless error.

14. Jury's function usurped by "were-they-lying" questions

In *Hunter v. State*, 397 Md. 580, 597 (2007), the Court of Appeals held that it was impermissible for a prosecutor to ask a witness if they believed that another witness was lying. The "were-they-lying" question improperly encroaches on the province of the jury by asking a witness to judge the credibility of other witnesses.

In *Tyner v. State*, 417 Md. 611 (2011), the getaway driver gave a taped statement and testified that she saw the Defendants shoot the victims. She testified in exchange for murder charges against her being dismissed. The detective testified that she had a "deal" with the State contingent on her truthful testimony. The detective, over objection, testified that telling the truth was part of her deal with the State. During closing argument, the prosecutor stated that the witness had an agreement with the State to tell the truth, but that it was up to the jury "to judge whether or not she did that." The Court of Appeals upheld the trial court's allowance of the detective's testimony and the State's remarks during closing, stating:

> [T]he State's direct examination of [the detective] involved not the substance of [the witness'] taped statement, but the context in which it was given . . . The prosecutor elicited only from [the detective] "why" [the witness] gave the taped statement and whether "tell[ing] the truth" was part of the agreement. Stated differently, the State used [the detective's] testimony to verify the existence and terms of a cooperation agreement entered into by one of its key witnesses. Therefore, *in these circumstances*, [the detective's] testimony did not infringe upon the. jury's fact finding obligations.

Id. at 621. In *Bohnert v. State*, 312 Md. 266 (1988), the Court of Appeals reversed the Defendant's conviction for child abuse when an "expert" was allowed to opine that the victim was abused by the Defendant and testified truthfully, even though (a) there was no physical evidence of abuse; (b) a foundation had not been laid for the testimony; and (c) the credibility of the child was crucial to the case. The Court held that "the expert's opinion was inadmissible[. I]t encroached on the jury's function to judge the credibility of witnesses and weigh their testimony . . ." *Id.* at 279.

15. Failure of the State to comply with discovery obligations

In *Massey v. State*, 173 Md. App. 94, 118-19 (2007), the Court of Special Appeals determined that the trial court's failure to order the State to produce a report prepared by an officer who testified for the State was not harmless because it was the testifying officer who solely searched the Defendant upon arrest and found drugs.

16. Admission of documents in violation of the Sixth Amendment

In *Carter v. State*, 149 Md. App. 509 (2003), the Court of Special Appeals held that it was not harmless error for the trial court to admit, and for the State to make beneficial use of, documents prepared by the Defendant at the request of his counsel, which were found during a search of the Defendant's cell, and were protected by the attorney-client privilege. The constitutional right to counsel is violated when the attorney-client privilege of a person facing criminal charges is "undermined by state agents." *Id.* at 523.

17. Admission of polygraph evidence

In *Akonom*, 40 Md. App. 676, the Court of Special Appeals held that the admission of polygraph evidence, by its nature unreliable, was not harmless error.

18. Un-admitted evidence submitted to the jury

In *Merritt v. State*, 367 Md. 17 (2001), the Court of Appeals held that allowing un-admitted evidence into the jury room was subject to harmless error analysis, but that, in this case, it was not harmless error to allow an un-admitted application for a search warrant into the jury room. In *Sherman v. State*, 288 Md. 636 (1980), the Court of Appeals held that it was not harmless error for the trial court to allow the jury to take the indictment into the jury room.

19. Admission of evidence obtained in violation of the Defendant's right to counsel

In *United States v. Wade*, 388 U.S. 218, 242 (1967), the Supreme Court reversed the Defendant's conviction based on a courtroom identification of the Defendant when the Defendant was identified by the witnesses in a post-indictment lineup in the absence of counsel. The error was not harmless.

20. Improper restriction of cross-examination in violation of the Confrontation Clause

In *Lee v. Illinois*, 476 U.S. 530, 547 (1986), the Supreme Court held that the trial court's reliance on a Co-Defendant's statement, in violation of the Confrontation Clause, was not harmless error.

21. Exclusion of testimony regarding circumstances surrounding the Defendant's confession

In *Crane v. Kentucky*, 476 U.S. 683 (1986), the Supreme Court held that it was not harmless error for the trial court to exclude testimony regarding the circumstances of the Defendant's confession.

22. Denial of an indigent Defendant's right to counsel during a critical stage of the proceedings

In *Coleman v. Alabama*, 399 U.S. 1, 11 (1970), the Supreme Court held that the Defendant, an indigent, was denied his right to counsel at a preliminary hearing conducted to determine if there was sufficient evidence for the case to be tried. The Court remanded the case for a determination as to whether the error was harmless.

23. Jury instructions containing a conclusive presumption

In *Carella v. California*, 491 U.S. 263, 266-67 (1989), the Supreme Court held that the trial court's instructions, which contained conclusive presumptions, were not harmless error.

24. Failure to instruct the jury on an element of an offense

In *California v. Roy*, 519 U.S. 2, 5 (1996), the Supreme Court held that the failure to instruct on an element of an offense was not harmless error.

25. Admission of a coerced confession

In *Arizona v. Fulminante*, 499 U.S. 279, 302 (1991), the Supreme Court held that the admission of a coerced confession was subject to the harmless error rule, but that the admission of such a confession, in that case, was not harmless error.

C. Errors that cannot be harmless because they constitute a structural error & are reversible

1. Structural defects are not harmless error

In *Fulminante*, 499 U.S. 279, the Supreme Court defined structural errors as errors that result in structural defects affecting the framework from which the trial proceeds and not simply an error in the trial process. The Court stated that "structural defects [differ] in the constitution of the trial mechanism and thus defy analysis by the harmless-error standard," whereas a traditional trial error may be quantitatively assessed in view of other evidence to discover whether its admission was harmless. *Id.* at 280-81.

2. Defective reasonable doubt instruction is a structural defect

The standard of proof in a criminal case is guilt beyond a reasonable doubt. This standard gives substance to the presumption of innocence, designed to prevent unjust convictions and reduce the risk of factual error in criminal trials. Proof beyond a reasonable doubt is an essential element of Fourteenth Amendment due process and, therefore, any conviction that occurs based on less than guilt beyond a reasonable doubt must be reversed because it cannot constitutionally stand. *Jackson v. Virginia*, 443 U.S. 307, 317 (1979). In *Fulminante*, the Supreme Court stated:

> [It is] impossible to analyze in terms of harmless error the failure to instruct a jury on the reasonable-doubt standard, because it is impossible to determine the effect the omission of the instruction may have upon a jury, thus raising the absence of the instruction from a "trial error" to an error that distorts the very structure of the trial because it creates the risk that the jury will convict the Defendant even if the State has not met its required burden of proof.

499 U.S. at 291.

3. Racial or gender discrimination in grand or petite jury composition

Racial or gender discrimination in the selection of a grand jury or a petit jury is a structural defect, requires reversal, and cannot be harmless error. *Batson v. Kentucky*, 476 U.S. 79 (1986).

4. Denial of the right to trial by jury

In *Boulden v. State*, 414 Md. 284, 307 (2010), the Court of Appeals held that denial of the right to a trial by jury is a structural defect, requires reversal, and cannot be harmless error.

5. Denial of the right to a public trial

In *Carter v. State*, 356 Md. 207, 224-25 (1999), the Court of Appeals held that denial of the right to a public trial is a structural defect, requires reversal, and cannot be harmless error.

6. Total deprivation of the right to counsel

Denial of the right entitled to counsel during all stages of the trial is a structural defect, requires reversal, and cannot be harmless error. *See Fulminante*, 499 U.S. at 294.

7. Denial of the right to an impartial judge

Denial of the right to an impartial judge is a structural defect, requires reversal, and cannot be harmless error. *See Tumey v. Ohio*, 273 U.S. 510 (1927).

8. Denial of the right to represent oneself

Denial of the constitutional right to self-representation is a structural defect, requires reversal, and cannot be harmless error. *McKaskle v. Wiggins*, 465 U.S. 168, 177 n.8 (1984).

9. Denial of the right to select counsel of one's choice

For a Defendant who is not indigent, there is a constitutional right to choose counsel. Denial of that right is a structural defect, requires reversal, and cannot be harmless error. *United States v. Gonzalez-Lopez*, 548 U.S. 140, 148-51 (2006).

10. Denial of the right to consult with counsel during recess

In *Geders v. United States*, 425 U.S. 80, 91-92 (1976), the Supreme Court held that the Defendant's denial of the right to consult with counsel during a 17-hour overnight recess violated the Sixth Amendment right to counsel, was a structural defect, requires reversal, and cannot be harmless error.

11. Failure to inquire into a possible conflict of interest

In *Holloway v. Arkansas*, 435 U.S. 475, 487-91 (1978), the Supreme Court held that requiring Co-Defendants to be tried jointly, with one counsel who had a conflict of interest violated the Sixth Amendment right to counsel, was a structural defect, requires reversal, and cannot be harmless error.

Chapter 33

Collateral Review

§ I. Overview

If a Defendant is found guilty at trial, or enters a guilty plea, the Defendant has appellate options, including (a) application for leave to appeal; (b) direct appeal to an appellate court of right; (c) discretionary appeal to a state court of last resort; and/or (d) a discretionary appeal to the Supreme Court. The appellate process is referred to as a "direct" attack on one's conviction. At the appellate level, the Defendant challenges the legal rulings and actions of the trial judge and, if not the first appeal, the legal rulings of earlier appellate courts. In other words, the appellate process places one or more judges "on trial."

If a Defendant loses on appeal, the Defendant's direct attack is concluded. At that point, the Defendant usually has one of more levels of collateral review that are available. Unlike appeals, during which the Defendant challenges the legal action of judges, on collateral review, the Defendant usually challenges the legal action of attorneys, meaning defense counsel and the prosecutor. Defense counsel is usually challenged for having denied the Defendant the Sixth Amendment right to effective assistance of counsel. The prosecutor is usually challenged for having denied the Defendant the due process right to disclosure of exculpatory evidence under *Brady v. Maryland* and its progeny.

At common law, there was a remedy for prisoners illegally held was known as habeas corpus. A petition for habeas corpus relief argued to the jailer "that you have the body" and demanded release. *Black's Law Dictionary* 728 (8th ed. 2004). The English writ dates to the Habeas Corpus Act of 1679. The common law writ of habeas corpus became part of the United States Constitution. U.S. Const. art. I, § 9, cl. 2 provides that "[t]he Privilege of the Writ of Habeas Corpus shall not be suspended, unless when in Cases of Rebellion or Invasion the public Safety may require it."

In addition, the states adopted habeas corpus as a means to challenge an illegal conviction or sentence. Today, in most states, such proceedings are litigated under the Uniform Post Conviction Procedures Act. In Maryland, since 1958, this statutory remedy has permitted "convicted" persons to (a) challenge the conviction, i.e., the judgment and/or the sentence, based on a violation of the federal or state constitution or the laws of Maryland. For individuals who are not convicted persons within the meaning of the statute, i.e., not incarcerated, not on probation, and not on parole, they may accomplish the same thing through a petition for a writ of error coram nobis.

Since 2009, Maryland has also permitted convicted persons to challenge their conviction through a petition for a writ of actual innocence based on newly discovered evidence.

§ II. The right to effective assistance of counsel

Most typically, the theory of a collateral attack is ineffective assistance of counsel. This theory was first recognized as a constitutional right in *Powell v. Alabama*, 287 U.S. 45, 72-73 (1932). Because *Powell* was decided 31 years before the Sixth Amendment right to counsel was incorporated against the states, the right to effective assistance of counsel was a due process right.

The right to effective assistance of counsel is based on the theory that the Defendant's right to counsel includes, of necessity, a right to effective assistance of counsel. If counsel is ineffective, it is as if the Defendant has no counsel at all. If the Defendant has no counsel, when the Defendant did not make a knowing and intelligent waiver of the right to counsel, the result of the proceeding is void and must be vacated.

A. The right to effective assistance of counsel applies equally whether counsel is retained or appointed

In *Cuyler v. Sullivan*, 446 U.S. 335, 344 (1980), the Supreme Court held that the standard for effective assistance of counsel is the same whether counsel is retained or appointed. *Accord Rhodes v. Warden, Maryland Penitentiary*, 7 Md. App. 423, 427 (1969); *Swann v. State*, 7 Md. App. 309, 311 (1969) ("no valid distinction between paid and court appointed counsel").

B. The right to effective assistance of counsel applies equally whether the right to counsel is based on the Sixth Amendment or based on a statute that provides for counsel even when not constitutionally required

In *State v. Flansburg*, 345 Md. 694 (1997), the Court of Appeals held that counsel must be effective, regardless of whether the source of counsel is the Constitution or a state statute: "Regardless of the source, the right to counsel means the right to effective assistance of counsel." *Id.* at 703 (citing *Kimmelman v. Morrison*, 477 U.S. 365, 377 (1986); *McMann v. Richardson*, 397 U.S. 759, 771 n.14 (1970); *Grandison v. State*, 341 Md. 175, 164 (1995); *Brosan v. Cochran*, 307 Md. 662, 673 (1986)).

C. The two-pronged conjunctive *Strickland v. Washington* test for ineffective assistance of counsel

In *Strickland v. Washington*, 466 U.S. 668, 687 (1984), the Supreme Court established a two-prong test for ineffective assistance of counsel. *Accord United States v. Cronic*, 466 U.S. 648 (1984). In *Rompilla v. Beard*, 545 U.S. 374 (2005), the Supreme Court held that the two prongs of *Strickland* each present distinct issues.

1. The performance prong

To satisfy the performance prong of *Strickland*, the Defendant must demonstrate that the acts or omissions of counsel constituted serious attorney error, and counsel's performance fell below the objective standards of competence under the prevailing professional norms. *Nix v. Whiteside*, 475 U.S. 157, 166-67 (1986); *Oken v. State*, 343 Md. 256, 283 (1996); *Williams v. State*, 326 Md. 367, 373 (1992); *Harris v. State*, 303 Md. 685, 697 (1985); *Cirincione v. State*, 119 Md. App. 471, 484 (1998). Serious attorney error requires an error to the extent that counsel was not functioning as the counsel that is guaranteed by the Sixth Amendment. *Strickland*, 466 U.S. at 687.

Serious attorney error does not include errors that are part of legitimate trial strategy

There is a presumption that defense counsel's performance was reasonable and counsel's decisions were part of a sound trial strategy. Tactical decisions made by trial counsel must be judged as of the time the decision was made and not with the benefit of hindsight. Most choices "affecting conduct of the trial," such as objections, arguments, and witnesses, are within the purview of defense counsel. *Gonzalez v. United States*, 553 U.S. 242, 249 (2008); *Yarborough v. Gentry*, 540 U.S. 1, 5-6 (2003). In *State v. Thomas*, 325 Md. 160 (1992), the Court of Appeals held:

> Judicial scrutiny of counsel's performance must be highly deferential. It is all too tempting for a Defendant to second-guess counsel's assistance after conviction or adverse sentence, and it is all too easy for a court, examining counsel's defense after it has proved unsuccessful, to conclude that a particular act or omission of counsel was unreasonable. A fair assessment of attorney performance requires that every effort be made to eliminate the distorting effects of hindsight, to reconstruct the circumstances of counsel's challenged conduct, and to evaluate the conduct from the counsel's perspective at the time. Because of the difficulties inherent in making the evaluation, a court

must indulge a strong presumption that counsel's conduct falls within a wide range of reasonable professional assistance; that is, the Defendant must overcome the presumption that, under the circumstances, the challenged action "might be considered sound trial strategy."

Id. at 171 (quoting *Strickland*, 466 U.S. 668 (other internal citations omitted)). In *Gilliam v. State*, 331 Md. 651 (1993), the Court of Appeals stated: "The Sixth Amendment does not require the best possible defense or that every attorney render a perfect defense." *Id.* at 665. In *State v. Matthews*, 58 Md. App. 243 (1984), the Court of Special Appeals stated: "An attorney is not required to raise all possible defenses, but is permitted to make tactical decisions as to which defenses to pursue and which to abandon." *Id.* at 245.

Counsel's failure to permit the Defendant to make certain decisions that can be made only by the Defendant is serious attorney error

Certain decisions can only be made by the Defendant and cannot be made by defense counsel. These include (a) whether to accept a guilty plea; (b) whether to be tried in a court trial or to exercise the right to trial by jury; (c) whether to exercise the Fifth Amendment right ot testify or the Fifth Amendment right not to testify; and (d) whether to file a plea of "not criminally responsible by reason of insanity" (NCR), assuming that the Defendant is competent to stand trial.

Lack of experience insufficient to demonstrate serious attorney error

Lack of experience, without more, cannot establish serious attorney error. In *State v. Glover*, 355 S.E.2d 631 (W. Va. 1987), the court stated:

[E]very lawyer who handles criminal matters has once handled his first criminal matter. Not every lawyer would be guilty of ineffective assistance the first few times he appeared in court. The test is whether his performance was below what would be expected of a lawyer with experience, not whether he in fact had that experience.

Id. at 639.

Physical or mental impairment of counsel

Physical or mental impairment of counsel may materially impair the attorney's ability to represent the Defendant and may be serious attorney error. MRPC 1.16(a). For example, an attorney's alcohol use during trial may be used to establish that counsel was ineffective, but it is not ineffectiveness per se. *Frye v. State*, 235 F.3d 907 (4th Cir. 2000); *Burnett v. Collins*, 982 F.2d 922, 930 (5th Cir. 1993); *Fowler v. Parratt*, 682 F.2d 746, 750 (8th Cir. 1982).

2. The prejudice prong

The Defendant must demonstrate that counsel's deficient performance prejudiced the Defendant. There is a presumption of prejudice only when (a) the Defendant is deprived of counsel during a critical stage of a criminal proceeding, *see, e.g., Geders v. United States*, 425 U.S. 80 (1976); *Herring v. New York*, 422 U.S. 853 (1975); *Brooks v. Tennessee*, 406 U.S. 605 (1972); *White v. Maryland*, 373 U.S. 59 (1963); *Ferguson v. Georgia*, 365 U.S. 570 (1961); *Hamilton v. Alabama*, 368 U.S. 52 (1961); *Williams v. Kaiser*, 323 U.S. 471 (1945); or (b) counsel "'*entirely* fails to subject the prosecution's case to meaningful adversarial testing.'" *Bell v. Cone*, 535 U.S. 685, 697 (2002) (quoting *Cronic*, 466 U.S. at 659).

Showing prejudice in a case that went to trial

For cases that are tried and result in a guilty verdict, the Defendant must demonstrate that there is either a reasonable probability, or a substantial or significant possibility, that, but for the serious attorney error, the result would have been different, i.e., not guilty on one or more counts.

In *Lockhart v. Fretwell*, 506 U.S. 364 (1993), the Supreme Court clarified the *Strickland* "prejudice prong." In a death sentence case, the Defendant was convicted of felony murder and sentenced to death. The verdict of guilty of felony murder and the sentence of death were both based on the aggravating factor that the murder was committed for pecuniary gain. A 1985 case (later overruled) held that it was unconstitutional for the Defendant to be sentenced based on an aggravating factor that was also an element of the offense. The Defendant's counsel failed to preserve this issue for appeal.

The Court held that counsel's failure to object, although probably error, was not prejudicial for purposes of Sixth Amendment effective assistance of counsel, stating that the Defendant must show that the attorney error was so serious (a) that it deprived the Defendant of a fair and reliable trial; and (b) that the outcome of the trial might have been different. In *Lockhart*, the Court held that the Defendant's trial was neither unreliable nor fundamentally unfair. *Id.* at 372 ("unreliability or unfairness does not result if the ineffectiveness of counsel does not deprive the Defendant of any substantive or procedural right which the law entitles him").

In *Hiligh v. State*, 375 Md. 456 (2003), the Court of Appeals held that counsel's failure to argue involuntariness of the confession, based on failure to comply with the prompt presentment requirement, constituted prejudicial ineffective assistance of counsel because there was a significant possibility that the trial court would have found the confession involuntary or, in the alternative, would have been required to submit the issue to the jury.

In *State v. Peterson*, 158 Md. App. 558, 595 (2004), the Court of Special Appeals held that trial counsel's failure to investigate and argue battered spouse syndrome as a defense to murder when there was ample evidence to show that the victim suffered a long history of abuse by her spouse, constituted ineffective assistance as it would have generated the defense of imperfect self-defense and it was reasonably probable that the result of the proceeding would have been different.

In *State v. Jones*, 138 Md. App. 178, 223-24 (2001), *aff'd on other grounds*, 379 Md. 704 (2004), the Court of Special Appeals held that counsel's error in failing to object to a hearsay statement was prejudicial for the purposes of ineffective assistance when the State lacked any physical or forensic evidence tying him to the crime. In *Redman v. State*, 363 Md. 298, 310 (2001), the Court of Appeals held that defense counsel's failure to inform the Defendant of his absolute right of removal in a capital case amounted to substandard performance, but that the Defendant failed to show prejudice because he was sentenced to life in prison.

In *Walker v. State*, 391 Md. 233 (2006), the Court of Appeals held that prejudice will not be presumed solely because a case is tried in absentia. For prejudice to be presumed there must be a complete denial of counsel or complete failure to subject the State's case to adversarial testing. Defense counsel's decision to participate minimally at trial was a strategic decision based on the Defendant having absconded before trial and not a complete failure of counsel. *Id.* at 251.

Showing prejudice in a case that resulted in a guilty plea

Approximately 94% of state cases and 97% of federal cases result in a guilty plea. *See Missouri v. Frye*, 132 S. Ct. 1399 (2012); *Lafler v. Cooper*, 132 S. Ct. 1376 (2012). To establish prejudice in a guilty plea, the Defendant must demonstrate that there is either a reasonable probability, or a substantial or significant possibility, that, but for the serious attorney error, the Defendant would not have accepted the guilty plea, but would have gone to trial. *Hill v. Lockhart*, 474 U.S. 52, 59 (1985); *Yoswick v. State*, 347 Md. 228, 245-46 (1997).

Cases in which the Defendant did not have an appeal or post-sentencing motions

If, because of serious attorney error, the Defendant lost the opportunity for (a) an appeal; (b) a motion for modification or reduction of sentence; or (c) an application for review of sentence by a three-judge panel, the Defendant is not required to demonstrate that he or she would have won the appeal or would have be given a lesser sentence. Instead, to show prejudice, the Defendant is only required to demonstrate the "lost opportunity" for an appeal or for a post-sentencing sentence proceeding. *Roe v. Flores-Ortega*, 528 U.S. 470, 486 (2000) (appeal); *Matthews v. State*, 161 Md. App. 248, 252 (2005) (post-sentencing proceeding).

3. Cumulative effect of errors

Though a single error of defense counsel may not be enough for a court to declare counsel's performance ineffective, the cumulative effect of multiple errors may be. *Gilliam v. State*, 331 Md. 651, 685-86 (1993); *Bowers v. State*, 320 Md. 416, 436-37 (1990); *Schmitt v. State*, 140 Md. App. 1, 19-20 (2001); *Cirincione*, 119 Md. App. at 506. The cumulative effect of the errors may be applied to either prong of the *Strickland* test. *Mendes v. State*, 146 Md. App. 23, 52 (2002). In *Cirincione*, 119 Md. App. 471, the Court of Special Appeals held:

> Even when no single aspect of the representation falls below the minimum standards required under the Sixth Amendment, the cumulative effect of counsel's entire performance may still result in a denial of effective assistance. Apparently, this cumulative effect may be applied to either prong of the *Strickland* test. That is, numerous non-deficient errors may cumulatively amount to a deficiency, or numerous non-prejudicial deficiencies may cumulatively cause prejudice. As ever, the touchstone is whether, in view of all the circumstances, our confidence in the result has been undermined by counsel's failings.

Id. at 506 (citations omitted).

4. Ineffective assistance of counsel litigated in proceedings other than a post conviction proceeding

A post conviction proceeding is the appropriate—and usually the only—state forum to raise ineffective assistance of counsel. *Perry v. State*, 344 Md. 204, 227 (1996); *Davis v. State*, 285 Md. 19, 36 (1979), *Bratt v. State*, 62 Md. App. 535, 537 (1985). In most cases, if there was ineffective assistance of counsel, the Defendant would not have known of the ineffective assistance of counsel, much less have had an opportunity to litigate the ineffectiveness, in the very proceeding in which counsel was ineffective. *Ware v. State*, 360 Md. 650, 706 (2000); *Walker v. State*, 338 Md. 253, 262 (1995).

Because ineffective assistance of counsel can almost never be litigated at trial, and certainly not if the same counsel represents the Defendant through the trial, sentencing, and post-trial motions, ineffective assistance of counsel is almost always raised for first time in a post conviction proceeding. *See Mosley v. State*, 378 Md. 548, 558-60 (2003); *Davis v. State*, 285 Md. 19, 36 (1979).

Ineffective assistance of counsel may, on rare occasion, be reviewed at trial in post-trial motions. As a general rule, ineffective assistance of counsel is almost never litigated in the very proceeding in which counsel is ineffective. *Kimmelman*, 477 U.S. at 378; *see Ware*, 360 Md. at 706; *Walker*, 338 Md. at 262; *Harris v. State*, 295 Md. 329, 337-38 (1983); *Colvin v. State*, 299 Md. 88, 112-13 (1984).

However, in *Harris v. State*, 299 Md. 511 (1984), *vac. & remanded*, 312 Md. 225 (1988), the Court of Appeals held that it was appropriate for the trial court to hear the Defendant's ineffective assistance of counsel claims in a post-trial motion under the unique circumstances of that case. The Court stated:

> Where, as here, the Defendant has pled guilty to murder and related offenses and is awaiting a capital sentencing proceeding, where the ineffective assistance of counsel allegations relate to the guilty pleas and thus can be adjudicated in a collateral evidentiary proceeding[,] where the Defendant has made a detailed evidentiary proffer that his counsel was ineffective and that he was misled into pleading guilty, where the Defendant is represented by new counsel, and where his prior attorney is available to testify concerning that prior representation, it is desirable for the trial court to resolve the claims of counsel incompetency . . . instead of delaying the matter until a post conviction application is filed.

Id. at 518.

Similarly, ineffective assistance of counsel is rarely reviewed on direct appeal. In *Johnson v. State*, 292 Md. 405 (1982), the Court of Appeals held: "[U]nder the settled rules of appellate procedure, a claim of ineffective assistance of counsel not presented to the trial court generally is not an issue which will be reviewed initially on direct appeal." *Id.* at 434.

However, an appellate court occasionally addresses ineffective assistance of counsel. In *Testerman v. State*, 170 Md. App. 324, 343-44 (2006), the Court of Special Appeals held that there was ineffective assistance of counsel when counsel failed to make what would have been a successful MJOA. In *In re Parris W.*, 363 Md. 717, 726 (2001), the Court of Appeals held that an ineffective assistance of counsel claim may be evaluated on appeal when the record is sufficiently developed to permit a fair review of the claim. *Accord Whitney v. State*, 158 Md. App. 519 (2004); *accord Mosley*, 378 Md. at 564 n.9 (ineffective assistance of counsel heard only on direct appeal when the critical facts of the ineffectiveness are not in dispute).

When there is a violation of the attorney-client privilege or there is attorney conflict of interest, the appellate court is more likely to review ineffective assistance of counsel. In *Smith v. State*, 394 Md. 184 (2006), the Court of Appeals held that when counsel violated the attorney-client privilege, ineffective assistance of counsel could be reviewed on direct appeal because a separate hearing, beyond the existing record, was not necessary, stating: "Our refusal to address [the Defendant's] claim on direct appeal would constitute a waste judicial resources." *Id.* at 201.

In *Lettley v. State*, 358 Md. 26, 32 (2000), the Court of Appeals held that when the record is clear and the ineffective assistance claim is based on a conflict of interest, the court will hear the claim on direct appeal. *Accord Stewart v. State*, 319 Md. 81, 92

(1990). *Compare Austin v. State*, 327 Md. 375, 394 (1992) (challenge based on defense counsel's conflict of interest did not need to wait for post conviction); *with Pugh v. State*, 103 Md. App. 624, 639 (1995) (although conflict of interest may be heard on direct appeal, if the issue was not raised at trial, and the record is silent on the issue, post conviction is the preferred method).

Even in a conflict of interest scenario, the court is more likely to defer review until post conviction. In *Reed v. State*, 52 Md. App. 345 (1982), the Court of Special Appeals held:

> The record before us has not been sufficiently developed with respect to such issues as whether trial counsel perceived a potential conflict of interest when he consented to consolidation of [the Defendant's case with his co-Defendant's]; whether [the Defendant] was adequately informed regarding any potential conflict, and, if so, whether he voluntarily agreed to joint representation; whether trial counsel's strategy and ability to cross-examine were actually impaired . . . Until such matters are explored more thoroughly we are unable to conduct a full and fair assessment of that issue. We therefore conclude that [the Defendant's] contention regarding ineffective assistance of counsel is not properly before us at this time.

Id. at 354-55.

D. At which stages of the proceeding does a Defendant have the right to effective assistance of counsel?

The Defendant has the right to effective assistance of counsel throughout (1) the preparation for trial and the entire trial; (2) the plea bargaining and guilty plea process; (3) in preparation for and at sentencing; (4) on appeal; and (5) on post conviction.

1. Throughout the trial

The effectiveness of counsel must be viewed at the time of the conduct and not based on subsequent history. There is no ineffective assistance of counsel if counsel's conduct is a legitimate trial strategy, even if the strategy proved to be bad or unsuccessful. In *State v. Borchardt*, 396 Md. 586, 623 (2007), the Court of Appeals held that it was legitimate trial strategy (a) to not call a mitigation specialist; and (b) to limit the testimony of a neurologist. In *Knowles v. Mirzayance*, 556 U.S. 111, 122-23 (2009), the Supreme Court held that it was legitimate trial strategy, and not serious attorney error, to abandon an insanity defense that had virtually no chance of success.

In *State v. Latham*, 182 Md. App. 597, 616-18 (2008), the Court of Special Appeals held that counsel's decision (a) to not request a self-defense jury instruction; (b) to not request curative measures after a juror saw the Defendant in shackles; and (c) to not present evidence that the Defendant wore a bullet-proof vest, because of his involvement in prior shootings, were reasonable trial strategy decisions and not serious attorney error.

In *Wood v. Allen*, 558 U.S. 290 (2010), the Supreme Court held that counsel's decision to not introduce evidence of the Defendant's mental deficiencies was trial strategy and not serious attorney error. The Court stated that it is trial strategy if "it is a conscious choice between two legitimate and rational alternatives. It must be borne of deliberation and not happenstance, inattention, or neglect." *Id.* at 307.

In *Kimmelman*, 477 U.S. at 386-87, the Supreme Court held that it was serious attorney error and ineffective assistance of counsel to fail to conduct discovery and to fail to file a motion to suppress semen-stained bed sheets that were seized without a search warrant.

Counsel's failure to argue battered spouse syndrome may be serious attorney error

In *Peterson*, 158 Md. App. at 597, the Court of Special Appeals held that failure to investigate or pursue a battered spouse syndrome defense, in a murder case, despite ample evidence of prolonged abuse, was serious attorney error.

Counsel's failure to argue a motion to suppress evidence may be serious attorney error

In *Evans v. State*, 151 Md. App. 365, 380-81 (2003), the Court of Special Appeals held that it was serious attorney error to fail to file and to argue a motion to suppress drugs that were seized from a male Defendant, during a daytime rectal search in public, by officers and not by trained medical personnel, with both male and female officers present. In *Perry v. State*, 357 Md. 37, 87 (1999), the Court of Appeals held that it was serious attorney error to fail to file and to argue a motion to suppress the Defendant's statement that was recorded in violation of Maryland's wiretap law.

Counsel's failure to conduct adequate investigation before abandoning NCR & voluntary intoxication, without consulting the Defendant, may be serious attorney error

In *State v. Johnson*, 143 Md. App. 173, 195-96 (2002), the Court of Special Appeals held that it was serious attorney error to fail to pursue the defenses of NCR and voluntary intoxication, without discussing these issues with the Defendant or conducting adequate investigation of the effects of PCP.

Counsel's failure to object to inadmissible evidence is serious attorney error

In *Jones*, 138 Md. App. at 242-43, the Court of Special Appeals held that the failure to object to inadmissible evidence in a witness's written statement, admitted after the witness recanted a prior written statement, was serious attorney error.

Failing to argue an MJOA that would have been successful is serious attorney error

In *Testerman*, 170 Md. App. at 343-44, the Court of Special Appeals held that it was ineffective assistance of counsel to fail to make what would have been a successful MJOA.

Not objecting to admission of evidence may be reasonable trial strategy

In *Jones*, 138 Md. App. 178, the Court of Special appeals held that trial counsel's failure to object to the admission of a co-conspirator's conviction for murder was reasonable trial strategy when counsel had conceded that the Defendant had taken part in the underlying robbery prior to the murder, but sought to place the blame for the murder on the co-conspirator. The Court stated that "[b]ased on defense counsel's strategy, [the Defendant] was not tainted by [the co-conspirator's] conviction, because [the Defendant] admitted some degree of culpability, but contended that he was not involved in the murders." *Id.* at 221. *See Oken v. State*, 343 Md. 256 (1996) (noting that failure to object is often part of trial strategy).

2. During plea bargaining & the guilty plea

Plea bargaining is an indispensable part of the criminal justice system, and "when properly utilized, aid[s] in the administration of justice and, within reason, should be encouraged." *Cuffley v. State*, 416 Md. 568, 577 (2010); *see Santobello v. New York*, 404 U.S. 257, 261 (1971). The Supreme Court has recognized that about 97% of federal convictions and 94% of state convictions result from plea bargaining. Nonetheless, this process almost always happens behind closed doors, and there is very little, if any, judicial supervision over (a) the negotiations between the State and defense counsel; and (b) the communication between the Defendant and defense counsel.

In *Missouri v. Frye*, 132 S. Ct. 1399 (2012), the Supreme Court recognized that the style and tactics of defense counsel "are so individual that it may neither be prudent nor practicable to try to elaborate or define detailed standards for the proper discharge of defense counsel's participation in the process." *Id.* at 1408. Accordingly, there is little authority to guide defense counsel (a) in preparing for and/or conducting plea bargaining; or (b) in fulfilling his or her obligations to the Defendant.

If there had been an open question of the requirement for effective assistance of counsel during the plea bargaining process and the entry of a guilty plea, the Supreme Court answered that question in the companion cases of *Lafler v. Cooper*, 132 S. Ct. 1376 (2012), and *Frye*, 132 S. Ct. 1399. In so holding, the Court provided some guidance to defense counsel.

In *Frye*, the Defendant was charged with driving on a revoked license. 132 S. Ct. at 1404. Based on three "priors" for the same crime, the Defendant was charged as a felon, subject to four years incarceration. *Id.* The prosecutor made a written plea offer for (a) a three-year felony sentence with a recommendation of ten days in jail; or (b) a one-year misdemeanor with a recommendation of 90 days in jail. *Id.*

Defense counsel failed to communicate the plea offer to the Defendant, who eventually pleaded guilty to the felony charge, with no agreement, and was sentenced to three years. *Id.* at 1404-05. The Defendant filed for post conviction relief, alleging ineffective assistance of counsel in the failure to inform him of the State's plea offer. *Id.* at 1405. The Defendant testified that he would have accepted the second option and plead to the misdemeanor charge, with the 90-day recommendation, against a one-year maximum. *Id.* After the post conviction court denied relief, the appellate court reversed and remanded for trial or the guilty plea, at the Defendant's option. *Id.*

The Supreme Court held that (a) plea negotiations is "almost always" a critical stage and the Defendant is entitled to effective assistance of counsel; (b) defense counsel has the duty to communicate to the Defendant formal plea offers made by the prosecution; and (c) to show prejudice based on an un-communicated offer, the Defendant must show a reasonable probability that he would have accepted the plea and neither the prosecution, nor the court, would have prevented the offer from being accepted and implemented. *Id.* at 1408-10.

The Court held that (a) defense counsel was deficient in failing to communicate the State's plea offer; (b) there was a substantial likelihood the Defendant would have accepted the misdemeanor plea, considering he pleaded guilty to a more serious crime with no promise of a sentencing recommendation; and (c) the case would be remanded to determine whether the State would have adhered to the plea agreement and whether the court would have accepted the plea. *Id.*

In *Lafler*, the Defendant was charged with assault with intent to murder. 132 S. Ct. at 1383. The State offered a recommended sentence of 51 to 85 months in return for a guilty plea. *Id.* The Defendant rejected the offer on advice of counsel, who urged him to reject the plea and go to trial, stating that the prosecution would not be able to establish intent to murder because the victim was shot below the waist. *Id.* The Defendant (a) went to trial; (b) was convicted; and (c) received a mandatory minimum sentence of 185 to 360 months. *Id.*

After an unsuccessful appeal, the Defendant filed a petition for habeas corpus relief, alleging ineffective assistance of counsel. *Id.* Both sides agreed that defense counsel's erroneous advice was serious attorney error under *Strickland. Id.* at 1384. Because counsel's representation was deficient, the Court addressed "how to apply *Strickland*'s prejudice test where ineffective assistance results in a rejection of the plea offer and the Defendant is convicted at the ensuing trial." *Id.*

The Court held that, in order to demonstrate prejudice under *Strickland*, in the context of a rejected plea offer, the Defendant must show that (a) but for the ineffective advice of counsel, there is a reasonable probability that the Defendant would have accepted the plea; (b) the prosecution would not have withdrawn the plea, and the trial court would have accepted the plea; and (c) the sentence pursuant to the plea would have been lower than the sentence actually imposed. *Id.* at 1385. The Court held that the Defendant satisfied the prejudice prong.

The remaining issue was the remedy. The Court held that, if the Defendant can show that counsel was deficient in erroneously recommending rejection of a plea offer, "[t]he correct remedy . . . is to order the State to reoffer the plea agreement[, and presuming the Defendant] accepts the offer, the trial court must then determine whether (1) to vacate the conviction and resentence . . . pursuant to the plea agreement, (2) to vacate only some of the conviction and resentence, or (3) leave the conviction and sentence from trial undisturbed." *Id.* at 1391.

In both *Frye* and *Lafler*, the State argued that allowing post conviction relief when defense counsel (a) incorrectly advises the Defendant about a plea offer; or (b) fails to communicate a plea offer to the Defendant, would open the floodgates to frivolous post conviction claims. *Frye*, 132 S. Ct. at 1409; *Lafler*, 132 S. Ct. at 1389-90. The Court rejected this argument.

The Court noted that when a formal plea offer is made, it "can be documented so that what took place in the negotiation process becomes more clear if some later inquiry turns on conduct of earlier pre-trial negotiations." *Frye*, 132 S. Ct. at 1409. Defense counsel should document, in writing, the fact that a plea offer has been extended. Moreover, if an offer is accepted or rejected, defense counsel should document why the offer was accepted or rejected and any advice on which that decision was made.

The Court noted that "states may elect to follow rules that all offers must be in writing . . . to ensure against later misunderstandings or fabricat[ions]." *Id.* For example, one state mandates that "[a]ny plea offer to be made by the prosecutor shall be made in writing and forwarded to the Defendant's attorney." N.J. Ct. Rule 3:9-1(b). Maryland does not require that plea offers be in writing. Requiring plea offers to be in writing would reduce (a) frivolous claims that a plea offer was made when it was not; and (b) self-serving misrepresentations about the terms of a plea.

The Court suggested that "formal offers can be made part of the record at any subsequent plea proceeding or before a trial on the merits . . . to ensure that a Defendant has been fully advised before those proceedings commence." *Frye*, 132 S. Ct. at 1409. The Court noted that one state requires such procedure. *See State v. Donald*, 10 P.2d 1193 (Ariz. Ct. App. 2000).

Frye and *Lafler* provide Defendants with the ability to vacate a guilty plea if trial counsel (a) provided legally erroneous advice regarding whether to accept or reject a plea offer; or (b) failed to communicate to the Defendant a prosecutor's plea offer. Because, in Maryland, there is a ten-year statute of limitation on filing a petition for post conviction relief, defense counsel should preserve all Defendants' files. Defense counsel should take steps to (a) effectively represent the Defendant during the plea process; and (b) create a paper trail to document that representation. Defense counsel should obtain written authorization to discuss a possible plea with the prosecutor.

Defense counsel should speak early and often with the prosecutor about a possible plea and document both the fact of, and the content of, conversations with the prosecutor. If the prosecutor makes a plea offer, or there is progress toward a plea agreement, defense counsel should document such conversations. Defense counsel should request that the prosecutor place any plea offer in writing. If there is a plea offer or progress toward a plea agreement, defense counsel should immediately communicate the plea offer or plea negotiations.

If the State makes a plea offer, defense counsel should make an oral recommendation to the Defendant, if possible, followed by a written version regarding whether to (a) accept the plea offer; (b) reject the plea offer; or (c) make a counter plea offer. Defense counsel should include (a) the recommendation to the Defendant; and (b) the rationale for the recommendation, including facts known, facts unknown, and uncertainties in the law. Defense counsel should do this with any subsequent recommendation, based on a different plea offer and an evolving understanding of the case.

If defense counsel takes these steps, if a competent counsel might make such a recommendation, courts will almost always defer to defense counsel's judgment and strategy. A court's unwillingness to defer to defense counsel will almost certainly be limited to situations in which defense counsel does nothing.

Counsel's failure to advise of the maximum sentence when advising the Defendant to accept a guilty plea is serious attorney error

In *Williams v. State*, 326 Md. 367, 379 (1992), the Court of Appeals held that failure to advise the Defendant, who rejected a ten-year plea, that the maximum possible sentence was a 25-year mandatory sentence, was serious attorney error.

In *McMann*, 397 U.S. 759, the Supreme Court recognized that, merely because, in hind sight, it turned out to be a good or bad decision to accept a plea offer is not dispositive, or else every decision would be vulnerable. The Court stated that it does not matter whether "counsel's advice [is] right or wrong, but on whether that advice was within the range of competence demanded of attorneys in criminal cases." *Id.* at 770-71.

In *Premo v. Moore*, 131 S. Ct. 733, 742-43 (2011), the Supreme Court held that the failure to file a motion to suppress the Defendant's statements made to police, prior to advising the Defendant to plead guilty, was not serious attorney error.

Counsel's failure to advise the Defendant of immigration consequences of a guilty plea is serious attorney error

In *Padilla v. Kentucky*, 559 U.S. 356 (2010), the Supreme Court held that deportation is an integral part of the consequences whenever a Defendant is not a U.S. citizen and is considering whether to plead guilty. Counsel's failure to advise the Defendant of the deportation consequences is serious attorney error. In *Chaidez v. United States*, 133 S. Ct. 1103 (2013), the Supreme Court held that the holding of *Padilla* was not retroactive because it "breach[ed] the previously chink free wall between direct and collateral consequences . . . If that does not count as breaking new ground or imposing a new obligation, we are hard pressed to know what would." *Id.* at 1110 (internal citations & alterations omitted).

In *Denisyuk v. State*, 422 Md. 462 (2011), the Court of Appeals held that *Padilla* applies to post conviction claims arising from guilty pleas obtained after the enactment of the Illegal Immigration Reform & Immigrant Responsibility Act, which was effective on April 1, 1997. The Defendant in that case pleaded guilty to assault in exchange for a ten-year sentence, with all but two years suspended. At the plea hearing, the Defendant was not advised by the Court, by the State, or by defense counsel regarding the immigration consequences of the plea. As a result of the plea, the Defendant faced deportation. The Defendant did not file an application for leave to appeal from the guilty plea.

The Defendant filed a petition for post conviction relief, seeking to vacate the conviction and obtain a new trial, arguing that (a) the plea was involuntary because he was not advised of its immigration consequences; and (b) failure of defense counsel to inform him that he would face immigration consequences was ineffective assistance of counsel in violation of the Sixth Amendment.

The post conviction court agreed that the failure to advise the Defendant of the immigration consequences of his plea was ineffective assistance of counsel, but the Court of Special Appeals reversed, pre-*Padilla*, holding: "The Sixth Amendment does not impose on a lawyer a duty to inform a client about collateral consequences generally or the risk of deportation specifically." *Id.* at 469.

The Court of Appeals reversed the Court of Special Appeals, holding that the failure to advise a Defendant of the immigration consequences of his plea, post-April 1, 1997, was ineffective assistance of counsel. The Court stated that the central issue was "whether the holding of *Padilla* applies of collateral review of [the Defendant's] conviction." *Id.* at 478.

The Court analyzed whether *Padilla* was a "new rule" for purposes of applying its holding retrospectively, stating: "*Padilla* is an application of *Strickland* to a specific set of facts. *Padilla*, decided March 31, 2010, instructs that, '[f]or at least 15 years, professional norms have generally imposed an obligation on counsel to provide advice on the deportation consequences of a client's plea.' That 15-year span approximately matches the 1996 amendments to federal immigration law that made deportation 'practically inevitable' for noncitizens convicted of removable offenses." *Id.* at 481.

The Court held that *Padilla* outlined "what has been expected of defense counsel" since 1996 and, in failing to meet those expectations, the Defendant's counsel was deficient, causing prejudice (because the Defendant would not have pled guilty absent that advice and insisted on going to trial), which entitled the Defendant to a new trial. *Id.*

In *Miller v. State*, 207 Md. App. 453 (2012), the Defendant argued, in a petition for a writ of error coram nobis, that his guilty plea was involuntary because his attorney never informed him of the immigration consequences of that plea. The Court of Special Appeals held that an attorney's performance may be deficient for failing to inform a client about the immigration consequences of his or her plea, but this deficiency does not render a plea involuntary per se, stating:

> [W]e do not consider our decision in this case to be controlled by either *Padilla* or *Denisyuk*; those cases have no direct bearing on [this] case. They were both dealing with the Sixth Amendment right to effective assistance of counsel generally and with the performance prong of *Strickland v. Washington* specifically. . . . The coram nobis petition raised only [the Defendant's] claim that his guilty plea was not voluntary. [T]he effective assistance of counsel and the voluntariness of a guilty plea are separate and distinct issues. They are not joined at the hip. A finding of ineffective assistance would by no means compel a finding that a guilty plea was involuntary . . .

Id. at 485. Although the holding in *Miller* did not require it, the Court of Special Appeals analyzed *Denisyuk*, explaining that "[a] genuine concern for the law's repose in this case . . . behooves us to go further. There is something fundamentally disturbing about revisiting a guilty plea in a case that became final 13 years ago." *Id.* at 486.

The Court surveyed federal and state cases existing in 1999, which was when the Defendant's conviction became final, and contrary to Court of Appeals holding in *Denisyuk*, concluded: "[T]here was no 'existing precedent' as of September 1, 1999, that would have compelled or dictated . . . a legal ruling that the failure to advise a criminal defendant about deportation consequences would constitute ineffective assistance of counsel according to the Sixth Amendment." *Id.* at 519.

The Supreme Court's holding in *Chaidez* will likely not affect the Court of Appeals' holding in *Denisyuk*, in which the Court of Appeals noted that, "even if the Supreme Court ever were to hold that *Padilla* is not retroactive under *Teague*, that holding would have no adverse effect" on its holding. *Denisyuk*, 422 Md. at 480 n.8.

Failure to learn of prior felony convictions before advising the Defendant to plead guilty may be legitimate trial strategy

In *Hill v. Lockhart*, 474 U.S. 52 (1985), the Defendant pleaded guilty based on advice of counsel that he would be eligible for parole after serving one-third of his sentence. This information was incorrect because the Defendant had a prior felony conviction, which was unknown to trial counsel, and which required the Defendant to serve longer before being eligible for parole. The Defendant argued that his guilty plea was involuntary because it resulted from serious attorney error.

The Supreme Court held that, in a guilty plea, the Defendant must show that, but for trial counsel's error, the Defendant would not have pleaded guilty and would have gone to trial. The Defendant did not allege that, had counsel correctly informed him of parole eligibility, he would have pleaded not guilty and gone to trial. The Defendant did not allege special circumstances demonstrating that he placed particular emphasis on parole eligibility in deciding whether to plead guilty. Moreover, the Defendant signed a statement that he did not have a prior felony conviction, making it reasonable for counsel not to investigate further.

3. At sentencing

The Defendant has the right to effective assistance of counsel at sentencing and, if sentencing counsel is ineffective, the Defendant has the right to a new sentencing. In *Wiggins v. Smith*, 539 U.S. 510, 524 (2003), the Supreme Court held that, in a death penalty case, it is serious attorney error and ineffective assistance of counsel to fail to investigate the Defendant's background or present evidence of the Defendant's traumatic childhood. *Accord Rompilla*, 545 U.S. at 383-84 (serious attorney error and ineffective assistance of counsel to fail to investigate mitigating evidence in a capital case).

In *State v. Tichnell*, 306 Md. 428, 453-55 (1986), the Court of Appeals held that failure to present character and psychiatric evidence, in a capital sentencing, is legitimate trial strategy, and not serious attorney error, and not ineffective assistance of counsel when not doing so was consistent with defense counsel's trial strategy.

In *Flansburg*, 345 Md. at 700, the Court of Appeals held that the Defendant has a right to effective assistance of counsel, under the Maryland Public Defenders Act, when filing a motion for modification or reduction of sentence regarding a sentence that was re-imposed on revocation of probation. If the Defendant requests counsel to file a motion for modification or reduction of sentence, it is serious attorney error and ineffective assistance of counsel to fail to file such motion. In *Matthews v. State*, 161 Md. App. 248 (2005), the Court of Special Appeals held:

> "We . . . make explicit what was merely, but clearly, implicit in [*Flansburg*, 345 Md. 694]: The failure to follow a client's directions to file a motion for modification of sentence is a deficient act, and such failure is prejudicial because it results in a loss of any opportunity to have a reconsideration of sentence hearing. Accordingly, when a Defendant in a criminal case asks his attorney to file a motion for modification of sentence, and the attorney fails to do so, the Defendant is entitled to the post conviction remedy of being allowed to file a belated motion for modification of sentence, without the necessity of presenting any other evidence of prejudice.

Id. at 252.

4. On appeal

The Defendant has the right to effective assistance of counsel on appeal and, if appellate counsel is ineffective, the Defendant has the right to a new appeal. In *Douglas v. California*, 372 U.S. 353, 357-58 (1963), the Supreme Court rejected a state system in which indigent Defendants were provided counsel only after their appeal was deemed to have merit. *See Wilson v. State*, 284 Md. 664, 679 (1979).

In *Ross v. Moffitt*, 417 U.S. 600, 610 (1974), the Supreme Court held a Defendant does not have a constitutional right to counsel on a discretionary appeal to a state court of last resort or the Supreme Court. In *Wainwright v. Torna*, 455 U.S. 586, 588 (1982), the Supreme Court held that when the Defendant does not have the right to counsel, e.g., a discretionary appeal, the Defendant has no right to effective assistance of counsel. However, in *Evitts v. Lucey*, 469 U.S. 387, 397 (1985), the Supreme Court held that, even though there is no constitutional right to counsel at state expense, e.g., a non-indigent on direct appeal, if the Defendant has counsel, due process requires that counsel be effective.

In *Roe v. Flores-Ortega*, 528 U.S. 470, 486-87 (2000), the Supreme Court held that it is serious attorney error to fail to file a notice of appeal. Counsel has a duty to consult with the Defendant when there is reason to think that (a) a rational Defendant would want to take an appeal; or (b) the Defendant demonstrated an interest in taking an appeal.

"Consulting" means explaining the advantages and disadvantages of taking an appeal and making reasonable efforts to discover the Defendant's wishes. When the conduct of defense counsel causes the Defendant to be denied an entire judicial proceeding, it is presumptively serious attorney error. When a Defendant is denied an appeal of right, through the inaction of counsel, and through no fault of the Defendant, the Defendant is entitled to a belated appeal without having to show a likelihood of success on appeal. The Defendant simply has to show the lost opportunity. *Accord Garrison v. State*, 350 Md. 128, 138 (1998).

Failure to raise a claim on direct appeal may be legitimate trial strategy

In *Smith v. Murray*, 477 U.S. 527 (1986), the Supreme Court held that the failure to raise an issue on appeal was not serious attorney error. During a death penalty sentencing, trial counsel objected to the testimony of a court-appointed psychiatrist regarding the Defendant's admission that once he tore a girl's clothes off on a school bus and then decided to rape her. The Defendant sought habeas relief, arguing that admission of this testimony violated his Fifth Amendment privilege against compelled self-incrimination, and that appellate counsel committed serious attorney error in failing to raise this issue on direct appeal. The Court held that appellate counsel's failure to raise this issue on appeal was a tactical decision based on existing state law.

In *Oken v. State*, 343 Md. 256 (1996), the Court of Appeals held that counsel's decision not to raise an issue regarding jury instructions on appeal was a tactical deci-sion and that "[t]he decision whether to raise an issue on appeal is quintessentially a tactical decision of counsel." *Id.* at 271. *See Hunt v. Smith*, 856 F. Supp. 25, 257 (D. Md. 1994), *aff'd sub nom. Hunt v. Nuth*, 57 F.3d 1327 (4th Cir. 1995), *cert. denied*, 516 U.S. 1054 (1996).

Failing to argue an issue on appeal within reasonable professional judgment

Failing to raise a particular issue on appeal does not constitute serious attorney error if the Defendant's attorney had a reasonable basis for believing the argument would fail. In *Carter v. State*, 73 Md. App. 437 (1988), the Court of Special Appeals held:

> [Defendant's] counsel was confronted with a record that would have present-ed a novel issue which, according to her interpretation of a recent Court of Appeals opinion, had not been preserved for appellate review. Whether legal-ly right or wrong, that interpretation was certainly not unreasonable. Since counsel's decision to forego the restricted impeachment issue was supported by a reasonable professional judgment, her representation of [the Defendant] cannot be deemed ineffective.

Id. at 445.

No serious attorney error when neither the Sixth Amendment nor state law requires counsel

In *Torna*, 455 U.S. at 587-88, the Supreme Court held that failure to timely file an appli-cation for a discretionary appeal was not serious attorney error because there is no right to counsel on a discretionary appeal.

5. On collateral attack

In *Pennsylvania v. Finley*, 481 U.S. 551, 555 (1987), the Supreme Court held that when the Defendant has no right to counsel in a state post conviction proceeding and has no right to counsel for a federal habeas corpus proceeding, there is no right to effective assistance of counsel. The Court stated: "We think that since a Defendant has no federal constitutional right to counsel when pursuing a discretionary appeal on direct review of his conviction, *a fortiori*, he has no such right when attacking a conviction that has long since become final upon exhaustion of the appellate pro-cess." *Id.* at 554.

In Maryland, a Defendant has a right counsel, at state expense, if indigent, for a post conviction proceeding. In *Stovall v. State*, 144 Md. App. 711 (2002), the Court of Special Appeals recognized that a "Defendant has a broader right to counsel under the Maryland Public Defender Act than under the United States Constitution." *Id.* at 721 (citing *McCarter v. State*, 363 Md. 705, 713 (2001); *Flansburg*, 345 Md. 694).

In *Stovall*, 144 Md. App. at 722-23, the Court held that, because Maryland provides counsel, at state expense, in a post conviction proceeding, the Defendant has a right to effective assistance of counsel. *See Flansburg*, 345 Md. at 703 (1997) (citing *Kimmelman*, 477 U.S. at 377; *McMann*, 397 U.S. at 771 n.14; *Grandison v. State*, 341 Md. 175, 264 (1995); *Brosan v. Cochran*, 307 Md. 662, 673 (1986)).

§ III. Prosecutorial misconduct

If the State failed to disclose, under *Brady v. Maryland*, 373 U.S. 83 (1963), (a) exculpatory evidence that may exonerate the Defendant because he is innocent; (b) mitigating evidence that may make the Defendant's crime less serious or sentence smaller; or (c) impeachment evidence that may be used to impeach a State's witness, e.g., evidence of favorable treatment of State's witness in return for testimony, the Defendant may be entitled to a new trial.

In sum, *Brady* material includes all information that, if believed, would be favorable to Defendant, and, at the time of the required disclosure, it must be assumed that the material would be believed by the fact finder. *See United States v. Agurs*, 427 U.S. 97, 110-11 (1976); *Giglio v. United States*, 405 U.S. 150, 154 (1972); *Ware v. State*, 348 Md. 19, 38 (1997).

One source of exculpatory evidence is prosecutor's file, and one source of exculpatory evidence is the police file. The Defendant may obtain access to the prosecutor's file and the police file, subject to limited exceptions, by filing a request under Maryland Public Information Act (MPIA).

A. Exculpatory evidence

Exculpatory evidence is evidence that, if believed, would tend to negate the Defendant's guilt. *See Strosnider v. Warden, Maryland Penitentiary*, 228 Md. 663, 667 (1962); *Johnson v. Warden, Maryland Penitentiary*, 16 Md. App. 227, 233-34 (1972); *Smith v. Warden, Maryland Penitentiary*, 7 Md. App. 579, 583 (1969).

B. Mitigation evidence

Mitigation evidence is evidence that, if believed, would tend to mitigate the degree of the Defendant's guilt or tend to lessen the sentence to which the Defendant would be subjected. In *Cone v. Bell*, 556 U.S. 449, 476 (2009), the Supreme Court held that the prosecution's failure to disclose evidence of the Defendant's long history of drug use, when the Defendant stated that he was on drugs during the murders, was a *Brady* violation, and the case was remanded.

C. Impeachment evidence

Impeachment evidence is evidence providing a basis for impeaching a State's witness, e.g., a favorable "deal" for the witness in return for testifying for the State. Evidence of an actual or implied agreement between the State and a witness for favorable action by the State in return for testimony is *Brady* material because it affects the witness's credibility. *Giglio*, 405 U.S. at 155); *Wilson v. State*, 363 Md. 333, 346 (2001). In *Ware*, the Court of Appeals stated: "In *Giglio*, the Supreme Court made clear that the prosecutor's duty to disclose applies to *any* understanding or agreement between the witness and the State." 348 Md. at 41-42. This includes a reasonable belief by the witness of favorable treatment.

In *Williams v. State*, 152 Md. App. 200 (2003), the Court of Appeals held that the fact that the State's witness is a paid informant is exculpatory and material. In *Smith v. Cain*, 132 S. Ct. 627, 630 (2012), the Supreme Court held that the prosecution violated *Brady* when it withheld an investigating officer's notes, stating that a witness could not identify the Defendant, and that witness testified at trial that the Defendant was the perpetrator. The Defendant was entitled to a new trial because there was no other evidence linking the Defendant to the crime.

In *Agurs*, 427 U.S. at 112-13 n.21, the Supreme Court stated: "[The witness's] testimony was the *only* evidence linking [the Defendant] to the crime. [The witness's] undisclosed statements directly contradict his testimony . . ."

However, the Defendant is not entitled to a new trial if the evidence impeaching an eyewitness is not material because the State's other evidence is strong enough to sustain the conviction. The State is not required to disclose impeachment evidence prior to entering a plea agreement. *United States v. Ruiz*, 536 U.S. 622, 629-33 (2002).

D. Known perjured testimony

The prosecution's use of known perjured testimony entitles the Defendant to a new trial. *Strosnider v. Warden, Maryland Penitentiary*, 228 Md. 663, 667 (1962). The Defendant must show that the prosecution *knowingly* used perjured testimony. *Hamm v. Warden, Maryland Penitentiary*, 238 Md. 633, 635 (1965); *Duckett v. Warden, Maryland House of Correction*, 230 Md. 621, 625-26 (1962); *Washington v. Warden, Maryland House of Correction*, 225 Md. 623, 625 (1961) (mere claim of perjured testimony insufficient); *Fisher v. Warden, Maryland House of Correction*, 225 Md. 642, 643 (1961) (perjured testimony without the State's knowledge is insufficient).

Moreover, the perjured testimony must go to a material issue in the case. *Kulbiki v. State*, 207 Md. App. 412, 382 (2012) (expert witness perjury regarding credentials not material).

§ IV. DNA evidence

"[T]he purpose underlying [Md. Code Ann., Crim. Proc. § 8-201] is to provide a means for incarcerated persons to produce exculpatory or mitigating evidence relevant to a claim of wrongful conviction or sentencing . . ." *Arey v. State*, 400 Md. 491, 506 (2007) (*Arey I*).

A. Homicide cases & sex offense cases

In homicide cases and sex offense cases, when criminal agency is the issue, the Defendant is entitled to DNA testing of evidence in the chain of custody, if not previously tested under a method accepted within the relevant scientific community, assuming that there is a reasonable probability of relevant exculpatory evidence.

B. Substantial possibility of a different result

In *Arrington v. State*, 411 Md. 524 (2009), the Court of Appeals held that DNA testing raised a substantial possibility that the jury would have reached a different outcome had the DNA evidence been available at trial. The State must preserve evidence, during the Defendant's period of incarceration, if there is reason to believe it contains DNA material. In *Thompson v. State*, 411 Md. 664, 680 (2009), the Court of Appeals held that, to obtain a new trial, a Defendant must show a "substantial possibility" of innocence and not "actual innocence."

The court must dismiss the petition if the results of DNA testing is unfavorable to the Defendant. If the results of DNA testing are favorable to the Defendant, the court must initiate post conviction proceedings. Md. Code Ann., Crim. Proc. § 8-201; *Simms v. State*, 409 Md. 722, 731-32 (2009). In *Gregg v. State*, 409 Md. 698, 719-20 (2009), the Court of Appeals held that the Defendant, convicted of murder, could petition for post conviction relief to produce and test available DNA evidence when he offered sufficient factual basis that the DNA evidence was exculpatory and carried a "substantial possibility" of innocence, and the State offered no contradictory evidence.

C. Destroyed DNA evidence

In *Washington v. State*, 424 Md. 632, 666-67 (2012), the Court of Appeals stated that in homicide cases and sex offense cases, under Md. Code Ann., Crim. Proc. § 8-201(j), the State has a duty to preserve scientific evidence. However, the State's duty to preserve did not commence until the effective date of the statute (January 1, 2009), and is not retroactive. In *Horton v. State*, 412 Md. 1, 15 (2009), the Court of Appeals held that the State was required to (1) prove that DNA evidence had been destroyed; or (2) conduct a thorough search for DNA evidence.

The State, as the custodian of evidence, has a duty to conduct a reasonable search for the requested evidence. *Washington*, 424 Md. at 659; *Blake v. State*, 418 Md. 445, 463 (2011) (*Blake II*); *Horton*, 412 Md. at 7-8. If the State claims that the evidence no longer exists, in *Arey I*, the Court held that the initial burden is on the State to show that the requested evidence no longer exists, and searching the evidence control unit, alone, is insufficient to satis this burden.

If the State establishes a prima facie case that the DNA evidence no longer exists, the burden shifts to the Defendant to show that DNA evidence does exist. The Defendant must be given an opportunity to respond to the State's assertion that the evidence no longer exists. The Defendant is not entitled to a hearing on a petition for DNA testing. In *Blake v. State*, 395 Md. 213, 228 (2006) (*Blake I*), the Court of Appeals held:

> Fundamental fairness requires that [the Defendant] be given an opportunity to respond and to challenge the State's representation. When it is the State's position that the evidence sought to be tested no longer exists, the circuit court may not summarily dismiss the petition requesting DNA testing. The court must give [the Defendant] notice of and an opportunity to respond to the State's allegation . . . that the evidence is unavailable.

Id. at 228. In *Arey v. State*, 422 Md. 328, 339 (2011) (*Arey II*), the Court of Appeals reversed an order of the trial court dismissing the request for DNA testing, which was issued just two days after the State submitted an affidavit from a lab technician, stating that the evidence was destroyed. The Court held that the summary denial of the request denied the Defendant an opportunity to respond to the State's assertions. A trial court's factual determinations regarding the State's search for the evidence in question will not be reversed unless clearly erroneous. *Arey II*; *Blake II*.

In *District Attorney's Office for the Third Judicial Circuit v. Osborne*, 557 U.S. 52, 73-75 (2009), the Supreme Court held that, although a legislature may proscribe otherwise, there is no constitutional right to access evidence used at trial in order to facilitate DNA testing.

D. No right to counsel

There is no right to counsel for a post conviction DNA collateral attack. *Blake I*; *Trimble v. State*, 157 Md. App. 73, 78 (2004). However, the court has the authority to appoint counsel if it so chooses. In *Arey I*, the Court of Appeals held: "We conclude that although there is no constitutional or statutory right to counsel at the time a [Defendant] files for DNA testing, a court has the inherent power to appoint counsel at any stage of the proceedings . . ." Id. at 508.

§ V. Illegal sentence

A sentence may be challenged as an illegal sentence at any time under a motion to correct illegal sentence under Md. Rule 4-345(a). If a motion to correct illegal sentence is unsuccessful, the Defendant is entitled to a direct appeal and not merely an application for leave to appeal. *State v. Kanaras*, 357 Md. 170, 184 (1999). An illegal sentence may also be challenged in a petition for post conviction relief.

§ VI. Litigating a collateral attack under the Maryland's Uniform Post Conviction Procedure Act (the Act)

A. Who may litigate under the Act

Under the Act, a Defendant may file a petition for post conviction relief by alleging that the judgment or the sentence violates the federal or state constitution or the laws of Maryland. Md. Code Ann., Crim. Proc. § 7-102(a). *See Perry v. State*, 344 Md. 204, 227 (1996); *Davis v. State*, 285 Md. 19, 36 (1979); *Bratt v. State*, 62 Md. App. 535, 538 (1985). The Act is procedural only and does not grant substantive rights to the Defendant. *Wilson v. State*, 284 Md. 664, 671 (1979); *Jordan v. State*, 221 Md. 134, 140 (1959); *State v. D'Onofrio*, 221 Md. 20, 28-29 (1959).

Under Md. Rules 4-401 to 4-408, the Act provides for a post conviction proceeding for a Defendant who was convicted of a crime and is in custody, which means (1) incarcerated, (2) on parole, or (3) on probation. Md. Code Ann., Crim. Proc. § 7-101; *Ruby v. State*, 353 Md. 100, 106 n.3 (1999); *Fairbanks v. State*, 331 Md. 482, 492 n.3 (1993); *Randall Book Corp. v. State*, 316 Md. 315, 321 (1989). In *McMannis v. State*, 311 Md. 534, 547 (1988), the Court of Appeals held that the Defendant must be in custody, i.e., confinement, probation, parole, or detainer in Maryland and not in another jurisdiction.

However, in *Barrow v. State*, 318 Md. 644, 645 (1990), the Court of Appeals held that a Defendant who is serving a Maryland sentence out of state is in Maryland custody under the Act if the sentence imposed out of state was made to run consecutive to the Maryland sentence.

The judge who presided over the trial, may not be the post conviction judge, unless the Defendant consents. Md. Rule 4-406(b); *Pfoff v. State*, 85 Md. App. 296, 300 (1991).

In *Obomighie v. State*, 170 Md. App. 708, 713 (2006), the Court of Special Appeals held that there is no right to litigate a petition for post conviction relief when the Defendant is no longer on probation, even if he filed prior to the expiration of probation. In *Gakaba v. State*, 84 Md. App. 154, 157 (1990), the Court of Special Appeals held that probation before judgment (PBJ), as opposed to a probation after judgment, is not a conviction for post conviction purposes, and the Defendant may not seek post conviction relief from a PBJ, unless probation is revoked and a formal judgment of conviction is entered.

In *Smith v. State*, 115 Md. App. 614 (1997), the Defendant was sentenced to a term of probation after a trial and filed a petition for post conviction relief, which was denied. Subsequently, the Defendant's probation was revoked, and the Defendant filed another petition for post conviction relief, raising issues related to the revocation. The State argued that the Defendant had already filed his one petition. The Court of Appeals held that a probation revocation hearing was a "trial" and, as long as the petition raises new issues apart from those that arose out of the initial trial, the Defendant was entitled to file a petition relating to the revocation hearing. *Id.* at 625.

B. Right to counsel under the Act

Although an indigent Defendant is not entitled to counsel in a post conviction proceeding at government expense under either the federal or state constitution, an indigent Defendant is entitled to counsel at the state expense under the Act. Md. Code Ann., Crim. Proc. § 7-108(a). *See O'Connor v. Director, Patuxent Institution*, 238 Md. 1, 2 (1965); *Hobbs v. Warden, Maryland Penitentiary*, 219 Md. 684, 686 (1959). In *Stovall v. State*, 144 Md. App. 711, 721-22 (2002), the Court of Special Appeals recognized that the right to counsel in a post conviction proceeding means the right to effective assistance of counsel in a post conviction proceeding.

An indigent Defendant is not entitled to counsel, at state expense, on a motion to reopen a closed post conviction proceeding. In *Taylor v. Director, Patuxent Institution*, 1 Md. App. 23, 24 (1967), the Court of Special Appeals held that appointment of counsel on a motion to reopen a closed post conviction proceeding is within the court's discretion. The Defendant is virtually never awarded counsel.

C. Number of petitions

From 1958, when the Act was enacted, until 1986, Defendants could file an unlimited number of post conviction petitions. From 1986 to 1995, Defendants could file two post conviction petitions, and the two petition limit was not retroactive. Thus, regardless of the number of post conviction petitions filed before July 1, 1986, Defendants could file two post conviction petitions after the 1986 amendment. *Mason v. State*, 309 Md. 215, 219 (1987). Since October 1, 1995, inmates have been limited to one post conviction petition, which applies retroactively. Md. Code Ann., Crim. Proc. § 7-103(a); *see Grayson v. State*, 354 Md. 1, 9 (1999). Thereafter, after October 1, 1995, no Defendant may file a second post conviction petition.

However, a Defendant may file an unlimited number of motions to reopen a closed post conviction proceeding. Md. Code Ann., Crim. Proc. § 7-104. Unlike in a post conviction proceeding, in a motion to reopen a closed post conviction proceeding, the Defendant is entitled to "reopen" the closed post conviction proceeding only when "the action is in the interest of justice." *Id.* In *Gray v. State*, 388 Md. 366, 382 (2005), the Court of Appeals held that the court is not required to give detailed written ruling denying a motion to reopen.

Although the Defendant is entitled to counsel at state's expense, if indigent, in a post conviction proceeding, the Defendant is not entitled to counsel at state's expense, if indigent, in a motion to reopen a closed post conviction proceeding. The court, within its discretion, may award counsel on a motion to reopen a closed post conviction proceeding, but this virtually never happens. Md. Code Ann., Crim. Proc. § 7-108(b).

D. Statute of limitation

Prior to 1995, there was no statute of limitation for filing a petition for post conviction relief. For a Defendant sentenced after September 30, 1995, a petition for post conviction relief must be filed within ten years after sentence, unless the Defendant can show "extraordinary cause." Md. Code Ann., Crim. Proc. § 7-103(b). In *Poole v. State*, 203 Md. App. 1, 14 (2012), the Court of Special Appeals held that the ten-year statute of limitation had not run on the Defendant's amended petition, filed by an appointed counsel, when the Defendant had timely filed a pro se petition.

For Defendants sentenced before October 1, 1995, there is no statute of limitation, and statute of limitation is not retroactive. In *State v. Williamson*, 408 Md. 269, 277-78 (2009), the Court of Appeals held that post conviction relief was available for a 1968 conviction when the post conviction petition was filed in 2007, because the ten-year statute of limitation only applies as of October 1, 1995.

Although there is a statute of limitations for filing a petition for post conviction relief as of 1995, the doctrine of laches does not apply. In *Lopez v. State*, 205 Md. App. 141, *cert. granted*, No. 226 (Md. Sept. 21, 2012), the Court of Special Appeals held that the doctrine of laches applies to a post conviction petition filed in a case in which the Defendant was sentenced prior to October 1, 1995. The Court held:

> [T]he filing of a post conviction petition in a case where petitioner was sentenced prior to October 1, 1995, may be barred under the affirmative defense of laches. [T]he State, must show by a preponderance of the evidence that: (1) there was an unreasonable or impermissible delay in asserting a particular claim; and, (2) that the delay prejudiced the State.

Id. at 175. The Court of Special Appeals remanded because the record was insufficient to conclude that the Defendant's claim was barred by laches. *Id.*

E. Venue

A petition for post conviction relief must be filed in the Circuit Court of the county in which the Defendant was convicted. Md. Rules 4-401 & 4-402; Md. Code Ann., Crim. Proc. § 7-102(a). *See McMannis v. State*, 311 Md. 534, 536 (1988); *Williams v. State*, 292 Md. 201, 204 (1981).

F. Pleadings

Under Md. Rule 4-402(a), a petition for post conviction relief must include the following, and failure to include all required information in a petition may result in dismissal of the petition. The petition for post conviction relief must include (1) the Defendant's name; (2) the Defendant's place of confinement; (3) the Defendant's DOC #; and (4) whether the Defendant is able to retain counsel and pay costs. It must include (1) the date and place of the offense(s); (2) the offense(s) for which the Defendant was convicted; and (3) the sentence(s) imposed. Md. Rule 4-404(a)(2).

1. Allegations of error & relief sought

The petition for post conviction relief must include (a) the alleged error(s), based on violations of the federal or state constitution and/or Maryland law; (b) the facts of the case; and (c) the relief sought. Md. Rule 4-402(a)(3). In *Williams v. Director, Patuxent Institution*, 4 Md. App. 721 (1968), the Court of Special Appeals held that a "bald assertion of a denial of constitutional rights without specification . . . affords no grounds for relief." *Id.* at 714. The Defendant must set forth specific facts supporting the alleged error(s). *See Cirincione*, 119 Md. App. at 504. In *Pfoff v. State*, 85 Md. App. 296 (1991), the Court of Special Appeals held:

> [I]f the petition is so deficient that the court cannot reasonably determine the nature of the complaint, it may be denied on that basis, as failing to comply with the requirements of the Rule. But where that is not the case—where, despite some vagueness in the language, the nature of the complaint is ascertainable—the court may not use imprecise language as an excuse not to give full consideration to the complaint. [The Defendant] may, indeed should, be held to substantial compliance with the requirements of Rule 4-402(a), but if the person *does* substantially comply, it must be given due and fair consideration.

Id. at 201-02; *see Tucker v. Warden, Md. Penitentiary*, 243 Md. 331, 332-33 (1966); *Husk v. Warden, Maryland Penitentiary*, 240 Md. 353, 356 (1965); *Matthews v. Warden, Maryland House of Correction*, 223 Md. 649, 651 (1960); *Daniels v. Warden, Maryland Penitentiary*, 222 Md. 606, 607-08 (1960).

2. Amendment to the petition for post conviction relief

A petition for post conviction relief may be freely amended. Md. Rule 4-402(c).

3. State's response

The State must file a response within 15 days of notice of filing or later if the court permits. Md. Rule 4-404.

4. Withdrawal of a petition

A post conviction petition may be withdrawn, without prejudice, at any time before the hearing date and for good cause shown thereafter. Md. Rule 4-405.

5. Issues must not be "finally litigated" & must not be "waived"

A post conviction petitions is limited to issues that have not been "finally litigated" or "waived." Md. Code Ann., Crim. Proc. §§ 7-102 & 7-106. *Evans v. State*, 396 Md. 256, 280-81 (2006) (issue finally litigated when previously addressed by both Maryland and federal courts); *see Gorman v. State*, 67 Md. App. 398, 406-07 (1986). Guilt/innocence issues and sufficiency of the evidence have either been finally litigated or waived by the post conviction stage. *Greene v. Warden, Maryland Penitentiary*, 238 Md. 651, 652 (1965). Most errors of the judge must be raised on appeal, and a post conviction proceeding is not a substitute for an appeal. *Prokopis v. State*, 49 Md. App. 531, 534 (1981).

Allegations become "finally litigated" when there is a ruling on the merits of the issue by the Court of Special Appeals or the Court of Appeals. Md. Code Ann., Crim. Proc. §§ 7-102 & 7-106(a); *see Buettner v. Superintendent, Maryland Correctional Institution for Women*, 239 Md. 710, 711 (1965) (issue finally litigated on direct appeal); *accord Walker v. Warden, Maryland Penitentiary*, 1 Md. App. 534, 536 (1967). In *State v. Hernandez*, 344 Md. 721 (1997), the Court of Appeals held that an issue is not finally litigated by inclusion in an application for leave to appeal that is denied.

Allegations are waived when they could have been previously raised, but were not. *See State v. Rose*, 345 Md. 238, 250 (1997). For example, if the trial court gives an unconstitutional "beyond a reasonable doubt" jury instruction, for which counsel makes no objection, the Fourteenth Amendment right to due process is waived for appeal and for post conviction. What is not waived when counsel failed to object to the unconstitutional jury instruction is the Sixth Amendment right to effective assistance of counsel for post conviction.

A petition for post conviction relief must plead facts of special circumstances to demonstrate non-waiver. Md. Code Ann., Crim. Proc. § 7-102(b); Md. Rule 4-402(a)(7). Defendants are generally bound by the tactical decisions of counsel when counsel decides what "not to do," which results in waiver. *Hunt v. State*, 345 Md. 122, 136-37 (1997); *Curtis v. State*, 284 Md. 132, 147 (1978); *see Davis v. State*, 285 Md. 19, 36 (1979); *State v. Merchant*, 10 Md. App. 545, 550 (1970).

If a Defendant pleads guilty but, thereafter, fails to file an application for appeal, there is a rebuttable presumption that the Defendant waived the right to challenge his conviction in a post conviction proceeding. In *McElroy v. State*, 329 Md. 136, 146 (1993), the Court of Appeals, in consolidated appeals, held that the Defendants failed to rebut the presumption that they knowingly and intelligently waived their right to challenge alleged errors in their guilty pleas when they alleged no such errors in their application for leave to appeal. *See Walker v. State*, 343 Md. 629, 644-45 (1996).

In *State v. Torres*, 86 Md. App. 560 (1991), the Court of Special Appeals held:

> [W]hen an allegation of error is raised in a post conviction case, the judge deciding the case should consider whether the allegation could have been raised before. If it could, the judge must decide whether the allegation has been waived. In order to make this decision, he must first determine whether the allegation is premised upon a fundamental right or non-fundamental right. If the right is a fundamental right, waiver measured by the "intelligent and knowing" standard must be proved. If the right is a non-fundamental right, however, the "intelligent and knowing" standard does not apply, and waiver is determined by general legal principles.

Id. at 568. Regarding applications for leave to appeal from a guilty plea, the waiver provisions apply whether or not an application was filed. *State v. Gutierrez*, 153 Md. App. 462, 473 (2003).

For non-fundamental rights, there can be waiver through inaction. *See Wyche v. State*, 53 Md. App. 403, 408 (1983). In *State v. Romulus*, 315 Md. 526, 540 (1989), the Court of Appeals held that an issue of a defect in the charging document is deemed waived for post conviction purposes after sentencing.

6. Special circumstances may excuse waiver

Failure to raise an allegation creates a rebuttable presumption of a knowing and intelligent waiver, which may be excused by special circumstances. *See Conyers v. State*, 367 Md. 571, 595-96 (2002) (no waiver of *Brady* exculpatory evidence violation when not discovered until post conviction); *State v. Romulus*, 315 Md. 526, 539-40 (1989); *State v. Gutierrez*, 153 Md. App. 462, 475 (2003) (rebuttable presumption that waiver of an issue was made intelligently and knowingly, with the burden on the Defendant to rebut the presumption or show "special circumstances"); *accord Curtis*, 284 Md. at 140; *see State v. Geppi*, 17 Md. App. 639, 645 (1979); *Holmes v. State*, 401 Md. 429, 473-75 (2007).

7. Impact of a "new rule"

An issue is not finally litigated or waived if (a) the Supreme Court, Court of Appeals, or Court of Special Appeals holds that the federal or state constitution adopts a procedural or substantive standard not previously recognized; and (b) the "new rule" was intended to apply retroactively. Md. Code Ann., Crim. Proc. § 7-106(c). In *Greco v. State*, 427 Md. 477 (2012), the Court of Appeals held:

> Determining whether a principle of law qualifies as "not previously recognized" is a question best answered by examining the legal landscape before and after issuance of the decision setting forth the legal principle at issue. If a rule does

not squarely amend a prior rule, but merely clarifies it or comments on dicta associated with it, then it will not qualify as a "not previously recognized.'"

Id. at 493 (citations omitted).

8. Hearing

The Defendant is entitled, by statute, to a hearing on petition for post conviction relief. Md. Rule 4-406(a); *Wilson*, 284 Md. at 675; *Vernon v. Warden, Maryland Penitentiary*, 11 Md. App. 340, 341-42 (1971); *Franklin v. Warden, Maryland Penitentiary*, 8 Md. App. 395, 396 (1970); *Yopps v. Warden, Maryland Penitentiary*, 1 Md. App. 537, 540 (1967). The Defendant has the right to be present at any post conviction hearing. Md. Rule 4-406(d).

The trial judge may not serve as the post conviction judge, unless the parties agree otherwise. Md. Rule 4-406(b); Md. Code Ann., Crim. Proc. § 7-204(a); *Pfoff v. State*, 85 Md. App. 296, 300 (1991); *Montague v. Director, Patuxent Institution*, 2 Md. App. 642, 643 (1967). *See Ware v. Warden, Maryland Penitentiary*, 2 Md. App. 728, 730 (1968) (judge who was the prosecutor at trial may not serve as the post conviction judge). *Cf. Berman v. Warden, Maryland Penitentiary*, 232 Md. 642, 643 (1963) (judge not disqualified to hear post conviction proceeding after serving on the board of the Division of Correction at the time the Defendant was incarcerated).

Because "trial," for post conviction purposes, means a proceeding in which guilt/innocence is decided, a judge who presided over a suppression hearing may hear the post conviction proceeding. *Hernandez v. State*, 108 Md. App. 354 (1996), *aff'd*, 344 Md. 721 (1997).

Although the Defendant is entitled to a prompt hearing, because a post conviction hearing is not a criminal prosecution, the right to a speedy trial under the Sixth Amendment and Md. Decl. of Rights art. 21 does not apply. *See Burke v. Warden*, 3 Md. App. 719, 721 n.2 (1968).

9. Evidence

The rules of evidence are relaxed in post conviction proceedings. Evidence may include (a) live testimony; (b) affidavits; (c) depositions; and (d) other forms of evidence within the court's discretion. Md. Rule 4-406. When the Defendant alleges ineffective assistance of trial counsel, appellate counsel, or post conviction counsel, the Defendant should subpoena the allegedly ineffective attorney. If the Defendant fails to call counsel as a witness, the court may infer, but is not required to infer, that anything that counsel did, or failed to do, was done or not done as part of legitimate trial strategy. *Cirincione*, 119 Md. App. at 497.

10. Defendant's burden of persuasion

The Defendant must persuade the court of the entitlement to post conviction relief by a preponderance of the evidence. However, it is not necessary to establish each prong (performance prong and prejudice prong) by a preponderance of the evidence. To establish the prejudice prong, there must be a "reasonable probability" or "substantial or significant possibility," which is less than 50-50. See *Shelton v. Warden, Maryland Penitentiary*, 4 Md. App. 368, 370 (1968).

11. Disposition

The post conviction court is required to make a written order (which may be dictated into the record and transcribed) as to each allegation, which must be provided to the Defendant, defense counsel, and the State. *Wilson*, 284 Md. at 675; *Bauerlien v. Warden, Maryland Penitentiary*, 236 Md. 346, 349 (1964); *Fennell v. Warden, Maryland Penitentiary*, 236 Md. 423, 425 (1964); *Duff v. Warden, Maryland Penitentiary*, 234 Md. 646, 648 (1964); *Smith v. Warden, Maryland Penitentiary*, 22 Md. 613 (1960).

The judge must make findings of facts as to every claim. *Davis v. State*, 285 Md. 19, 36 (1979); *Farrell v. Warden, Md. Penitentiary*, 241 Md. 46, 49 (1965); *Conley v. Warden, Md. Penitentiary*, 10 Md. App. 251, 252 (1969); *Sample v. Warden, Md. Penitentiary*, 6 Md. App. 103, 109 (1969); *Prevatte v. Director, Patuxent Inst.*, 5 Md. App. 406, 414 (1968); *Shelton v. Warden, Md. Penitentiary*, 4 Md. App. 368, 370 (1968); *Szukiewicz v. Warden, Md. Penitentiary*, 1 Md. App. 61, 63 (1967).

In *Daniels v. Warden, Maryland Penitentiary*, 222 Md. 606, 607 (1960), the Court of Appeal held that, unless the post conviction court rules that an issue has been abandoned, the failure of the court to consider all contentions results in a remand to address any un-addressed issues. *See, e.g., Duff v. Warden, Maryland Penitentiary*, 234 Md. 646 (1964); *Ellinger v. Warden, Maryland Penitentiary*, 221 Md. 628 (1960). A remand is unnecessary if the issue can be resolved by a review of the record. *State v. Borchardt*, 396 Md. 586, 637 (2007); *Gilliam v. State*, 331 Md. 651, 693 (1993). The post conviction court need not decide issues not raised in the petition. *Cirincione*, 119 Md. App. 471.

12. Appeal

The non-prevailing party has no right to appeal, but may file an application for leave to appeal to the Court of Special Appeals. Applications are granted about 5% of the time. Md. Rule 4-408; Md. Code Ann., Crim. Proc. § 7-109(a). The Court of Appeals lacks certiorari jurisdiction over a decision of the Court of Special Appeals to grant or deny an application. The appellate court will not disturb the factual findings of the post conviction court unless clearly erroneous. *Wilson*, 363 Md. at 348; *Gilliam v. State*, 331 Md. 651, 672 (1993); Md. Code Ann., Cts. & Jud. Proc. § 12-202(1); *Sherman v. State*, 323 Md. 310, 311 (1991); *Williams v. State*, 292 Md. 201, 210 (1981).

In *Jourdan v. State*, 275 Md. 495 (1975), the Court of Appeals held:

> [T]his Court has no jurisdiction to review a decision of the Court of Special Appeals granting or denying leave to appeal in a post conviction proceeding.

However, once the Court of Special Appeals grants leave to appeal in such a case and transfers the case to its appeal docket, the matter takes the posture of a regular appeal, and we do have jurisdiction . . . to review the Court of Special Appeals' decision on the appeal itself.

Id. at 506 n.4.

G. Motion to reopen a closed post conviction proceeding

Effective October 1, 1995, the number of permissible post conviction proceedings was reduced from two to one. Md. Code Ann., Crim. Proc. § 7-103(a). At the same time, the legislature established a motion to reopen a closed post conviction proceeding. There is no limit on the number of motions to reopen that may be filed, and there is no statute of limitation on filing a motion to reopen a closed post conviction proceeding. Md. Code Ann., Crim. Proc. § 7-104. It is unclear whether the Defendant may file a motion to reopen a closed post conviction proceeding if the Defendant failed to file a timely petition for post conviction relief.

1. Waiver & "special circumstances"

Allegations are rebuttably presumed to be waived if they could have been—but were not—raised in a petition for post conviction relief or in a prior motion to reopen a closed post conviction proceeding, unless the Defendant can demonstrate non-waiver and/or special circumstances. Md. Rule 4-402(a)(7); Md. Code Ann., Crim. Proc. §§ 7-102 & 7-104.

2. Standard to reopen a closed post conviction proceeding

The Defendant is not entitled to a hearing on a motion to reopen a closed post conviction proceeding. Whether to reopen the closed post conviction proceeding is within the court's discretion. The standard for "reopening" is the "interests of justice" standard. Md. Rule 4-406(a). In most venues, the motion to reopen a closed post conviction proceeding is assigned to the judge who heard the petition for post conviction relief, unless retired, deceased, or elevated to another court. In *Gray v. State*, 388 Md. 366, 382 (2005), the Court of Appeals held that, if the court elects not to reopen the closed post conviction proceeding, there is no requirement for a written opinion.

If there was ineffective assistance of post conviction counsel, the Defendant is entitled to reopen a closed post conviction proceeding. In *Harris v. State*, 160 Md. App. 78, 112-13 (2004), the Court of Special Appeals held that the Defendant has a right to reopen a closed post conviction proceeding by asserting facts that, if proven, show that post conviction relief would have been granted, but for ineffective assistance of post conviction counsel. In *Stovall v. State*, 144 Md. App. 711, 715 (2002), the Court of Special Appeals held that if post conviction counsel renders ineffective assistance, it is in the "interests of justice" to reopen the closed post conviction proceeding if the allegations, if correct, would entitle the Defendant to post conviction relief.

After the 1995 creation of the motion to reopen a closed post conviction proceeding, courts would either (a) deny the motion to reopen the closed post conviction proceeding; or (b) grant the motion to reopen the closed post conviction proceeding, and treat the motion to reopen in the same way that it would treat a petition for post conviction relief. In recent years, many circuit court judges have added a third step, as follows: (a) deny the motion; (b) grant a proffer hearing for the limited purpose of permitting oral argument on what will be established if the court grants a hearing on the merits; and (c) with or without a "proffer" step, reopen the closed post conviction proceeding.

§ VII. Litigating a collateral attack in a petition for a writ of error coram nobis

A. Applicability

A petition for a writ of error coram nobis is mostly the equivalent of a petition for post conviction relief or a motion to reopen a closed post conviction proceeding. Coram nobis relief may be sought to correct an error of law or an error of fact. *Skok v. State*, 361 Md. 52, 78 (2000). A coram nobis petition may be filed by a person who (a) is not incarcerated, not on parole, and not on probation; (b) who faces significant collateral consequence from a conviction; and (c) has no other common law or statutory remedy. Md. Rule 15-1201 et seq.; *Parker v. State*, 160 Md. App. 672, 678 (2005).

Although PBJ is not a conviction for purposes of a petition for post conviction relief, a PBJ is a conviction for purposes of coram nobis. *Rivera v. State*, 409 Md. 176, 191-93 (2009); *Abrams v. State*, 176 Md. App. 600, 617 (2007). *But see Holmes v. State*, 401 Md. 429 (2007) (when an individual enters a guilty plea after having been informed of their right to file an application for leave to appeal and subsequently fails to file an application for leave to appeal, a presumption arises that they have waived their right to file a petition for a writ of coram nobis).

B. Subject matter jurisdiction

A petition for a writ of error coram nobis must be filed in the Circuit Court or the District Court in which the conviction occurred. Md. Rule 15-1202(a).

C. Doctrine of laches

There is no statute of limitation for filing a petition for a writ of error coram nobis, but the doctrine of laches applies to coram nobis petitions. *Moguel v. State*, 184 Md. App. 465, 471 (2009).

D. Content of petition

To succeed, the Defendant must demonstrate (1) serious attorney error and prejudice in a trial or a plea; (2) actual or potential significant collateral consequences, e.g., deportation or sentencing enhancement in federal court based on a prior conviction; and (3) non-waiver or special circumstances. *See, e.g., Skok v. State*, 361 Md. 52, 56-57 (2000); *Parker v. State*, 160 Md. App. 672, 697-88 (2005). A coram nobis petition must include the following and may be amended freely when justice permits. Md. Rule 15-1202(e).

The coram nobis petition must include (1) the name of the Defendant; (2) the date and place of the trial; (3) the offense(s) for which the Defendant was convicted (or received PBJ); (4) the sentence(s) imposed; (5) all previous proceedings and disposition; (6) allegations of error; (7) a statement explaining non-waiver; (8) actual or potential significant collateral consequences; (9) the fact that no other remedies are available; (10) a demand for relief and argument(s) in support of that demand; and (11) points and authorities. Md. Rule 15-1202 (a)-(b).

The State must file a response within 30 days after receiving notice or within the time ordered by the court. Md. Rule 15-1204.

E. Hearing

A hearing is discretionary on a petition for a writ of error coram nobis. The court may deny the petition without a hearing, but may grant the petition only if there is a hearing. The court may permit relaxed rules of evidence, except as to competency of witnesses. Md. Rule 15-1205(a).

F. Disposition

The court must prepare an order, addressing each allegation. If the petition is granted, the court must provide appropriate relief. Md. Rule 15-1207.

G. Appeal

Unlike with a petition for post conviction relief, which permits the non-prevailing party to file only an application for leave to appeal, in a coram nobis petition, the non-prevailing party may file a direct appeal from the court's order to the Court of Special Appeals. *Skok*, 361 Md. at 65-66; *State v. Hicks*, 139 Md. App. 1, 6 (2001).

§ VIII. Litigating a collateral attack through a federal petition for habeas corpus relief

A federal petition for habeas corpus relief must be filed in the United States District Court. A federal habeas corpus petition may be used to address illegal state convictions and illegal federal convictions.

A. Full & fair opportunity to litigate a constitutional claim in state court

The Defendant may seek federal habeas corpus relief if a state court denied a "full and fair opportunity" to litigate a federal constitutional claim. In *Stone v. Powell*, 428 U.S. 465, 489 (1976), the Supreme Court held that, because the Fourth Amendment claim had been fully litigated in state court, it could not be brought in a federal habeas corpus petition.

However, some constitutional claims may be litigate in a federal habeas corpus petition, even though there was a full and fair opportunity to litigate the issue in state court. The Defendant may use federal habeas corpus to challenge a reasonable doubt jury instruction, *Jackson v. Virginia*, 443 U.S. 307, 315-17 (1979); a denial of equal protection, *Rose v. Mitchell*, 443 U.S. 545, 561-62 (1979) (discrimination in selection of the grand jury); a denial of the Sixth Amendment right to effective assistance of counsel, *Kimmelman*, 477 U.S. at 374; and a denial of the Fifth Amendment privilege against compelled self-incrimination, *Withrow v. Williams*, 507 U.S. 680, 689-94 (1993).

B. 1996 Anti-Terrorism & Effective Death Penalty Act

1. Federal review is limited to state court decisions that are contrary to well-established law or render an unreasonable application of clearly established federal law

In 1996, Congress enacted the Anti-Terrorism & Effective Death Penalty Act (AEDPA), which provides for a hearing on a federal habeas corpus petition only if a state court decision is (a) contrary to well-established federal law; or (b) involved an unreasonable application of clearly established federal law. 28 U.S.C. § 2254. In *Williams v. Taylor*, 529 U.S. 362, 412-13 (2000), the Supreme Court stated:

> [U]nder the "contrary to" clause, a federal habeas court may grant the writ if the state court arrives at a conclusion opposite to that reached by this Court on a question of law or if the state decided a case differently that this court on a set of materially indistinguishable facts. Under the "unreasonable application" clause, a federal habeas court may grant the writ if the state court

identifies the correct governing legal principle from this Court's decisions but unreasonably applies that principle to the facts of the prisoner's case.

Id. at 412-13.

To demonstrate an "unreasonable applicable," the Defendant must demonstrate that the state court's error was more egregious than just an error in application of the law. In *Williams v. Taylor*, 529 U.S. 362 (2000), the Supreme Court held: "For the purposes of today's opinion, the most important point is that an *unreasonable* application of federal law is different from an *incorrect* application of federal law." *Id.* at 410 (emphasis in original). *See Cavasos v. Smith*, 132 S. Ct. 2, 5-8 (2011) (state court did not unreasonably apply *Jackson v. Virginia*). *Compare Harrington v. Richter*, 131 S. Ct. 770, 790-93 (2011) (state court's application of *Strickland* was not unreasonable); *Wiggins v. Smith*, 539 U.S. 510 (2003) (state court's application of *Strickland* was unreasonable, noting: "[T]he 'unreasonable application' prong of § 2254(d)(1) permits a federal habeas court to grant the writ if the state court identifies the correct governing principle from this Court's decisions but unreasonably applies that principle to the facts of petitioner's case." *Id.* at 520 (internal citations & quotations omitted)), *with Carey v. Musladin*, 549 U.S. 70, 77 (2006) (state court correctly held that the Defendant was not prejudiced by spectators wearing buttons with the picture of the murder victim); *Yarborough v. Alvarado*, 541 U.S. 652, 664 (2004) (state correctly applied *Miranda*); *Lockyer v. Andrade*, 538 U.S. 63, 72-76 (2003) (state court correctly applied Supreme Court's Eighth Amendment jurisprudence); *Price v. Vincent*, 538 U.S. 634 (2003) (state court correctly applied the Double Jeopardy Clause).

Some rules, e.g., when is a suspect in custody for purposes of *Miranda*, may have more flexibility in interpretation of the law than do the majority of legal rules. In the areas in which the law is a little less certain, it is less likely that a state interpretation of federal constitutional law will be deemed unreasonable. *See, e.g., Yarborough v. Alvarado*, 541 U.S. 652, 664 (2004). In essence, the AEDPA eliminated the full and fair hearing exception. Under the AEDPA, federal courts may review state court decisions, following a full and fair hearing in state court, only if there is clearly erroneous application of federal constitutional law when viewed at the time the state court rendered its decision, as determined by using the record that was before that court.

In *Cullen v. Pinholster*, 131 S. Ct. 1388, 1398 (2011), the Supreme Court held: "We now hold that review under § 2254(d)(1) is limited to the record that was before the state court that adjudicated the claim on the merits." *Id.* at 1398; *see Greene v. Fisher*, 132 S. Ct. 38, 44 (2011). Thus, since 1996, federal habeas corpus relief from a state ruling is almost non-existent. In *Renico v. Lett*, 559 U.S. 766 (2010), the Supreme Court held that the AEDPA permits federal review of state decisions only when a state's application of federal law is "objectively unreasonable," and not merely incorrect. In *Cullen*, 131 S. Ct. at 1403-04, the Supreme Court held that the state's application of *Strickland* was not unreasonable.

Furthermore, a state trial court's determination is entitled to great deference when it involves a credibility determination. *See, e.g., Felkner v. Jackson,* 131 S. Ct. 1305, 1307 (2011). Review of a state court decision, under 28 U.S.C. § 2254(d)(1), is limited to the record before the state court when that court's decision was made on the merits. *Cullen,* 131 S. Ct. 1388. A Defendant may introduce new evidence only on claims that were not adjudicated in the state court. *Id.* at 1398.

2. Claims are limited to issues under the United States Constitution

Federal habeas corpus claims are limited to challenges based on the United States Constitution. In *Wilson v. Corcoran,* 131 S. Ct. 13 (2010), the Supreme Court held: "[I]t is only noncompliance with *federal* law that renders a State's criminal judgment susceptible to collateral attack in the federal courts." *Id.* at 16. In *Fay v. Noia,* 372 U.S. 391 (1963), the Supreme Court stated:

> [T]he traditional characterization of the writ of habeas corpus as an original (save perhaps when it is issued by this Court) civil remedy for the enforcement of the right to personal liberty, rather than as a stage of the state criminal proceedings or as an appeal therefrom, emphasizes the independence of the federal habeas proceedings from what has gone before. This is not to say that a state criminal judgment resting on a constitutional error is void for all purposes. But conventional notions of finality in criminal litigation cannot be permitted to defeat the manifest federal policy that federal constitutional rights of personal liberty shall not be denied without the fullest opportunity for plenary federal judicial review.

Id. at 423-24; *see Brown v. Allen,* 344 U.S. 443, 447 (1953). In *Swarthout v. Cooke,* 131 S. Ct. 859 (2011), the Defendants were denied parole from state prison and were denied relief by state courts. The Defendants then filed for federal habeas relief, which was granted based on a "liberty interest" in parole protected by the Due Process Clause, which was violated by the State's incorrect application of the evidentiary standard required for granting parole. The Supreme Court reversed, holding:

> Whatever liberty interest exists is, of course, a *state* interest created by [state] law. There is no right under the Federal Constitution to be conditionally released before the expiration of a valid sentence, and States are under no duty to offer parole to their prisoners. When, however, a State creates a liberty interest, the Due Process Clause requires fair procedures for its vindication—and federal courts will review the application of those constitutionally required procedures.

Id. at 862. Furthermore, a review of those procedures "should have been the beginning and the end of the federal habeas courts' inquiry into whether [the Defendants] received due process. Instead, however, the Court of Appeals reviewed the state courts' decisions on the merits and concluded that they had unreasonably determined the facts in light of the evidence." *Id.* at 862, In *Wilson*, 131 S. Ct. 13, the Supreme Court stated: "It is not enough to note that a habeas petitioner *asserts* the existence of a constitutional violation; unless the federal court agrees with that assertion, it may not grant relief." *Id.* at 17.

In *Herrera v. Collins*, 506 U.S. 390, 416-17 (1993), the Supreme Court held that a federal habeas corpus petition may not raise claims of actual innocence, even if such claim is couched as a violation of the Eighth Amendment prohibition against cruel and unusual punishment.

3. Default under state procedural rules

Federal habeas corpus relief is limited to federal constitutional issues previously raised in (a) a state appeal; (b) a state post conviction proceeding; or (c) another state collateral proceeding. In *Keeny v. Tamayo-Reyes*, 504 U.S. 1 (1992), the Supreme Court stated: "Just as the State must afford the petitioner a full and fair hearing on his federal claim, so must the petitioner afford the full and fair opportunity to address and resolve the claim on the merits." *Id.* at 10. The claims presented in a habeas corpus petition must be the same as those presented to the state courts. In *Duncan v. Henry*, 513 U.S. 364 (1995), the Supreme Court held that "mere similarity of claims is insufficient to exhaust." *Id.* at 366. In *Anderson v. Harless*, 459 U.S. 4 (1982), the Supreme Court stated:

> In *Picard v. Connor*, 404 U.S. 270 (1971), we made clear that 28 U.S.C. § 2254 requires a federal habeas petitioner to provide the state courts with a "fair opportunity" to apply controlling legal principles to the facts bearing upon his constitutional claim. It is not enough that all the facts necessary to support the federal claim were before the state courts, or that a somewhat similar state-law claim was made. In addition, the habeas petitioner must have "fairly presented" to the state courts the "substance" of his federal habeas corpus claim.

Id. at 6 (internal citations omitted). If a state Defendant failed to raise a claim in an earlier proceeding, as required by state law, it may not be raised for the first time in a federal petition for habeas corpus relief unless it goes to actual innocence or is barred because there are no adequate or independent state grounds. In *Walker v. Martin*, 131 S. Ct. 1120 (2011), the Supreme Court held that a state court's decision, holding that the Defendant's state habeas petition was time barred by application of state time limits for filing a state petition for habeas corpus relief, had an independent and adequate state ground and thus barred federal habeas relief. *Id.* at 1131.

The only exception to the inability to raise procedurally defaulted claims is if the Defendant can show cause for previously failing to raise a claim and can show prejudice. *Wainwright v. Sykes*, 433 U.S. 72, 87 (1977). In *Cone*, 556 U.S. at 469, the Supreme Court, addressing a *Brady* violation, held that federal courts may consider issues that state courts dismissed on state procedural grounds. In that case, the state court rejected a *Brady* claim, stating that the state supreme court had decided the issue or it was not preserved. The Supreme Court held that that was not a ground that bars federal habeas corpus review.

4. Actual innocence exception

In *Kuhlmann v. Wilson*, 477 U.S. 436 (1986), the Supreme Court held that if a constitutional violation probably resulted in conviction of an innocent person, the Defendant is entitled to habeas corpus review, stating:

> In light of the historic purpose of habeas corpus and the interests implicated by successive petitions for federal habeas relief from a state conviction, we conclude that the "ends of justice" require federal courts to entertain such petitions only where the prisoner supplements his constitutional claim with a colorable showing of actual innocence.

Id. at 454. The Defendant must show a fair probability that, in light of all the evidence, the trier of fact would have had reasonable doubt. To establish actual innocence, the Defendant must prove that it is more likely than not that no reasonable juror would have convicted. *Schlup v. Delo*, 513 U.S. 298, 327 (1995).

5. "Fugitive forfeiture" exception

In *Beard v. Kindler*, 558 U.S. 53, 62-63 (2009), the Supreme Court held that a state law that permits courts discretion to bar, from federal habeas corpus relief and other collateral review, state Defendants who had been convicted of the crime of escape, was constitutional.

6. Cause & prejudice

A procedural default in state court may be excused if the Defendant can show cause for the default and prejudice stemming from that default. In *Coleman v. Thompson*, 501 U.S. 722 (1991), the Supreme Court held:

> In all cases in which a [Defendant] has defaulted his federal claims in state court pursuant to an independent and adequate state procedural rule, federal habeas review of the claims is barred unless the [Defendant] can demonstrate cause for the default and actual prejudice as a result of the alleged violation of federal law, or demonstrate that failure to consider the claims will result in a fundamental miscarriage of justice.

Id. at 750. *See Wainwright v. Sykes*, 433 U.S. 72, 86-87 (1977). In *Francis v. Henderson*, 425 U.S. 536 (1976), the Supreme court stated that procedural default in state court requires "not only a showing of 'cause' . . . but also a showing of actual preju-dice." *Id.* at 542. Defense counsel's negligence will not excuse a procedural default. In *Coleman*, the Supreme Court stated: "In the absence of a constitutional violation, the [Defendant] bears the risk in federal habeas for all attorney errors made in the course of representation . . ." *Coleman*, 501 U.S. at 754.

Ineffective assistance of counsel

If the Defendant is claiming ineffective assistance as the cause for his state procedur-al default, the Defendant must have raised an ineffective assistance of counsel claim in state court. *Edwards v. Carpenter*, 529 U.S. 446, 452 (2000). However, in *Martinez v. Ryan*, 132 S. Ct. 1309 (2012), the Supreme Court held that a Defendant may raise a claim of ineffective assistance of counsel to excuse a state procedural default in a federal habeas proceeding if an attorney failed to raise ineffective assistance of coun-sel in the only proceeding in which such a claim could have been raised. The Court stated:

> To protect prisoners with a potentially legitimate claim of ineffective assis-tance of trial counsel, it is necessary to modify the unqualified statement in *Coleman* [*v. Thompson*, 501 U.S. 722 (1991)], that an attorney's ignorance or inadvertence in a post conviction proceeding does not qualify as cause to excuse a procedural default. . . . Inadequate assistance of counsel at an initial-review collateral proceeding may establish cause for a prisoner's pro-cedural default of a claim of ineffective assistance of trial counsel.

Id. at 1315. The Court held that this rule applies only to situations in which counsel fails to raise an ineffective assistance of counsel claim in the "first designated pro-ceeding for a prisoner to raise a claim of ineffective assistance of counsel . . ." *Id.* at 1317. Thus, the rule in *Coleman*, that attorney negligence is generally not an excuse for procedural default remains. The Court stated: "*Coleman* held that an attorney's negligence in a post conviction proceeding does not establish cause, and this remains true except as to initial-review collateral proceedings for claims of ineffective assis-tance of counsel at trial. *Id.* at 1319.

State interference

If actions by a state or a state actor results in the Defendant's procedural default, that default will be excused. In *Strickler v. Greene*, 527 U.S. 263, 282 (1999), the State's *Brady* violation was deemed to be cause for the Defendant's procedural default, but the Defendant's claim was denied due to a lack of prejudice. In *McClesky v. Zant*, 499 U.S. 467, 501 (1991), the Supreme Court held that the State's failure to disclose a recorded statement was not cause because that statement was not "critical" to the Defendant's Sixth Amendment claim.

Prejudice stemming from default

In order to show prejudice, the Defendant must demonstrate a "reasonable probability" of a different outcome. *Strickler*, 527 U.S. at 298.

Fundamental miscarriage of justice

If a Defendant cannot meet the "cause-and-prejudice" test, he still may have his habeas corpus claims heard if the failure to allow those claims to go forward would result in a fundamental miscarriage of justice. In *Schlup v. Delo*, 513 U.S. 298 (1995), the Supreme Court discussed *Murray v. Carrier*, 477 U.S. 478 (1986), which set forth what was necessary for a showing of a "fundamental miscarriage of justice." The Court stated:

> *Carrier* requires a [Defendant] to show that he is "actually innocent" . . . To satisfy the *Carrier* gateway standard, a [Defendant] must show that it is more likely that not that no reasonable juror would have found [the Defendant] guilty beyond a reasonable doubt. Several observations about this standard are in order. The *Carrier* standard is intended to focus the inquiry on actual innocence. In assessing the adequacy of [the Defendant's] showing, therefore, the district court is not bound by the rules of admissibility that would govern at trial. Instead, the emphasis on "actual innocence" allows the reviewing tribunal also to consider the probative force of relevant evidence that was either excluded or unavailable at trial.

513 U.S. at 327. In *House v. Bell*, 547 U.S. 518 (2006), the Supreme Court held that the Defendant made the requisite showing of actual innocence necessary to excuse his procedural default. In that case, the Defendant was convicted of murder and sentenced to death. In his habeas corpus petition, he presented evidence that showed (a) another person may have been responsible for the murder; (b) the DNA evidence showed that the semen found on the victim was not his; and (c) evidence calling into doubt forensic evidence presented by the State at trial.

The Supreme Court stated that this was sufficient to meet the requirements for claiming actual innocence, stating: "[A]lthough the issue is close, we conclude that this is the rare case where . . . it is more likely than not that [a] reasonable juror viewing the record as a whole would lack reasonable doubt." *Id.* at 540-41.

In *Bousley v. United States*, 523 U.S. 614 (1998), the Supreme Court applied the actual innocence standard to a Defendant seeking review of his guilty plea. The Court stated: "'[A]ctual innocence' means factual evidence, not mere insufficiency. . . . In case where the Government has foregone more serious charges in the course of plea bargaining, [the Defendant's] showing of actual innocence must also extend to those charges." *Id.* at 623-24.

In *Sawyer v. Whitley*, 505 U.S. 333 (1992), the Supreme Court applied the actual innocence standard in a death penalty case, and required the Defendant to "show by clear and convincing evidence that but for a constitutional error no reasonable juror would find the [Defendant] eligible for the death penalty." *Id.* at 336.

7. Procedural requirements

In order to file a federal petition for habeas corpus relief, the Defendant must meet following requirements:

Exhaustion

The state Defendant must have exhausted all state remedies for relief based on alleged violations of the United States Constitution. 28 U.S.C. § 2254(b)(1). In *O'Sullivan v. Boerckel*, 526 U.S. 838 (1999), the Supreme Court held:

> Because the exhaustion doctrine is designed to give state courts a full and fair opportunity to resolve federal constitutional claims before those claims are presented to the federal courts, we conclude that state prisoners must give the state courts one full opportunity to resolve any constitutional issues by invoking one complete round of the State's established appellate review process.

Id. at 845. In *Rose v. Lundy*, 455 U.S. 509 (1982), the Supreme Court held: "The exhaustion doctrine is principally designed to protect the state courts' role in enforcement of federal law and prevent disruption of state proceedings." *Id.* at 518. In *Ex Parte Hawk*, 321 U.S. 114, 116-17 (1944), the Supreme Court stated:

> "Ordinarily an application for habeas corpus by one detained under a state court judgment of conviction for crime will be entertained by a federal court only after all state remedies available, including all appellate remedies in the state courts and in this Court by appeal or writ of certiorari, have been exhausted.

Id. at 116-17. *See Ex Parte Royall*, 117 U.S. 241 (1886). Exhaustion may be waived by the State, but must be done so expressly. 28 U.S.C. § 2254(b)(3). If a Supreme Court decision is released, subsequent to the Defendant filing for habeas corpus relief, and it casts doubt on the Defendant's conviction, the Defendant must then reapply for state relief before his federal habeas corpus petition will be adjudicated. However, if the highest state court alters its interpretation of existing Supreme Court precedent, the Defendant need not reapply to state court for relief. *Roberts v. LaValle*, 389 U.S. 40, 42-43 (1967).

Furthermore, a Defendant need not return to state court if the statute under which he was convicted has been held unconstitutional by state courts subsequent to the Defendant being convicted. In *Francisco v. Gathright*, 419 U.S. 59 (1974), the Supreme Court stated: "[S]tate courts had a full opportunity to determine the federal constitutional issues before resort was made to a federal forum, and the policies served by the exhaustion requirement would not be furthered by resubmission of the claims to state courts." *Id.* at 63; see *Brown*, 344 U.S. at 447-50; *Picard*, 404 U.S. at 275.

28 U.S.C. § 2254(b)(2) provides that a federal habeas corpus petition "may be denied on the merits, notwithstanding the failure of the applicant to exhaust the remedies available in the courts of the State."

Limited exceptions to exhaustion

Even if all avenues for State relief are not exhausted, the AEDPA provides that the Defendant may file a federal petition for habeas corpus relief when "there is an absence of available State corrective process, or circumstances exist that render such process ineffective to protect the rights of the applicant." 28 U.S.C. § 2254(b)(1)(B)(i) & (ii).

Petition containing both exhausted & un-exhausted claims—"stay and abeyance"

A petition advancing both exhausted and un-exhausted claims may be stayed, with the exhausted claims held in abeyance, while the un-exhausted claims are finally litigated provided: "(a) the petitioner had good cause for his failure to exhaust; (b) his unexhausted claims are potentially meritorious; and (c) there is no indication that the [Defendant] engaged in intentionally dilatory litigation tactics. In such circumstances, the district court should stay, rather than dismiss, the mixed petition." *Rhines v. Weber*, 544 U.S. 269, 278 (2005).

8. Filing multiple petitions

Although state Defendants may file multiple federal habeas corpus petitions, if a given claim is raised for the second time, it must be dismissed. 28 U.S.C. § 2244(b)(1). Moreover, if the Defendant failed to raise the claim in the first petition, that claim is barred in subsequent petitions, unless

> the applicant shows that the claim relies on a new rule of constitutional law, made retroactive to cases on collateral review by the Supreme Court, that was previously unavailable, [or] the factual predicate for the claim could not have been discovered previously through the exercise of due diligence[, and] the fact underlying the claim, if proven and viewed in light of the evidence as a whole, would be sufficient to establish by clear and convincing evidence that, but for constitutional error, no reasonable fact finder would have found the [Defendant] guilty of the underlying offense.

28 U.S.C. § 2244(b)(2). 28 U.S.C. § 2244(b)(3) provides that, before a Defendant may file a second or successive application, a three-judge panel of the Court of Appeals

must determine whether the Defendant's second or successive petition meets the criteria. The three-judge panel's decision is not appealable.

9. Custody

To eligible to file a federal petition for habeas corpus relief, the Defendant must be in custody, which means (a) incarceration; (b) parole; or (c) release on recognizance. *Compare Justices of Boston Municipal Court v. Lydon*, 466 U.S. 294, 300-02 (1984) (release on personal recognizance pending a *de novo* trial was "in custody"); *Hensley v. Municipal Court*, 411 U.S. 345, 351-53 (1973) (release on personal recognizance pending execution of his sentence was "in custody"); *Jones v. Cunningham*, 371 U.S. 236, 242-43 (1963) ("being on parole fulfilled the custody requirement; [i]t is not relevant that conditions and restrictions such as these may be desirable and important parts of the rehabilitative process; what matters is that they significantly restrain [the Defendant's] liberty to do those things which in this country free men are entitled to do. Such restraints are enough to invoke the help of the Great Writ. Of course, that writ always could and still can reach behind prison walls and bars. But it can do more. It is not now and never has been a static, narrow, formalistic remedy; its scope has grown to achieve its grand purpose—the protection of individuals against erosion of their right to be free from wrongful restraints on their liberty. [Although the Defendant's] parole releases him from immediate physical imprisonment, it imposes conditions which significantly confine and restrain his freedom; this is enough to keep him in 'custody' . . ."), *with Maleng v. Cook*, 490 U.S. 488, 492-93 (1989) (rejecting the Defendant's argument that he was "in custody" because of the possibility that his conviction would be used to enhance the sentence for a subsequent conviction).

Release from custody prior to final adjudication

In *Carafas v. LaValle*, 391 U.S. 234 (1968), the Defendant was convicted of burglary. He filed for both federal and state habeas relief based on alleged constitutional violations. The Defendant's claims were rejected and he subsequently filed an appeal. The Second Circuit dismissed his appeal, but the Supreme Court granted certiorari. Prior to the case being heard, the Defendant was unconditionally released from custody and the State argued that the Defendant's appeal was moot as he had already been released from custody. The Supreme Court disagreed and held that the case could move forward because the Defendant filed while he was in custody and the case was not moot. The Court stated:

> [The Defendant's] cause is not moot. In consequence of his conviction, he cannot engage in certain businesses; he cannot serve as an official of a labor union for a specified period of time; he cannot vote in any election held in New York States; he cannot serve as a juror. Because of these disabilities or burdens (which) may flow from [the Defendant's] conviction, he has a sub-

stantial stake in the judgment of conviction which survives the satisfaction of the sentence imposed on him. On account of these collateral consequences, the case is not moot.

Id. at 237-38 (internal citations & quotations omitted). In *Garlotte v. Fordice*, 515 U.S. 39, 45-46 (1995), the Supreme held that the Defendant, who was serving the second of two consecutive sentences, could challenge his first sentence, even though he had already served the entirety of the first sentence. In *Peyton v. Rowe*, 391 U.S. 54, 66-67 (1968), the Supreme Court held that the Defendant could challenge the second of two consecutive sentences while still serving the first sentence. In *Braden v. 30th Judicial Circuit Court of Kentucky*, 410 U.S. 484, 495 (1968), the Supreme Court held that the Defendant, who was incarcerated in one state, could challenge pending charges in another state.

10. State court claims must be finally adjudicated

Federal habeas corpus claims will be heard only after the Defendant's claims have been "adjudicated on the merits" in state court. 28 U.S.C. § 2254(d). In *Harrington v. Richter*, 131 S. Ct. 770 (2011), the Defendant filed a habeas petition in state court, which was denied in a one-sentence opinion without reasoning. Despite the absence of a state court opinion or rationale, the Supreme Court held that the summary one-sentence denial was an adjudication on the merits for the purposes of 28 U.S.C. § 2254(d). *Id.* at 785. When a state court addresses some of [the Defendant's] claims, but does not specifically address federal constitutional claims, as in *Richter*, it is presumed that those unaddressed claims were "adjudicated on the merits."

In *Johnson v. Williams*, 133 S. Ct. 1088 (2013), the Supreme Court held: "Where a state court's decision is unaccompanied by an explanation, the habeas petitioner's burden must be met by showing there was no reasonable basis for the state court to deny relief." *See Richter*, 131 S. Ct. at 784.

11. Filing deadlines

One year after a judgment becomes final

Under the AEDPA, a federal petition for habeas corpus relief must be filed within one year after the judgment became final. A state conviction is final after the time for filing for certiorari in the Supreme Court has passed or the Court has denied certiorari. *Sawyer v. Smith*, 497 U.S. 227, 232 (1990).

A request for counsel will not substitute for filing, and the Defendant must seek relief on the merits. In *Woodford v. Garceau*, 538 U.S. 202 (2003), the Supreme Court stated: "[A] habeas suit begins with the filing of an application for habeas corpus relief—the equivalent of a complaint in an ordinary case." *Id.* at 208. For state Defendants, the one-year period does not include any time during which a state collateral proceeding is pending.

In *Wall v. Kholi*, 131 S. Ct. 1278, 1287 (2011), the Supreme Court held that a motion to reduce a sentence filed under state law qualified as a collateral proceeding. *See Carrol v. Saffold*, 536 U.S. 214 (2002); *Duncan v. Walker*, 533 U.S. 167, 172-73 (2001); *Artuz v. Bennett*, 531 U.S. 4, 10-11 (2000). However, the limitation period is not tolled while a petition for a writ of certiorari, from the denial of a state post conviction relief, is pending before the United States Supreme Court.

In *Lawrence v. Florida*, 549 U.S. 327 (2007), the Supreme Court stated: "This tolling rule would provide an incentive for prisoners to file certiorari petitions—regardless of the merit of the claims asserted—so that they receive additional time to file their habeas applications." *Id.* at 336. In *Wall v. Kholi*, 131 S. Ct. 1278 (2011), the Supreme Court defined "collateral review" as the "a judicial reexamination of a judgment or claim in a proceeding outside of the direct review process." *Id.* at 1285.

In capital cases, the deadline is six months from the final state court affirmance of the conviction. A court may raised the issue of timeliness sua sponte, provided that the court affords the Defendant an opportunity to present his or her position. *Day v. McDonough*, 547 U.S. 198, 209-11 (2006). In *Jimenez v. Quarterman*, 555 U.S. 113, 120 (2009), the Supreme Court held that a judgment was not final, for federal habeas corpus purposes, when a state court granted state post conviction relief in the form of the right to file a belated direct appeal in state court.

Equitable tolling

"Extraordinary circumstances" may provide for equitable tolling. In *Lawrence v. Florida*, 549 U.S. 327, 336-37 (2007), the Supreme Court held that defense counsel's miscalculation of dates was not an "extraordinary circumstance" to justify equitable tolling.

Amended petition

In *Mayle v. Felix*, 545 U.S. 644, 649-50 (2005), the Supreme Court held that a federal habeas corpus petition could be amended after the limitations period had run. However, the amended petition will not relate back if it relies on facts not set forth in the original petition.

No right to stay due to incompetence

In *Ryan v. Gonzalez*, 133 S. Ct. 696 (2013), the Supreme Court held that a Defendant seeking federal habeas corpus relief is not entitled to a tolling of the statute of limitations under the AEDPA when the Defendant is deemed incompetent. The Court stated:

> Given the backward looking, record-based nature of most federal habeas proceedings, counsel can generally provide effective representation to a habeas petitioner regardless of the petitioner's competence. . . . Attorneys are quite

capable of reviewing the state-court record, identifying legal errors, and mar-
shaling relevant arguments, even without their client's assistance.

Id. at 704-05.

12. Retroactive application of cases decided while a habeas petition is pending

In *Teague v. Lane*, 489 U.S. 288 (1989), the Defendant was convicted in state court.
Thereafter, the Defendant filed a federal habeas corpus petition, alleging racial
discrimination in the prosecutor's use of peremptory challenges to exclude Afri-
can-Americans from the jury. While his petition was pending, the Supreme Court
decided *Batson v. Kentucky*, which held that racially discriminatory use of peremptory challenges is unconstitutional. The Defendant argued that the holding in *Batson*
should be applied retroactively to his case.

The Supreme Court disagreed, holding that the Defendant's conviction would be
examined in light of the law prevailing at the time of his conviction. A "new rule" will
generally not apply to federal habeas corpus petitions. In *O'Dell v. Netherland*, 521
U.S. 151 (1997), the Supreme Court held that a determination of whether a given rule
will be applied to a Defendant's habeas petition requires a three-step process. The
Court stated:

> First, the date on which the Defendant's conviction became final is deter-
> mined. Next, the habeas court considers whether a state court considering
> [the Defendant's] claim at the time his conviction became final would have
> felt compelled by existing precedent to conclude that the rule [he] seeks was
> required by the Constitution. If not, then the rule is new. If the rule is deter-
> mined to be new, the final step in the *Teague* analysis requires the court to
> determine whether the rule nonetheless falls within one of the two narrow
> exceptions to the *Teague* doctrine.

Id. at 157 (internal citations omitted).

Determining whether a rule is "new"

In *Teague*, 489 U.S. 288, the Supreme Court explained what a "new" rule is, stating:
"[A] case announces a new rule when it breaks new ground and imposes obligations
on the States or Federal government. To put it differently, a case announces a new
rule if the result was not dictated by precedent existing at the time the Defendant's
conviction became final." *Id.* at 301 (citing *Rock v. Arkansas*, 483 U.S. 44, 62 (1987);
Ford v. Wainwright, 477 U.S. 399, 410 (1986); *Truesdale v. Aiken*, 480 U.S. 527, 528-29
(1987)). *Compare Penry v. Lynaugh*, 492 U.S. 302 (1989) (not a new rule); *Stringer
v. Black*, 503 U.S. 222 (1992) (not a new rule); *with Butler v. McKellar*, 494 U.S. 407
(1990) (new rule); *Mills v. Maryland*, 486 U.S. 367 (1988) (new rule).

Exceptions to non-retroactivity

In *Teague*, 489 U.S. 288, the Court recognized two exceptions to non-retroactivity, as follows: "First, a new rule should be applied retroactively if it places certain kinds of primary, private individual conduct beyond the power of the criminal law-making authority to proscribe. Second, a new rule should be applied retroactively if it requires the observance of those procedure that . . . are implicit in the concept of ordered liberty." *Id.* at 307 (internal citations & quotations omitted).

Individual conduct beyond the power of the criminal law-making authority to proscribe

A new rule comes within one of the *Teague* exceptions if it "decriminalize[s] a class of conduct" or prohibits the execution of certain individuals, for example, mentally handicapped persons. *Graham v. Collins*, 506 U.S. 461 (1993); *Penry v. Lynaugh*, 492 U.S. 302 (1989). Although decided before *Teague*, *United States v. United States Coin & Currency*, 401 U.S. 715 (1971), provides an example of a rule to be applied retroactively, when the Court found that a law criminalized behavior, in violation of the Fifth Amendment, applied retroactively.

Observance of procedures implicit in the concept of ordered liberty

The Supreme Court addressed this *Teague* exception in *Beard v. Banks*, 542 U.S. 406 (2004), stating:

> We have repeatedly emphasized the limited scope of the second *Teague* exception, explaining that it is clearly meant to apply only to a small core of rules requiring observance of those procedures that . . . are implicit in the concept of ordered liberty. And, because any qualifying rule would be so central to an accurate determination of innocence or guilt [that it is] unlikely that many such components of basic due process have yet to emerge, it should come as no surprise that we have yet to find a new rule that falls under the second *Teague* exception.

Id. at 417 (internal citations & quotations omitted). In *Gray v. Netherland*, 518 U.S. 152, 170 (1996), the Supreme Court held that a rule requiring notice of evidence to be used at sentencing does not fall with the second *Teague* exception. In *Caspari v. Bohlen*, 510 U.S. 383, 396 (1994), the Supreme Court held that a rule barring successive sentencing proceedings based on double jeopardy does not fall within the second *Teague* exception. In *Graham*, 506 U.S. at 477-78, the Supreme Court held that a rule requiring certain jury instructions in death penalty cases does not fall within the second *Teague* exception.

In *Sawyer v. Smith*, 497 U.S. 227 (1990), the Supreme Court held that a rule barring prosecutors from implying that appellate courts have the final responsibility for determining whether a death sentence is warranted does not fall within the second *Teague* exception because it did not "alter our understanding of the *bedrock procedural elements* essential to the fairness of the proceeding." *Id.* at 242 (emphasis in original) (internal quotations & citation omitted).

13. Presumption that factual determinations of the trial court are correct

In federal habeas corpus cases, there is a presumption that the factual findings of the trial court are correct, which the Defendant must rebut by clear and convincing evidence. 28 U.S.C. § 2254(e)(1). In *Miller-el v. Dretke*, 545 U.S. 231 (2005), the Supreme Court stated: "[W]e presume the [state] court's factual findings to be sound unless [the Defendant] rebuts the 'presumption of correctness by clear and convincing evidence.'" *Id.* at 240 (internal citations & quotations omitted). 28 U.S.C. § 2254(d)(2) provides that relief will not be granted unless the federal court finds that the trial court's factual determinations are "an unreasonable determination of the facts in light of the evidence presented in the State court proceeding."

14. Hearing

A Defendant is not entitled to a hearing unless he can show that his claim relies on (a) a new rule of constitutional law, made retroactive to cases on collateral review by the Supreme Court, that was previously unavailable; or (b) a factual predicate that could not have been previously discovered through the exercise of due diligence and the fact facts underlying the claim would be sufficient to establish by clear and convincing evidence that, but for the constitutional error, no reasonable fact finder would have found the Defendant guilty of the underlying offense. 28 U.S.C. § 2254(e)(2).

Due diligence requires "a reasonable attempt, in light of the information available at the time, to investigate and pursue claims in state court; it does not depend . . . upon whether those efforts could have been successful." *Williams v. Taylor*, 529 U.S. 420, 435 (2000).

§ IX. State petition for habeas corpus relief

A. Who may file a state habeas corpus petition in Maryland?

Anyone committed, detained, confined, or restrained, who is entitled to immediate release, may file a state petition for habeas corpus relief. Md. Code Ann., Cts. & Jud. Proc. § 3-702; *Pollock v. Patuxent Institution Board of Review*, 358 Md. 656, 668-69 (2000) (habeas corpus limited to release but may result in a new parole hearing).

B. Where to file a state habeas corpus petition?

A state petition for habeas corpus relief may be filed with any judge of any Circuit Court or appellate court (not with the court, but with a judge on the court). The judge must immediately (1) resolve the petition; or (2) refer the petition to the Circuit Court in which the Defendant was convicted, but it may not be heard by the trial judge. Md. Code Ann., Cts. & Jud. Proc. §§ 3-701 & 3-702.

C. Disposition of a state habeas corpus petition

If the habeas court holds that the Defendant is being held unlawfully, the Defendant must be released. *Id.* §§ 3-704 & 3-706.

§ X. Petition for a writ of actual innocence

A. Newly discovered evidence of actual innocence

Md. Code Ann., Crim. Proc. § 8-301 provides a Defendant an opportunity to seek a new trial based on newly discovered evidence of actual innocence. In *Douglas v. State*, 423 Md. 156 (2011), the Court of Appeals held: "It is settled that questions of guilt or innocence cannot be raised in petitions for post conviction relief. It is just as well settled that a petition for post conviction relief is not a substitute for a motion for a new trial." *Id.* at 175-76.

A Defendant convicted in Circuit Court may, at any time, file a petition for a writ of actual innocence in the court in which the Defendant was convicted, based on newly discovered evidence that (1) creates a substantial or significant possibility that the result may have been different, as that standard has been judicially determined; or (2) could not have been discovered in time to file a motion for a new trial under Md. Rule 4-331. Md. Code Ann., Crim. Proc. § 8-301(a).

B. The petition

1. Required contents of the petition

The written petition for a writ of actual innocence must contain (a) the court in which the charging document was filed and the file number; (b) the court to which the case was removed, if any; (c) each offense for which the Defendant was convicted and the sentence(s); (d) if appealed, (i) the appellate case number, (ii) the issues raised on appeal, and (iii) the date of the appellate mandate; (e) for each motion or petition for post-judgment relief, (i) the court in which filed, (ii) the case number of each proceeding, (iii) the issues raised, the result, and the date of disposition; (f) the fact of newly discovered evidence that, even with due diligence, would not have been discovered in time to file a motion for a new trial under Md. Rule 4-331; (g) (i) description of the newly discovered evidence, (ii) how and when discovered, and (iii) if the issue was previously raised, the identity of the proceeding in which raised, and how this evidence is different; (h) the fact that newly discovered evidence creates a substantial possibility that the result may have been different; (i) an assertion that the Defendant is factually innocent; (j) if no counsel, and if the Defendant cannot afford counsel, whether the Defendant wishes appointed counsel; (k) statement that the petition has been mailed to the State's Attorney's office; (l) the relief requested; and (m) a request for a hearing. Md. Rule 4-332(d); Md. Code Ann., Crim. Proc. § 8-301(b).

2. Amendment & response

The Defendant may amend the petition. The State may respond within 90 days of receipt of the petition and any amendment. Md. Rule 4-332(e) to (i).

C. Hearing

The court is required to grant a hearing unless the petition fails to state grounds for relief. Md. Code Ann., Crim. Proc. § 8-301(e). In *Douglas*, the Court of Appeals held that section 8-301

> imposes a burden of pleading, such that [the Defendant] is entitled to a hearing on the merits of the petition, provided the petition sufficiently (1) pleads grounds for relief under the statute; (2) includes a request for a hearing; and (3) complies with the filing requirements of § 8-301(b) . . . The pleading requirement mandates that the trial court determine whether the allegations could afford a petitioner relief, if those allegations would be proven at a hearing, assuming the fact in the light most favorable to the [Defendant] and accepting all reasonable inferences that can be drawn from the petition[.] This standard does not require that a trial court take impossibilities as truths.

423 Md. at 165. The victim or victim's representative must be notified of the hearing and be permitted to attend the hearing. Md. Code Ann., Crim. Proc. § 8-301(d); Md. Rule 4-332(e)(2) & (j)(2). If the Defendant requests counsel, based on indigency, the Court must send the petition to the Public Defender's office. Md. Rule 4-332(e)(3). A hearing is required when the petition substantially complies with Md. Rule 4-332(d) and a hearing is requested. Md. Rule 4-332(j)(1). The burden of persuasion is on the Defendant. Md. Code Ann., Crim. Proc. § 8-301(g); Md. Rule 4-332(k).

D. Ruling & appeal

The court may dismiss the petition for failure to contain the necessary averments. If so, the court may grant leave to amend. Md. Rule 4-332(i)(1). If the court reaches the merits, the court may (1) set aside the verdict and grant a new trial; or (2) re-sentence the Defendant or correct the sentence. Md. Code Ann., Crim. Proc. § 8-301(f). The reasons for the court's ruling must be stated on the record. Md. Rule 4-332(k)(2). An order denying a petition for a writ of actual innocence is immediately appealable, regardless of whether the court holds a hearing. *Douglas*, 423 Md. 156.

§ XI. Collateral challenge to predicate convictions during a recidivist enhancement sentencing proceeding

In the recidivist sentencing proceeding, the State is required to prove the predicate conviction beyond a reasonable doubt. *Bowman v. State*, 314 Md. 725, 733-34 (1989). The State may use an authenticated and facially valid judgment to meet this standard because of the strong presumption of regularity that attaches to final judgments.

In *Fairbanks v. State*, 331 Md. 482 (1993), the Defendant argued that his enhanced sentence was based on an unconstitutional predicate conviction because the State had not shown that he knowingly and intelligently waived his right to trial by jury in the case that resulted in the predicate conviction. The Court of Appeals held that the Defendant was not entitled to challenge his prior conviction during the recidivist sentencing proceeding. *See State v. McGhee*, 331 Md. 494, 488 (1993).

However, the Court recognized that a collateral challenge to a prior conviction may be made in some limited circumstances. The Court stated that "[w]hen the evidence relied upon by the State to establish the previous conviction on its face strongly tends to undermine the constitutional validity of the conviction, the strong presumption of regularity that accompanies a facially valid conviction is not present, and further inquiry will be required to determine admissibility." *Id.* at 486.

The Court will not consider an un-counseled predicate conviction as facially valid unless it contains a docket entry or affirmative statement by the Defendant of waiver of the right to counsel. If the record lacks such evidence, the burden is on the State to show that a knowing and voluntary waiver actually occurred.

In *Fairbanks*, the Court stated: "A Defendant seeking to challenge a facially valid prior conviction on grounds of constitutional invalidity has no right to do so as part of the recidivist sentencing proceeding, but may pursue other available avenues of collateral attack and, if successful, seek subsequent relief from the enhanced sentence that was imposed." 331 Md. at 486.

Chapter 34

Parole, Pardon, & Clemency

§ I. Parole

A. Paroleable sentences versus sentences without parole

Maryland and most states have a parole system. Federal law eliminated parole for federal inmates in 1987. 18 U.S.C. § 3551; *Norwood v. Brennan*, 891 F.2d 179, 180-81 (7th Cir. 1989). Even with a parole system, legislatures sometime establish sentences that are not eligible for parole or establish sentences that have a certain period of non-parole eligibility. In Maryland, most executed sentences in the Division of Correction (DOC) are paroleable sentences within the discretion of the Maryland Parole Commission (MPC). In *Lewis v. State*, 348 Md. 648, 659 (1998), the Court of Appeals held that if the legislature intends a sentence to be without parole, it must be clearly stated in the statute.

1. Life versus life without parole

In Maryland, the only offense that is subject to life without parole is first degree murder. In Maryland, the only three offenses that are subject to life with parole are first degree murder, first degree rape, and first degree sex offense (plus their inchoate forms of attempt, solicitation, and conspiracy).

2. Life with parole arguably treated as life without parole

In Maryland, the only sentence for which parole requires action by both the MPC and the Governor is "life." In 1995, the Governor announced that he would no longer parole those serving "life." Thus, the Governor treated "life with parole" the same as "life without parole." In *Lomax v. Warden*, 356 Md. 569, 577, 580-81 (1999), the Court of Appeals upheld the Governor's action. Since that time, no Maryland "lifer" has been paroled, although some lifers have had their sentences commuted to a term of years. *See State v. Kanaras*, 357 Md. 170, 185 (1999) (the Governor's announcement that he would not approve parole for lifers did not render the Defendant's sentence illegal).

3. Legislative response

On April 4, 2011, the Maryland General Assembly enacted House Bill 302, which changed the role of the Governor in the parole process for inmates serving a sentence of "life with parole." Md. Code Ann., Corr. Serv. § 7-301. Prior to the new law, if the MPC determined that a lifer should be paroled, that determination went to the Governor as a recommendation. For more than a decade and a half, no MPC recommendation for parole had been approved by the Governor. By doing nothing with the recommendation, and taking no action, the Governor had rejected the recommendation. House Bill 302 took some of the Governor's power away in the parole process for lifers.

Under the new law, if the MPC recommends parole for a lifer, the Governor has 180 days to deny, in writing, the recommendation for parole. Md. Code Ann., Corr. Serv. § 7-301(d)(5)(iii). If the Governor adopts the recommendation for parole, or fails to deny the recommendation, in writing, the lifer is paroled. *Id.*

The new law, requiring affirmative "rejection" of parole by the governor does not apply to all lifers. In order for an inmate to be eligible to have the Governor affirmatively reject, or else the inmate will be paroled, the new law requires a Defendant to serve 25 years, not counting diminution credits. In other words, for a lifer who has not yet served 25 years, that life must still obtain the approval of the Governor and not merely the disapproval of the Governor.

B. Mandatory "without parole" sentences

1. Use of a firearm in the commission of a felony or crime of violence

The offense of "use of a firearm in the commission of a felony or crime of violence" has a 20-year maximum sentence and a five-year mandatory minimum sentence. Md. Code Ann., Crim. Law § 4-204(c)(1) Moreover, whatever sentence is imposed, the first five years of the sentence are "without parole." *Id.*; Md. Code Ann., Pub. Safety § 5-133(c)(1-(3).

2. Crimes of violence—"three-time loser"

Maryland has a three-time loser statute. Md. Code Ann., Crim. Law § 14-101(d)(1). The statute provides a 25-year sentence, without parole, for a Defendant convicted for a third crime of violence if the Defendant has previously served at least one term of confinement in a correctional facility for a crime of violence.

In *McGlone v. State*, 406 Md. 545, 556 (2008), the Court of Appeals held that the intervening terms of confinement is not required for the predicate convictions, *id.* at 558, and the sentence enhancement does not require the predicate convictions be imposed sequentially. *Id.* at 560. In *Taylor v. State*, 333 Md. 229, 237 (1994), the Court of Appeals held that parole ineligibility applies only to the first 25 years of a life sentence.

3. Crimes of violence — "four-time loser"

Maryland has a four-time loser statute. The statute provides a life sentence, without parole, for a Defendant convicted for a fourth crime of violence if the Defendant served three separate terms of confinement in a correctional facility as a result of three separate convictions of a crime of violence. Md. Code Ann., Crim. Law § 14-101(c)(1).

4. Eligibility for parole for inmates subject to a "without parole" sentence

A Defendant sentenced to a mandatory without parole sentence is eligible for parole if the Defendant (a) is at least age 65, and (b) served at least 15 years of a "without parole" sentence. Md. Code Ann., Crim. Law § 14-101(g)(1).

C. Diminution of confinement credits

1. Term of confinement

Under Md. Code Ann., Corr. Serv. § 3-701, a "term of confinement" is the length of a sentence from first day of the sentence through the last day of the sentence for (a) concurrent sentences; (b) partially concurrent sentences; (c) consecutive sentences; or (d) a combination of concurrent and consecutive sentences. *See Beshears v. Wickes*, 349 Md. 1, 9 (1998).

2. Earning diminution credits

Under Md. Code Ann., Corr. Serv. § 3-704, diminution credits are earned by inmates to reduce the term of confinement. Diminution credits are earned for (a) good behavior; (b) special projects; (c) work tasks; and (d) education. Unless the Defendant is paroled, release occurs when the Defendant has accumulated sufficient diminution credits to be released. Each diminution credit reduces the term of confinement by one day. *Beshears*, 349 Md. at 5-6.

3. Revocation of diminution credits

Under Md. Code Ann., Corr. Serv. § 3-709, if the Defendant violates a prison disciplinary rule, the Division of Parole & Probation (DPP) may revoke some or all diminution credits that were earned for good behavior or special projects, but the DPP may not revoke diminution credits awarded for work tasks or education. *Id.* § 3-709(a) & (b); *Frost v. State*, 336 Md. 125, 139 (1994).

4. When diminution credits apply

In Maryland, for all inmates serving a paroleable sentence less than life, diminution credits do not influence parole eligibility, because the diminution credits apply only at the "back end" of the sentence. However, for inmates serving a paroleable life sentence, diminution credits apply to the parole eligibility date, meaning that diminution credits count at the "front end" of the sentence.

For an inmate serving a life sentence, the inmate is eligible for parole (a) after serving 15 years (less diminution credits) if the State did not seek the death penalty; or (b) 25 years (less diminution credits) if the offense is first degree murder and the State unsuccessfully sought the death penalty. Md. Code Ann., Corr. Serv. § 3-806. Since 1995, no Maryland "lifer" has been paroled, although some lifers have had their sentences commuted by the Governor to a term of years less than life.

5. Effect of a parole violation on diminution credits

Under Md. Code Ann., Corr. Serv. § 3-711, if a Defendant is convicted of, and sentenced for, a crime that was committed while on parole, the Defendant's parole will be revoked, and the Defendant will lose diminution credits that were earned prior to release. *Jones v. Filbert*, 155 Md. App. 568, 573 (2004).

D. Parole eligibility

For inmates serving a sentence less than life, the MPC has the power to parole, and the power to grant discretionary conditional release into the community, with the inmate continuing to serve the sentence, but serving the sentence under the supervision of DPP, rather than under the supervision of the DOC. Md. Code Ann., Corr. Serv. § 7-101(i); *Mitchell v. State*, 58 Md. App. 113, 117 (1983). When a Defendant has served the minimum portion of the sentence that makes the Defendant parole eligible, and has served any mandatory portion of the sentence, the Defendant is eligible for parole and is entitled to a parole hearing. Md. Code Ann., Corr. Serv. § 7-301(a)(1).

Although inmates who are described in the previous paragraph have a right to a parole hearing, they have no right to parole, which is a discretionary function of the MPC. In *Richardson v. State*, 89 Md. App. 259 (1990), the Court of Special Appeals stated that parole is a privilege and not a constitutional right. *Id.* at 272 n.9 (citing *Greenholt v. Inmates of Nebraska Penal & Correctional Complex*, 442 U.S. 1 (1979); *Woods v. Steiner*, 207 F. Supp. 945, 951 (D. Md. 1962)). Eligibility for parole is calculated based on (1) the offense(s) for which the inmate was convicted and the "consecutive-concurrent" nature of the sentence(s); and (2) the amount of time that the inmate has served on that conviction.

1. Eligibility after serving 25% of the sentence

For non-violent offenses, inmates are entitled to a parole hearing, and are eligible for parole, after serving 25% of the aggregate sentence. Md. Code Ann., Corr. Serv. § 7-301(a)(2).

2. Eligibility after serving 50% of the sentence

For violent offenses for which the inmate was sentenced on October 1, 1994, or later, inmates are entitled to a parole hearing, and are eligible for parole, after serving the greater of (a) 50% of the aggregate sentence for violent crimes; or (b) 25% of the total aggregate sentence. *Id.* § 7-301(c)(2). Inmates sentenced for violent crimes on or after October 1, 1994, with both a paroleable sentence and a non-paroleable sentence, are eligible for parole after serving the greater of (a) 50% of total aggregate sentence for violent crimes; (b) 25% of the total aggregate sentence; or (c) the period equal to the term of confinement, during which ineligible for parole. *Id.* § 7-301(c)(1)(ii).

3. Eligibility if sentenced to life

If the State did not seek the death penalty or life without parole, an inmate sentenced to life will be eligible for parole after 15 years or less, when subtracting diminution credits. *Id.* § 4-305(b)(1). However, if the State sought death or life without parole, but the inmate was sentenced to a paroleable life, the inmate is not eligible for parole until he or she has served 25 years or less, when subtracting diminution credits. *Id.* § 4-305(b)(2).

In either of the scenarios in the previous paragraph, if the MPC believes that the inmate should be paroled, that determination goes as a recommendation to the Governor. The Governor may reject the recommendation of the MPC. However, if the Governor does not affirmatively reject the recommendation, in writing, within 180 days, the inmate is paroled. Md. Code Ann., Corr. Serv. § 4-305(b)(4).

4. Eligibility at any time for non-violent inmates who are drug dependent

Inmates may be released on parole at any time to undergo drug or alcohol treatment if the inmate (a) is not serving a sentence for a crime of violence under Md. Code Ann., Crim. Law § 14-101; (b) is not serving a sentence for (i) a fourth drug offense as a dealer, kingpin, or importer, (ii) use of a weapon in relation to a drug trafficking offense, (iii) possession of a firearm as a convicted drug felon, or (iv) use of a minor to manufacture or distribute drugs, *id.* §§ 5-608(d), 5-609(d), 5-612 to 5-614, 5-621 to 5-622, & 5-628; and (c) has been determined to be amenable to drug or alcohol treatment. Md. Code Ann., Corr. Serv. § 7-301(a)(3).

E. The parole process

1. Institutional review of inmate progress

At the start of the term of confinement, and at five-year intervals thereafter, the MPC conducts an "institutional review" of the inmate's progress while incarcerated. The institutional review is designed (a) to ensure that the Defendant's file is complete; (b) to develop a chronological record of the period of incarceration; and (c) to send a written notice to the Defendant and the institution regarding parole eligibility, the steps that the Defendant should take to increase the chance of being paroled, and the timeframe for a parole hearing.

2. Steps in the parole process

Prior to a parole hearing, the MPC must provide the inmate with (a) written notice of the date, time, and place of the hearing; (b) written notice of the factors the MPC hearing examiner will consider in determining whether the inmate is suitable for parole; and (c) notice of the right to request any document that the MPC or the hearing examiner will use in determining whether the inmate is suitable for parole. *Id.* § 7-303(a) & (b)(1)(i)-(iii).

There are two separate "parole hearing" tracks. In the majority of cases, the parole hearing is conducted by one hearing examiner, as assigned by the MPC chair. *Id.* § 7-306(a)-(c). If (a) the crime victim died, or (b) the sentence is life, the parole hearing is conducted by two parole Commissioners. If both parole Commissioners agree that the inmate should be paroled, the inmate is paroled, if not serving life, and is recommended for parole, if serving life. *Id.* § 7-301, 7-305. If the two parole Commissioners disagree, the decision goes to a panel consisting of thee parole Commissioners. *Id.* § 7-307(a)(1)-(b)(1)(ii).

3. Factors & information to be considered by the MPC

Under section 7-305, in determining whether an inmate is suitable for parole, the primary focus is the assessment of the risk that the inmate will re-offend. The greater the risk to public safety, the longer the inmate will serve before being paroled. In assessing whether to grant parole, the MPC panels and hearing examiners consider enumerated factors. *See Kanaras*, 357 Md. at 185; *Lomax*, 356 Md. at 578.

The factors are (a) circumstances surrounding the crime; (b) physical, mental, and moral qualifications of the inmate; (c) progress while confined (including academic progress if in a mandatory education program); (d) drug and alcohol evaluation (including recommendations for amenability to treatment and availability of an appropriate treatment program); (e) probability of obeying the law; if released; (f) safety of society, if released; (g) an updated VIS and the original VIS, if one exists; and (h) recommendation of the sentencing judge. Md. Code Ann., Corr. Serv. 7-305.

In *York v. State*, 56 Md. App. 222, 235 (1983), the sentencing judge's statement that the Defendant should never be paroled did not make the sentence a non-paroleable sentence, but rather was a "recommendation" to the MPC regarding parole.

4. MPC hearing

The MPC considers any information presented during the meeting with the victim and any testimony presented to the MPC by the victim or the victim's representative. Md. Code Ann., Corr. Serv. § 7-305(1)-(10). The MPC hearing is an interview with the inmate to obtain information from the inmate and information about the inmate. *Id.* § 7-304.

Parole hearings are closed to the public, except that parole hearings may be open to adult victims or surviving family members of a deceased victim for crimes of violence, child abuse, or crimes in which the victim suffered physical injury or death. *Id.* § 7-801(a)(1)-(4). The MPC or a panel of Commissioners retains the right to limit those in attendance at an open hearing, based on security and space. *Id.* § 7-304(d).

5. Parole decision

In making its parole decision, the MPC focus on the inmate's risk of re-offending. The MPC considers (a) the amount of time the inmate has been incarcerated; (b) the inmate's treatment needs; (c) the inmate's institutional adjustment; (d) the inmate's participation in programs; and (e) the inmate's home plan (where and with whom will the inmate live) and work plan (where and with whom will the inmate work), if released. *Campbell v. Cushwa*, 133 Md. App. 519, 530-31 (2000). Subsequent to the parole hearing, the MPC provides the inmate with the parole decision. *Id.* §§ 7-306(d)(1) & 7-307.

Grant immediate parole

If the inmate meets the pre-release conditions, including a verified and approved home plan, the MPC may grant immediate release.

Grant parole upon a fixed, future release date

The MPC may set a delayed release date, ranging from three months to three years, conditioned on satisfaction of pre-release requirements.

Delay a parole decision, pending obtaining additional information

The MPC may delay the parole decision because information is lacking. Upon receipt of that information, a decision may be issued without another hearing.

Deny parole & set a future rehearing date

The MPC may set a re-hearing date, following a "set off" or "hit" period, making recommendations for interim accomplishments, which may include participation in educational or other programs.

Deny parole & deny future parole hearings

The MPC may refuse parole because the MPC believes that parole, either now or in the future, is inappropriate. However, even in such cases, in which the inmate is denied parole, the inmate may "get back in parole system" two years later.

6. Post-hearing procedures
Parole order

If the MPC determines to parole non-life, the MPC provides a written order to the inmate, which becomes effective, once accepted. *Id.* § 7-308. Parole entitles an inmate to leave the correctional facility and, if in compliance with the terms and conditions in the parole order, to serve the remainder of the sentence outside the correctional facility. *Id.* § 7-308(a)-(b). In *Simms v. State*, 65 Md. App. 685, 689 (1986), the Court of Special Appeals stated that parole is an act of executive clemency. It is a conditional release, which requires compliance with all terms and conditions in the parole order. *See Murray v. Swenson*, 196 Md. 222, 230 (1950); *DeLeon v. State*, 102 Md. App. 58, 73-74 (1994).

Pre-release conditions must be met or parole approval may be suspended

Inmates must meet standard pre-release conditions, including an approved and verified home plan and work plan. Md. Code Ann., Corr. Serv. § 7-308. If the inmate fails to meet the pre-release conditions or breaks institutional rules, parole approval may be suspended and another hearing may be ordered. *Id.* § 7-401.

Restitution

If the MPC grants parole to an inmate who was ordered by a court to make restitution, as part of the sentence or as a condition of probation, the inmate is required by the MPC to make restitution while on parole. *Id.* § 7-701. In *Simms*, 65 Md. App. at 689, the Court of Special Appeals held that a court cannot impose restitution as a parole condition because parole is an executive branch function. In *Mitchell*, 58 Md. App. at 119-20, the Court of Special Appeals held that a court may not impose restitution, based on a violation of parole, if restitution was not part of the original sentence.

In *Lopez-Sanchez v. State*, 155 Md. App. 580, 600 (2004), *aff'd*, 388 Md. 214 (2005), the Court of Special Appeals stated that restitution is part of the sentence. It is not to compensate the victim, which is handled by the civil justice system. In *Sumrall v. Central Collection Unit*, 150 Md. App. 290, 300 (2003), the Court of Special Appeals held that when restitution is part of the sentence, the requirement to pay restitution is not terminated by revocation of parole.

Parole fees

An inmate with a sentence that exceeds one year, who is paroled or released under mandatory supervision, is assigned to a DPP agent. Md. Code Ann., Corr. Serv. § 7-702. A parolee is evaluated every six months to assess the risk of recidivism and to determine the level of supervision required. A parolee must pay a $40-per-month assessment fee.

Modification of parole

Upon recommendation of the DPP, or by the MPC on its own initiation, the MPC may modify the conditions of parole for good cause. The modification may include home detention as a parole condition. Before modifying parole conditions, the MPC must allow an inmate an opportunity to present information showing that the parole conditions should not be modified. This does not require another hearing. *Id.* § 7-402(a)(1)-(b)(2).

7. Revocation of parole

Parole violations

Violations of parole include (a) technical violations, i.e., violation of parole conditions, but no commission of a criminal offense; and (b) commission of a criminal offense. *Id.* §§ 7-403 & 7-401.

Conviction of a crime while on parole

Under section § 7-403, if a parolee is convicted of a crime, while on parole, and is sentenced to incarceration on the new crime, the court must determine whether the sentence will run concurrently or consecutively to any sentence imposed as a consequence of the parole violation. If the parolee is convicted in another state, while on parole, and is sentenced to incarceration in the other state, the MPC shall file, with the correctional facility in the other state, a statement of the violation of parole, which serves as a detainer on the parolee's release from the out-of-state correctional facility. *Id.* § 7-403.

Parole is not a term of confinement for purposes of consecutive sentencing for a conviction of a crime committed on parole

For sentencing purposes, parole is not incarceration or a sentence being served. In *Stouffer v. Pearson*, 390 Md. 36, 41 (2005), the Court of Appeals held that, when a parolee is sentenced for a new crime, prior to the parole revocation hearing, the sentencing judge may not treat parole as an existing term of confinement, and the new sentence may not be served consecutive to the parole term because parole is not confinement.

Imposing a sentence consecutive to the term of confinement for which on parole

If parole is revoked before the parolee is sentenced, a consecutive sentence begins after the original sentence expires. Md. Code Ann., Corr. Serv. § 9-202(c)(1). If parole is not revoked before the parolee is sentenced, the sentence begins on the date that the consecutive sentence is imposed. *Id.* § 9-202(c)(2); *see Stouffer*, 390 Md. 36.

"Retake" & revoke parole

If the MPC believes that the parolee violated the conditions of parole, the MPC may seek to revoke parole and re-incarcerate the Defendant until the expiration of the sentence. The MPC will issue a "retake" warrant. When the parolee is apprehended, the parolee is placed in a correctional facility awaiting a parole revocation hearing. *Stouffer*, 390 Md. at 49. The MPC conducts a parole revocation hearing before a parole Commissioner. *Gantt v. State*, 81 Md. App. 653, 657 (1990). The burden of persuasion is on the State by a preponderance of the evidence. *Wink v. State*, 317 Md. 330, 332 (1989).

Result of a parole hearing

If the parolee is found guilty of violating the conditions of parole, the parole Commissioner may re-impose, within his or her discretion, all, part, or none of the sentence from which the parole was paroled. Md. Code Ann., Corr. Serv. §§ 7-401, 7-403(a). In addition, the parole Commissioner may forfeit all, some, or none of the diminution credits that the parolee earned prior to release. *Id.* § 7-401(d). Even if the parole Commissioner finds that the inmate violated parole, the MPC may continue the inmate on parole, with or without a modification of parole conditions, including home detention.

Judicial review

If, as a result of the hearing, the inmate's parole is revoked, the inmate may seek judicial review in the Circuit Court, if filed within 30 days after receipt of the MPC decision. Md. Code Ann., Corr. Serv. § 7-401; *see Bergstein v. State*, 322 Md. 506, 515 (1991). The standard of review is substantial evidence. *Pollock v. Patuxent Institution Board of Review*, 374 Md. 463, 468 n.3 (2003).

§ II. Pardon

Pardon is act of clemency by the Governor, as to state criminal convictions, or the President, as to federal criminal convictions. A pardon is a written order that absolves the Defendant of guilt and exempts the Defendant from the penalties previously imposed. Md. Code Ann., Corr. Serv. § 7-101(h). Upon giving notice, as required by the State Constitution, the Governor may (a) commute or modify a death sentence to a period of confinement; or (b) pardon a convicted Defendant or remit part of a sentence. Both pardon and remission may be subject to conditions. *Id.* § 7-601(a)(1)-(3). Pardons may be conditional, partial, or unconditional.

A. Conditional pardon

A conditional pardon requires the Defendant to adhere to specified conditions in the pardon. *Id.* § 7-101(f). In *State ex rel Murray v. Swenson*, 196 Md. 222 (1950), the Court of Appeals held:

> There is a difference between a parole and a conditional pardon. A parole is conditional release from imprisonment which entitles the grantee to leave the institution in which he is imprisoned, and to serve the remainder of his term outside the confines thereof, if he shall satisfactorily comply with all the terms and conditions provided in the parole order. Thus, a parole order does not vacate the sentence, but merely suspends the execution of the penalty and releases the [Defendant] from imprisonment temporarily upon conditions, which he may accept or reject. Generally, a pardon is an act of clemency, evidenced by an executive order signed by the Governor, absolving the

convict from the guilt of his criminal acts and exempting him from any pains and penalties imposed upon him therefor[e] by law. A conditional pardon is defined as a pardon whose legal operation is dependent upon the performance of such conditions as the Governor may specify in the order.

Id. at 229.

The Governor is the sole judge of whether a condition of a conditional pardon has been violated and is subject to revocation by the Governor. Md. Code Ann., Corr. Serv. § 7-602(a) & (b); *Swenson,* 196 Md. 222. If a conditional pardon is revoked by the Governor, the Defendant must (1) serve the un-served portion of the sentence that was originally imposed; and (2) not be credited for any time on release prior to violating the conditional pardon. Md. Code Ann., Corr. Serv. § 7-603(1) & (2).

The Governor is not required to conduct a hearing before revoking a conditional pardon, however, "this does not mean that the Governor can exercise his power arbitrarily or upon whim, caprice, or rumor." *Wright v. Herzog,* 182 Md. 316, 322 (1943). A prisoner may challenge an arbitrary revocation of a conditional pardon through a habeas corpus proceeding. *Id.*

B. Partial pardon

A partial pardon is a pardon limited by the terms set forth by the Governor in a written order granting the pardon. A partial pardon has "less effect" than full pardon. *Id.* § 7-101(k). All pardons or commutations of sentence must be in written executive order signed by Governor. *Id.* § 7-601(b)(1). The order granting a pardon or a conditional pardon must indicate "on its face" whether it is a partial or full pardon. *Id.* § 7-601(b)(1) & (2). There is a presumption that the recipient of a Governor's pardon was lawfully convicted, unless the pardon states conclusively that person pardoned was convicted in error. *Id.* § 7-601(c).

§ III. Commutation of sentence

A commutation of sentence is an act of clemency in which the Governor, by written order, substitutes a lesser penalty. *Id.* § 7-101(d).

If the victim, or the family representative of a deceased victim, made written request to the DPP and maintains a current address on file, the DPP is required to notify the victim or representative, in writing, that the Defendant is being considered for (a) commutation of sentence; (b) pardon; or (c) remission of sentence, and permit written input to the Governor. The DPP must subsequently notify the victim or family representative of the decision regarding commutation of sentence or pardon. *Id.* § 7-805(b) & (f).

Table of Cases

*References are to chapter and section number (e.g., **8**: VI.I.5; **9**: XVI.A.13 refers to section VI.I.5 in Chapter 8 and to section XVI.A.13 in Chapter 9.) Alphabetization is letter-by-letter (e.g., "Greenleaf" precedes "Green Party").*

E

H

M

N

W

Z

Table of Authorities

*References are to chapter and section number (e.g., **8**: VI.I.5; **9**: XVI.A.13 refers to section VI.I.5 in Chapter 8 and to section XVI.A.13 in Chapter 9.)*

U.S. Constitution (U.S. Const.)

Articles

art. I, § 8 . . . *17:* I.B.1, I.B.3

art. I, § 8, cl. 3 . . . *17:* I.B.1

art. I, § 8, cl. 6 . . . *17:* I.B.1

art. I, § 8, cl. 10 . . . *17:* I.B.1

art. I, § 8, cl. 17 . . . *17:* I.B.1

art. I, § 8, cl. 18 . . . *17:* I.B.1

art. I, § 9, cl. 2 . . . *33:* I

art. I, § 9, cl. 3 . . . *2:* III.A

art. I, § 10, cl. 1 . . . *2:* III.A

art. II, § 2 . . . *1:* II.A.2

art. II, § 3 . . . *13:* III.A

art. III, § 2 . . . *32:* I.A.1

Amendments

amend. IV . . . *2:* VIII.C; *5:* I.G; *6:* II.B.2; *7: passim; 8: passim; 9: passim; 10: passim; 11: passim; 13:* I.A.8, I.C.3, I.H; *14:* I.A, II.D.2, II.D.3, III.B, III.F; *15:* VI; *16:* IX.A, IX.F.3; *19:* I.A, II.A, II.D.1, II.D.4, IV; *32:* I.A.7, XII.A.15; *33:* VIII.A

amend. V . . . *1:* I.3, IV.B.3; *2:* IV.A; *3:* VI.D.1, VII.C.1, IX.C; *5:* I.C, IX.H.2; *9:* XI.E.3; *11:* I.B, II; *12: passim; 13: passim; 14:* I.C, II.A, II.D.3, III.A, III.F, IV; *15:* VI; *16:* I.A, VI.A, VI.C, IX.B, X.A; *17:* I.A, I.B.1, I.B.4; *19:* II.D.1, II.D.3; *20:* I.D.3, II.E.2; *21:* I.A, I.D.1, II.C.2; *22:* I.B.3, II.E.4; *23:* I.A; *25:* II.C.2; *26:* III.K.6; *27:* I.M, VII.E.6; *28:* I.G.1, IV; *29:* II; *30:* IV.C.3, XII.A, XII.B; *32:* I.A.6; *33:* II.A.1

amend. VI . . . *1:* I.A.2; *5:* I.A, I.B.1, I.D, I.E, I.F.2, II, IX.L.1; *9:* XII.A, XII.B; *13:* III.D.4, III.E.6, III.E.7, IV; *14:* I.E; *15:* I, III, V.A; *16:* IX.C, IX.D, XIII.A, XIV.A; *17:* II.D; *18:* II.D.1, III.C; *19:* IV.A, IV.B, IX; *20:* I.A.1, I.C.3; *22:* I, II.A, IV.A; *23:* I.B, I.C; *24:* II, IV.A, IV.A.4, IV.A.8, IV.B.1, IV.B.2, IV.B.6, IV.B.8, IV.B.16; *26:* I.B.1, II.G.5, VI.B.1; *27:* I, II, IV.B.1, VIII.C; *28:* I, III.A, III.B, V.G, V.J; *29:* I.A, II, V.G.3; *30:* III; *32:* I.A.7, XII.A.14, XII.A.16; *33:* I, II

amend. VIII . . . *10:* VIII.D.1; *11:* I.B; *19:* III.E.1, III.E.2; *30:* XX.C.3; *32:* I.A.7; *33:* VIII.B.1, VIII.B.2

amend. X . . . *17:* I.B.2

amend. XIV . . . *1:* I.B.3, II.B, IV.B.3; *2:* IV.A, VIII.C; *3:* VII.C.1; *4:* IX.C; *5:* I.E, I.F, I.G; *8:* I, VI.B; *9:* III.E.3; *11:* I.B, VII; *12:* I; *13:* I, II, III.H, IV.A, IV.B; *14:* I.B, I.C, I.D.3, III.B, III.D, III.F; *15:* IV.B; *16:* I.A, XII.A; *17:* I.A, I.B.2, I.B.4, II.D; *19:* II.D.2; *21:* I.A; *22:* I.A; *23:* I.D, III.B.3; *24:* II.A.1, IV.A.3, IV.A.4, IV.B.1, IV.B.22, IV.B.24; *25:* II.C.2; *27:* I, II.B; *28:* I, II; *29:* I.A; *30:* IX.H, XII.B; *32:* I.A.6–I.A.8, XII.C.2; *33:* VI.F.5

United States Code (U.S. Code)

18 U.S.C. § 13 . . . *1:* II.C; *17:* I.B.1

18 U.S.C. § 17(a) . . . *20:* II.C.1

18 U.S.C. § 51(a) . . . *4:* IX.B.5

18 U.S.C. § 921 . . . *1:* IV.C.12

18 U.S.C. § 924 . . . *30:* VIII.A

18 U.S.C. § 1361(e) . . . *22:* III.C

18 U.S.C. § 1361(h) . . . *22:* III.E

18 U.S.C. § 1361(h)(1)(F) . . . *22:* III.D.5

18 U.S.C. § 1361(h)(3)(A) . . . *22:* III.D.3

18 U.S.C. § 1361(h)(3)(B) . . . *22:* III.D.3

18 U.S.C. § 1361(h)(4) . . . *22:* III.D.4

18 U.S.C. § 1361(h)(5) . . . *22:* III.D.6

18 U.S.C. § 1361(h)(6) . . . *22:* III.D.7

18 U.S.C. § 1361(h)(7) . . . *22:* III.D.8

18 U.S.C. § 1362 . . . *22:* III.H

18 U.S.C. § 1362(a)(2) . . . *22:* III.F

18 U.S.C. § 2255 . . . *2:* XII.N

18 U.S.C. §§ 2510–2522 . . . *7:* III.F

18 U.S.C. § 2703(d) . . . *7:* III.D.2

18 U.S.C. § 3109 . . . *8:* X.K.1, X.L

18 U.S.C. § 3161 . . . *1:* II.C; *22:* III

18 U.S.C. § 3161(b) . . . *22:* III.A

18 U.S.C. § 3161(c)(2) . . . *22:* III.B

18 U.S.C. § 3161(h) . . . *22:* III.D.1

18 U.S.C. §§ 3165–3166 . . . *22:* III

Federal Rules of Criminal Procedure (Fed. R. Crim. P.)

Federal Rules of Evidence

Maryland Constitution (Md. Const.)

Courts and Judicial Proceedings (Cts. & Jud. Proc.)

Criminal Law (Crim. Law)

Criminal Procedure (Crim. Proc.)

Education (Educ.)

Election Law (Elect. Law)

Family Law (Fam. Law)

Health – General (Health-Gen.)

Health Occupations (Health Occ.)

Uniform Statutory Construction Act (USCA)

Law Reviews, Treatises, and Secondary References

Allen, Ronald J., & M.K. Mace, The Self-Incrimination Clause Explained & Its Future Predicted, 94 J. Crim. L. & Criminology 243 (2004) . . . *11:* II

Amar, Akil R., & Renee B. Lettow, Fifth Amendment Principles: The Self-Incrimination Clause, 93 Mich. L. Rev. 857 (1995) . . . *11:* II

Attorney Grievance Comm'n of Maryland 35th Annual Report (July 1, 2009 to June 30, 2010) . . . *5:* IX.A.6

Black's Law Dictionary (8th ed. 2004) . . . *33:* I

Broun, Kenneth S., McCormick on Evidence (6th ed. 2006) . . . *13:* II.B.2; *26:* III.G.3

Chitty, A Practical Treatise on the Criminal Law (1819) . . . *1:* I.B.3

Clark, William L., & William L. Marshall, A Treatise on the Law of Crimes (Marion Quinn 7th ed. 1967) . . . *3:* II.A; *1:* II.A.1

Demarco, Anne M. & Elisa Scott, Confusion Among the Courts: Should the Contents of Personal Papers be Privileged by the Fifth Amendment's Self-Incrimination Clause, 9 St. John's J. Legal Comment 219 (1993) . . . *11:* II

Ginsberg, Hyman, & Isidore Ginsberg, Maryland Criminal Law & Procedure (1940) . . . *1:* I.B, I.B.1

Helmholz, R.H., Origins of the Privilege Against Self-Incrimination: The Role of the European Ius Commune, 64 N.Y.U.L. Rev. 962 (1990) . . . *11:* II

Hochheimer, Lewis, The Law of Crimes & Criminal Procedure (2d ed. 1904) . . . *1:* I.B.1, I.B.3; *2:* I.A.1

LaFave, Wayne R., Criminal Law (5th ed. 2010) . . . *1:* I.B.3, I.C, II.C, IV.B.1, IV.C.1; *3:* II.A, II.A.2, IV.A.1, IV.B, VI.A; *4:* I.F.4, II.C, V.A, VI, VII, IX, IX.B.4, IX.C; *25:* II.A.3

Leipold, Andrew D., Why Grand Juries Do Not (And Cannot) Protect the Accused, 80 Cornell L. Rev. 260 (1995) . . . *16:* III.F

Levy, Leonard W., Origins of the Fifth Amendment & Its Critics, 19 Cardoza L. Rev. 821 (1997) . . . *11:* II

Macnair, M.R.T., The Early Development of the Privilege Against Self-Incrimination, 10 Oxford J. Legal Stud. 66 (1990) . . . *11:* II

Maryland Judiciary, Annual Statistical Abstract (2010) . . . *5:* I.F.3

McLain, Lynn, Maryland Evidence (2d ed. 2001 & Supp. 2010) . . . *13:* II.B.2; *26:* III.G.3

Murphy, Joseph F., Jr, Maryland Evidence Handbook (4th ed. 2010) . . . *13:* II.B.2; *26:* III.G.3

The Rights of Criminal Defendants & the Subpoena Duces Tecum: The Aftermath of *Fisher v. United States*, 95 Harv. L. Rev. 683 (1982) . . . *11:* II

Singer, Norman J., Sutherland on Statutes & Statutory Construction (7th ed. 2007) . . . *1:* IV, IV.C.1

Sloan, Amy E., Appellate Fruit Salad & Other Concepts: A Short Course in Appellate Process, 35 U. Balt. L. Rev. 45 (2005) . . . *32:* V

Stuntz, William J., Self-Incrimination & Excuse, 88 Colum. L. Rev. 1227 (1988) . . . *11:* II

Thompson, David C., & Melanie F. Waddell, An Empirical Analysis of Supreme Court Certiorari Procedures: The Call for Response and the Call for the Views of the Solicitor General, 16:2 Geo. Mason L. Rev. 238 (2009) . . . *32:* I.A.2

West Key Number System Statutes key #174-361 . . . *1:* IV

Witt, John F., Making the Fifth: The Constitutionalization of American Self-Incrimination Doctrine, 1791-1903, 77 Tex. L. Rev. 825 (1999) . . . *11:* II

Index

Introductory Note

*References are to chapter (bolded number) followed by section number (e.g., **1:** I.B.3; **5:** I.E.1 refers to section I.B.3 in Chapter 1 and to section I.E.1 in Chapter 5). Alphabetization is letter-by-letter (e.g. "Arrests" precedes "Arrest warrants").*

Cross-references ("See" and "See also") generally refer users to another main heading where related information may be found. When the phrase "subheading:" is included in the cross-reference, it directs users to a particular sublevel under a main heading. These "pinpoint" cross-references save users time when turning to lengthy main headings. Within a heading, an internal cross-reference may be provided; this type of cross-reference sends the user from one sublevel under a main heading to another sublevel under that same heading. The phrase "this heading" (at the end of the cross-reference) indicates this type of internal cross-reference.

Cross-references within the Index to the Table of Authorities refer users to that separate finding aid for complete lists of all statutory and rule citations within the text.

G

Gagging Defendant, *27*: V.C.3

Gender

in statutory construction, *1*: IV.C.19

Gender discrimination

in grand or petite jury composition, *32*: XII.C.3

impermissible sentencing considerations, *30*: IV.C.2

General anesthetic surgery

search warrants, *8*: X.O.3

General intent, *4*: VIII

specific intent vs., *4*: I.G.3

Gerstein v. Pugh **initial appearance/ non-adversarial preliminary hearing, rights at**, *5*: II.B.2; *9*: XII; *19*: IV

Good character evidence

jury instructions, *26*: III.K.10

"Good faith" exception to exclusionary rule. *See* Exclusionary rule

Governmental action

civil rights suits. *See* Qualified immunity

Fourth Amendment applicability, *7*: II.A. *See also* Fourth Amendment

Government employees

Fourth Amendment rights, *7*: II.A.2

GPS device, use of

good faith exception to GPS tracking devices attached prior to *Jones*, *7*: III.D.1

Jones warrant requirements, *7*: III.C.2

privacy and technology issues as domain of legislature, *7*: III.F

reasonable expectation of privacy in one's home, *7*: IV.B.3

trespass violation, *7*: III.C.1

in vehicles when tracked for extended period, *7*: IV.B.11

Grand jury proceedings, *Ch.* 16

challenges

to composition of jurors, *16*: III.D

to decision to prosecute, *16*: XVI

to indictment, *16*: IX.F

constitutional rights of witnesses, *16*: IX

discovery in Circuit Court, *23*: III.D.18

due process, *16*: IX.E

equal protection challenges

to decision to prosecute, *16*: XVI.A

to indictment, *16*: IX.F.1

evidence, *16*: VII

grand juror discovered evidence, *16*: VII.B

inadmissible and illegal evidence, *16*: VII.A

indictment based on, *16*: VIII

use of evidence that is inadmissible at trial, *16*: IX.F.2

evolution and history of grand jury, *16*: II

exclusionary rule not applicable, *11*: VII.A.1

fair trial, right to, *27*: III.C

disclosure by Defendant of own testimony, *27*: III.C.2

disclosure by grand jury witnesses, *27*: III.C.2

disclosure to non-prosecuting government officials, *27*: III.C.2

inadmissible evidence, use in grand jury, *27*: III.C.3

limitations on secrecy and permissible or required disclosure, *27*: III.C.2

secrecy, *27*: III.C.1

unconstitutionally seized evidence, use in grand jury, *27*: III.C.4

withholding exculpatory evidence from grand jury, *27*: III.C.5

felony charges, *1*: I.B.3

federal charges requiring indictment, *16*: I.A

grand jury indictment vs. criminal information, *16*: I.B

indictment, *16*: X.A

Fifth Amendment privilege against compelled self-incrimination, *16*: IX.B

collective entity (e.g., corporation) not entitled to privilege, *16*: IX.B.2

Miranda warnings not applicable, *16*: IX.B.5

Guilty pleas.

See Pleas of not guilty or guilty

Guns. *See* Weapons offenses

H

Habeas corpus relief

Anti-Terrorism and Effective Death Penalty Act, *33*: VIII.B. *See also* Anti-Terrorism and Effective Death Penalty Act of 1996 (AEDPA)

collateral review, *33*: VIII

disposition of state habeas corpus petition, *33*: IX.C

exclusionary rule not applicable, *11*: VII.A.2

federal petition for, *2*: XII.N

filing state habeas corpus petition, *33*: IX.B

full and fair opportunity to litigate in state court, *33*: VIII.A

no constitutional right to counsel, *5*: I.F.4

pre-trial release determination, *19*: III.E.6

state petition for, *2*: XII.P; *33*: IX

who is entitled to file in Maryland, *33*: IX.A

Habitation, crimes against, *1*: I.D

malice, *4*: IV.C

specific intent, *4*: III.H

willfully committed, *4*: II.D

Hair samples

compelled self-incrimination, *12*: VII.H

Handcuffing Defendant, *9*: XV.A.4; *27*: V.C.3, V.C.4. *See also* Restraints on Defendant

Handguns. *See* Weapons offenses

Harassment

judicial harassment of defense witness, *29*: IV.E

solicitation by attorney, *5*: IX.A.4

Harmless error, *32*: XII

Brady material, *23*: II.D.1

Defendant's right to be present, *28*: II.E

errors that cannot be harmless because of structural defect, *32*: XII.C

conflict of interest, failure to inquire about, *32*: XII.C.11

consulting with counsel during recess, denial of right to, *32*: XII.C.10

defective reasonable doubt instruction, *32*: XII.C.2

impartial judge, denial of right to, *32*: XII.C.7

public trial, denial of right to, *32*: XII.C.5

racial or gender discrimination in grand or petite jury composition, *32*: XII.C.3

right to counsel, deprivation of, *32*: XII.C.6

selection of counsel of one's choice, denial of right to, *32*: XII.C.9

self-representation, denial of right to, *32*: XII.C.8

structural defects, *32*: XII.C.1

trial by jury, denial of right to, *32*: XII.C.4

evidence, erroneous admission of

of another responsible party, *32*: XII.A.8

attorney-client privilege violation, *32*: XII.A.11

cross-examination of expert witness, *32*: XII.A.9

DNA evidence, *32*: XII.A.5

hearsay evidence, *32*: XII.A.4

un-admitted evidence allowed in jury room, *32*: XII.A.10

voice stress test, *32*: XII.A.6

examples of, *32*: XII.A

Co-Defendant's statements admitted in violation of Confrontation Clause, *32*: XII.A.16

failing to sustain objection to improper prosecutor arguments, *32*: XII.A.18

failure to change venue, *32*: XII.A.3

failure to swear jury at start of trial, *32*: XII.A.2

M

Magistrates

"good faith" exception to exclusionary rule, *11*: VII.C.4

neutral and detached magistrates, *8*: III

conflict of interest, *8*: III.B.1

executive branch, *8*: III.A

federal system, *8*: III.B.4

judge who issues warrant able to preside over motion to suppress evidence obtained from that warrant, *8*: III.B.3

judicial branch, *8*: III.B

magistrate not a judge, *8*: III.B.2

Maryland system, *8*: III.B.4

not required to be judges, *8*: III.B.2

probable cause determination, *8*: VI.L.1

Mail

international mail receipt akin to crossing international border, *10*: VI.B

prison inmates' mail, search of, *10*: VIII.D.3

reasonable expectation of privacy (REP), *7*: IV.B.13

service by, *2*: VII.C

Malfeasance. *See* Misconduct in office

Malice, *4*: IV

arson, *4*: IV.A.1

depraved heart murder, *4*: IV.B.1

felony murder, *4*: IV.B.1

habitation, crimes against, *4*: IV.C

homicide offenses, *4*: IV.C

justification or excuse, *4*: IV.B.2

Local Government Tort Claims Act (LGTCA), *11*: VIII.D.4

malicious destruction of property, *4*: IV.A.2

mayhem, *4*: IV.A.3

mitigation, *4*: IV.B.2

murder. *See* Malice in murder

non-murder criminal offenses containing malice, *4*: IV.A

offenses with malice in their mens rea, *4*: IV.C

serious bodily harm likely to result in death, *4*: IV.B.1

transferring specific intent, *4*: III.D.3

Malice in murder, *4*: IV.B

actus reus, *3*: V.O, VIII.D

"back end" of malice mens rea, *4*: IV.B.2

"front end" of malice mens rea, *4*: IV.B.1

rebuttably presumed, *25*: III.A.1

specific vs. general intent, *4*: I.G.3

Malicious destruction of property, *4*: IV.A.2

no merger doctrine, *30*: XII.A.11

Malum in se, *1*: I.C; *4*: X.B.3

Malum prohibitum, *1*: I.C; *4*: X.B.3

Mandatory sentencing, *1*: I.B.3; *32*: II.B.4

Mandatory vs. directory language, in statutory construction, *1*: IV.C.16

Manslaughter

actus reus, *3*: V.P

jury instruction for mitigation, *26*: III.K.8

vehicular manslaughter

arrest for, *19*: I.A.1

driving under influence of alcohol or drugs, *16*: XIII.H

merger doctrine, *30*: XII.A.10

Mapp v. Ohio

exclusionary rule in states, *11*: I.B

fruit of the poisonous tree doctrine, *11*: VI.A

incorporation of Fourth Amendment to states, *32*: I.A.7

Marbury v. Madison, *32*: I.A.1

Marital status discrimination

impermissible sentencing considerations, *30*: IV.C.2

Maryland Annotated Code (Md. Ann. Code, pre October 2002), *1*: II.B

Maryland Circuit Courts. *See* Circuit Courts, Maryland

U.S. Attorney General

qualified immunity as defense against civil damages, *11*: VIII.C.6

U.S. Supreme Court. *See* Supreme Court, U.S.

"Use and derivative use" immunity, *12*: VIII.B, VIII.C, VIII.E, VIII.H, VIII.I, VIII.L.2

grand jury subpoena, *16*: VI.A–VI.C

Kastigar ruling on grand jury subpoena, *16*: VI.C

"Use" immunity, *12*: VIII.H

Uttering

merger doctrine, *30*: XII.B.7

V

Vagueness, *1*: IV.B.3

Valuation, *28*: V.F.16

Vehicle Identification Number (VIN)

police obtaining without warrant, *10*: IV.C.2

removal or defaced, *25*: II.C.4

Vehicles. *See* Motor vehicles; Search warrants and exceptions, *subheading:* automobile exception to warrant requirement; Traffic offenses

Vehicular manslaughter. *See* Manslaughter

Vengeance

improper prosecutorial remarks on, *27*: VII.E.7

Venue, *17*: V

burden of persuasion, *17*: V.A

burden of production, *17*: V.A

common law and statutory venue, *17*: V.B

failure to change, *32*: XII.A.3

fresh pursuit conducted by Maryland officer outside venue, *10*: I.L

pre-trial motions, *2*: VIII.C

rebuttably presumed, *25*: III.B.2

waiver, *2*: VIII.C

Verb tense, in statutory construction, *1*: IV.C.20

Verdict, *26*: VI. *See also* Jury trials

absence of verdict on a count pursuant to court's instructions regarding verdict sheet, *21*: II.B.2

collateral estoppel, *21*: IV.A.1

complete vs. partial, *26*: VI.C

completion of verdict sheet, *26*: III.M

confirming, *26*: VI.B

Defendant's right to be present at verdict announcement by jury, *28*: II.A.10

guilty verdict on greater offense and silence on lesser included offense, *21*: II.B.3

hearkening jury, *26*: VI.A.2–VI.A.6, VI.A.3

hung jury. *See* Hung jury

impeachment by jury, *26*: VI.F

inconsistent, *26*: VI.E

post-*Price* decision, *26*: VI.E.4

pre-*Price* (pre-2008), *26*: VI.E.1

preservation of *Price* issue, *26*: VI.E.3

Price (2008), *26*: VI.E.2

insanity/not criminally responsible (NCR), *20*: II.E.5

verdict of "guilty" on guilt/innocence issue and verdict of "NCR" on NCR issue, *20*: II.E.7

legally inconsistent, preservation of issue for appeal, *32*: IX.F.3

motion to correct illegal sentence when verdict not announced in open court, *30*: XX.C.3

new trial motions based on verdict against weight of evidence, *31*: III.D.2

not guilty verdict, State has no right to appeal, *32*: II.B.2

polling jury, *26*: VI.A.1, VI.A.3

post-verdict motions for new trial, *31*: II

receiving, *26*: VI.A

sealed, *26*: VI.A

trial court not to direct verdict of guilty, *25*: II.D.4

Vicarious liability, *3*: VI.C

non-strict liability, *3*: VI.C.1

strict liability, *3*: VI.C.2

W

Waiver

of adversarial preliminary hearing, *19*: VI.B

of allocution, *30*: VII.D

court costs, *30*: XVIII.A

jury trials

Circuit Court, *24*: III.C

peremptory challenges, when failure to exhaust, *24*: IV.B.17

peremptory challenges, when no objection raised, *24*: IV.B.28

unanimous jury, waiver of, *24*: III.D

waiver of 12-person jury, *24*: III.D

of *Miranda* rights. *See* Interrogations and confessions

overlap of Fifth Amendment and Sixth Amendment in confession law, *13*: IV.F

of prompt presentment requirement, *9*: XI.D

of right to appeal, *32*: II.A.3

of right to counsel. *See* Right to counsel

of self-incrimination privilege applies to only one proceeding at a time, *12*: III.M

speedy trial, *22*: III.G, IV.D

unrepresented Defendant, waiver of rights not valid, *27*: III.B.3

venue, *2*: VIII.C

Warnings

prosecutor allowed to make, *27*: VII.A.2

prosecutor issuing about dangerous behavior, *5*: IX.G.2

"Warrant Clause," 8: I

Warrantless arrests

common law defenses, *1*: I.B.3

exclusionary rule, *11*: III.D.5

preliminary hearings, *19*: I.A.1

Warrantless searches. *See also* Search warrants and exceptions, *subheading:* exceptions to warrant requirement

automobiles, *8*: I.B.8; *10*: IV. *See also* Motor vehicles; Search warrants and exceptions, *subheading:* automobile exception to warrant requirement

persons, warrantless intrusions into, *8*: X.O

probable cause

determination and review of determination, *8*: VI.L.1, VI.L.2

staleness, *8*: VI.K.2

when required, *8*: VI.G.2, VI.G.5

Warrants, *16*: X.F. *See also* Arrest warrants; Search warrants and exceptions

confrontation, right to, *28*: V.F.11

"retake" warrant for parole revocation, *34*: I.E.7

Weapons offenses, *1*: I.D

concealed weapons

arrest for possession, *19*: I.A.1

no merger doctrine, *30*: XII.A.11

felony committed with firearm

mandatory "without parole" sentences, *34*: I.B.1

merger doctrine, *30*: XII.A.10

no merger doctrine, *30*: XII.A.11

knowledge, *4*: V.F

possession of firearm as unit of offense/unit of criminality, *16*: XIII.D.3

possession of firearm in relation to drug trafficking offense

inconsistent verdict, *26*: VI.E.2

inferring nexus, *25*: II.C.4

unit of offense/unit of criminality, *3*: VIII.C

specific intent, *4*: III.H

transporting firearm in vehicle

merger doctrine, *30*: XII.A.10

presumption of knowing mental state, *25*: II.C.6, III.A.2

unit of offense/unit of criminality, *16*: XIII.D.3

Weapon use by criminal.
See also Armed and dangerous

eyewitness identifications, factor in, *15*: VII.A.6

Weapon use by law enforcement

pointing weapon at Defendant, *9*: XV.A.4